WINNING UGLY

WINNING UGLY
NATO's War to Save Kosovo

Ivo H. Daalder
Michael E. O'Hanlon

Brookings Institution Press
Washington, D.C.

Copyright © 2000
THE BROOKINGS INSTITUTION
1775 Massachusetts Avenue, N.W., Washington, D.C. 20036
www.brookings.edu
All rights reserved

Library of Congress Cataloging-in-Publication data

Daalder, Ivo H.
   Winning ugly : NATO's war to save Kosovo / Ivo H. Daalder and Michael
E. O'Hanlon.
      p.   cm.
Includes bibliographical references and index.
   ISBN 0-8157-1696-6 (cloth)
   1. Kosovo (Serbia)—History—Civil War, 1998– 2. North Atlantic
Treaty Organization. I. O'Hanlon, Michael E. II. Title.
   DR2087 .D33 2000   00-009198
   949.71—dc21   CIP

9 8 7 6 5 4 3 2 1

The paper used in this publication meets minimum requirements of the
American National Standard for Information Sciences—Permanence of Paper
for Printed Library Materials: ANSI Z39.48-1984.

Typeset in Minion

Composition by Cynthia Stock
Silver Spring, Maryland

Maps by Parrot Graphics
Stillwater, Minnesota
Map images by Mountain High Maps
Copyright © 1993 Digital Wisdom

Printed by Phoenix Color
Hagerstown, Maryland

Foreword

IN MARCH 1998, violence again erupted in the Balkans, this time in Kosovo—an ethnic cauldron in the heart of the former Yugoslavia. For the third time in a decade, the violence was caused by the nationalist politics of Serbia's long-standing dictator, Slobodan Milosevic. Whereas Milosevic had relied primarily on local Serb surrogates in the Croatian and Bosnian wars, the violence in Kosovo was directly controlled by him and involved land within Serbia itself that was of great historical, cultural, and religious importance to all Serbs.

For years, it had been widely feared that a violent conflict in Kosovo was likely to be both bloody, given the long-held animosity between Serbs and Albanians, and highly destabilizing, in view of the large Albanian populations just to Kosovo's south. For these reasons, the United States and its European allies were determined to avoid an escalation in the conflict. Once violence erupted in Kosovo in March 1998, Washington and its allies sought to stop it, and to forge agreement on a political solution that would provide the Kosovar Albanians with increased autonomy (though short of the independence virtually all Albanians sought). These efforts failed—and the result was NATO's decision in March 1999 to intervene militarily in order to achieve by force what it could not achieve through negotiations.

NATO made the decision to go to war in the belief that a few days of limited bombing in the Balkans would likely suffice to persuade Milosevic to end the attacks on the Kosovar Albanian population and accept a political formula for restoring Kosovo's autonomy. That proved to be a major miscalculation. Rather than bowing to NATO's will, Milosevic escalated his violent campaign against the local population—forcibly removing 1.3 million people from their homes and pushing 800,000 people entirely out of Kosovo. Rather than undertaking a limited use of coercive force, NATO became engaged in the most extensive combat operations in its fifty-year history.

In this book, Ivo Daalder and Michael O'Hanlon provide the first comprehensive examination of the causes, course, and consequences of the conflict in Kosovo. Their focus is the immediate period of crisis of 1998 and 1999 that culminated in the eleven weeks of bombing. Daalder and O'Hanlon critically assess the policies of the Clinton administration and other NATO governments over this time period, with particular emphasis on three main questions: Was the war avoidable (and if so, how)? Did NATO win the war, not only in narrow military terms but also in a broader political and strategic sense? And why did Slobodan Milosevic, after seventy-eight days of bombing, finally relent and accept NATO's terms for a cessation of the war? From this historical and policy analysis, they draw lessons for future situations in which the United States and its allies might consider using force to save lives and shore up the stability of critical regions of the world.

The authors draw for their analysis on an extensive body of primary and secondary literature. But this book would not have been possible without the assistance of many U.S. and European officials who were directly involved in making and executing policy and consented to be interviewed. These officials include Joachim von Arnim, Samuel Berger, Edgar Buckley, General Wesley Clark, Ambassador Charles Crawford, Ambassador Robert Gelbard, Ambassador Sir John Goulden, Ambassador Phillippe Guelluy, General Sir Charles Guthrie, Morton Halperin, Ambassador Richard Holbrooke, Colonel Gregory Kaufmann, General Klaus Naumann, James O'Brien, Ambassador Francisco Olivieri, Christian Pauls, John Sawers, Gregory Schulte, William Shapcott, Jamie Shea, General Rupert Smith, Ambassador Alexander Vershbow, Lieutenant General David Weisman, and Brigadier General Klaus Wittmann. Daalder and O'Hanlon are exceedingly grateful for their cooperation.

This book could not have been written in such a short period of time without the indefatigable research assistance of Karla Nieting and Micah Zenko, who never tired of searching for additional sources and information and provided critical assistance in tracing the chronology of the conflict. Additional assistance was provided by Brian Finlay and Jason Forrester, for which the authors are grateful. They would also like to thank Susan Jackson for her work in verifying the manuscript, and Jessica Friedman for preparing the verification materials that enabled the process to be completed in short order. Kate O'Hanlon also helped her brother with useful and important insights. The production staff at the Brookings Institution Press, notably Diane Hammond, who edited the volume, and Carlotta Ribar and Sherry

Smith, who proofread and indexed the pages, also made possible the very short publication turnaround.

The authors benefited greatly from reviews of a draft of the manuscript by Robert Art, Michael Brown, and Warren Zimmermann, as well as informal reviews by Hans Daalder, David Ochmanek, and Richard Ullman. Aside from reading and commenting on the manuscript twice, Richard Haass assisted in innumerable ways throughout the project. They all have the authors' heartfelt thanks.

Just as important, the authors would like to thank both the German Marshall Fund of the United States and the John M. Olin Foundation for their financial support of this effort.

The views expressed here are those of the authors and should not be ascribed to those acknowledged above or to the trustees, officers, or other staff members of the Brookings Institution.

Michael H. Armacost
President

Washington, D.C.
April 2000

To our wives
Elisa Harris and Cathryn Garland

Contents

Kosovo and Its Neighbors

Kosovo

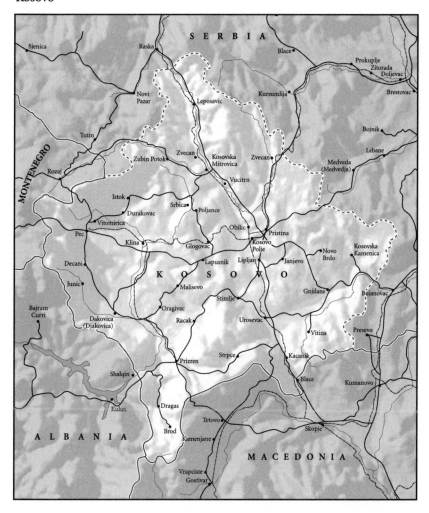

CHAPTER ONE

Introduction

O N MARCH 24, 1999, NATO went to war for the first time in its fifty-year history. Its target was not a country, but a man. As the Serb leader of Yugoslavia, Slobodan Milosevic had been most responsible for a decade of violence that accompanied the breakup of Yugoslavia. Well over a hundred thousand people had been killed and millions displaced in Croatian and Bosnian wars during the first part of the 1990s. Now a similar humanitarian catastrophe threatened in Kosovo, part of Serbia, the heart of the former Yugoslavia. Milosevic's security forces were arrayed against the Kosovo Liberation Army (KLA), a small insurgent force, and the ethnic Albanians who dominated the area's population. In the previous year of fighting, nearly two thousand people had been killed and many hundreds of thousands were driven from their homes. A full-scale war in Kosovo between Serbs and Albanians would likely have been particularly brutal, leaving untold death and destruction in its wake. Compounding the likely humanitarian disaster was the potential for large numbers of refugees engulfing the fragile border countries of Macedonia and Albania, with consequences for stability and security across the entire region.

So NATO went to war. For a decade, the alliance had wavered in its resolve to confront Milosevic. At times, the Serb leader had proven a willing partner in negotiating a halt to the region's violence. More often, he had been the source of that violence. For more than a year, the United States and its principal European allies had tried to head off a military confrontation by seeking to engage the man most responsible for the carnage that had befallen Kosovo, an approach similar to that followed in Croatia and Bosnia earlier in the decade. The Kosovo effort failed, not least because Milosevic displayed little interest in defusing a confrontation with a NATO alliance he assumed would soon founder in disagreement over how and to what extent to prosecute a war.

Late on the night of March 24, NATO warplanes began what was expected to be a brief bombing campaign. The purpose of the campaign was to force Milosevic back to the negotiating table so that NATO could find a way short of independence to protect Kosovo's ethnic Albanian population from Serb violence and political domination. This bombing campaign, it was emphatically stated, was not a war, and none of the NATO leaders had any intention of waging one.

Politics at home and abroad were believed to constrain the United States and its partners in the use of force. When hostilities began, President Bill Clinton had just survived his impeachment ordeal. He faced a Congress that was not just politically hostile but also increasingly wary of U.S. military action designed to serve humanitarian goals, including in the Balkans. Although Clinton had authorized the use of military force several times in his presidency, he had not ordered American soldiers into situations in which some were likely to be killed since the Somalia operation had gone tragically wrong in late 1993. Against this backdrop, the president failed to prepare the country for the possibility that NATO's initial bombing raids might be the opening salvo of a drawn-out war. Nor were he and his top advisers really prepared for this possibility themselves.

As alliance aircraft revved up their engines to start a short air campaign focused primarily on Serb antiaircraft defenses, the expected operation had the flavor of a number of other recent, short, and antiseptic uses of Western airpower. Three months earlier the United States and Great Britain had conducted a four-day bombing campaign against Iraq, and in August 1998 the Clinton administration had launched cruise missile strikes against suspected terrorist facilities in Afghanistan and Sudan in retaliation for the bombings of two U.S. embassies in Africa by the Osama bin Laden network. Neither of those recent military operations had achieved core U.S. strategic objectives. Saddam Hussein had not allowed weapons inspections to resume in Iraq, and the bin Laden network remained intact and, by all accounts, poised to strike again. These generally unsuccessful attacks did little to enhance the credibility of the United States. They were designed more to punish, and to "send a message," than to compel an adversary to change his behavior or directly achieve concrete strategic objectives.

NATO's security interests seemed even less engaged in the Balkans than they had been with Saddam Hussein or bin Laden. This was apparent in the alliance's goals for Kosovo, which were quite nuanced. NATO did not seek to defeat the Serb-dominated Yugoslav armed forces, cause a regime change in Belgrade, or gain Kosovo its independence. Rather it sought to convince

Milosevic to resume negotiations that would allow an armed international force into Kosovo to quell the violence that had erupted there in March 1998. Beyond that the alliance objective was nothing more than autonomy for the ethnic Albanian majority in Kosovo. As a major inducement to Milosevic, it even promised to disarm the KLA. Under such circumstances, a protracted NATO bombing campaign seemed disproportionate—and thus unlikely—to most onlookers, be they in Belgrade, Brussels, Washington, or elsewhere.

However, what had started very much as a foreign ministers' battle soon became NATO's first real war. Seventy-eight days later, it finally ended as Serb forces left Kosovo and a NATO-led international force of 50,000 began to move in. But over the intervening weeks a great deal of destruction was wrought, by Serbs against ethnic Albanians and by NATO against Serbia.

Despite the fact that most of the world's best air forces were conducting combat missions over Yugoslavia from March 24 onward, the early phases of the conflict were dominated militarily by Serb units in Kosovo. NATO lost the war in the initial going, and the Kosovar Albanian people paid the price. Up to 10,000 or so died at Serb hands, mostly innocent civilians; thousands more were raped or otherwise brutalized. Some 800,000 people were forcefully expelled from Kosovo, and hundreds of thousand more were displaced within the territory. Ultimately perhaps 1,000 to 2,000 Serbs perished as well, both civilians killed inadvertently and regular and irregular Serb forces killed on the battlefield.

In the end, NATO prevailed. Although there was no clear turning point, the NATO summit in Washington on April 23–25, 1999—organized originally to celebrate the alliance's fiftieth anniversary—may represent the best dividing line between losing and winning the war. Before that time, the vast majority of Kosovar Albanians were forced from their homes. Despite an intensification of its air campaign, NATO remained powerless to prevent atrocities on the ground or to establish a public perception that it was truly committed to winning the war.

But the summit revealed an alliance unified in its conviction that the war against Serbia must be won. War planning became more systematic, and further increases in NATO's air armada were authorized. The alliance steeled itself sufficiently that even the accidental bombing of the Chinese embassy on May 7 by a U.S. B-2 bomber did not seriously threaten continuation of the war effort. Perhaps most significantly, on April 25 Russian President Boris Yeltsin called Bill Clinton, resuming U.S.-Russian ties that had been effectively frozen when the war began. Yeltsin, though still upset,

committed to do what he could to end the war, setting in motion a negotiating process that would ultimately put a 360-degree diplomatic squeeze
on Milosevic.

When it was all over, the alliance was able to reverse most of the damage
Serbia had caused in the early period of the war. Notably, of the nearly 1.3
million ethnic Albanians driven from their homes, virtually all were able to
return within a few short weeks of the end of the war. Serb forces left Kosovo,
with NATO-led units assuming physical control of the territory. An international administration was set up to run Kosovo, effectively wresting political
control over the area from Belgrade.

Although overall political momentum began to shift in NATO's favor
around the time of the Washington summit, the military tide of battle turned
most dramatically in late May. By then, NATO air assets had nearly tripled
and the weather had improved, making precision bombs far more effective.
In addition, the alliance's political leadership had authorized attacks against
a much wider range of targets in Belgrade and elsewhere. The KLA, though
still a modest militia force, had begun to conduct limited offensives against
Serb positions within Kosovo, in some cases forcing Serb troops to expose
themselves, at which point they became more vulnerable to NATO attack
aircraft.

By early June Serbia was reeling. In Kosovo Serb forces had lost substantial amounts of the equipment with which they had begun, and Serb soldiers were finding themselves at considerable personal risk. In Serbia
electricity grids were being severely damaged, water distribution was ad-
versely affected in all major cities, and the businesses and other assets of
Milosevic's cronies were being attacked with growing frequency.

During the eleven-week air campaign, NATO flew nearly 40,000 combat
sorties, about one-third the number flown in six weeks during the 1991
Desert Storm campaign. Fourteen of the alliance's nineteen members participated in the attacks.[1] The air campaign was conducted very profession-
ally and precisely by the armed forces of the United States and other NATO
member countries. Although some 500 Serb and ethnic Albanian civilians
were killed accidentally by NATO bombs, that toll is modest by the standards of war. Moreover, only two alliance jets were shot down in combat,
and only two NATO troops died—U.S. Army pilots who perished in an
Apache helicopter training accident in neighboring Albania.

NATO's air war had two main thrusts: a strategic campaign against the
Serb heartland and a tactical campaign against the Serb forces doing the

killing and the forced expulsions in Kosovo. NATO supreme commander General Wesley Clark rightly argued that, for understanding how NATO won the war, "the indispensable condition for all the other factors was the success of the air campaign itself." The Pentagon's report on the war reached a similar conclusion.[2] But neither ultimate victory nor historically low losses demonstrate that the air war was well designed or properly conceived by top decisionmakers in Washington and other NATO capitals.

Final victory required more than bombing. Two critical factors occurred on the political front: NATO's demonstrated cohesion as an alliance and Russia's growing willingness to cooperate in the pursuit of a diplomatic solution. On the military front, NATO's talk of a possible ground war (which alliance leaders had unwisely ruled out when the bombing began) and the well-publicized decisions to augment allied troop strength in Macedonia and Albania proved to be crucial as well. Whereas the air war inflicted mounting damage, these other factors probably convinced Milosevic that no plausible escape remained. Once that became clear to him, capitulation became his best course, both to minimize further damage to Serbia and its military and to secure his position in power.

Although U.S. domestic politics complicated the conduct of the conflict at times, and did much to shape the limited way in which it was initially fought, they did not fundamentally threaten the operation once it was under way. Most polls showed clear, though hardly overwhelming or impassioned, majorities of the U.S. public supporting NATO's air campaign.[3] Indeed, once the war started, the Clinton administration faced more criticism from those who felt its war plan to be excessively cautious than from those who believed the use of force to be wrongheaded in the first place. As columnist E. J. Dionne Jr. wrote, liberals in particular supported this war for its humanitarian dimensions, getting over their "Vietnam syndrome" in the process.[4] And while some conservatives objected to the war as not serving U.S. interests, much of the Republican foreign policy elite felt strongly that the conflict had to end in a NATO victory.

In this book, we trace the causes, conduct, and consequences of the Kosovo conflict, analyzing the prelude to war in 1998 and 1999, the period when the KLA first came into direct conflict with Serb forces in Kosovo and the latter began a deliberate escalation of the conflict. We also critically assess the key decisions in NATO policymaking over the eighteen-month period from early 1998 through mid-1999: the October 1998 Holbrooke-Milosevic agreement to place unarmed international monitors in Kosovo, the Rambouillet negotiations of early 1999, the alliance's decision to begin bombing, and its gradual realization that it would have to win a war, whatever that ultimately required. We conclude by drawing lessons from the conflict that may be relevant to managing similar crises and conducting other such interventions in the future.

Our basic thesis is summarized in the book's title, *Winning Ugly.* NATO did meet reasonable standards of success in its 1999 war against Serbia. The outcome achieved in Kosovo, while hardly without its problems, represented a major improvement over what had prevailed in the region up to that point and certainly over what would have happened had NATO chosen not to intervene. It is in that relative sense that the policy was successful, not because it was properly designed at most major stages and not because it achieved the best plausible outcome to which NATO might have aspired.

Operation Allied Force was far from a perfect diplomatic and military accomplishment. The United States and its allies succeeded only after much suffering by the ethnic Albanian people on the ground. They prevailed only after committing a number of major mistakes, which future interventions must seek to avoid. In fact, NATO's mistakes were so serious that its victory was anything but preordained. Had Milosevic not escalated the conflict dramatically by creating the largest forced exodus on the European continent since World War II, and had alliance leaders not then realized they had to radically overhaul their military strategy, NATO could have lost the war. That would have held very serious implications for the future of the alliance and even worse implications for the peoples of the region.

The Roots of War

The immediate cause of the conflict in Kosovo was Slobodan Milosevic, and his oppression of Kosovar ethnic Albanians in the preceding decade. Oppression ultimately gave rise to violent opposition to Serb rule, first in the formation of the KLA and then in the spiral of violence of 1998 and 1999. But the antecedents of the war go back many centuries. The most famous historic event of the millennium in the territory was probably the 1389 Battle of Kosovo, in the Field of the Blackbirds, near Kosovo's present-day capital of Pristina. There, Serb forces attempted to fend off the invading Turks, with ethnic Albanians probably fighting on both sides in the battle. A subsequent battle in Kosovo in 1448 between the Ottoman Turks and the Hungarians, together with the fall of Constantinople to the Ottomans in 1453, sealed the fate of the region. The Ottoman Empire would soon dominate the region and it in fact controlled Kosovo into the twentieth century. Looking back on these momentous events, nineteenth- and twentieth-century Serb nationalists mythologized the 1389 battle and, more generally, the role of Kosovo in their nation's history. In the process, they portrayed the primarily Muslim Albanians essentially as sympathizers of the victorious Turkish invaders. The complex interaction of Serbs, Albanians, and Turks over the ensuing centuries provided the ground for all parties' competing historical perceptions, myths, fears, and vendettas.[5]

Kosovo's population became increasingly ethnic Albanian during the period of Ottoman rule. A decisive turning point, politically and demographically, was the large Serb exodus from the region (ultimately into Hungary) in the late seventeenth century. It was caused by Ottoman armies pressing north, ending in their defeat at Vienna against the Habsburg dynasty during the Ottoman-Habsburg War of 1683–99. That war spelled the beginning of the end for Ottoman rule in the Balkans, though as noted it survived in Kosovo for another two hundred years.

In the early twentieth century, the Ottoman Empire was driven out of the Balkans by Serb, Macedonian, and Bulgarian forces, shortly before its complete collapse. Serbia, having itself regained de facto independence in the early 1800s and formal state status in the 1878 Treaty of Berlin, asserted control over Kosovo in 1912. That was the same year in which an independent Albanian state was created for the first time, with many of the key moves on the road to independence occurring in Kosovo, conferring on the territory a historic importance for the Albanian people comparable to that for the Serbs.[6] Serbia lost control of Kosovo during World War I. After the war both Serbia and Kosovo were integrated into the new country of Yugoslavia, with Kosovo a province of Serbia.

At various times over the last century, Serbs drove large numbers of ethnic Albanians from Kosovo in what would be antecedents to Slobodan Milosevic's 1999 campaign to effectively empty the territory of nearly all of them.[7] Nonetheless, ethnic Albanians remained the majority population throughout the century, representing an increasingly high percentage of all Kosovars in recent decades. Serbs and Montenegrins constituted slightly less than 30 percent of the population in the early years of Tito's rule, which lasted from 1945 until his death in 1980. They gradually declined to less than half that percentage in recent times due to Serb departures and high Albanian birth rates.[8]

Whatever the recent population proportions, Kosovo is a land to which both Serbs and Albanians have important and long-standing claims.[9] For that reason, claims by extremists on both sides that they have exclusive rights to the land are false, as are claims that the peoples are so different from each other as to be innately incapable of coexistence.[10] The fact that Kosovo's Albanians are now effectively in charge in the province—and that they should remain in control of at least most of it, whether through autonomy within Serbia, republic status within Yugoslavia, or eventual independence—has nothing to do with original claims to the land. It has instead to do with the treatment of the Kosovar Albanians by Slobodan Milosevic and his fellow Serb nationalists in recent times.

Problems became serious even before the rise of Milosevic in 1987. As early as 1981, a year after the death of Tito, a student uprising in Pristina gave rise to provincewide demonstrations against Yugoslav authorities and perhaps dozens or even hundreds of deaths of ethnic Albanians. For Serbs the uprising was surprising in that Kosovo had been granted greater autonomy and rights, including Albanian-language schools, under the 1974 revision of the Yugoslav constitution. For Albanians these new rights only made them hunger for more, and the deteriorating economic conditions in the province together with their second-class status exacerbated the political tension. Additional incidents through the 1980s further divided Serbs from Albanians.[11]

In early 1989, as part of his effort to consolidate power as president of Serbia (the position he held from 1987 until becoming president of Yugoslavia in 1997), Milosevic stripped Kosovo of its autonomy. That denied the territory the special status within the Yugoslav Federation that it had enjoyed since the adoption of the 1974 constitution. In response to growing Serb oppression, Albanians established parallel state structures that were championed by Ibrahim Rugova and his Democratic League of Kosovo (LDK), officially founded in December 1989 and committed from the outset to opposing Serb sovereignty over the Kosovar Albanian people. In the following years, Rugova would be elected and reelected as Kosovo's "president" in unofficial elections among the region's ethnic Albanian population.[12]

Rugova and the LDK hoped that in demonstrating their ability to run the territory in all but name, the West would come to recognize Kosovo's right to be independent, as it had for four Yugoslav republics in the early 1990s. Support for separation from Yugoslavia was essentially universal. According to a 1995 survey, 43 percent of all Kosovar Albanians wanted to join Albania, and the remaining 57 percent desired outright independence, with none favoring any other solution (including the status of an independent republic within Yugoslavia, which by then included only Serbia and the much smaller Montenegro).[13] That hope and expectation proved to be misplaced. Kosovo was not at the center of U.S. and European Balkan policy and, as long as violence did not escalate, it would not be at the center of that policy.

Yet the United States and its European allies recognized that Kosovo was a powder keg in the middle of a highly volatile region. With Albanians living in at least four countries (Albania, Greece, Macedonia, and Yugoslavia), anything that stoked Albanian nationalism could be highly destabilizing for Kosovo's neighbors. Probably of most concern was Macedonia, whose population is a potentially volatile mix of Slavs with a large minority of Albanians. The fragility of Albania itself was also a reason for concern. Widespread violence in Kosovo was therefore to be avoided, even if that required direct U.S. military action. This together with congressional pressure explains why the Bush administration, which otherwise had a hands-off policy toward Yugoslavia's breakup, decided in late 1992, in response to indications that Serbia might be contemplating a violent crackdown against the Albanian population in Kosovo, to issue a stern warning that such action would lead to U.S. military action. In a letter to Milosevic, President Bush warned that "in the event of conflict in Kosovo caused by Serbian action, the United States will be prepared to employ military force against the Serbs in Kosovo and in Serbia proper."[14] This so-called Christmas warning was reiterated by the Clinton administration within a month of taking office in 1993, when the new secretary of state, Warren Christopher, stated, "We remain prepared to respond against the Serbians in the event of conflict in Kosovo caused by Serb action."[15]

On the whole, however, Kosovo occupied a distinctly secondary place in U.S. and Western policy toward the region. Indeed, unlike Bosnia, Croatia, and the other former Yugoslav republics, Kosovo was regarded as an integral part of Serbia rather than as a constituent part of the federation that broke up in the early 1990s. Whereas the republics were regarded as new states that emerged from Yugoslavia's dissolution and thus enjoyed sovereign rights, this status did not apply to Serbia's autonomous provinces (Kosovo and Vojvodina), even though these had enjoyed many of the same prerogatives the republics had, including their own constitutions, governments, judiciaries, central banks, and seats alongside the republics in Yugoslavia's eight-member federal presidency.[16] As a result, the issue for Western policy in Kosovo was not self-determination or national rights but how to protect minority and human rights.

Almost from the beginning, therefore, U.S. and European policy toward Kosovo was limited to increasing pressure on Belgrade to improve the human rights situation in the territory and establish conditions for greater autonomy and self-government. These demands were raised as a matter of course in all diplomatic dealings with the Belgrade government. The chief U.S. negotiator for ending the Bosnian war, Richard Holbrooke, also raised the issue of Kosovo with Milosevic during their Bosnia negotiations in Dayton in 1995. However, not only were the issues to be resolved in Dayton highly complex and the negotiations intense, the fact that Milosevic's cooperation was critical to success weakened the negotiators' leverage in exacting the concessions that would have been necessary for progress on Kosovo.[17]

Still, even after sanctions on Serbia were lifted as the reward for Milosevic's important role in concluding the Bosnian peace agreement, an "outer wall" of sanctions remained in place, partly to encourage the Serb government to improve its policies in Kosovo.[18] In 1996, moreover, the United States established an official government presence in Pristina, when it opened a cultural center run by the U.S. Information Agency that, in Holbrooke's words, amounted to "a virtual U.S. embassy." This step demonstrated U.S. concern over the deteriorating conditions in Kosovo. Finally, during the few meetings he had with Milosevic after successfully concluding the Dayton negotiations, Holbrooke consistently repeated the Christmas warning, even though he says that he was not 100 percent clear on what it was or exactly what it would mean in practice.[19]

Despite these limited efforts, there was no concerted attempt to resolve the Kosovo issue before it exploded in full violence (for example, by threatening to impose new sanctions unless Milosevic restored autonomy to the Kosovar Albanians). Although the failure to address Kosovo in Dayton was understandable, the lack of international attention to the issue dealt a major setback to Rugova's strategy of nonviolence. It became increasingly clear in the second half of the 1990s that the Serbs would not stop their repression of Kosovo's majority population and that the international community would do little to effect a change in Serb policy, let alone endorse the Kosovars' demand for independence. For many ethnic Albanians, one conclusion was inescapable: only violence gets international attention.[20] A previously unknown group—the Kosovo Liberation Army—took advantage of this realization and started to engage in sporadic violence, harassing and even killing Serb policemen and other authority figures. Its levels of violence were fairly modest; the KLA claimed to have killed ten Serbs in the two-year period up to early 1998. Nonetheless, the situation was deteriorating.[21]

Meanwhile, Rugova's efforts at nonviolent resistance were leading nowhere after Dayton. In 1996, he negotiated an agreement with Milosevic (with the assistance of Communitá di Sant'Egidio, an Italian Catholic charity) that would have given the educational systems run by ethnic Albanians access to official government buildings. Milosevic failed to implement the accord. Rugova was also hurt when the Sali Berisha government in Albania, from which he had received support, fell in 1997 as a result of the spectacular collapse of a nationwide pyramid scheme. The ensuing chaos in Albania led to looting of weapons stocks in many parts of Albania, some of them undoubtedly winding up in the hands of the KLA.[22]

In March 1998 Serb security forces stoked the fires by massacring eighty-five people in a brutally indiscriminate attempt to stem the KLA's growing importance in Kosovo. At that point, the violence in Kosovo reached a critical threshold and demanded sustained international attention. Unless stopped by a third party, the ethnic Albanian population and Slobodan Milosevic's Serb nationalists were headed for war. The only remaining questions were two. First, did the United States and its allies care enough about Kosovo to be true to Washington's 1992 Christmas warning? Second, would they find an integrated strategy involving both diplomacy and the threat of force that would succeed in getting the local parties off their collision course? The respective answers to these questions were yes and no.

This book explains how these and other questions were raised, and answered, during the critical eighteen-month period from early 1998 through mid-1999, when Kosovo was a top concern of Western policymakers. Chapters 2 and 3 focus on the prewar period, up to and including the Rambouillet negotiations of early 1999. Chapters 4 and 5 trace the seventy-eight-day violent conflict, including the ups and downs of NATO's, Serbia's, and the Kosovar Albanians' fortunes, and identify its key elements and milestones. The conclusion addresses three key policy questions: Was the war inevitable? Did NATO win? And why did Milosevic ultimately capitulate? It also draws several lessons for future policy regarding coercive diplomacy, the use of force, and humanitarian intervention.

Before addressing these questions, however, it is necessary to spell out the main argument of the book: that NATO's cause was worthy, and its efforts ultimately were reasonably successful, but that the strategy it chose to pursue its cause was seriously flawed.

NATO's Worthy Cause

NATO had moral and strategic rectitude on its side in using military power in the Balkans. First, upholding human rights and alleviating humanitarian tragedy are worthy goals for American national security policy. Doing so reinforces the notion that the United States is not interested in power for its own sake but rather to enhance stability and security and to promote certain universal principles and values. Second, the United States and its allies have a special interest in upholding these values in Europe, a continent that has become generally free and undivided since the cold war ended but that remains conflict ridden in the Balkans. Third, in addition to these humanitarian and normative rationales, traditional national interest argues for quelling violence in the Balkans because instability there can affect key allies more directly than instability in most other parts of the world.

I would reverse this order [margin note]

A number of critics of NATO's approach to the Kosovo crisis either disagree with these arguments or argue that the alliance should have found a way to solve the problem without going to war. More specifically, critics of the alliance argue the following: that the level of violence in Kosovo did not justify NATO military action, especially given the predictable fallout such an action would have on relations with Russia and China; that a more tactically creative and balanced negotiating strategy in the years before the conflict, and particularly at Rambouillet in the winter of 1999, might have averted war; and that even after Milosevic capitulated to most of NATO's main demands in June, conditions in Kosovo did not improve enough to deem the outcome successful. On all of these points, however, critics have overstated their case.[23]

NATO created greater viol. ag. Albanians [margin note]

Certainly the levels of violence in Kosovo before March 24, 1999, were modest by the standards of civil conflict and compared to what ensued during NATO's bombing campaign. The violence had caused the deaths of an estimated 2,000 people in the previous year. This was not an attempted genocide of the ethnic Albanian people. However, there was good reason to believe that, without intervention, things would have gotten much worse. Milosevic and his fellow Serb extremists had already displayed their true colors earlier in the decade in Bosnia, where at least 100,000 people, mostly Muslims and Croats, had been killed. More recently, and more to the point, in 1998, before the October agreement between Milosevic and U.S. special envoy Richard Holbrooke, Milosevic and his henchmen had driven some 300,000 Kosovar Albanians from their homes, with 50,000 winding up, vulnerable and exposed, hiding in the hills of the province. It was one of the world's five largest crises involving refugees and internally displaced persons in 1998 and the only one in a country subject to cold winters.[24] What the alliance has since learned about Milosevic's planned Operation Horseshoe only confirms these judgments. Recognizing that the KLA was probably becoming too strong and too popular within ethnic Albanian society for him to defeat using classic counterinsurgency techniques, he chose to expel much of the civilian population instead. If this policy was conceived to serve a military purpose, it had a real political appeal for Milosevic too, being the surest way to restore Kosovo to complete Serb control and to free land for Serbs displaced from other parts of the former Yugoslavia in recent conflicts.

At the very best, had Milosevic been left to his own devices, hundreds of thousands of ethnic Albanians would have been driven permanently out of the province, possibly causing serious economic and political consequences in Albania and Macedonia. Fewer Kosovar Albanians might have died in a slower campaign of forced expulsion than the number who died in the actual war, but even that is not certain. It is equally plausible that, once Milosevic saw NATO's lack of resolve in protecting the Kosovars, he would have reverted to the style of warfare perpetrated in Bosnia, killing far more than the 10,000 or so who ultimately perished.

As for the effects on Russia and China, both of these countries had supported previous UN Security Council resolutions demanding an improvement in the human rights situation in Kosovo. Yet neither offered any constructive or serious alternatives to NATO's adopted strategy. The damage to relations with Moscow and Beijing was deeply regrettable; the NATO May 7 bombing of the Chinese embassy in Belgrade was both tragic and incompetent; and the need to act without a UN Security Council resolution was unfortunate. But NATO could not allow itself to be prevented from stopping a mass murderer in its own backyard by unreasonable demands from foreign capitals. In fact, there may even have been a silver lining, in that NATO demonstrated to Russia and China that it would not be intimidated by their protests over a matter that did not concern them directly—and that they seemed uninterested in trying to solve in any case.

NATO's war against Serbia will remain an irritant in Western relations with both China and Russia, perhaps for years, but it was already fading in salience by late 1999 and early 2000. By that point, most normal ties between Western capitals and Moscow and Beijing had been resumed, the U.S.-China relationship had moved on to trade issues and Taiwan security matters, and the U.S.-Russian agenda had refocused on nuclear and economic issues as well as on achieving a smooth transition from Boris Yeltsin to Vladimir Putin. The UN Security Council had restored its ability to function effectively, as evidenced by resolutions proposing a new weapons inspection regime for Iraq and peacekeeping forces for East Timor and Congo. Despite the charges of some, it is not plausible that NATO's war over Kosovo was a chief cause of Russia's resumed conflict in Chechnya or of China's tense relations with Taiwan. Both of those problems are far too central to those countries' core interests to be blamed on Western military action in the Balkans. Operation Allied Force was clearly bad for the West's relations with China and Russia, but it was hardly a turning point. Ultimately, both China and Russia have more important things to worry about and more important matters to discuss with the United States and its allies.

What about the possibility of protecting the ethnic Albanians without going to war? Critics argue, for example, that NATO essentially ignored the Kosovo problem throughout the 1990s, doing little to make the 1992 Christmas warning credible. Others argue that NATO made a deal with Milosevic impossible when it demanded at Rambouillet that its troops have access to all Yugoslav territory and that a plebiscite on Kosovo's future be held three years after the signing of an accord. Still others assert that partitioning Kosovo between Albanians and Serbs might have prevented war or that arming the KLA might have allowed NATO to stay out of the violent conflict once it did begin.

It is true that NATO's tendency to neglect Kosovo throughout the 1990s was a mistake. At a minimum, once the 1995 Dayton Accords were signed and NATO troops deployed to Bosnia, the United States and its allies should have threatened to impose sanctions as conditions in Kosovo deteriorated in the ensuing years. They no longer needed Milosevic to establish or keep the peace in Bosnia and could thus hold him up to reasonable standards of behavior in his own backyard. However, it is doubtful that doing so would have convinced Milosevic to back down; he had already demonstrated his willingness to accept sanctions as the price of trying to gain land in Bosnia for Serbs, and if anything he cared more about Kosovo than about Bosnia. Moreover, by the time of Rambouillet Milosevic knew the tide had turned against him in Kosovo and that to keep his hold over the territory he would have to wipe out the KLA rather than simply restore autonomy to the ethnic Albanians (which it is doubtful that he wished to do in any event). Having watched NATO troops become ensconced in Bosnia, he probably also doubted whether NATO troops, once allowed in, would ever leave Kosovo.

NATO did err in insisting on military access to all of Serbia at Rambouillet. It clearly failed to recognize that the kind of language common in status-of-forces agreements it had negotiated previously (including with Croatia) might be wrongly interpreted, but this provision was almost certainly not the decisive factor in Milosevic's thinking. The Serbs never raised it during the negotiations, focusing their opposition instead on the proposed deployment of a NATO-led force inside Kosovo. Had they objected to the provision, negotiators would surely have recommended that alliance military authorities change their position. NATO made this demand as a matter of military convenience and nothing else. As the later Kosovo Force (KFOR) operation showed, NATO did not need access to northern and central Serbia to carry out its mission in Kosovo.

The conflict in Kosovo was fundamental: only NATO troops could have protected the Kosovar Albanians reliably enough to convince the KLA to disarm, but such troops were anathema to Milosevic, as was the idea of Kosovo's autonomy or independence. The parties were on a collision course for war, and a different negotiating strategy could not itself have changed that fact. It may still have been worth making one last offer to Milosevic, partly to allow Russia a somewhat greater role in setting the terms of NATO's ultimatum. But the practical purpose of doing so would have been more to limit the fallout between NATO and Moscow once the war began than to avoid war. Only a very credible threat of massive NATO military action—a demonstrated willingness to achieve by force what negotiations could not— might have been enough to convince the butcher of Belgrade to relent. Yet critics do not generally make that argument, focusing instead on secondary or tactical issues, where their case is unconvincing.   *ugh. overused.*

What about partitioning Kosovo between Serbia and the ethnic Albanian population? It would have run counter to the views of virtually all NATO governments, which believed that partitioning *within* the various republics of the former Yugoslavia, such as Bosnia, was a bad idea. That is not itself sufficient reason to dismiss the idea analytically. However, while partitioning can help produce stable peace accords in civil conflicts, it is doubtful it would have worked in this particular instance. Ethnic Albanians, who were the overwhelming majority of Kosovars, would have insisted on, and had rights to, the majority of Kosovo's territory. Yet that would surely have been too high a price for Milosevic, who viewed Kosovo as key not only to his own rise to power a decade before but also to the territorial integrity of the Serb nation. Both sides essentially wanted all of the province. Perhaps partition would have been moderately preferable, in Milosevic's eyes, to having NATO throughout all of Kosovo. But either way, serious NATO threats or the use of force would have been necessary to convince him to give up most of a territory that he and his countrymen held very dear.

Arming the KLA might have contributed to an eventual battlefield success once war was under way, but it could hardly have prevented violence or allowed the Kosovar Albanians to win a quick victory. Leaving aside the fact that the KLA was an organization with goals for Kosovo's independence that NATO governments and Russia did not share, arming it would not have achieved any of the stated goals. An organization with only a few thousand ragtag fighters into early 1999, it could not have become strong enough to take on tens of thousands of Serb soldiers and police—or to prevent Milosevic's campaign of "ethnic cleansing"—in the space of a few short months of equipping and training by NATO.[25] Arming the KLA might have prevented Serbia from consolidating its control over the province but only at the price of turning Kosovo into another Afghanistan or Angola. That was not the right way to pursue a policy focused first and foremost on humanitarian goals.

Finally, many critics argue that postwar Kosovo, beset by problems like the exodus of local Serbs, is little improved from conditions that prevailed when Serbia ran the province. This claim is wrong. The level of per capita violence in Kosovo remains too high, but it dropped tenfold within the nine months after the war ended on June 10, 1999.[26] Serbs have left in great numbers, many out of a very real fear for their lives, but the displacement of some 100,000 Serbs since the end of the war is a far less severe violation of human rights than what Milosevic did to the ethnic Albanians—and for the most part it happened much less violently. Two wrongs do not make a right. But people who have been discriminated against for decades, oppressed for the last decade, brutalized for a year, and then driven from their homes and their land—often with the collaboration of local Serbs—can be forgiven a certain paranoia, even if their revenge attacks against Serbs cannot be condoned. To be sure, enough problems remain in Kosovo that NATO's victory cannot yet be called permanent. But the international community is now in a very favorable position to maintain basic military peace in the territory and to gradually improve its economic and social conditions. With good policymaking, it should be able to consolidate its victory, at least by standards that are reasonable to apply to a place, such as Kosovo, that has recently suffered a vicious civil war.

NATO's—and Washington's—Key Mistakes

The story of the Kosovo crisis is largely a saga of NATO and its major international partners doing the right thing but in the wrong way. From the beginning of the Kosovo crisis, U.S. and European leaders shared a common belief that they had to "do something" about the situation in this small territory in the heart of the former Yugoslavia. They just could never agree what that "something" was. When Milosevic's forces engaged in a brutal crackdown on the KLA in early March 1998, the Clinton administration knew it had to act for political, strategic, and moral reasons. Politically, Milosevic's actions challenged U.S. and NATO policy in other parts of the Balkans, including the decision to reward the Yugoslav leader for his cooperation in helping stabilize the situation in Bosnia. Strategically, widespread violence pitting Serbs against Albanians could rapidly spread to other parts of the Balkans, notably to Albania and Macedonia and even to Greece and Bulgaria. Morally, after what the world had witnessed in Croatia and Bosnia earlier in the decade, it was not difficult to imagine what Milosevic and his henchmen might be capable of doing against an ethnic Albanian population long despised by much of the Serb majority in Yugoslavia.

The choice for the Clinton administration and its European allies was not whether to act but how. The administration's fundamental failure in dealing with the Kosovo crisis was that it never decided what it was prepared to do, except incrementally and reactively. It was likely not until May 1999— six-plus weeks into NATO's war against Serbia—that President Clinton finally determined that, if necessary, the United States would do whatever was required to prevail, probably even including a U.S.-led allied invasion of Kosovo to end the war and ensure safety and autonomy for the Kosovar Albanians.

In the year and a half leading up to that point, the Clinton administration resorted to speaking loudly and carrying a small stick. It threatened largely unspecified action, hoping that would be sufficient to influence the parties to enter a dialogue leading to a political settlement. That approach was never adequate. Slowly but surely, the United States and its NATO allies moved down a slippery slope of making threats, planning for military action and demonstrations, backing up the threats by deploying military assets, issuing ultimatums, using airpower, intensifying strategic bombing, and finally being on the verge of committing to a ground invasion of Kosovo. No one thought that the policy would eventually end up there. Indeed much of the effort was designed to prevent the use of force—and certainly to prevent the use of ground forces, even in a peacekeeping mode.

The failure in Kosovo was the result of policymakers in Washington and elsewhere who proved unwilling or unable to set political objectives and to consider how far they were prepared to go to achieve them militarily. To be sure, the broad goals were widely agreed on: to end the violence and to establish conditions for the political autonomy of Kosovo within Yugoslavia.

But since this broad objective proved unacceptable to the Serb authorities, who wanted to maintain the political status quo, and to many Kosovars, who wanted independence, an international protectorate of the territory was the only real alternative. It took the alliance nearly a year to arrive at that conclusion. Even when it finally did, it failed to develop a reliable strategy for establishing such a protectorate-like arrangement in Kosovo. It had a hope, but not a plan.

NATO stumbled into war, unready either for countering Serbia's massive campaign to forcefully expel much of the ethnic Albanian population from Kosovo or to do militarily what it would take to achieve its stated objectives. Even if the war itself was not easily or demonstrably avoidable, NATO leaders should have been better prepared. That required knowing what the objective was and then committing to achieve it with the necessary military might. Instead NATO went to war in the hope it could win without much of a fight. It was proven wrong.

NATO's campaign plan was unsound in the war's early going. The fault did not lie in the alliance's decisionmaking processes or in specific foreign capitals like Paris and Berlin, as some have argued.[27] Rather, the fault lay in the basic strategy espoused for the war by the United States and its allied partners as a group. The basic idea of using bombing as an element of coercive diplomacy against Milosevic was pushed incessantly by Washington, and most specifically by the State Department, with strong support from NATO's military leadership. The U.S. government generally expected air strikes to last only a few days—a couple of weeks at the outside—as interviews with key officials and other sources convincingly attest. The United States did not even envisage hard-hitting attacks during that short period: on March 24 it had made available only about one-third the number of aircraft it ultimately devoted to the war, and days earlier it had pulled its only nearby aircraft carrier out of the Mediterranean region and thus away from the war zone. During the war's early going, NATO's limited number of strike sorties focused largely on attacking Serb air defenses, due largely to a body of U.S. Air Force doctrine that requires that air supremacy be established in the early phase of any war.[28] NATO's policy of keeping aircraft above 15,000 feet above sea level, which limited the effectiveness of the tactical bombing—severely so in the war's early going, given the predictably poor Balkan early spring weather— was primarily due to Washington's preference to avoid casualties at nearly any cost. In short, the frequent postwar tendencies of Clinton administration officials, particularly at the Pentagon, to blame the allies for the slow start of Operation Allied Force is almost entirely without foundation.

Operation Allied Force was in its early weeks a textbook case of how *not* to wage war. The blindness of NATO's major members to the possibility that the war might not end quickly was astounding. As a result of that blindness, the alliance was caught entirely unprepared for what followed. Had NATO not enjoyed such a huge military advantage over Serbia, the alliance might well have lost its first real war. The losers would have included the Kosovar Albanians as well as NATO itself, since a defeat would have called into doubt not only NATO's raison d'être but even its basic competence in the post–cold war world.

NATO's shortsightedness, and its cavalier attitude toward the use of force, could have had extremely serious consequences. Had Milosevic's henchmen in Kosovo been more brutal—for example, on the scale of what Ratko Mladic's Bosnian Serb forces did in Srebrenica in July 1995—or had food supplies in the hills and forests of Kosovo not held up for the many thousands of people who had to hide outdoors during the war, far more people might have died, with NATO powerless to save them. Had these things happened, NATO's ultimate victory would have been Pyrrhic.

Finally, had Milosevic not upped the stakes in the conflict by drastically escalating his forced expulsion campaign, NATO could easily have lost the war. He so repulsed Western publics with his barbaric actions that the alliance found a resolve it would almost certainly not have otherwise displayed. If Milosevic had hunkered down and restrained his military and paramilitary forces during the bombing, support within NATO countries for sustaining the operation probably would have quickly dissipated.

Perversely, Milosevic came to NATO's rescue. In a way that alliance leaders did not anticipate, he shored up their resolve and cohesion by his brutal treatment of the ethnic Albanians. Without it, NATO would probably have bombed for a few days and then been obliged to desist, even had Milosevic continued to resist an international armed presence in Kosovo. This argument is supported by our interviews with numerous NATO government officials, the Desert Fox precedent in Iraq from the previous December, and the alliance's limited enthusiasm for coming to the military aid of the KLA. True, Milosevic would have had to expect stronger economic sanctions in the aftermath of such an unsuccessful bombing campaign, but he had proven he could live with that. Moreover, Washington had already demonstrated the December before in the bombing campaign against Iraq—which was both short and ineffective—that it could "bomb and forget" even more heinous and dangerous adversaries affecting even more important U.S. interests. Milosevic had ample reason to think that NATO would bomb for a spell, declare victory, and stop. He could have then proceeded to a more patient form of ethnic expulsion, gradually, over a period of many months or even years, pushing ethnic Albanians out of large swaths of Kosovo while also weakening the KLA's hold in those areas. That he did not adopt such an approach may have been his greatest mistake of the war.

Since the day the war ended U.S. officials from President Clinton on down have concluded that the alliance "did the right thing"—which is true—and that it also did so in "the right way"—which is not.[29] Their argument rests on the twin contentions that in the end NATO prevailed and that the alliance could not have fought any other way given its internal political constraints. However, making war by accepting political constraints that impede sound military preparations can be a prescription for defeat—and nearly was in this case. Particularly for the United States, the alliance's undisputed leader, accepting alliance political constraints rather than working to mold them in support of the U.S. perspective was bad policy. It is true that NATO is, and must be, a committee. But in this war it was a committee without a chairman, particularly in the conflict's early going.

What was NATO's real alternative to its policy of diplomatic caution and military gradualism? Before the war, the proper approach would have been a muscular NATO threat to Milosevic, with the goal of convincing him to allow the establishment of a de facto international protectorate over Kosovo that would ensure the safety of civilians and demilitarize the KLA. Either in the fall of 1998 or in the immediate aftermath of the January 1999 Racak massacres, NATO should have promised a much more extensive and open-ended bombing campaign. Ideally it should also have deployed forces into the region to conduct a ground invasion if necessary.

This approach might have produced a negotiated settlement allowing international peacekeeping troops into the province. If not, once it began bombing NATO would have had the option of intervening quickly had massive slaughters been undertaken by the Serbs or if a lack of food supplies had led to widespread starvation. That it would have been extremely hard for the Clinton administration to convince Congress and the NATO allies to support such a strategy and that there was no guarantee that such a threat would then have worked, we acknowledge. But there is no excuse for not trying. Whatever the outcome would have been on preparing a possible invasion option, moreover, Washington could have and should have convinced NATO to pose a far more daunting aerial threat from the war's beginning. And it should never have ruled a ground force option off the table.

Conclusion

Operation Allied Force, the last war in Europe in the twentieth century, was ultimately an accomplishment for which NATO, the Clinton administration, and a number of other key actors can take satisfaction. The ethnic Albanian people of Kosovo, who suffered significant oppression under Slobodan Milosevic, are today far better off than they would have been had NATO stood aside. Their violent reprisal against Serbs in Kosovo since the war ended, while highly regrettable, does not begin to compare to what had happened before. The war's damage to Western relations with Russia and China, though real, is generally reparable and has already been largely attenuated. Moreover, NATO as an alliance distinguished itself by showing the political will to do what was right, on humanitarian and political grounds, even in the face of strident opposition from Moscow and Beijing. The demands the war placed on NATO military forces, in budgetary terms and human terms, were modest and were largely compensated for by important lessons the alliance's members learned about how to improve their individual and combined military capabilities for the future.

But this book is not, primarily, a laudatory history of NATO's first real war. It is a critique and, in places, a rather severe one. NATO in general, and the Clinton administration in particular, missed key opportunities in 1998 and early 1999 to reduce the odds of war. The alliance then undertook armed hostilities when it was unprepared for real combat, unwisely confident that its short campaign of coercive bombing would work. Its poor preparation and early lack of resolve extended the conflict; luckily that did not exact an enormous price in civilian or military lives lost, but it was risky—and unnecessary.

NATO's war in Kosovo was difficult enough, and unpleasant enough on many grounds, that it is unlikely to be seen by Western governments as a precedent for frequent humanitarian intervention. But the post–cold war world has already seen major Western military interventions designed to save lives or uphold democratic principles in Panama, northern Iraq, Somalia, Haiti, Bosnia, Kosovo, and East Timor. That track record, and the continuing prevalence of civil conflict around the world, suggests that Western countries need to learn as much as they can from NATO's 1999 war against Serbia, for better and for worse. This war will not be the last time that NATO governments use force to save lives.

CHAPTER TWO

The Escalating Crisis

L ONG IN THE MAKING, the Kosovo conflict finally turned violent in early 1998 when Serbia decided to crack down on the Kosovo Liberation Army, a small group of rebels bent on achieving independence through violence. From the moment violence exploded, the battle lines were drawn. On one side stood the Belgrade government, led by Yugoslav president Slobodan Milosevic and backed by the armed might of his Interior Ministry police troops (the MUP) and the Yugoslav army (the VJ). Its goal was both to prevent any further disintegration of what remained of Yugoslavia and to keep Kosovo firmly within Serbia's orbit. On the other side stood the Kosovar Albanians, who constituted the overwhelming majority of Kosovo's population and who had suffered under Serb repression for nearly a decade. Although divided over the means to be employed—with much of the political leadership under Ibrahim Rugova favoring peaceful resistance and the KLA preferring the use of violence—the Kosovar Albanians were united in their quest for the territory's independence not only from Serbia but also from the Federal Republic of Yugoslavia.

The United States and European countries had long been concerned about Kosovo and the consequences of a violent eruption in the area. But they had failed to translate this concern into effective action to prevent the conflict's slide into bloodshed. Once the Serb assault commenced in early March 1998, however, international attention was immediate and involved the highest levels of the U.S. and allied governments. From the start, these governments shared several key assumptions on how best to approach the conflict, including that they had to act promptly to avoid what had happened in Bosnia, that unity of effort and American leadership were necessary to forge a viable strategy, that concerted pressure on Milosevic would be necessary to reach a settlement, and that a solution short of Kosovo's independence would have to be found.

Throughout much of 1998, however, U.S., European, and NATO policy toward Kosovo was haphazard and marked by a tendency to avoid making difficult decisions. The focus of the initial effort was on economic sanctions and on encouraging a dialogue between the parties in order to arrive at a settlement of Kosovo's political future. The desire to halt an escalation in the fighting and to forge a political solution did not, at least initially, extend to a willingness to consider a forceful intervention to bring these results about. Rather than exposing themselves to the inevitable risks that any military option entailed, the Clinton administration and its European allies were content to defer for as long as possible having to make a choice among the unpalatable options of letting the Serbs get away with their murderous campaign against the KLA, supporting ethnic Albanian aspirations for independence, and taking the decisive action necessary to avoid either of these two outcomes. And once they were prepared to threaten force, they did so only tentatively and irresolutely.

This indecisiveness continued even in October 1998, when Richard Holbrooke, the Clinton administration's special Balkans envoy, traveled to Belgrade in an effort to persuade Slobodan Milosevic to end his forces' attacks on the Kosovar population (which by that time had forced some 300,000 people from their homes, including upward of 50,000 into the mountains). Backed by the threat of NATO airpower, Holbrooke succeeded in gaining Milosevic's apparent commitment to cease attacks on civilians, withdraw some of his security forces from the region, grant access to humanitarian relief agencies, allow refugees and displaced persons to return to their homes, and acquiesce to an international presence in Kosovo to verify his compliance with these commitments. However, key details of the Holbrooke-Milosevic agreement remained ill defined, and whatever NATO commitment existed to enforce compliance with its terms was effectively nullified by the decision to deploy unarmed monitors to the region. Consistent with U.S. and European efforts throughout the crisis, the Holbrooke mission was one more indication that the aim was less to find a viable and lasting solution to the conflict than to push the final reckoning as far into the future as possible. In doing so, however, this overall approach may well have sown the seeds of an even more violent conclusion to the conflict, as developments in 1999 would make clear.

Policy Assumptions and Contradictions

When violence exploded in the Kosovo hillsides in the first days of March 1998, the six Contact Group nations (France, Germany, Great Britain, Italy, Russia, and the United States) reacted swiftly. Within days of the Serb crackdown that left eighty-five people dead, foreign ministers from the six countries met in London to condemn the attack and take stock. The ministers demanded that Milosevic agree to cease all action by Serb security forces against the civilian population, withdraw Serb special police units from the territory within ten days, allow humanitarian groups to enter Kosovo, and commence an unconditional dialogue with the Albanian community. Failure to meet these demands, the ministers warned, would lead to imposition of an arms embargo, a denial of travel visas for senior Yugoslav and Serb officials, a moratorium on export credits for trade and investment, and a freeze on funds held abroad.[1] The six countries also committed themselves to remain on top of the issue, agreeing to meet by the end of March to assess Belgrade's actions and, if necessary, to agree to additional steps.

This prompt, high-level, and unified response to the eruption of violence in Kosovo reflected a number of assumptions the six Contact Group countries had derived from their shared experience in dealing with the Bosnian conflict earlier in the decade. First, all agreed that they had to act rapidly in order to avoid a repeat of the Bosnian horrors. As U.S. Secretary of State Madeleine Albright noted just days after the massacres: "We are not going to stand by and watch Serb authorities do in Kosovo what they can no longer get away with doing in Bosnia."[2] President Bill Clinton suggested much the same in his first public comments: "We do not want the Balkans to have more pictures like we've seen in the last few days so reminiscent of what Bosnia endured."[3] The need for a strong condemnation of and response to the Serb crackdown was underscored by Albright in the London meeting with her European colleagues on March 9, 1998. "History is watching us," she told the gathering assembled in Lancaster House. "In this very room our predecessors delayed as Bosnia burned, and history will not be kind to us if we do the same."[4]

A second assumption was that successful intervention required unity of effort as well as American leadership. Both had been absent in Bosnia. In that case, U.S. and European perceptions of the conflict and how best to approach its resolution diverged as a result of the decision by European countries to deploy troops on the ground. Instead of joining them in this effort, Washington decided (with Europe's full support) to cede leadership to Europe. With Europe exposed to risks that the United States avoided, the two sides' perspectives on the conduct of the war consequently diverged.[5] In the Kosovo case, the Clinton administration determined not to make this mistake. From day one, Albright forcefully took the lead in devising an appropriate response to the violence. Aside from a strong response, her goal was to ensure allied unity rather than division and to forge a path that would keep the Russians on board. This explains why the six-nation Contact Group, which had been founded to minimize disagreements over Bosnia, was chosen as the vehicle for developing a common approach to Kosovo.

A third assumption of Western policy was that only concerted pressure on Milosevic would prove effective in convincing Belgrade to end the violence and commence a dialogue with the Albanian community in Kosovo. A policy of carrots had failed. In November 1997, Milosevic spurned a European Union offer to improve diplomatic and trade relations with Belgrade and support its reentry into international institutions in return for accepting a negotiating process between the Kosovar, Serb, and Yugoslav authorities that would be supported by third-party mediation.[6] Days before the violence in Kosovo in March, the United States had lifted a number of sanctions as a reward for Milosevic's assistance in moderating the Bosnian Serb leadership, only to find Belgrade planning a major crackdown in Kosovo.[7] As Albright put it, "by his actions in Kosovo, Slobodan Milosevic has made it clear that he is spurning incentives that the United States and others have offered him in recent weeks—unfortunately the only thing he truly understands is decisive and firm action."[8]

A final assumption guiding the international response to violence in Kosovo was to rule out independence as a solution to the conflict. Independence posed two major problems. First, it could destabilize the rest of the region. The fragile interethnic consensus in Macedonia would be severely shaken, providing the minority Albanian population there with an incentive to join their Kosovar and Albanian neighbors in the quest for a Greater Albania. Macedonia's destabilization, in turn, could reignite territorial and other ambitions among its neighbors—Bulgaria, Greece, and Serbia—which in the early twentieth century had fought two wars over the territory. A second concern fueling opposition to independence was that independence in Kosovo would set a precedent for Bosnia, where Bosnian Serb and Croat claims for independence—or for merger with neighboring states—were at least as strong as those of the Kosovar Albanians. Having found what still appeared to be a viable solution to the Bosnia crisis, no one wished to promote a policy for Kosovo that would call that resolution into question.

Although these four assumptions of Western policy toward Kosovo were widely shared, they contained at least three contradictions. First, there was a conflict between the desire to act quickly and decisively, and the perceived need to forge a consensus on policy not only with key NATO allies but also with Russia. Given the range of views within the Contact Group on how to respond to the crisis—with the Russians and, to some extent, the Italians, favoring a policy of relying on positive incentives and the Americans and British preferring a more confrontational policy—forging a consensus on decisive action proved difficult. At times, however, this conflict was bypassed when the need for action outweighed getting the agreement of all Contact Group members, as when Russia abstained from decisions to impose economic sanctions on Belgrade and when NATO, in threatening to use force, bypassed the UN Security Council and a certain Russian veto.

A second contradiction concerned the belief that a solution to the Kosovo crisis lay in pressing Milosevic to end the violent crackdown in Kosovo—while at the same time NATO relied on him to negotiate a final settlement with the Albanian community. This meant that the ability to apply pressure on Milosevic to end the violence would at every turn be constrained by the realization that in the end the Yugoslav president was central to any successful negotiations. This constraint was compounded by the belief that the success of Western policy in Bosnia also depended crucially upon Milosevic's cooperation. It was therefore never really apparent who had leverage over whom: the United States and its allies over Milosevic, or vice versa.

A third contradiction was pressuring Milosevic to end the violence while hoping not to encourage the ethnic Albanians in Kosovo to push their maximalist claims for independence. Having rejected independence as an acceptable outcome of the conflict, Western policymakers had to constantly balance their pressure against Belgrade with the need to discourage the Kosovars from pressing their case for secession.

These policy contradictions were not inevitable.[9] Some of the assumptions underlying Western policy could have been relaxed or even abandoned altogether. For example, the decision to rely on consensus within the Contact Group inevitably resulted in least-common-denominator policies, hardly the kind of approach necessary to convince Belgrade to change course. Moreover, the best way to pressure Milosevic without encouraging the Kosovars to seek immediate independence would have been if NATO countries had been prepared to deploy ground forces in Kosovo as part of an agreement with Belgrade to protect ethnic Albanians, demilitarize the KLA, and guarantee their territory's continued inclusion in the Federal Republic of Yugoslavia. None of these options would have ensured success, but all would have improved the prospects for a peaceful settlement. Conversely, if the use of force was to remain a true option of last resort so as to maintain domestic and allied support for the policy, then abandoning opposition to Kosovo's independence in favor of pursuing partition might have been worth an attempt. Rather than making these choices, however, the United States and its European partners sought to defer making difficult decisions, preferring instead to muddle through in the hope that somehow and someway a solution would present itself that would at once end the violence, provide a firm political basis for a settlement, and avoid confronting the international community with the need to use massive force.

Responding to Violence

By early 1998, there were indications that the low-level violence that had beset Kosovo the previous year would escalate into a major conflagration. The Central Intelligence Agency warned in mid-January that the Serb authorities were contemplating a crackdown on ethnic Albanians. A month later it warned senior U.S. officials that Serb armored units were beginning to mobilize and that Interior Ministry police troops were moving toward the Kosovo border.[10] In late February, Robert Gelbard, the Clinton administration's senior envoy for the region, traveled to Belgrade to warn both sides that violence would solve nothing. In private talks with Milosevic, Gelbard indicated that Belgrade faced a choice: either cooperate in resolving the Kosovo problem (as it had in helping to bring peace in Bosnia by promoting a more moderate Bosnian Serb government), and be rewarded with a relaxation of sanctions, or face further isolation "into a downward spiral of darkness" if violence in Kosovo mounted.[11]

Gelbard's warnings notwithstanding, Serb security forces launched a major offensive against key KLA strongholds just days after his departure. On February 28, Serb forces killed some two dozen people in Qirez and Likosane in central Kosovo. Days later a major assault on Srbica and other villages in the Drenica valley left another fifty-one people dead, including a KLA leader, Adem Jashari, and twenty members of his family. Those killed included at least eleven children and twenty-three women. Within a week, eighty-five people were murdered by Serb security forces.[12] Serb officials justified their use of force as a necessary response to a "terrorist group," arguing that the attack on the village of Donji Prekaz where the Jashari family lived, had "wiped out . . . the biggest and most important one."[13]

Strong Rhetoric and Weak Sanctions

Within days of the first reports of the Serb massacres in Kosovo, Secretary Albright traveled to Europe to consult with her Contact Group counterparts to set the course for a united response. Her main purpose was to push the European allies, American public opinion, and even her own government toward concerted action designed to avert the kind of human tragedy that had happened in Bosnia. Her leverage was neither a plan of action nor a U.S. commitment to threaten or use force but rather her strong rhetoric.[14] It was a rhetoric steeped in a determination to avoid the appearance of another Munich (and the delay witnessed in Bosnia) and lacked the fear of another Vietnam-type quagmire that seemed to haunt some of her colleagues in Washington and elsewhere.[15] In London, Albright urged her colleagues not to delay and to push for immediate action rather than rely on rhetoric and diplomacy alone:

> When the war in the former Yugoslavia began in 1991, the international community did not react with sufficient vigor and force. Each small act of aggression that we did not oppose led to larger acts of aggression that we could not oppose without great risk to ourselves. Only when those responsible paid for their actions with isolation and hardship did the war end. It took us seven years to bring Bosnia to this moment of hope. It must not take us that long to resolve the crisis that is growing in Kosovo; and it does not have to if we apply the lessons of 1991. This time, we must act with unity and resolve. This time, we must respond before it is too late.[16]

The Contact Group accepted the logic of Albright's position. In a statement issued on March 9, 1998, the ministers not only condemned Milosevic's actions but also demanded that he act within ten days, halting attacks by Serb security forces against the civilian population and withdrawing all Serb special police units from the province. They also insisted that Belgrade cooperate with the international community to monitor implementation of this demand by allowing the UN High Commissioner for Refugees (UNHCR) to visit Kosovo, granting access to investigators of the International Criminal Tribunal for the former Yugoslavia (ICTY) to gather evidence of possible war crimes, supporting the return of the Organization for Security and Cooperation in Europe (OSCE) to Kosovo and other regions of Yugoslavia (where it had been briefly deployed in the early 1990s), and providing access to Kosovo for Contact Group diplomats to monitor implementation of these commitments. To back up their demands, five of the six Contact Group nations agreed to consider additional measures, including instituting a complete arms embargo, denying visas to senior Serb government and security officials, placing a halt on export credit financing, and freezing Serb-held funds abroad.[17]

It would take another two months for all Contact Group members but Russia to accept the need to impose the economic sanctions first mentioned in the London meeting. Verbal commitments by Belgrade to accede to the Contact Group's demands just before the meeting in Bonn in late March were sufficient to delay imposition of the sanctions though not to forestall agreement on an arms embargo.[18] The latter was imposed by the UN Security Council on March 31 (with China abstaining), after Russia succeeded in eliminating any reference to the situation in Kosovo as constituting a threat to international peace and security (which might have justified subsequent enforcement action). Instead, the embargo was to remain in effect until Milosevic initiated a "substantial dialogue" with the Kosovar leadership, withdrew Serb police, and allowed access to Kosovo by UNHCR, the OSCE, humanitarian organizations, and Contact Group diplomats.[19] After the United States threatened to abandon the Contact Group's process because of its least-common-denominator approach, the European members did finally agree to freeze Serb funds abroad in late April and to tighten a ban on new investments in early May.[20]

The Absence of Force

Conspicuously absent from the list of sanctions was any threat or discussion of military force. This absence was the more notable since both the Bush and the Clinton administrations had warned Milosevic in 1992 and 1993 that the U.S. response to the kind of violent crackdown that occurred in Kosovo in early March 1998 would be air strikes, including against targets in Serbia proper. Yet although senior Clinton administration officials never ruled out using force and insisted that all options were open, no one repeated this so-called Christmas warning, and any question about whether the warning was still in effect was consistently deflected.[21] Given the belief that only pressure could work to convince Milosevic, why not explicitly include the ultimate form of pressure: military force?

There were at least two reasons that the United States did not push the issue of threatening the use of force. First, there was very little appetite in Washington for another potential military adventure at this particular time.

Quite apart from the fact that the White House was then embroiled in a major scandal involving the president, few top administration officials believed that Milosevic's transgressions warranted threatening force, at least at this stage.[22] Aside from the relatively small scale of atrocities—then still less than a hundred killed and no more than a few thousand made homeless—the Clinton administration was still recovering from its previous round of threatening force (in Iraq in the spring of 1998, due to an impasse over weapons inspections). If only for that reason, the White House, led by Clinton's national security adviser, Samuel ("Sandy") Berger, was wary about threatening force. This became apparent during a meeting in Berger's office in mid-May 1998 that Secretary Albright had requested in order for the national security adviser to hear the case for threatening the use of force as a way to increase the pressure on Milosevic. At the meeting, Bob Gelbard made the case for threatening air strikes, noting that General Wesley Clark, NATO's Supreme Allied Commander Europe (SACEUR), had developed a list of targets that, if struck, could convince Milosevic to end his attacks. Berger summarily and angrily rejected the idea, noting that NATO had not even begun drawing up plans and that no one had yet thought through what might happen if air strikes did not have their intended effect.[23]

A second reason that force remained off the table was the belief that any threat of military action would have to involve the NATO allies. Berger had long believed that the Christmas warning, a threat of unilateral American military action, had been overtaken by events. As Berger recalled, "We wanted to avoid empty rhetoric as we tried to multilateralize the threat of force."[24] By the time violence broke out in Kosovo in 1998, NATO had become the principal instrument for exerting military pressure and influence in the region. The large presence of NATO—primarily European—troops in neighboring Bosnia only added to the conviction that military action would have to involve allied consent. One U.S. official said that "the idea of us using force over the objection of allies who have troops on the ground, subject to retaliation, is fantasy-land. Allies do not do that to each other."[25]

The question can be raised whether the threat of force at this early stage could have prevented the major humanitarian catastrophe that was to unfold and could have produced a workable political settlement.[26] At this initial stage of the conflict, tempers had not yet flared, and positions, though seemingly irreconcilable, had yet to be set in stone. The credible threat of force might have convinced Milosevic to end the violence and agree to a mediated negotiation for greater Albanian autonomy in Kosovo (though NATO would, of course, have needed to be prepared to carry out the threat, if necessary, with all the risks that doing so would have entailed). A commitment to ensure the security of the local population (if necessary, by deploying a NATO military presence) might have convinced the ethnic Albanians to abandon the armed struggle and settle for at least an interim period of autonomy within the Federal Republic of Yugoslavia.

Would the European allies in NATO have gone along with this strategy? They were even less inclined in this direction and at least as worried about inadvertently supporting the KLA as was Washington. Under these circumstances, Berger may have been right when he later observed that "moving that alliance to act is a Herculean undertaking, which would happen only in the most egregious circumstances."[27] Without a concerted effort by Washington to persuade them, it is almost certain that the allies would not have supported the threat—or use—of force. Yet during these initial months of the conflict the Clinton administration never tried to reach a NATO consensus on the issue, not only because it thought the allies politically might not go along but also, and more important, because it was worried that the use of force was not sustainable at home. As U.S. Defense Secretary William Cohen recalled, "I was absolutely convinced that the United States could not afford to take any kind of unilateral action, from a political viewpoint, and certainly we were not going to recommend to the president and to the Congress that we intervene unilaterally without NATO consensus and support."[28] In hindsight, however, it would seem that this may have been a lost opportunity to end the conflict before the violence escalated later that summer and fall.

Enter NATO

Even though the United States and its NATO allies ruled out threatening or using force in the initial months of the conflict, the allies were determined to ensure that, unlike in Bosnia, this time the alliance would be involved from the beginning. NATO's chief political body, the North Atlantic Council (NAC), issued its first of many statements on the crisis on March 5, 1998, four days before the Contact Group convened. Initial efforts focused on assisting Kosovo's poor and unstable neighbors (Albania and Macedonia) to cope with the possible consequences of the crisis next door, including assisting refugees who were flowing out and stemming the arms flowing into Kosovo. In addition to providing direct assistance for securing their borders and preparing to assist UNHCR in the event of a major refugee crisis, NATO's principal means for helping to "promote security and stability in these Partner countries" was planning to conduct a series of Partnership for Peace exercises in and around their territories, using NATO ground, air, and naval forces.[29]

It was not until three months into the conflict that the NATO countries began to consider how they could use their own military capabilities to affect the situation inside Kosovo. Meeting in Luxembourg in late May, NATO foreign ministers announced that "in order to have options available for possible later decisions and to confirm our willingness to take further steps if necessary, we have [also] commissioned military advice on support for UN and OSCE monitoring activity as well as on NATO preventive deployments in Albania and the former Yugoslav Republic of Macedonia."[30] In explaining this decision, NATO Secretary-General Javier Solana pointedly noted that NATO "will consider further deterrent measures, if the violence continues. Let me stress, nothing is excluded."[31]

The deteriorating situation on the ground in Kosovo following further escalation by Milosevic's forces in early June forced the allies to consider the additional measures Solana had warned about. Meeting in Brussels on June 11, 1998, NATO defense ministers directed the NATO military authorities to undertake the following:

—Conduct an appropriate air exercise in [Albania and Macedonia] as quickly as possible, with the aim of demonstrating NATO's capability to project power rapidly into the region.

—Develop a full range of options with the mission of halting or disrupting a systematic campaign of violent repression and expulsion in Kosovo; supporting international efforts to secure the agreement of the parties to a cessation of violence and disengagement; and helping to create the conditions for serious negotiations toward a political settlement.

—Accelerate the provision of advice mandated by NATO foreign ministers on possible support for UN and OSCE monitoring activity and on possible NATO preventive deployments in Albania and the former Yugoslav Republic of Macedonia.[32]

Four days after the NATO defense ministerial meeting, more than eighty warplanes from thirteen NATO countries participated in Operation Determined Falcon, a flyover of Albanian and Macedonian territory that put NATO aircraft within fifteen miles of the border of the Federal Republic of Yugoslavia.[33] According to Secretary-General Solana, the objective of the exercise was "to demonstrate NATO's capability to project power into the region."[34] Privately, NATO military authorities warned that the exercise might have the opposite effect—advertising NATO's weakness—and they accordingly advised against its conduct.[35]

It is unclear whether the exercise did have this intended effect.[36] Few could have doubted that NATO possessed the ability to fly dozens of aircraft near the Serb border. However, did this mean that NATO was prepared to drop the missiles and bombs slung under the wings of their aircraft on Serb targets? Or was the exercise more a demonstration of how little the allies were in fact prepared to do to forcefully end the fighting in Kosovo? The chairman of the NATO Military Committee, General Klaus Naumann, left little doubt about his views when he suggested that Milosevic "rightly concluded that the NATO threat was a bluff . . . and finished his summer offensive."[37]

Whatever their ultimate intention, key NATO members believed that a demonstration of the allies' ability to project power rapidly was not enough. As the German defense minister, Volker Rühe, explained:

> We cannot afford any longer to focus on hollow solutions of rather symbolic character like border-securing missions in Albania or Macedonia, thus sealing off Kosovo from the outside. What we now have to focus on in order to support the ongoing political process is to elaborate credible military options aiming at the core of the problem: the extensive use of violence by Serb security or military forces against the Albanian population in Kosovo.[38]

The range of options NATO considered in response to the defense ministers' request was extensive. Two sets of options were examined—preventive deployments and intrusive measures—and the entire panoply was briefed to the North Atlantic Council in July and August 1998.[39] The ten preventive options included NATO support for OSCE monitoring efforts in Albania, support for monitoring compliance with the UN arms embargo against the Federal Republic of Yugoslavia, preventive deployments in Albania or Macedonia to deter a spillover of the conflict, and deployment of NATO troops in Albania to assist in anti–arms smuggling operations. These options required the deployment of between 7,000 and 23,000 troops.

NATO military authorities also prepared a set of intrusive measures, including a phased air campaign and a full range of options for using ground forces. Unlike the 1995 bombing operation in Bosnia, the air campaign would involve a major attack to destroy the extensive Serb air defense network, which included some sixty fixed surface-to-air missile sites and 241 combat aircraft. Aside from conducting strikes to suppress Serb air defenses in the first phase of the campaign, two additional phases were contemplated: in phase 2 NATO would strike below the forty-fourth parallel against Serb military targets conducting or supporting operations in Kosovo; in phase 3 it would engage in a countrywide bombing campaign designed to force the Belgrade political and military leadership to accept NATO's terms.

As for ground forces, four options were developed, two for deploying troops in Kosovo with the consent of the parties to the conflict (options A and A–) and two for a forced entry into the area (options B and B–).

—Option A was NATO enforcement of a cease-fire agreement reached by the parties while maintaining an environment conducive to negotiating a peace settlement; this option would have required 50,000 NATO troops.

—Option A– was NATO enforcement of a peace settlement reached by the parties; this option would have required 28,000 NATO troops.

—Option B was NATO's forced entry into all of Yugoslavia, with the mission of "subjugating" the Yugoslav government in order to facilitate negotiation of a cease-fire and a peace settlement in Kosovo; this option required 200,000 NATO troops.

—Option B– was NATO's forced entry into Kosovo, with a mission of defeating the Yugoslav army and the Serb Interior Ministry police and of neutralizing the KLA in order to facilitate negotiation of a cease-fire and a peace settlement; this option would have required 75,000 NATO troops.

The last two options would have been linked to a phased air campaign.[40]

General Naumann briefed the NAC in July and August on the initial results of the military analysis, presenting the assembled ambassadors with options ranging from indirect support to OSCE monitoring activities outside Kosovo to an invasion of Yugoslavia. There was very little interest within the NAC in the forced entry options (options B and B–), which were subsequently shelved (though not discarded). Instead, the NAC instructed the military authorities to focus on the ten preventive options and to further refine the air option as well as the option for using ground forces in a consensual or "permissive" environment.[41]

While the NATO machinery went through its normal planning process, developments on the ground in Kosovo and in NATO capitals were calling into question the likelihood of an allied decision to threaten or use military force to stem the fighting. Three obstacles to developing an allied consensus emerged. First, some allies feared that NATO intervention against Serb forces would favor the military and political fortunes of the KLA. Second, even among those who supported intervention in principle, there was disagreement on how to do so most effectively and with least risk. Third, with Russia threatening a veto of any UN resolution authorizing NATO's use of force, there was considerable disagreement on what, if anything, would constitute the legal basis of a NATO decision.

One reason for placing the military option on the back burner was the apparent shift in the military tide in Kosovo in early summer. Responding perhaps to a request by Moscow, Serb forces had moderated their actions in mid-June, following Milosevic's visit with Yeltsin. At the same time, an increasingly large, active, well-armed, and even brazen KLA was taking advantage of relative Serb passivity, seizing control of large swaths of territory, especially in rural areas. By mid-July the KLA claimed control of as much as 40 percent of Kosovo's territory. Its ranks had swollen to many thousands, with new recruits joining even from the extensive Albanian diaspora. Money and weapons were flowing freely across the border with Albania, where a sympathetic populace was supportive of the KLA's cause. Inside Kosovo the rebels' popularity reached an all-time high, as a disaffected population turned away from the pacifist policies of their erstwhile "president," Ibrahim Rugova, and embraced the only forces that promised—and sometimes even provided—protection from the Serb onslaught.

As a result of these shifting fortunes, the NATO allies began to fear that military intervention would strengthen the KLA more than it would weaken Milosevic's desire to wreak havoc. As Secretary Cohen recalled, "my concern was that if there was going to be any kind of action taken, it must be consistent with making sure that we were entirely neutral, that the KLA was not going to use NATO to serve its own purposes. And for many months, I made the statement that we will not be the air force for the KLA."[42] By mid-July U.S. defense and intelligence officials were actively discouraging the notion that intervention was imminent or even likely. Speaking at a background briefing, one U.S. official noted that "from a policy perspective, we're not anywhere near making a decision for any kind of armed intervention in Kosovo right now. The situation is fluid." The more the KLA improved militarily, the less likely NATO planning would lead to intervention: "This [planning] is all about preserving the territorial integrity of the FRY [Federal Republic of Yugoslavia], and it's also about not supporting Kosovo independence. . . . They [the KLA] need to know and NATO has made clear, the U.S. government has made this clear, that the cavalry is not coming."[43]

A second reason accounting for the absence of a NATO consensus on threatening the use of force was the disagreement among allied governments over how the alliance ought to intervene, a disagreement that stemmed from different calculations about the risks individual countries were willing to run. Arguing most strongly in favor of the possible use of force was Great Britain, where as of early June the mood had hardened "from the top down." According to one British official, London now firmly believed that the "only thing that would change Milosevic's actions would be [military] actions in and over Kosovo itself."[44] Aside from seeking agreement in New York on a UN Security Council resolution authorizing the use of "all necessary means" to stabilize the region, Britain also suggested that NATO had to consider deploying ground forces to enforce any agreement that might be reached.[45]

London found few supporters within the alliance for its more assertive approach; the idea of sending ground forces for anything other than monitoring Kosovo's border with Albania and Macedonia had no other supporters. But the alternative of relying on airpower also had its detractors. In view of Serbia's extensive air defense network, limited air strikes were prudent only if conducted by cruise missiles, which only the United States possessed in abundance, and Washington had rejected the option of using force on its own. That left strikes by manned aircraft. To be effective and minimize risks, an attack would have to begin by taking out Serb air defenses. Few NATO members were at this point prepared to threaten, let alone launch, what would amount to a smaller-scale version of the air war phase of Desert Storm.[46] Given these constraints, the alliance was left with little choice but to defer a decision on military force until a later date.

Even if the allies had been able to agree on how they might threaten to intervene, however, they were deeply divided over the legal mandate for such action. As a defensive military alliance, NATO had traditionally considered using force only if one or more of its members were attacked, a right enshrined in Article 51 of the UN Charter. The case of Kosovo was different. Not only did NATO members agree that Kosovo was an integral part of Yugoslavia and, indeed, should remain so, but they were considering threatening or using force against a sovereign country in order to persuade the Belgrade government to cease violent attacks against its Albanian population. This was not, therefore, a question of self-defense. Accordingly, under one interpretation of international law, the alliance could use force in this instance only with the explicit authorization of the UN Security Council. However, this view, which was strongly argued by France and Germany and supported by Britain and most other European governments, posed a dilemma for NATO. For Russia had made clear that it would veto any resolution authorizing the use of force against Serbia in Kosovo, a position also held by China. To prevent a possible veto of NATO action by Russia, the United States maintained that it should be possible to threaten or use force without explicit UN authorization. As Secretary Cohen argued with regard to a possible UN mandate, "The United States does not feel it's imperative. It's desirable, not imperative."[47] But as long as some NATO members insisted on UN authorization before agreeing to threaten or use force, efforts to move the alliance toward considering such action remained stalled.

Encouraging a Political Solution

The main purpose of exerting pressure on the Milosevic regime, aside from forcing an end to the violence, was to encourage a political solution to the Kosovo problem. However, the search for such a solution faced at least three major obstacles. First, the differences among the parties over what constituted an acceptable solution were wide and growing. Second, because Belgrade regarded the conflict as strictly an internal matter, it rejected outright any suggestion of an international role in the search for a possible resolution. Third, political divisions among the Kosovar Albanians—which mounted as the KLA's effectiveness, strength, and popularity increased—stymied efforts to start a dialogue with Belgrade. Having learned a lesson from Bosnia, Washington decided early on that it would have to take the lead in trying to overcome these obstacles.

The most basic and, at the same time, most important obstacle to reaching a political solution in Kosovo was the difference in views on how the conflict might be resolved. To Belgrade, which in 1989 had stripped Kosovo of its constitutional autonomy and instituted a repressive form of rule, the issue was simple. Serbia and, indeed, the Federal Republic of Yugoslavia were under attack from the "terrorist" Kosovo Liberation Army. The central authority had every right, even the duty, to suppress the rebellion and eliminate the terrorists. As for Kosovo's political future, the area was not only an integral province of Serbia—the largest of Yugoslavia's two republics—but was also seen as the area in which modern Serbia had its historical foundation. There was therefore no question of giving up Kosovo in any political sense—and certainly not in response to terrorist actions.

Not surprisingly, the Albanian population of Kosovo viewed matters quite differently. Albanians had lived in the territory for centuries and by the end of the twentieth century constituted the overwhelming majority of Kosovo's population. Despite that, the majority population had been stripped of its autonomy in 1989 and had borne the brunt of Serb repression during the subsequent nine years. Through much of 1998 it suffered tremendously from the violent Serb suppression of the KLA's revolt. Hundreds would be killed and hundreds of thousands expelled from their homes, many of which were subsequently burned to the ground. Under these circumstances, the thought of restoring the autonomy Kosovo had enjoyed before 1989 was regarded by all Kosovar Albanians as insufficient. A true and final solution to the conflict had to include the prospect—if not the immediate promise—of independence. This was the demand not only of the KLA (some of whose supporters championed independence as a first step toward establishing a greater Albania, which would comprise Kosovo, Albania, and the Albanian-populated areas of Macedonia and even of Greece) but also of the more moderate political leadership associated with Ibrahim Rugova.

Squaring this political circle would be difficult under any circumstances, but the effort was further complicated by the fact that the main international actors—including the Contact Group and the UN Security Council—sided with Belgrade on the basic issue of Kosovo's political future. Fearing the precedent that independence would set both for other disaffected territories around the world and for stability in the immediate region, the United States, its European allies, and all other major powers steadfastly opposed the demand for independence expressed by the overwhelming majority of Kosovo's population. Instead, the Contact Group settled on the ambiguity of supporting a double negative—approving of "neither independence nor the maintenance of the status quo"[48]—and trying to cajole Belgrade and the Kosovars to begin a political dialogue designed to arrive at a solution somewhere between these positions.

To jump-start the process, Washington sent Richard Holbrooke to the area. A seasoned diplomat with extensive experience in the region, Holbrooke had successfully negotiated a Bosnian peace agreement with Milosevic in 1995. As a result of that earlier triumph, Holbrooke was widely regarded as the one person able to convince Milosevic to reach a political settlement with the Kosovar Albanians.

Holbrooke's initial efforts focused on symbolic rather than substantive movement in the diplomatic process, reflecting his oft-stated belief that diplomacy, like jazz, is a constant improvisation on a theme.[49] Within days of arriving on the scene in early May, Holbrooke announced an "important procedural breakthrough": a first-ever meeting between Rugova and Milosevic.[50] As the first meeting of senior Albanian leaders with the ruling regime in Belgrade since Tito's time, it was designed to set the stage for regular, lower level meetings to address substantive issues. Although Milosevic had little to lose from meeting with Rugova so long as it remained purely bilateral, Rugova took a risk by meeting with the person who was responsible for indiscriminate attacks against Kosovar civilians. A photograph of his meeting with Milosevic, in which he appeared to be smiling, weakened his standing within Kosovo, especially among hard-liners. Indeed, Rugova agreed to attend only after Holbrooke promised to arrange a meeting for him with President Clinton in Washington later in the month.[51]

Aside from arranging the Rugova-Milosevic agreement, Holbrooke made progress on two other procedural fronts.[52] First, Milosevic agreed that a U.S. mediator could try to move the process from this symbolic first meeting into a substantive dialogue about Kosovo's political future. This task fell to Christopher Hill, the U.S. ambassador to Macedonia and part of Holbrooke's negotiating team at Dayton. Hill would spend many months trying to move the sides closer together. Second, Holbrooke convinced Milosevic to accede to the long-standing demand by the Contact Group to allow diplomatic observers to travel from Belgrade to Kosovo to take stock of the situation on the ground. This agreement laid the basis for establishing the Kosovo Diplomatic Observer Mission (KDOM), which by summer 1998 evolved into a permanent foreign monitoring presence in the area.[53]

Despite these procedural advances, there was little progress in the succeeding months in the search for a diplomatic solution to the Kosovo conflict. Hill's task was close to impossible. Notwithstanding Belgrade's acceptance of Hill's presence in the area, Milosevic continued to reject a role for foreign mediation in any direct discussions with Kosovar Albanians. Hill also faced fundamental differences among the Albanians about who should constitute a negotiating team. The KLA was divided even on the question of whether there could be any negotiations at all; its only point of agreement was to reject Rugova as the sole interlocutor. Through the summer, Hill strove valiantly to put a Kosovar negotiating team together. In late June Washington abandoned its resistance to including the KLA in a negotiating effort, recognizing that its participation would be necessary to make any deal stick. Both Holbrooke and Gelbard met with KLA leaders publicly and privately to convince them to participate.[54] But recognition of a critical KLA role was one thing; getting the KLA and other Albanian leaders to agree on a common negotiating team proved to be impossible for the remainder of the year.

Above all, Hill's efforts went for naught because neither of the two sides nor the international community could agree on an appropriate political framework for resolving the Kosovo crisis. The logical options for Kosovo's future were three: independence, partition, or autonomy. Though it was the option preferred by the vast majority of Kosovo's population, independence was ruled out by Belgrade and all other governments. Partition offered an appealing solution in principle, though it was difficult to envisage how it could be done in practice, since both sides felt entitled to most of Kosovo's territory. Moreover, the United States and its European allies were bound to oppose any movement in this direction for fear of the precedent it would set in Bosnia, the formal partition of which had been avoided at Dayton. That left autonomy as the least-worse option, but this concept offered no real solution either, for the Serbs and Albanians remained far apart on the extent and nature of autonomy.

With direct negotiations stymied by the Kosovars' internal division and Milosevic's rejection of a foreign mediation role—and in the absence of an acceptable negotiating framework—the Contact Group could do little to move the process forward. Instead of focusing on direct talks, the six nations agreed in July to draw up a plan for autonomy in Kosovo that could provide the basis for discussions between the parties and, eventually, agreement by them on how to proceed.[55] Hill was tasked by the Contact Group to meet with the Belgrade and Albanian leadership to gain agreement on what were termed "principles to guide discussions and negotiations" presented by the United States to the Contact Group meeting in Bonn.[56] The key concept of the principles focused on the means for implementing autonomy in Kosovo in the short term and left the issue of the area's political future to be decided years later.[57] On September 2, 1999, Hill announced that Milosevic and Rugova had agreed to work toward an interim plan for Kosovo and to postpone a final decision on Kosovo's political status for three to five years. However, in yet another indication of the Albanian divisions, KLA leaders indicated they thought Rugova's agreement to postpone discussion of possible independence a mistake.[58]

The Summer Offensive

Compounding the uncertainty about the prospects for a diplomatic process was a major Serb offensive launched in late July 1998. The offensive was designed to deliver a punishing blow against the KLA, which had exploited the previous period of relative Serb restraint by succeeding in taking control of a substantial part of Kosovo. However, during this offensive, Serb military, paramilitary, and interior police forces left little unscathed. In August alone, 100,000 Kosovars were forced to flee their homes (see figure 2-1). Although many found shelter with family and friends, mostly in urban areas, about one-third of those left homeless did not, taking refuge instead in the forests and mountains surrounding their villages and homes. In late July, while visiting areas where Serb forces had completed their offensive, a senior German diplomat described Kosovo as "an empty country, a wasteland."[59]

Figure 2-1. Refugees and Internally Displaced Persons, Kosovo, March 1998 to March 1999

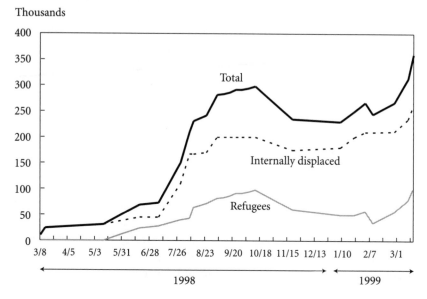

Thousands

Source: UN High Commissioner for Refugees, "Briefing Notes"; and *UN Interagency Update on Kosovo Situation Reports*, various dates (www.reliefweb.int [accessed March 2000]).

Quite apart from the sheer brutality of Serb actions, the international community was now confronted with a potential humanitarian crisis on a vast scale. While people could live outside during the summer and early fall, winter arrives early in this mountainous territory. Snow could fall as early as mid-October, threatening the many tens of thousands of people exposed to the elements with starvation and the possibility of literally freezing to death. This prospect finally concentrated minds in Washington and elsewhere. The fighting had to end; Serb military and police forces had to withdraw; international relief agencies had to enter to assist those displaced from their homes, and a real political dialogue had to begin without preconditions and with international involvement.

It would take more than a month of tough negotiations for the UN Security Council to pass a resolution to formally make these demands of the Yugoslav authorities. One key sticking point was Russia's opposition to passing a resolution implying that force could be used to enforce the Security

Council's demands. In the end, Moscow agreed only to a resolution under Chapter VII of the UN Charter (which relates to "threats to or breaches of international peace and security") and continued to oppose any reference to enforcing the demands in case Belgrade failed to comply.[60] On September 23, 1998, the Security Council passed Resolution 1199 (see appendix C) by a vote of fourteen to zero (with China abstaining), stating inter alia that Yugoslavia

—cease all actions by the security forces against the civilian population and order the withdrawal of security units used for civilian repression;

—enable effective and continuous international monitoring in Kosovo by diplomatic missions accredited to Yugoslavia;

—facilitate, in agreement with the UNHCR and the International Committee of the Red Cross (ICRC), the safe return of refugees and displaced persons to their homes;

—allow free and unimpeded access for humanitarian organizations and supplies;

—enter into and make rapid progress on a meaningful dialogue without preconditions and with international involvement to end the crisis and to negotiate a political solution to the issue of Kosovo.[61]

Enforcing the UN Demands

Passage of the UN resolution answered the question of what needed to be done, but it provided no answer on how to ensure that these demands would be met. Still missing was a consensus even within and between NATO governments on what they were prepared to do. This was not for lack of military planning. By early August NATO military authorities had completed "planning for a full range of options to bring an end to violence and to create the conditions for negotiations" and presented them for possible approval by the North Atlantic Council. The plans included "the use of ground and air power and in particular a full-range of options for the use of air power alone. They ensure that NATO can act swiftly and effectively should the need arise."[62] The air-only options consisted of a limited air response (demonstration strikes against a few key targets) and a full-fledged phased air campaign. The ground options were notional plans for enforcing a peace settlement or a cease-fire agreement as well as for a ground invasion of Kosovo and Yugoslavia in conjunction with an air campaign.[63] After reviewing these options, the North Atlantic Council authorized the military authorities "to approach nations informally about the forces which they would be ready to commit to possible air operations." There was no formal decision about ground force options.[64]

With ground forces effectively ruled out, only airpower could back up threats designed to persuade Belgrade to accept the UN Security Council's demands. The case for such action was forcefully made during an informal NATO defense ministerial meeting in Portugal on September 23–24, 1998. Secretary-General Solana argued that following its numerous warnings and threats, the alliance's credibility was now on the line. Serb actions were not only beyond the pale but actually mocked the allies by keeping the offensive at a level that Belgrade believed would prevent a NATO decision to use force. To underscore the point, Solana noted that a Serb diplomat had even joked that "a village a day keeps NATO away."[65] Secretary Cohen forcefully supported Solana's plea for allied action, agreeing that NATO's credibility was on the line: "NATO has a choice now. They must go forward with this, or it will be seen as simply a hollow warning." Milosevic's crackdown in Kosovo was "a challenge I don't think NATO can afford to walk away from. We can't simply ignore what he continues to do."[66]

The arguments by Solana, Cohen, and others at the meeting persuaded the North Atlantic Council to move one step closer to using force. On September 24, the council approved the issuing of an "activation warning" (ACTWARN) for both limited air strikes and a phased air campaign.[67] The ACTWARN allowed NATO commanders to identify the forces they would need to implement either of these options. It did not amount to a decision to use force, or even to threaten it explicitly, but rather enabled the alliance to prepare for such a decision in short order. As a senior Pentagon official explained, the decision put NATO in a position "to be ready to act very quickly. It is not a decision to use force, but it is a sign of recognition by the Alliance and all of its members of the increasing seriousness and urgency of the situation. . . . It will allow the Alliance to move within a matter of days from a situation of being ready to execute."[68]

Debating the Mandate for NATO Action

Five days after the alliance moved closer to threatening air strikes against Belgrade reports of another Serb massacre of Kosovar Albanians raised the ante. The massacre in Gornji Obrinje was particularly brutal, involving twenty-one women, children, and the elderly, ranging in age from four to ninety-five; in a neighboring village thirteen more were killed. Among those slaughtered was a woman, seven months pregnant, whose stomach had been slit open.[69] For the United States, the gruesome tales and pictures represented a breach in the "atrocities threshold," as Sandy Berger called it.[70] However, while Washington pressed its NATO allies to issue an ultimatum for

Belgrade to comply with the international community's demands, the alliance still had to overcome a key obstacle concerning the question of NATO's mandate for using force other than for self-defense.

Even though the allies had debated the mandate question for many months, by early October 1998 they were no closer to a resolution than they had been at the start.[71] The problem confronting NATO was the fact that Russia and China had made clear that they would veto any UN Security Council resolution that mandated the use of force against a sovereign country for what they regarded as an issue that was purely the internal affair of Yugoslavia. For that reason, China had failed to support Resolution 1199, believing it went too far, and Russia had conditioned its approval of Resolution 1199 on the understanding that it not authorize the threat or use of force. To emphasize the point, Moscow warned publicly in early October that it would "definitely" veto any resolution authorizing the use of force.[72]

The absence of UN authorization posed a problem for many European countries, which had long argued that NATO could not use force for other than self-defense purposes unless the UN Security Council first approved an explicit mandate for such an operation. With Security Council action blocked by the certainty of Russian and Chinese vetoes, achieving agreement as to what the legal justification for threatening or using force would be was no easy matter. Some NATO governments suggested that the 1948 Geneva Convention on warfare had been violated. Others argued that while Resolutions 1160 and 1199 did not authorize the use of force, a military threat to enforce their demands was in the "sense and logic" of both. Yet other governments maintained that the human rights rules and norms adopted by the OSCE over the years, especially those regarding minority rights, suggested that a particularly high standard could be applied to the behavior of European states. Finally, some NATO governments explained that the urgency of the humanitarian situation, combined with the Security Council's inability to act, created a situation in which an exception to the agreed norm could be justified.[73] This last point, in the end, convinced even the French government of the necessity to act. As President Jacques Chirac explained on October 6,

> Any military action must be requested . . . by the Security Council. In this particular case, we have a resolution which does open the way to the possibility of military action. I would add, and repeat, that the humanitarian situation constitutes a ground that can justify an exception to a rule, however strong and firm it is. And if it appeared that the situation required it, then France

would not hesitate to join those who would like to intervene in order to assist those that are in danger.[74]

While the situation on the ground in Kosovo demanded vigorous action, the NATO alliance appeared unalterably divided on how to move forward. What started out as a largely theological debate ended up dividing NATO into three camps. There was, first, a "Catholic" camp (France and Italy), which insisted on the need for an explicit UN mandate while recognizing that, like sinning, this sacrosanct rule could be violated in exceptional circumstances such as these. In contrast, a "Lutheran" camp (including Britain and, later, Germany) sought to devise an alternative dogma to justify actions necessitated by the humanitarian crisis, notably the fact that the crisis was both overwhelming in nature and required an emergency response. A third camp (the United States) was "agnostic" in arguing that the rule requiring a UN mandate was neither sacrosanct nor absolute.

The absence of a consensus left NATO's secretary-general in the uncomfortable and unaccustomed position of having to devise a way to move the issue forward. Solana did so admirably when, on October 10, after some ten hours of debate on the issue in the North Atlantic Council, he summed up by stating that there was sufficient legal basis for moving forward with issuing a specific threat of force and, if necessary, proceeding with its implementation. Solana deliberately left unstated what constituted the exact basis of this judgment, knowing that while there was agreement on the former, the debate had demonstrated its absence on the latter. That decision opened the way for the council to approve an "activation order" (ACTORD), establishing a date for beginning air strikes. As one NATO diplomat put it, "the safety catch will be removed, the gun will be pointed, and we hope this will trigger a switch in Slobodan Milosevic's mind."[75] Even so, to get final approval for the ACTORD, all sixteen NATO members had to vote in the affirmative. To convince the last key recalcitrant allies to join ranks (notably Germany and Italy, both of which were in the midst of changing governments), a last-ditch diplomatic effort was made to persuade Milosevic to accept the UN's demands.

The Holbrooke-Milosevic Negotiations

While much of NATO waited for the publication in early October of a report by UN Secretary-General Kofi Annan on the extent to which Belgrade had complied with the demands spelled out in Resolution 1199 (passed two weeks earlier), the Clinton administration decided to send its chief Balkans diplomatic troubleshooter, Richard Holbrooke, back to Belgrade.[76] The purposes of the Holbrooke mission were twofold.[77] First, it was to demonstrate a commitment to go the extra mile in the search for a peaceful solution to the conflict, thus buttressing domestic political support in NATO countries in favor of a decision, now increasingly likely, to use force. Second, Holbrooke took along to Belgrade a detailed list of what Milosevic needed to do to come into compliance with the UN's demands. As reiterated by the Contact Group on October 8, these demands included:

—an end to offensive operations and hostilities;

—the withdrawal of Serb security forces to their positions before March and the withdrawal of heavy weapons;

—freedom of access for humanitarian agencies;

—full cooperation with the International War Crimes Tribunal to ensure that those who committed atrocities are brought to justice;

—the facilitation of the return of refugees to their homes without fear;

—a start to negotiations on the basis of proposals drafted by Christopher Hill after extensive consultations with both sides.[78]

Almost immediately upon Holbrooke's arrival in Belgrade on October 5, however, his negotiations with Milosevic blossomed into something much grander than securing Serb compliance with these demands.[79] One major thrust of Holbrooke's talks was to put into place a verification system designed to monitor Milosevic's compliance with the UN demands.[80] The need for such a system reflected a widespread belief within the Clinton administration that Milosevic could not be trusted—that he was, in Madeleine Albright's words, a "congenital liar."[81] Holbrooke focused his efforts on two different monitoring mechanisms. One related to the deployment of a large civilian presence, composed of retired and active duty military personnel and diplomats operating under the auspices of the OSCE, that would supplant the 150 monitors of the Kosovo Diplomatic Observer Mission, which had operated in the area since July. Holbrooke initially proposed deploying 3,000–4,000 unarmed observers, while Milosevic suggested the total be limited to 25–50. The other proposed mechanism consisted of aerial surveillance conducted by unarmed NATO reconnaissance planes over the Kosovo territory. Their purpose would be to ascertain that Serb military and security forces had been withdrawn to agreed levels and that the remainder were confined to agreed areas. Although the Yugoslav military regarded such surveillance as an intrusion upon Serb sovereignty, Milosevic did not dismiss the idea out of hand.

The second thrust of Holbrooke's discussions with Milosevic concerned the nature of a possible political dialogue between the Serbs and Kosovar Albanians. After months of shuttling between the two sides, Christopher Hill (who had accompanied Holbrooke to Belgrade) had a good sense of where the difficulties in any negotiation now lay. He and his small staff of State Department lawyers had shared with both sides multiple versions of an interim agreement that would grant Kosovo wide-ranging autonomy while postponing a final decision on its political status for three to five years.[82] It was on that basis that Holbrooke and Hill sought to narrow the gap dividing the two sides and to encourage a more forthcoming stance by Milosevic and the Serbs. During negotiations that eventually stretched into nine long days of talks, many central aspects of an interim settlement were broached, including the timing and purpose of holding elections, the composition of a local Kosovo police force, and the extent of autonomy granted to local governing institutions in Kosovo and the communes within that territory. In this veritable "mini-Dayton," as one participant characterized the talks, it was impossible to reach final agreement. After all, one of the two sides concerned was not directly involved in the talks (although discussions with the Kosovar Albanians, including by Holbrooke in person, were ongoing during this time). The goal was less ambitious: to narrow the differences between the sides and to establish a framework and timetable for commencing a direct dialogue that would be supported by international involvement.[83]

As the talks dragged on for hours, then days, and finally a week and more, it was increasingly clear that Holbrooke's ambitions to get a deal were foundering over Milosevic's belief that he had little to lose by stalling. Despite repeated threats and intimations that NATO was prepared to use force, the alliance had not formally moved to decide the question while talks proceeded in Belgrade. As Holbrooke reported to Secretary Albright on October 7, "This guy is not taking us seriously."[84] Even when President Clinton convinced the incoming German chancellor, Gerhard Schröder, to support a NATO decision on air strikes two days later, the fall of the Italian government appeared to give Milosevic new hope that he could outlast NATO.[85]

A deal was finally sealed as a result of a clever negotiating maneuver by Holbrooke. As talks entered their second week on Monday, October 12, Holbrooke put Milosevic on notice that, with the German and Italian governments having come around, NATO was about to approve an ACTORD for air strikes. He then told Milosevic that if he could go back to NATO and tell the allies that Serbia had accepted a "durable and independent" verification system of the kind they had been discussing, air strikes could probably be delayed. With Milosevic's agreement in hand, Holbrooke traveled to Brussels for a late-night briefing of the North Atlantic Council on the progress he had achieved. He ended by telling the ambassadors that their approval of an ACTORD would make the deal stick.[86] The allies obliged, voting in the early hours of October 13 "to issue activation orders—ACTORDs—for both limited air strikes and a phased air campaign in Yugoslavia, execution of which will begin in approximately 96 hours."[87]

After returning to Belgrade and engaging in two more hours of negotiations, Holbrooke emerged just before noon on October 13 to announce that he had reached an agreement with Milosevic, which, once implemented, would end the emergency that "brought us to the edge of the use of force." The agreement established a two-part verification system to monitor Serbia's compliance with UN Security Council Resolution 1199. The system's parts consisted of a ground element, the Kosovo Verification Mission (2,000 compliance verifiers operating under OSCE auspices) and an aerial element, conducted by noncombat aircraft flying over Kosovo under NATO command. Final details and binding agreements concerning both elements were to be negotiated by the OSCE and NATO, respectively, in the days immediately ahead. In addition, Holbrooke announced that Belgrade would "make a statement regarding the political process later.... A statement that is theirs and theirs alone." Holbrooke expressed the hope that it would "mark a turning point in the tortured and tragic relationships between the peoples— Albanian, Serb, others—in Kosovo." Elaborating, Hill noted that the statement, which contained points that Belgrade would want to see in an eventual agreement, "does provide the basis for establishing democratic self-government in Kosovo."[88]

The Holbrooke-Milosevic agreement was finalized in separate talks between OSCE, NATO, and Yugoslav authorities over the following days. On October 15, SACEUR concluded an agreement with Yugoslav military authorities for the right to conduct aerial surveillance flights over Kosovo.[89] To facilitate implementation, it was agreed that Yugoslav aircraft would not operate in Kosovo airspace or within a zone stretching twenty-five kilometers from the Kosovo border into Yugoslav territory while surveillance missions were ongoing. All air defense systems except early-warning radars would have to be removed from the area or placed in cantonment sites to ensure they would not operate for the duration of the mission. Finally, direct liaison cells placing Yugoslav officers in Vincenza, Italy, and NATO officers in Belgrade were to be established. The following day, the OSCE chairman in office, Polish Foreign Minister Bronislaw Geremek, signed an agreement with the Federal Republic of Yugoslavia for the deployment of 2,000 unarmed verifiers, whose safety and diplomatic immunity was guaranteed by Belgrade. The task of the Kosovo Verification Mission (KVM) was to verify compliance by all parties in Kosovo with UN Resolution 1199, to establish a permanent presence throughout Kosovo, and to supervise elections (which Belgrade promised could be held within nine months).[90] On October 24, the UN Security Council welcomed these agreements and demanded that Yugoslavia ensure their "full and prompt implementation," language that fell well short of implying possible forceful measures in case of noncompliance.[91]

The October Agreement: A Flawed Precedent

In summing up his negotiations with Slobodan Milosevic, Richard Holbrooke characterized their aim as a response to "an emergency inside a crisis." The emergency, Holbrooke argued, was "the military confrontation that brought us to the brink of NATO action," which the final agreement resolved, provided that Milosevic did not "backslide." But Holbrooke noted that "the crisis is Kosovo, and there has been no change in the political issues that caused the tragedy, the rampaging and the pillaging this summer."[92] This characterization of what did and did not transpire during the nine days of talks in Belgrade points to the limited focus of the effort, which addressed the immediate symptoms rather than the underlying causes of the situation.

The humanitarian emergency that finally galvanized NATO to threaten air strikes did ease in the immediate aftermath of the Holbrooke-Milosevic negotiations. Humanitarian agencies and other international organizations were granted access to the area to assist displaced persons to return home or to find shelter. The initial deployment of several hundred KVM personnel also contributed to a sense of security, enabling those who had fled to come down from the mountains. By the end of November, all displaced persons inside Kosovo had either returned to their villages or had found temporary shelter elsewhere.[93] In short, following the confrontation of October, the humanitarian situation in the territory improved to a point where the likelihood of the Kosovo winter claiming victims among the Kosovar population was drastically reduced. This was no mean achievement.

That said, the sequence of events does raise an important question: Aside from improving the humanitarian situation for the duration of the winter, what other benefits resulted from the Holbrooke-Milosevic agreement? Immediately following its conclusion, Holbrooke touted the "enormous concessions" Milosevic made as the reason for his success. These included the establishment of an aerial and ground verification regime to monitor Serb compliance with the demands set forth in UN Resolution 1199, the acceptance of Christopher Hill as an international mediator, and the agreement to a timetable for commencing talks with the Kosovar Albanians (including discussion of self-government, elections and setting up an ethnically balanced local police force).[94] The question remains: Did these add up to what Holbrooke argued could "retroactively or retrospectively later be regarded as turning points, perhaps arguably, historic turning points?"[95] Or was it a flawed agreement, at best an interim measure, that postponed a serious effort to resolve the underlying crisis—and perhaps did so in a manner that gave Milosevic the impression that the United States and its NATO allies were not committed either to resolve the conflict or to create an environment in which Kosovar Albanians could feel secure?

The Holbrooke-Milosevic agreement fell short in at least three respects.[96] First, for all the focus on verification, the details of what was to be verified (including how many Serb forces would have to be withdrawn from Kosovo) were left vague. Second, although the verification system set up in Kosovo was able to monitor Serb compliance, it was incapable of enforcing it. Indeed, the very vulnerability of unarmed monitors operating in an area teeming with Serb forces seriously undermined NATO's ability to threaten or use force in case of Serb noncompliance. Third, in ignoring the Albanian side of the equation, the agreement offered no effective way to prevent the Kosovar Albanians from attempting to exploit the opening created by the retreat of Serb forces. Thus not only was there no way to punish Serb noncompliance, there was also no way to prevent the KLA from exploiting Serb compliance and provoking a possibly violent Serb retort. In this way, the agreement may have contained within it the seeds of its own demise.

The Ambiguity of the Agreement

One major flaw in the Holbrooke-Milosevic agreement was substantial ambiguity about what exactly the monitors on the ground and in the air were supposed to verify. As previous experience with arms control agreements has demonstrated, any ambiguity about what needs to be verified is cause for trouble.[97] The same proved true in this case. One such ambiguity concerned the demand set forth in UN Security Council Resolution 1199, that Milosevic "cease all actions by the security forces affecting the civilian population." The resolution was silent about the use of security forces in ways that did not affect the civilian population. Would an attack against the KLA forces—either preemptively or in retaliation—constitute a violation? The answer, as subsequent experience was to show, was not clear.

A more problematic ambiguity in the Holbrooke-Milosevic agreement related to the nature and extent of any withdrawal by Serb security units from Kosovo. The Security Council resolution demanded "the withdrawal of security units used for civilian repression," and there was a general understanding that this included all interior ministry, paramilitary, and military forces that had been deployed to the area since February 1998. But how many interior police and army units could stay in Kosovo and how was their future disposition and use to be limited? Never codified in writing, the Holbrooke-Milosevic agreement was silent on this question.[98] Indeed, when pressed on the issue immediately after the agreement became public, Sandy Berger only said,

> I'm not going to get into a numbers game. We need to get forces that have been introduced into the area leaving; other forces, basically, that are in garrison or in other non-threatening situations; less roadblocks; less of police presence. This is an overall picture that we want to see on which the situation is less intimidating, less repressive, less violent, so that people can get back to their homes and a negotiating process can begin.[99]

As it turned out, the question of how many Serb security forces could remain in Kosovo and how many were to be withdrawn would bedevil NATO commanders when they traveled to Belgrade to finalize the verification agreement with Yugoslav authorities. In his talks with Holbrooke, Milosevic agreed to withdraw forces that had been deployed to the province since the outbreak of hostilities earlier that year and to keep those forces remaining in Kosovo in barracks and other peacetime deployment areas (including along the border with Albania). However, Holbrooke had left the specific details for NATO officials to negotiate, both because NATO would be responsible for verifying the withdrawal and because it would underscore that this was an alliance agreement, rather than a U.S. agreement.[100]

During subsequent negotiations on the details of the aerial verification regime, NATO's top military commanders, Generals Clark and Naumann, presented Yugoslav officials with a list of seven battalions that had to be withdrawn from Kosovo. The total included 4,000–5,000 regular army troops and 3,000–4,000 Interior Ministry police personnel.[101] Milosevic's acceptance of these terms appeared to be confirmed by the departure of some units from Kosovo starting on October 16, which led NATO to extend its original ninety-six-hour deadline for full compliance another ten days.[102] However, a week later it was clear that the pace of Serb withdrawals was insufficient to meet even this extended deadline. As a result, NATO ambassadors ordered both generals back to Belgrade to warn Milosevic that NATO was still prepared to launch air strikes if he did not comply by the October 27 deadline.[103]

After four sessions of exhausting talks, Clark and Naumann finally convinced Milosevic to codify his promise to withdraw a specific number of Serb security forces from Kosovo, thereby getting in writing the agreement that Holbrooke had only received orally (see appendix C). According to that agreement, the Serb army presence in Kosovo was to be limited to 12,000 troops. Of these, 1,000 troops could continue to augment the border guards. With the exception of three company-sized units deployed to protect critical lines of communication, the remaining army troops would have to return to their barracks and remain there. In addition, Serb Interior Ministry police units were to be limited to 11,000 personnel, which were to be stationed in twenty-seven sites around the territory.[104] These forces were to be stripped of all heavy weapons, and their movement was limited to conducting normal peacetime policing activities.[105]

NATO reported that there had been "substantial compliance" by the October 27 deadline. Most army troops had withdrawn by this date, although the largest unit to leave (the 211th Armored Brigade) did not actually return to its barracks in Nis. Moreover, more than 4,000 Interior Ministry police personnel departed only in the twenty-four hours preceding the midnight deadline.[106] Even so, NATO continued to keep in place the ACTORDs for both limited air operations and a phased air campaign, to ensure their execution, "subject to a decision and assessments by the North Atlantic Council" in case of "substantial non-compliance."[107] By the middle of November, the level of police forces had once again increased to 11,500, a level that would steadily rise in the months ahead.[108] The increasingly brazen Serb noncompliance would pose a major challenge to NATO, which had promised to enforce the agreement by using force, if necessary.

The Absence of Enforcement

The second problem with the Holbrooke-Milosevic agreement, however, was precisely its lack of a credible means of enforcement. This absence was the result of two decisions. First, Washington decided that there could be no NATO troops on the ground, even if their deployment would be part of any agreement that was to be negotiated. Making matters worse was a second decision, the proposal to substitute OSCE personnel for a NATO ground presence in Kosovo. Since these observers were unarmed and therefore highly vulnerable to intimidation or, worse, hostage taking, their deployment in

Kosovo effectively emasculated the credibility of NATO airpower as a possible enforcement threat. Although NATO would deploy a small ground force in Macedonia—the Extraction Force (XFOR, widely known as "the dentists")—to provide OSCE personnel some degree of protection, their basic vulnerability remained, thus undermining the threat of airpower at the point it would matter most.[109]

The critical flaw in this sequence was the Clinton administration's decision in 1998 to reject the idea of deploying ground forces in Kosovo no matter what the circumstances. At no time in 1998 did it give serious consideration to this option, fearing that it was bound to be rejected by the Congress at home and by the allies abroad. As early as July, U.S. officials even tried to remove any consideration of using ground forces in Kosovo from the menu of military options that NATO's military authorities were to present to the North Atlantic Council.[110] Although the attempt failed and a full panoply of options was presented by NATO military authorities in August, the administration still rejected the ground force options. A senior administration official recalled that "no one said yes, no one said no; it was taken off the table. . . . It was a complete eye-roller." A White House official confirmed that "the idea of troops never had any traction."[111]

Even when it began to consider threatening air strikes against Serbia in order to prevent a humanitarian nightmare during the winter, the administration never urged Milosevic to accept a NATO force in Kosovo as a means to stabilize the situation there. Richard Holbrooke, among others, had for months urged the administration to deploy a substantial "international security presence" in Kosovo—a point also made repeatedly by Alexander Vershbow, the U.S. ambassador to NATO.[112] Although the administration apparently considered briefly the possibility of sending a small, armed contingent of NATO soldiers to protect the headquarters of the civilian monitors, Holbrooke was under explicit instructions not to push for a large, armed presence in Kosovo.[113] That was, on the eve of the midterm elections, viewed as simply "a bridge too far."[114] As Albright later explained, "we didn't think it was necessary to make that decision at that time. . . . I didn't want to see something that was like the UN forces in Bosnia, who didn't have any real authority."[115]

The Clinton administration was convinced that Congress and the public would reject consideration of ground forces. That point was underscored by Secretary Cohen in later testimony before the Senate Armed Services Committee. In explaining why the administration had not considered deploying ground forces in October, Cohen said,

At that time, you may recall there was great discontent up here on Capitol Hill. If I had come to you at that time and requested authorization to put a ground force in—U.S., unilaterally, acting alone—I can imagine the nature of the questions I would have received. You'd say, "Well, No. 1, where are our allies? And No. 2, who's going to appropriate the money? No. 3, how long do you intend to be there? How many? How long? How much? And what's the exit strategy?" . . . And that would have been the extent of the debate and probably would have received an overwhelming rejection from the committee.[116]

Cohen's argument had three flaws. First, the implication that a decision to deploy ground forces in the region would have involved the United States acting on its own is wrong. In early August, the British government concluded not only that any solution to the crisis in Kosovo would involve the threat and likely use of military force, but also that ground forces would have to be deployed in Kosovo—if not to end the violence then to enforce the terms of any agreement that was reached. The cabinet also agreed that Britain would play a leading role in any military action and that London would therefore be prepared to deploy ground forces in large numbers.[117]

With Britain on its side, the United States could have made a powerful and probably decisive case in favor of a NATO decision to deploy ground forces to implement an agreement that ended the fighting in Kosovo. Indeed, there was some expectation at NATO headquarters in Brussels that Holbrooke would return from Belgrade with precisely such a plan to deploy ground forces. As one NATO diplomat recalled, "In our minds was the SFOR model, the deployment of a force like we had in Bosnia that would create a stable climate for negotiating a political settlement."[118] European intelligence had apparently even picked up indications that Milosevic would not reject this possibility out of hand.[119] Any doubt that this option would not gain allied support was erased in February 1999, when NATO decided to deploy just such a force to help implement any agreement the Serbs and Albanians might reach.

The logic of deploying an armed presence in Kosovo had been spelled out by Alexander Vershbow, the U.S. Ambassador to NATO, in a NODIS (no distribution) cable he sent to Washington on August 7, 1998. Drawing on his experience as a member of the National Security Council staff, where he had been a consistent, vocal, and strong advocate for forceful action in Bosnia, Vershbow compared the situation in Kosovo with the situation that the United States and its NATO allies had confronted three years earlier in Bosnia, when the Clinton administration decided to go for broke—to threaten major military action in order to negotiate an end to more than three years of bloody war. It worked then, Vershbow argued, and if tailored to the circumstances in Kosovo, it could work once again. Specifically, Vershbow proposed creating an international protectorate in Kosovo so as to bypass the question of its political future. The protectorate would be policed by outside forces provided by NATO. "Sooner or later we are going to face the issue of deploying ground forces in Kosovo," Vershbow wrote. "We have too much at stake in the political stability of the south Balkans to permit the conflict to fester much longer."[120] However, instead of making this case in Brussels, the administration decided that the ground force option would remain off the table. But that decision belonged to Washington, not the allies.

Second, contrary to Cohen's claim, it is highly unlikely that the administration would ever have gone to Capitol Hill to ask for its authorization—rather than its support—for deploying troops abroad, since it had never done so in the past. The issue was not one of congressional authorization but of making a case that Congress could support, at least in terms of providing funds for the operation. But not only did the administration fail to make a case for deploying ground forces, it in fact argued against such a deployment. Before briefing Congress in early October on what NATO air strikes might encompass, Cohen made clear that he would not even raise the question of ground forces. In a letter to Senate majority leader Trent Lott and eight other senior Republicans, President Clinton wrote with respect to involving ground forces in hostile action, "I can assure you the United States would not support these options."[121]

Finally, all of the questions Cohen raised about possible ground force deployment—its mission, size, and exit—were legitimate, and none would have been difficult to answer. Indeed, one would have hoped that these questions would have been asked and answered by the administration before going to the Hill to ask Congress for its support.

In short, it was the Clinton administration that ruled out the use of ground forces. The administration rejected their deployment in Kosovo out of hand in the summer of 1998 and did not reconsider this decision until January 1999. Although it is likely that Congress, already uneasy about the lengthy deployment of U.S. troops in Bosnia, would not have been enthusiastic about sending additional forces to Kosovo, the administration never tried to make a case for their deployment. The NATO allies were also unenthusiastic, though Britain had decided that troops would at some point be necessary, and it had also determined that London would make a substantial contribution. Further, our interviews with NATO and allied officials suggest that key allies (including France and Germany) might well have been prepared to send troops to help implement and enforce any agreement Holbrooke could reach in his talks with Milosevic.[122] Washington's refusal to consider this possibility left the allies with little choice but to follow the U.S. lead.[123]

Instead of pushing for an armed presence in Kosovo, Holbrooke suggested deploying unarmed observers to monitor Serb compliance with any deal they might reach. None of the NATO countries was consulted on this suggestion; even the OSCE, under whose auspices the observers would operate, was not informed of the idea of deploying unarmed observers until late on October 12.[124] With the United States pushing for a verification regime, the allies and OSCE had little choice but to make a go of what Holbrooke would call a "civilian army."[125] However, as an indication that personnel safety rather than effectiveness was uppermost for many NATO countries, key allies contributed troops to XFOR to ensure the monitors' protection. The United States did not, apparently fearing congressional opposition to any new potential combat role in the region.

There was, however, an inherent contradiction in the deployment of unarmed civilians to verify compliance with the agreement that Holbrooke and Milosevic had negotiated. The main reason for their presence was the oft-repeated insistence that Milosevic could not be trusted. As President Clinton warned when word of Holbrooke's agreement with the Serb leader first reached the United States, "Commitments are not compliance. Balkan graveyards are filled with President Milosevic's broken promises."[126] Whence the aerial and ground verification regimes. However, when critics of the agreement noted that unarmed observers were vulnerable to intimidation, and even hostage taking, administration officials claimed not to worry, believing Milosevic would do them no harm.[127] As Holbrooke explained, "Arms are not their best security. Their best security is unambiguous orders from both sides—the KLA and the Serb forces—not to harm them. After Dayton, Milosevic gave his word in Bosnia that no harm would come to the [heavily armed] NATO forces that went there. And he has kept his word on that. . . . He has signed a similar pledge with respect to the OSCE."[128] In other words, while the observers were needed because Milosevic could not be trusted to implement the agreement on his own, their safety was not an issue because the very same Milosevic had given his word![129]

In the end, the real flaw in the agreement was to confuse the ability to verify compliance with the ability to enforce it. This was a problem common to arms control also: tens of thousands of hours were spent constructing elaborate verification systems, but very little attention was paid to determining what to do in case the system detected noncompliance.[130] In both cases, this confusion of objectives had a price. Rather than demonstrating a commitment to seeing the agreement implemented, the emphasis on verification sowed doubts about the degree to which the United States and its NATO allies were prepared to use force to ensure Milosevic's compliance with UN demands. The failure to push for ground forces was one indication that NATO had limited interest in ensuring that Milosevic complied. The decision to use unarmed civilians deprived the allies of the ability to employ airpower effectively; before NATO could act, the safety of the OSCE personnel would have to be guaranteed, thus warning Serbia of the impending action.

Ignoring the KLA

The absence of a robust enforcement regime magnified the third major shortcoming of the Holbrooke-Milosevic agreement: the exclusion of the KLA and other Kosovars from the arrangement. Although the Security Council resolution called on all sides to cease hostilities, Holbrooke's focus was on Serb compliance. As Holbrooke told us, "I elected to use all leverage to pressure Milosevic, in part because there was no Albanian leadership to negotiate with us."[131] Yet it was entirely predictable that the KLA would attempt to exploit any opening provided by Serbia's reduced security presence in Kosovo following the withdrawal of its police and armed forces and the deployment of those remaining back to their barracks.[132] Indeed, the KLA had every incentive to do so. It could recapture ground lost to the Serbs in the latter's summer offensive. If its actions were to provoke the Serbs into violating the October agreement, NATO would be forced to intervene on what effectively was the Kosovars' side of the conflict. But other than report what was occurring (which the civilian monitors did within days of the agreement),[133] there was little the Kosovo Verification Mission or the NATO aerial verification regime could do to prevent this from happening. Not only would a KLA advance be perfectly legal under the Security Council resolution and the Holbrooke-Milosevic agreement, but as one senior Western diplomat acknowledged at the time, "We don't have leverage on the KLA. It is a missing element in our overall strategy."[134]

The failure to anticipate the likely KLA reaction to the agreement—or to put in place mechanisms that could have dissuaded it from seeking to take advantage of the Serb withdrawal—would prove to have major consequences for how the Kosovo crisis would evolve. It had been Milosevic's main concern during his negotiations with Holbrooke and later with Clark and Naumann. The Yugoslav president's opposition to limiting the number and disposition of his security and armed forces during these talks stemmed from his concern that the "terrorists" would move in as soon as the Serbs departed. Although they could not promise that the KLA would show restraint, Milosevic's interlocutors assured him that compliance on Serbia's part would place the onus for any violence in Kosovo squarely on the rebel movement. According to General Naumann, moreover, General Clark and he told Milosevic that the Kosovo Verification Mission and NATO would try to control the KLA. Shaun Byrnes, head of the Kosovo Diplomatic Observer Mission who had joined the two NATO generals in Belgrade during their talks, even suggested that the KVM could do so.[135]

While these assurances may have been necessary to get Milosevic's agreement to withdraw his forces, neither NATO nor the KVM was in any position to stop the KLA from exploiting this shift in the balance of forces to its advantage. When the KLA did act as Milosevic had expected, there was a price to be paid, one the Yugoslav president had hinted at in a chilling conversation with Generals Clark and Naumann in late October. As Clark recalled, Milosevic said, "'We know how to deal with the problem of these Albanians. We've done this before.' We asked where. 'In the Drenica region in central Kosovo in 1946,' he told us. We asked what the solution was. He said right out: 'We killed them. We killed them all. It took several years, but eventually we killed them all. And we had no problem.'"[136]

Viewing the KLA advances as proof that Holbrooke and NATO had somehow betrayed him during the negotiations, Milosevic appears to have decided sometime in November to take matters into his own hands.[137] He fired the head of his secret police, Jovica Stanisic, and the chief of the Yugoslav army, General Momcilo Perisic, and replaced them with well-known hardliners.[138] He put into effect a plan—dubbed Operation Horseshoe—for both eradicating the KLA and engineering a fundamental shift in Kosovo's ethnic balance.[139] The central idea of the plan, as Milosevic had told Clark and Naumann, involved employing Mao's favorite guerrilla tactic of draining the sea in which the fish swam; in the case of Kosovo, this meant emptying the villages of their Albanian population in order to isolate KLA fighters and supporters. The coordinated attack would involve a broad swath of territory in the shape of a horseshoe, moving from the northeast down to the west and back to the southeast of Kosovo along the Albanian and Macedonian borders. It also apparently entailed emptying the key cities of Prizren, Pec, and Pristina of their largely Albanian populations in order both to alter the ethnic balance in Kosovo in the Serbs' favor and to destabilize Kosovo's neighbors, who had to cope with the large influx of refugees.

In short, Operation Horseshoe was an audacious plan. No one could have foreseen that this would be the outcome of the KLA push to take advantage of Milosevic's decision to accept the UN and NATO demands that it withdraw some of his police and army forces from Kosovo. Only its authors and those who ultimately approved its implementation can be held responsible for the evil that the operation represented. It was neither a necessary nor even a logical outcome of the agreement that Holbrooke and Milosevic had negotiated, and it would be wrong to suggest otherwise. But there was also nothing in the October agreement that could have prevented this turn of events. The ability to enforce its terms was effectively neutralized by the presence of less than 2,000 unarmed observers, each one a potential hostage. Little thought had been given to how the KLA could be prevented from taking advantage of the changing balance of forces that resulted from the departure of some Serb security personnel. In other words, the agreement did nothing to prevent a return to fighting or to halt an escalation in violence, even though it was almost certain that both would soon occur.

Peace at a Price

The Holbrooke-Milosevic agreement did buy time—time that may well have proven important to get 50,000 people through the winter without exposing them to freezing temperatures and the risks of starvation. That outcome was important, and it may have been decisive in convincing those who were aware of the agreement's shortcomings to nevertheless support it. As one senior State Department official deeply involved in its negotiation said, "In the end, the benefits in terms of lives saved clearly outweighed its considerable shortcomings."[140]

Yet, when viewed as anything more than a temporary answer to an immediate humanitarian problem, the agreement was flawed in at least two respects. First, in focusing on resolving the immediate humanitarian crisis, those negotiating the accord appear to have ignored the fact that any outside intervention in conflicts has political consequences, even interventions undertaken solely for humanitarian purposes. Second, since the agreement offered no solution to the underlying reasons for the conflict, it was evident that it could not hold past winter, if that. By focusing only on efforts to improve the humanitarian situation, the United States and its

NATO allies failed to prepare for the all-but-inevitable resumption of fighting by spring 1999.

Like any intervention in internal conflicts, humanitarian interventions have political consequences. In a conflict pitting two or more sides against each other, there can generally be no truly impartial intervention.[141] That ought to have been the first lesson learned from the U.S. experience in northern Iraq, Somalia, Bosnia, and Haiti. It should have been evident in the Kosovo case as well. One can argue that NATO's threat and Holbrooke's negotiating talent succeeded in forcing the Serbs to cease their attacks on Kosovar Albanians, to withdraw a portion of Serb police and army forces from the region, and to deploy many of the troops that remained to barracks. That, combined with the international presence in the region, worked to reassure the displaced Albanian population to come down from the hills and seek shelter for the winter, thus averting a potentially catastrophic humanitarian disaster. But these same Serb actions also changed the military balance of forces inside Kosovo in the KLA's favor in ways that had a profound impact on the course of the conflict. The short-term humanitarian success must therefore be weighed against the longer term impact of ignoring the political consequences of achieving that success.

It was evident from the start that the Holbrooke-Milosevic agreement represented only a short-term palliative and Holbrooke and Hill repeatedly warned Washington of this fact after negotiations ended.[142] So did others, sometimes publicly. Thus, General Clark told NATO parliamentarians in November 1999, that the agreement had succeeded only in "dampening and containing the crisis" but not in resolving it. "At this very time both the KLA and the Serbs are re-arming and preparing for confrontation again. If even more destructive fighting is not to occur we must turn off the engines driving this conflict."[143] Absent the ability to enforce the agreement or a willingness to impose a solution, the only way to turn off these engines was to use the time available to devise a viable political solution, which in turn demanded a credible threat of decisive military force.

The unenviable task of finding a political solution in the few weeks before the conflict would again heat up was handed to Christopher Hill, who Milosevic had agreed could work as a mediator between the two sides as long as a face-to-face dialogue would not be convened. For lack of a better alternative, the Clinton administration and its European allies seized upon a set of perceived Serb concessions that had been worked out by Hill during the Holbrooke-Milosevic negotiations in Belgrade. In a unilateral statement issued after these talks concluded, the Serb government put forward eleven principles of a political solution and a proposed timetable for its implementation. Among the unilateral principles, two commitments were noteworthy: to hold within nine months, under OSCE auspices, "free and fair elections" for Kosovo's institutions; and to create a local police force reflecting the ethnic composition of Kosovo's population. In addition, the Serb government proposed a tight timetable for finalizing a political solution, including a commitment to reach agreement by early November 1998 "on the fundamental elements of a political solution . . . using the document proposed by the Contact Group on October 2, 1998, as a starting point."[144]

Although the Serb statement was unilateral and therefore unenforceable, it did provide a basis for Hill to restart his shuttle between Belgrade and Pristina in search of a viable political solution. Working feverishly, along with a small team of State Department lawyers, Hill sought to close the gap between the two sides. However, each time the draft interim agreement was adjusted to reflect the concerns of one side, the other side would raise new objections. The task of reconciling the seemingly irreconcilable proved to be frustrating and ultimately impossible. As one discouraged U.S. official commented in December, "Neither side is ready for a deal right now. Think of the Mideast. Think of Northern Ireland. Forget Bosnia. Forget the Dayton Accords" as appropriate models.[145]

The absence of progress on the political front reflected the fact that the underlying conflict between the Serbs and the Kosovar Albanians remained unresolved and—absent a robust NATO threat to use force as well as a NATO willingness to implement a peace accord—unresolvable. The two parties' positions had become diametrically opposed, a fact that Western governments continued to ignore. Not surprisingly, therefore, violence soon re-emerged in Kosovo. The occasional skirmishes that accompanied KLA advances on the heels of retreating Serb forces soon escalated into regular and increasingly intense confrontations.[146] Attacks affecting civilians increased in number—including the barbaric KLA attack in December on Serb teenagers in a tavern in Pec. As violence mounted, Serb army forces moved out of their garrisons without prior notification and Interior Ministry units that were required to withdraw from Kosovo soon returned to join in the fray. Despite violations of the agreement—communicated to the North Atlantic Council in detail on a daily basis—NATO did not act, making a mockery of the alliance's decision to keep the ACTORD for air strikes in place.[147] The Serbs were emboldened to the point that on December 24, 1998, security forces launched a major new offensive around the town of Podujevo, in violation of Security Council Resolution 1199. After witnessing the escalation, Ambassador William Walker, the head of the Kosovo Verification Mission, declared that "both sides have been looking for trouble and they have found it. If the two sides are unwilling to live up to their agreements, 2,000, 3,000, or 4,000 unarmed verifiers cannot frustrate their attempts to go after each other."[148]

Thus as 1999 approached, the Holbrooke-Milosevic agreement lay in tatters. In the short term, the agreement helped to forestall a major humanitarian crisis. In the long term, however, the deal resolved nothing. It was therefore incumbent upon NATO leaders to prepare for its inevitable breakdown. This they did not do, in part because U.S. officials oversold Holbrooke's success in Belgrade. As a result, Washington and allied capitals were caught largely unprepared when violence once again erupted in full force early in the new year. And their weak responses to early violations of the agreement told Milosevic that he might be able to get away with such violence, even on a massive scale.

CHAPTER THREE

The Road
to War

O N FRIDAY, JANUARY 15, 1999, marauding Serb paramilitary and armed forces moved through the village of
Racak in southern Kosovo, leaving devastation in their wake. Army artillery
had pounded the village for three days before Serb forces entered. When
they left, at least forty-five people had been slaughtered, including three
women, a twelve-year-old boy, and several elderly men. All had been ex-
ecuted. One person had been decapitated. Monitors of the Kosovo Verification Mission (KVM) organized by the Organization for Security and
Cooperation in Europe (OSCE) had been sent to the area as fighting escalated in the days and hours preceding the massacre. They entered Racak
within twenty-four hours of the killing and described a scene of unspeakable horror.

Surveying the sight, Ambassador William Walker, a seasoned American
diplomat who had witnessed his share of atrocities while serving in Central
America and who now headed the KVM, described what he had seen:

> I talked to several villagers . . . and started up the hill. In a gully above the
> village, I saw the first body. It was covered with a blanket, and when it was
> pulled back, I saw there was no head on the corpse—just an incredibly bloody
> mess on the neck. Somebody told me that the skull was on the other side of
> the gully and asked if I wanted to see that. But I said, "No, I've pretty much got
> this story." [Three more bodies appeared.] They looked like older men, with
> gray hair or white hair. . . . They had wounds on their heads, and there was
> blood on their clothes. [Then a larger group of bodies.] I didn't count them. I
> just looked and saw a lot of holes in the head—in the top of the head and the

back of the head. A couple had what appeared to be bullet wounds knocking out their eyes. I was told there were other bodies further up and over the crest of the hill, and I was asked by journalists and inspectors if I was going to go up and see the rest. I said, "I've seen enough."[1]

Once his inspection was over, Walker termed the massacre "an unspeakable atrocity" that constituted "a crime against humanity." He concluded that he would not "hesitate to accuse the government security forces of responsibility."[2]

Racak proved to be a turning point for the United States and its NATO allies. They had looked to the agreement worked out between Richard Holbrooke and Slobodan Milosevic the previous October as a vehicle to buy time to reach a political settlement before the resumption of the fighting that was expected in April. But as Secretary of State Madeleine Albright told National Security Adviser Samuel ("Sandy") Berger, Racak demonstrated that "spring has come early to Kosovo."[3] The October agreement failed to give Kosovo much of a respite from the fighting. The much-touted deployments of the OSCE verification mission and NATO aerial surveillance, while able to monitor developments, could not prevent violations of the agreement or enforce its implementation. Notwithstanding the efforts by Christopher Hill in leading a negotiating shuttle, it was evident that the Serb and Kosovar Albanian sides were no closer to reaching a political solution than they had been in mid-1998 when the diplomatic effort began.

After the massacre it was obvious to everyone within the Clinton administration that a new policy was needed, one that stressed decisive action; they abandoned the wait-and-see attitude that characterized U.S. and NATO policy following the conclusion of the October agreement. Yet a decision to use military force of any kind—from the air, on the ground, or both—still faced considerable obstacles. First, no one had made the case to the U.S. Congress or the public for large-scale use of military force in Kosovo. Instead, the October agreement had been hailed as a major achievement of American diplomacy backed by the threat of NATO force, and the Racak massacre was the first widely publicized indication that the situation on the ground was deteriorating. It would take time to make the case to the public for decisive military action.

Second, with few exceptions, the NATO allies were not prepared to take military action, as became clear when the North Atlantic Council met two days after the massacre. While reminding Milosevic that the NATO threat of air strikes issued the previous October was still in effect, the council decided to send its top military representatives to Belgrade rather than take military action. It was evident that some form of diplomatic activity would have to take place before all the allies would accept the need for stronger measures.

Third, there was extreme reluctance on the part of the Clinton administration to consider the use of military force—even if it was limited to air strikes. Some officials feared an antiseptic, limited use of airpower, which they sensed might fail. Others worried that the use of force would likely result in a long-term military commitment to the region, something they feared the United States could ill afford, especially in light of Congress's unhappiness with the extended deployment of American troops in Bosnia. Most officials were also concerned about the political impact of a decision to use force in an atmosphere poisoned by the impeachment procedures that were then ongoing. With the House having voted to impeach the president and the Senate in the midst of deciding on his possible removal from office, this was hardly a propitious time to lead NATO into war.

Finally, there was a widespread belief within the Clinton administration and among the NATO allies and authorities that decisive military action was not required. Instead, many believed that a credible threat of force—and possibly its demonstrative use—would suffice to convince Milosevic that NATO was serious and push him to make a political deal granting the Kosovar Albanians far-reaching autonomy. Equally important was the assumption of U.S. and NATO policy that once Milosevic was coerced into coming to the bargaining table, the Kosovars would follow suit and would settle for what Belgrade offered, especially if a security force, most likely led by NATO, was deployed to help enforce any agreement reached.

Given these considerations, the U.S. and NATO consensus in favor of some type of firmer action soon turned into an agreement to launch one last-ditch diplomatic effort to find a solution that would end the violence and provide greater autonomy to Kosovo. That effort took place at a medieval castle in the French village of Rambouillet, located just outside Paris. The talks at Rambouillet proved to be a disappointment. No agreement was reached between the parties, and even the Kosovars left the castle with only a commitment in principle to sign the accords at a future date (which they subsequently did).

The failure of the Rambouillet talks left the United States and NATO with little choice but to follow through on their frequent threats of force and commence military operations against Serbia. In doing so, Washington and its allies were convinced that a demonstration of NATO's military prowess was all that was needed to force Milosevic back to the bargaining table. As events showed, this did not happen. Instead, Milosevic escalated the conflict, forcing well over a million ethnic Albanians from their homes, and NATO ultimately had to fly one-third as many sorties as in the 1991 Desert Storm operation to prevail.

Could a different diplomatic strategy have succeeded where the Rambouillet talks failed? Was it necessary for the United States and NATO to use force once it became clear that neither the Serbs nor the Kosovar Albanians were interested in settling their differences peacefully? Although it is tempting to argue that the war was the result of a tactical error on the Clinton administration's part and could have been easily avoided with a wiser negotiating approach, we believe the record does not support that argument. War may not have been inevitable in early 1999. However, only the most Herculean of strategies (which virtually no one in any NATO country, inside or outside government, proposed) might have prevented war by this late date.

At least in theory, there were two alternatives to the approach taken at Rambouillet, one diplomatic, the other military. On the diplomatic front, the Clinton administration and its Contact Group allies could have approached the negotiations differently. One possibility was to try to negotiate a lasting settlement instead of settling for an interim agreement (which focused on Kosovo's autonomy and left the territory's final status unresolved). For example, the Contact Group could have proposed partitioning Kosovo into Serb and ethnic Albanian regions.[4] Partition offered a possible solution that, at least in theory, differed from two other unpromising options: the status quo and complete independence for all of Kosovo. And while both parties naturally insisted that they control the entire territory, partition offered a possible compromise—which voices in Serbia had raised in the past.[5]

Was partition negotiable in early 1999? Although it is impossible to know for certain, the answer is almost certainly no. There is no indication that Belgrade ever seriously contemplated a division of Kosovo; its political and military aim was to retain and strengthen its control over the territory by destroying the Kosovar rebel force and, if necessary, to forcefully change the internal ethnic balance.[6] The Kosovar Albanians might have settled for less than all of Kosovo if the remaining part could become independent, though it should be noted that there is no record of anyone suggesting that this would be an acceptable compromise.

What if NATO and the Contact Group had combined a partition proposal with a more credible threat to Belgrade? If that threat had included ground forces deployed to Kosovo's borders, there is a chance it might have worked. However, this strategy would have required a commitment to a very muscular use of force, probably every bit as credible and intimidating as what NATO would have needed to make the Rambouillet negotiations succeed. In other words, a partition proposal would not have changed the basic nature of the problem, since Serbia would likely have opposed it even more strongly than it opposed the Rambouillet approach.

If partition did not offer a viable compromise, another negotiating approach would have been to press for a more durable solution to the Kosovo conflict that was also more to Belgrade's liking. Negotiators could have rejected an interim solution and pushed for far-reaching autonomy and self-government as a final solution to the conflict. Doing so would have avoided the issue of a vote or referendum at the end of the interim period, a possibility that, given the large ethnic Albanian majority, Belgrade naturally found difficult to accept. Yet even if Belgrade would have accepted a substantial degree of autonomy for Kosovo, the Kosovar Albanians would not. The one thing uniting ethnic Albanians across the political spectrum in Kosovo was the preservation of the option for independence. Even if that obstacle could somehow have been overcome (and the presence of the KLA made that exceedingly unlikely), the Kosovars would have insisted on a large international security force to protect them against Serb military and police forces—the one provision of Rambouillet that Belgrade refused even to discuss. Without such a force, moreover, the KLA could not have been checked, leaving the ingredients in place for a worsening conflict down the road.

Diplomacy was clearly a hard sell in early 1999. The Serbs and Kosovars were miles apart and had little incentive to bridge the chasm that divided them. The best hope lay in the Contact Group's chosen negotiating strategy of seeking to narrow the differences step by step. That required putting aside the issue that divided the sides most deeply—Kosovo's future political status—and focusing instead on giving the vast majority of its population a greater say in the administration and government of the territory. It also meant addressing the immediate security requirements in the region, including both the Serb threat to the ethnic Albanian civilian population and the KLA challenge to the Serbs. The proposal offered at Rambouillet to limit the Serb military and security presence to a minimum, demilitarize the KLA, and deploy a substantial NATO force to the territory was designed to meet that immediate need. In the end, that effort failed to garner the support of both sides.

Once Rambouillet failed, was there an alternative military course open to NATO other than bombing? Here the answer is less clear-cut. At least in theory, the United States and its allies had three options. First, they could have walked away—as, indeed, they said they would if both sides chose not to sign the Rambouillet accords—and let the conflict run its course. A case can be made for this option.[7] Though there were indications that Belgrade was preparing militarily to inflict massive damage in its effort to destroy the KLA, the situation in Kosovo had not (yet) become a humanitarian disaster. U.S. and NATO interests at stake in the region may have been important (especially given the possibility of regional instability caused by open warfare and large movements of people), but they were hardly vital. Yet even though the alliance may have seemed to be off the "moral hook" to intervene when the Kosovar delegation failed to sign the Rambouillet accords, it retained a humanitarian interest in the well-being of the Kosovar Albanian people. What is more, the alliance was on the political and strategic hook to follow through on its frequent threats to use force to end large-scale violence in Kosovo. The U.S. commitment to oppose a violent Serb crackdown in Kosovo dated back to 1992; its interest in the stability of the Balkans dated back a half century, to the Truman Doctrine.

A second option after the failure at Rambouillet would have been to support the KLA and the Kosovar population in their quest for independence. NATO air strikes could have formed a part of that effort, which also would have had to include a program to arm and train the KLA to make it an effective fighting force. The problems with this option are many, however. A major concern propelling U.S. and NATO involvement in the conflict was humanitarian; arming the KLA and conducting air strikes would have failed to satisfy that concern. It could not prevent the Serb military and security forces from trying to drive out the ethnic Albanian population (if not slaughter large numbers of Kosovars). To the contrary, making the conflict about Kosovo's political future would likely have spurred the Serbs to accelerate their efforts to cleanse the territory of all Albanians. A Serb victory in the short run would not only have come at very large human cost but would also have produced a drawn-out guerilla campaign by a well-armed and well-trained rebel force, possibly turning Kosovo into a European Afghanistan. In the improbable event of a KLA victory , an independent Kosovo would have been achieved by force of arms. Not only would Belgrade have been unlikely to accept that outcome for long, but a self-confident and victorious KLA would have had every incentive to try to extend its triumph for Albanian nationalism to other parts of the region, especially Macedonia.

So the Clinton administration and its NATO allies had little choice but to secure by force what they sought to achieve through negotiations at Rambouillet: the creation of a de facto international protectorate that could both guarantee Kosovo's political autonomy and provide security for its people. That was the political goal of the alliance's bombing campaign. NATO proved unprepared to accomplish this task militarily. Rather than deploying the capabilities necessary to force Serb military and police forces out of Kosovo, the alliance adopted a strategy of using limited airpower to persuade Milosevic to accept this outcome. The allies assumed—wrongly, as it turned out—that the use of force by NATO would rapidly bring Milosevic around to accepting the political deal on the table. Equally important, there was a general sense that the limited stakes rendered the use of ground forces to wrest control of Kosovo from Serbia politically unsustainable and perhaps even militarily unwise, given the common view that U.S. armed forces were already overburdened around the world and that the American public can quickly turn against a military operation once there are substantial casualties. That assumption in effect meant that NATO would go to war in the hope, but without the certainty, that its military campaign would lead to victory.

The Rambouillet Strategy

From the very beginning of the conflict in Kosovo, Madeleine Albright believed that a strategy relying solely or even mainly on negotiations with Milosevic to achieve a political solution was likely to fail. This had been her steadfast view during the entire Bosnian war, when she persistently pressed for air strikes to bring an end to the conflict. From the moment violence mounted in Kosovo in 1998, Albright's rhetoric reflected her strong belief that Milosevic needed to be forcefully persuaded to accept Kosovo's autonomy. Yet throughout 1998, her perspective failed to prevail in Washington's corridors of power. Instead, the Clinton administration accepted the perspective of Richard Holbrooke and others, who believed an acceptable deal could be negotiated between Milosevic and the Kosovar Albanians. For much of the year, Albright deferred to Holbrooke, knowing that her own views lacked support in the White House and Pentagon. Even so, she never trusted Milosevic to deliver without a very large stick forcing him to do so. By December 1998, she appeared convinced that the Holbrooke strategy was failing. To underscore that view, she had her spokesman, James Rubin, declare publicly that "Milosevic has been at the center of every crisis in the former Yugoslavia over the last decade. He is not simply part of the problem; Milosevic is the problem."[8]

Bringing the Interagency on Board

As fighting in Kosovo escalated in late December, Albright began to consider alternatives to the policy of monitoring Serb noncompliance with the October agreement and hoping that a political solution might be achievable before spring, when everyone expected the violence to escalate once again. A meeting of National Security Council principals was called for January 15, 1999. Gathered in the White House Situation Room were Berger, Albright, Defense Secretary William Cohen, Joint Chiefs of Staff Chairman Henry Shelton, Director of Central Intelligence George Tenet, and their top aides. Lying before them was a thirteen-page Kosovo strategy paper, which tried to build on existing policy. It proposed beefing up the OSCE Kosovo Verification Mission with additional personnel, helicopters, and bodyguards and preparing to implement some of the key concessions Milosevic had made in October, including training an Albanian police force and planning for possible elections in Kosovo during the summer of 1999. The goal of these efforts was, as before, to "promote regional stability and protect our investment in Bosnia; prevent the resumption of hostilities in Kosovo and renewed humanitarian crisis; [and] preserve U.S. and NATO credibility."[9]

Albright came to the meeting armed with two pages of talking points. Rather than endorsing the strategy paper, she noted that the October agreement was about to fall apart, as the violence in northern Kosovo around Christmas showed. The KVM was good at "crisis management" but could not address, let alone solve, the underlying problem. Hill's negotiation efforts were stymied by Serb obstructionism and Albanian fragmentation. The administration now faced a "decision point." It had three options: "stepping back, muddling through or taking decisive steps."[10] As violence escalated and a new humanitarian crisis loomed, stepping back was not a real option. As for muddling through, at best it might postpone the inevitable collapse of the October agreement; at worst it amounted to what one senior NATO official termed "a strategy of incrementally reinforcing failure."[11] That left decisive steps. While Albright did not advocate immediate military action (be it air strikes or preparing a NATO ground force), she emphasized that "Milosevic needed to realize that he faced a real potential for NATO action. If he did not get that message, he would not make any concessions."[12]

Although Albright's cabinet colleagues agreed that Milosevic was in the process of "shredding" his promises of the previous October, none was yet prepared to follow her lead. The Pentagon—and none more so than its civilian chief, Secretary Cohen—was leery of getting involved militarily in yet another Balkan conflict, especially since there was no clear end to any such involvement. Led by Berger, the White House was skeptical about threatening military action for fear of having to follow through and implement the threats without having a sense of what the political objectives were and how they could best be achieved. The principals therefore opted for October-plus, as the Kosovo strategy paper was informally known. Albright could not hide her disappointment. "We're just gerbils running on a wheel," she exclaimed on her way back to her office in Foggy Bottom.[13]

The discovery of the Racak massacre within hours after the Principals Committee meeting called into question the continued viability of the incrementalist approach, which had just been endorsed. For Albright Racak confirmed that the United States and NATO should have acted sooner. "These were the kinds of things we were trying to avoid," she remembered thinking upon hearing the news. Others came to this conclusion more slowly. Berger's deputy, James Steinberg, recalled his reaction when he first heard about the massacre: "My first reaction is this is precisely what we feared. My second was, that's why we wanted the KVM in there, because it was going to be harder for them to cover this up."[14]

Just four hours after word of the Racak massacre reached Washington, Steinberg chaired a meeting of the NSC's Deputies Committee involving his counterparts from the State and Defense Departments, the Joint Chiefs of Staff vice chairman, and the CIA's deputy director. According to a person present at the meeting, State's representatives led the way in arguing for immediate military action, in the form of the limited air response involving the use of dozens of cruise missiles that NATO had devised for exactly that purpose. The Pentagon representatives were highly dubious that limited air strikes could work. What was the purpose of air strikes, they wondered. If it was just punishment, what tangible objective would that serve? If it was to end the fighting and persuade Milosevic to accept a political settlement, airpower alone might not be able to ensure success. Was the administration prepared to go in on the ground?[15] Without definitive answers to these questions, this and subsequent meetings held over the next few days ended without a decision on how to respond to the massacre.

In the days that immediately followed Racak, Albright worked with her staff on developing a new strategy that would go beyond the status-quo-plus policy the principals had endorsed on January 15. In developing the strategy, she and her staff drew on input from a cable written by Alexander Vershbow, the U.S. Ambassador to NATO, which reiterated his plea of the previous summer to establish an international protectorate in Kosovo by making a credible threat of force, including if necessary a willingness to impose a protectorate through a ground invasion.[16] Albright presented the result of this collective effort to her colleagues on January 19.

Albright's strategy consisted of an ultimatum to the parties to accept an interim settlement by a date certain. If the parties accepted the deal, NATO would commit to its enforcement with troops on the ground. However, if Belgrade refused to endorse the plan, NATO's standing orders to its military commanders to commence a phased air campaign would be implemented. Albright was explicit about the strategy's key assumptions. First, since the allies would not deploy their troops on their own for fear of having to repeat the disaster of Bosnia, American troops would have to be part of any international force. Second, Milosevic would never accept the need to negotiate seriously, let alone accept an interim settlement, if there was no credible bombing threat. Third, further negotiations would lead nowhere; therefore, an interim deal had to be imposed through the threat and, if necessary, the use of NATO airpower.

In presenting her ideas, Albright was essentially pushing on an open door. Although there was still some skepticism among Albright's colleagues—Cohen and Shelton, for instance, remained wary of including American troops in a NATO force—no one could come up with a better alternative to the proposal. That night, as the president delivered his State of the Union Address, the NSC staff prepared a memorandum for his approval of Albright's strategy. The president signed off on it the next day.[17]

After nearly a year of intermittent effort, Albright finally gained the interagency support she had long sought.[18] But that may have been the easy part. Success still required getting the allies and, if possible, the Russians on board. It also meant convincing the parties that a settlement was preferable to any alternative. Clearly, none of this would be easy.

Bringing the Allies and Russians on Board

In the days after the U.S. decision, Secretary Albright traveled to Moscow and other European capitals to fashion agreement on what would trigger NATO air strikes. The main obstacle, it turned out, was allied hesitancy. With the exception of Great Britain and, to some extent, France, none of the allies was yet prepared to use force even after the horrors of Racak became fully apparent. The main sticking points for resuscitating a serious threat of force were three, each one as sound as the next.[19]

First, contrary to initial indications from U.S. officials, key NATO allies insisted that force should not be threatened simply to punish Belgrade for its actions in Racak and violation of the October agreement. The restoration of the status quo ante—even a cease-fire buttressed by additional limitations on the movement of Serb military and police forces inside Kosovo and increased security for OSCE monitors—was not sufficient reason for NATO to use force. Instead, the threat of force should serve to promote a distinct political objective, including a notion of how the conflict in Kosovo could be settled.[20]

Second, with the experience of the previous October still fresh in many ② minds, the allies were concerned that they alone would be responsible for whatever emerged in the aftermath of NATO's bombing campaign. In particular, they worried that NATO troops would have to go into Kosovo to stabilize the situation and enforce a peace without American participation. Fearing a repeat of the disastrous experience in Bosnia, all allies (including Britain) made it clear that they could not support air strikes unless Washington was prepared to participate in whatever NATO ground operation would follow. A senior U.S. national security official seems to have understood this well, declaring that any "serious discussion on how to resolve Kosovo over the long term must explore all options, including American participation on the ground. It's just a fact of life that our allies are reluctant to support airpower against the Serbs in the absence of a strategy for what happens next on the ground."[21]

Finally, key NATO allies were concerned that the threat tied to the proposed U.S. ultimatum would be directed solely at Belgrade. However, as the experience of the previous fall demonstrated, the KLA was bound to exploit this threat to its own benefit. Its actions would invariably seek to provoke Serb forces into reacting in their predictably horrifying ways, thus forcing NATO to act against Serb forces—actions that, whether one liked it or not, would support the KLA's military aims. This concern was reflected in a conversation that President Bill Clinton had with British Prime Minister Tony Blair on January 21. Aware of European worries regarding the KLA, Clinton suggested that the KLA be urged to moderate its behavior. Blair responded affirmatively: "One of the dangers is if we go smack Milosevic and find the KLA moving on people who don't agree with them."[22]

All of the European concerns were not only valid but also useful correctives to the inclination of some Clinton administration officials to lash out violently against Milosevic without really having thought through the consequences of doing so. In response, the United States sought to refine its proposed strategy in a way that would garner NATO support. Washington agreed that the threat of force should be tied to specific political objectives and suggested that the most recent revision of the Hill plan provided a suitable framework for an interim settlement. The parties should be given a date certain by which to accept the plan or else face the consequences of their obstinacy. In that regard, U.S. officials agreed to condition the threat of air strikes against Serb forces in Kosovo and Serbia on KLA moderation and, ultimately, on the Kosovar Albanians accepting the political deal that was on the table.[23] The result was a coherent strategy that—like the U.S. strategy in Bosnia, on which this one was built and which ultimately led to the Dayton Accords—tied the stick of military action to clearly definable behavior at the negotiating table.

Finally, at least in private, U.S. officials indicated that the United States would participate in a NATO force deployed to enforce a negotiated agreement. However, reflecting the administration's sensitivity to congressional opinion, its public statements were far more circumspect. For example, on January 26 Sandy Berger stated that President Clinton remained opposed to deploying American ground forces. As for their possible participation in a force policing a negotiated settlement, Berger indicated, "We would have to look at that under those circumstances in consultation with Congress. Obviously, we've had no decisions along those lines."[24] Although Secretary Cohen and General Shelton indicated on February 3 that the Pentagon was planning to make 2,000–4,000 troops available for participation in a possible Kosovo Force (KFOR), President Clinton said the following day that "no decision has been reached." It was not until February 13, one full week into the Rambouillet conference and a day after the Senate concluded its trial of the president, that President Clinton used a regular Saturday radio address to announce his decision that "a little less than 4,000" U.S. troops might participate in KFOR.[25]

One other allied concern, shared by Washington, was to ensure that the emerging policy would receive Moscow's backing or at least not its active opposition. Even before Secretary Albright met with key allies to finalize a strategy, she traveled to Moscow for a meeting with Foreign Minister Igor Ivanov to try to enlist Russia's support. In discussions at the Bolshoi Theater during an intermission in La Traviata, Albright wondered whether Ivanov might agree that an ultimatum could convince Milosevic to accept a deal. Ivanov indicated that he understood Albright's reasoning without agreeing that this was the way to go.[26] Russia, it seemed, accepted the need to threaten force in order to get a deal, even if it could never accept the threat's actual implementation. Albright's informal talks with Ivanov over champagne and caviar at the Bolshoi suggested that there was sufficient common ground between the two countries to issue a joint statement that called upon Serb authorities to comply "without delay" with UN Security Council resolutions and other agreements previously negotiated, particularly with respect to the disposition and deployment of military and police units.[27]

With Russia on board, key European allies appeared to be more comfortable with endorsing the ultimatum strategy, including the possible use of force. German Foreign Minister Joschka Fisher, for instance, argued publicly for the consideration of force: "I am not a friend of using force, but sometimes it is a necessary means of last resort. So I am ready to use it if there is no other way. If people are being massacred, you cannot mutter about having no mandate. You must act."[28] The following day, British Prime Minister Blair and French President Jacques Chirac issued a joint statement declaring that they were "willing to consider all forms of military action, including the dispatch of ground forces, necessary to accompany the implementation of a negotiated agreement. If an early political agreement proves impossible, the two leaders believe that all options will need to be considered."[29] These statements underscored that basic agreement on the strategy had been reached among the allies, enabling Secretary Albright to announce that she would join her Contact Group colleagues from Britain, France, Germany, Italy, and Russia—something she had refused to do until a consensus was reached.[30]

The Strategy Rollout

The public rollout of the strategy came in a series of intricate and coordinated NATO, UN, and Contact Group statements. Although the precise sequencing of statements had been the subject of many difficult hours of high-level diplomacy, their import was unmistakable.[31] On January 28, UN Secretary-General Kofi Annan met with the North Atlantic Council and in a highly symbolic and important meeting endorsed the thrust of the emerging strategy. Annan urged the NATO countries to build on the lessons of Bosnia and "further refine the combination of force and diplomacy that is the key to peace in the Balkans, as elsewhere." In an implicit warning to Belgrade, Annan asserted that the "bloody wars of the last decade have left us with no illusions about the difficulty of halting internal conflicts—by reason or by force—particularly against the wishes of the government of a sovereign State. But nor have they left us with any illusions about the need to use force, when all other means have failed. We may be reaching that limit, once again, in the former Yugoslavia."[32] With this statement, the UN secretary-general implicitly provided his blessing to threatening and even using force against a sovereign state, even though such action was never explicitly authorized by the UN Security Council given the certainty of a Russian veto.

Within hours of Annan's statement, NATO Secretary-General Javier Solana emerged from a North Atlantic Council meeting and in a prepared statement affirmed NATO's readiness to act. Solana's statement called on the Serb and Kosovar Albanian sides to "agree to the proposals to be issued by the Contact Group for completing an interim political settlement within the timeframe to be established." NATO remains "ready to act and rules out no option to ensure full respect by both sides of the demands of the international community, and in particular observance of all relevant Security Council Resolutions." The council also declared that NATO would "increase its military preparedness to ensure that the demands of the international community are met" and would study how to stop arms smuggling into Kosovo.[33] Elaborating on the council's statement, Solana confirmed at a press conference that "NATO does not rule out any possibility. Therefore every possible option is open as it is stated."[34]

With NATO having expressed its willingness to act, the action moved next to the Contact Group, which met on January 29 in London. Foreign ministers from the six member countries emerged from the meeting with a call on both sides "to end the cycle of violence" and to negotiate a political settlement (see appendix C). Accordingly, the Contact Group

—insisted that the parties accept that the basis for a fair settlement must include the principles set out by the Contact Group;

—considered that the proposals drafted by the negotiators contain the elements for a substantial autonomy for Kosovo;

—recognized that the work done by the negotiators identified the limited number of points that required final negotiation between the parties;

—agreed to summon representatives from the Federal Yugoslav and Serb governments and representatives of the Kosovo Albanians to Rambouillet by February 6, to begin negotiations, with the direct involvement of the Contact Group;

—agreed that the participants should work to conclude negotiations within seven days. The negotiators should then report to Contact Group ministers, who would assess whether the progress made justified a further period (less than one week) to bring the negotiations to a successful conclusion.[35]

At a press conference immediately following the meeting, Secretary Albright underscored the one-week deadline for negotiations. "At the end of that time either parties will have agreed or they will not. If they have not, we will draw the appropriate conclusions. We have sent the parties an unmistakable message—get serious. Showing up is not going to be good enough."[36]

The strategy's final stepping-stone was laid the following day when NATO backed up the Contact Group's negotiating strategy with the explicit threat of force. In a statement issued by the North Atlantic Council, the allies declared that "NATO is ready to take whatever measures are necessary in the light of both parties' compliance with international commitments and requirements, including in particular assessment by the Contact Group of the response to its demands, to avert a humanitarian catastrophe, by compelling compliance with the demands of the international community and the achievement of a political settlement." To ensure NATO's responsiveness to the evolving situation, the council placed the decision "to authorize air strikes against targets on FRY [Federal Republic of Yugoslavia] territory" in the hands of the NATO secretary-general.[37]

At the end of this intricate series of statements, the preferred strategy for dealing with the Kosovo conflict was clear. One way or another, there would be a resolution of the conflict—or at least of NATO's role in it—in the next few weeks. Even though NATO's threat of force was designed to encourage a negotiated outcome, the actual nature of the conflict's resolution would be up to the parties. As Secretary Albright stated in a speech just before the opening of Rambouillet:

> Three outcomes are possible. If President Milosevic refuses to accept the Contact Group proposals, or has allowed repression in Kosovo to continue, he can expect NATO air strikes. If the Kosovo Albanians obstruct progress at Rambouillet or on the ground, they cannot expect the NATO and the international community to bail them out. Decisions on air strikes and international support will be affected, and we will find additional ways of bringing pressure to bear. If the two sides do reach agreement, we will need to concentrate our effort on making sure that it is successfully implemented.

Albright concluded by warning that there "should be no doubt on either side that the consequences of failure to reach agreement or to show restraint on the ground will be swift and severe."[38]

The Rambouillet Conference

By agreeing to attend the Rambouillet conference, the parties implicitly accepted the twenty-six principles that British Foreign Secretary Robin Cook had presented to them on January 30, immediately after the Contact Group ministerial.[39] The principles, drawn from the most recent Hill draft for a three-year interim settlement, addressed such matters as

—the governance of Kosovo, including setting up democratically accountable institutions to provide Kosovo a high degree of self-governance and representative police and judicial bodies;

—human rights, including an ombudsman and a role for the OSCE and other institutions in guaranteeing them;

—implementation, including the creation of dispute resolution mechanisms and participation by the OSCE and other international bodies;

—general principles, including an end to violence, agreement that the interim period would last three years, the territorial integrity of the Federal Republic of Yugoslavia, free and fair elections, an amnesty, and international involvement in implementation.[40]

None of the principles was negotiable, and any proposal for resolving the conflict peacefully had to be fully consistent with them.

The Rambouillet conference opened on February 6 under the formal chairmanship of the British and French foreign ministers (respectively, Robin Cook and Hubert Védrine). The actual negotiations were in the hands of three negotiators: Christopher Hill (representing the United States), Wolfgang Petritsch (for the European Union), and Boris Mayorski (for Russia). The negotiators were supported by a group of legal experts drawn from the Contact Group, which was headed by James O'Brien, the State Department's deputy director of policy planning and one of the principal drafters of the Dayton Accords.

Negotiations at Rambouillet were to proceed on the basis of the latest draft version of an agreement for a political settlement of the conflict, which was handed to the parties upon their arrival. Like the Dayton Accords, the document consisted of a brief framework agreement, accompanied by a series of annexes. The largest annex contained a new constitution for Kosovo; two smaller documents addressed elections and the role of the ombudsman. Additional annexes, including two on military and civilian implementation, were to be handed over to the parties at a later stage. The parties were invited to comment on the draft text and submit revisions. Those agreed to by both sides would be incorporated in the agreement, but no changes would be made in the text if only one party sought a modification. Finally, all proposed revisions were to be consistent with the nonnegotiable principles, and no significant changes could be made to the implementation annexes once these were tabled.[41]

The negotiations during the first week of the conference were hampered by the composition of the two delegations, the Serb refusal to engage in a serious give-and-take on the agreement's text, and squabbling among the NATO allies concerning the text of the security annex.

The first real obstacle to progress was the nature of the delegations themselves. One immediate indication of Serb intentions was the relatively low level of its delegation, which was led by Ratko Markovic, the deputy prime minister of the Serb Republic. Absent from the gathering were Yugoslav President Slobodan Milosevic, whose physical presence and full participation in Dayton proved crucial to its success. Even Milosevic's surrogate during the Bosnian peace negotiations, Serb President Milan Milutinovic, did not initially attend. Moreover, rather than staffing the delegation with legal and other experts, the Serb delegation included individuals from the different ethnic groups in Kosovo, including Albanians, Turks, Gorani, Roma, and Serbs. The delegation was informally called Belgrade's "rainbow coalition."[42]

As for the Kosovar Albanian delegation, its principal characteristic was fragmentation. At the suggestion of the negotiators, the Albanians arrived with a group of people representing constituencies that were significantly broader than those that had been Hill's principal interlocutors during much of the shuttle. In addition to representatives from Kosovo's "ruling" party headed by Ibrahim Rugova, the delegation included people from the main umbrella opposition party (the United Democratic Movement) as well as five representatives from the KLA. Missing, however, was the KLA's principal political representative, Adem Demaci, who failed to endorse let alone join the proceedings at Rambouillet. Somewhat to the negotiators' surprise, the delegation elected a twenty-nine-year-old KLA representative, Hashim Thaci, rather than Rugova as its head. If nothing else, this indicated the shift in power in Kosovo and suggested that even in his absence Demaci would influence what would go on inside the fourteenth-century castle in which the negotiations took place.

A second major obstacle to progress at least during the first week was the Serbs' refusal to engage in serious negotiations. While the Kosovars set about the difficult task of dissecting and commenting on the hastily drawn-up legal documents that would determine their future, the Serb delegation satisfied itself with singing patriotic songs deep into the night and indicating only that it was prepared to sign the twenty-six nonnegotiable principles before returning home. Indicative of the mood was its consumption of alcohol—some 300 bottles of red wine, 78 bottles of white wine, and 8 bottles of cognac for a few dozen people in the first five days alone.[43] Even if it wanted to negotiate seriously, moreover, the delegation's low-level representation meant that it could not. As a result, much of the first week was characterized by the Kosovar delegation indicating its general acceptance of the draft agreement and annexes (of which two more, on economic issues and humanitarian assistance, were tabled during that time), while providing detailed written comments that sought to clarify or improve on the proposed terms. In contrast, the Serb delegation was officially silent.

The third impediment to success was the internal wrangling within NATO on questions of detail in the security annex. Three basic issues were in contention. First, having failed to subordinate NATO to the Contact Group on the question of when and how to launch air strikes, France sought to have the NATO force that would be deployed to Kosovo in the event of an agreement receive its political guidance not from the North Atlantic Council but from the Contact Group. This was unacceptable to the United States and, indeed, to any of the other fourteen NATO allies. Second, supported by other European allies, Paris maintained that the deployment of KFOR had to be authorized by the United Nations, since NATO could not deploy outside its territory for reasons other than self-defense. The United States strongly resisted this demand for fear of setting a precedent by which a decision on whether or not to use force would rest with the UN Security Council (and thus implicitly with Moscow and Beijing) rather than with the alliance members. Both sides settled for a British proposal: that KFOR deployment would receive UN endorsement rather than authorization. Finally, there was a debate about the distribution of power between the security element of the implementation mission, to be provided by NATO, and the civilian element, to be provided by the OSCE. Early drafts of the annex would have given the civilian administration authority over the Serb interior police forces that were to remain, even though it lacked the military means to enforce compliance. In the end, NATO was assigned the task of ensuring compliance by the Serb police and armed forces with the terms of the agreement as well as of overseeing the demobilization of the KLA.[44]

These issues were not resolved until many days into the Rambouillet negotiations, and the final agreed text was not presented to the parties until after the first week of talks. Yet for all practical purposes the security annex was the very crux of the negotiations. The Kosovars were not going to sign onto an interim agreement unless a substantial military presence guaranteed their safety, while the Serbs were not going to accept an agreement if it required a foreign military presence on their soil. As a senior White House official told one of us at the time, "The issue is how much force can the Serbs accept and how little force can the Kosovars live with."[45] Yet that discussion did not take place at Rambouillet during the first week of the talks. Not surprisingly, therefore, the Contact Group ministers who convened in Paris at the end of the first week decided to extend the talks for another week, setting noon on February 20 as the new deadline.[46]

The dynamic of the second week of negotiations was quite different from that of the first. On the question of foreign troops, the Serb position remained unchanged. If anything, it hardened. Serb President Milutinovic, who joined the talks toward the end of the first week, underscored this position in his first press conference: "We're against any kind of foreign troops. ... If the agreement is good and fair and supported by a vast majority of residents of Kosovo, no foreign force is necessary to make them implement it."[47] As a result of this Serb stonewalling, senior Clinton administration officials decided to send Christopher Hill to Belgrade to meet with Milosevic in person. Although the hastily arranged trip from Paris to Belgrade evoked the image of "a sultan being visited in his redoubt,"[48] the fact remained that only Milosevic could force a breakthrough in the talks.[49] In three hours of talks with the Yugoslav leader, Hill presented the entire peace plan to Milosevic, including the security annexes, which the delegations in Rambouillet would not see until a day later.[50]

Hill's whirlwind visit to Belgrade seems to have had some impact, because suddenly the Serb side began a serious discussion on the specifics of the political documents before them.[51] The Serbs presented a lengthy paper commenting on the draft agreement, although much of it went contrary to the nonnegotiable principles and the structure of the agreement. Nevertheless, the negotiators engaged the Serb side and revised their draft of a political settlement to reflect some of the Serb concerns. In so doing, the negotiators violated their ground rules, which were that changes in the draft agreement were possible only if both sides agreed. What is more, the proposed changes were insufficient to get the Serbs on board. On February 19, Hill traveled once more to Belgrade to convince Milosevic to sign on, but this time the Yugoslav leader refused even to meet with him.[52]

Rather than bringing the negotiations to the brink of success, the final maneuvering before the noon deadline on February 20 may have made matters worse. The Serbs were no closer to accepting either the basic political framework of self-governance for Kosovo or the need for a foreign security presence in the region. What is more, the negotiators' departure from the ground rules to elicit a positive Serb response and Hill's ill-fated missions to Belgrade left the Kosovars distrustful of what the negotiators and their patrons were up to. In an effort to keep their options open, the Kosovars were particularly wary about the provisions in the security annex on the demobilization of the KLA, and they continued to demand that the final status of the region be decided by a popular referendum, which the forces in favor of independence were sure to win.

It was under these circumstances that Secretary Albright arrived at the talks in an effort to bring them to a conclusion. Despite President Clinton's admonition that "it would be a mistake to extend the deadline,"[53] the Europeans and Russians prevailed upon the United States to agree to a seventy-five-hour extension. Albright endorsed the extension, in part because she had been convinced by her aides that sufficient pressure on the Kosovars could elicit their agreement, at which point all the pressure would be focused on Milosevic and the Serbs, which is where she wanted it to be.

For three long days, Albright's efforts were almost entirely devoted to getting the Kosovars to sign onto the interim agreement. To reassure them of NATO's capability once KFOR was deployed, she arranged a briefing by General Wesley Clark, NATO Supreme Allied Commander Europe.[54] As an additional incentive, Albright offered the Kosovars a form of security partnership by promising to assist with the transformation of the KLA in ways consistent with the demobilization terms of the agreement.[55] Finally, Albright addressed the Kosovar demand for a referendum in two ways. First, she proposed to add "the expressed will of the people" as one of the elements that would be considered in determining a final settlement of Kosovo. The other elements included the "opinions of relevant authorities, each Party's efforts regarding implementation of [the Rambouillet] Agreement, and the Helsinki Final Act."[56] Second, Albright presented the Kosovars with an unsigned letter indicating that the United States would regard this formulation "as confirming a right for the people of Kosovo to hold a referendum on the final status of Kosovo after three years."[57] Yet Albright clearly indicated that the outcome of the referendum would be but one of four elements in determining Kosovo's final status, meaning that even a vote for independence would not guarantee independence. The secretary of state also warned that she would sign the letter and keep the implied commitment only if the Kosovars signed the entire agreement by the February 23 deadline.

Albright's efforts appeared to convince most Kosovar delegation members that the deal on the table was the best one available. Yet at least one delegation member, its elected head, Hashim Thaci, refused to sign the accords. Days before the deadline expired, Thaci visited with Adem Demaci, a vigorous partisan who spent decades in prison for his support of Kosovo's independence. Thaci returned to Rambouillet convinced that instead of signing a deal that did not guarantee Kosovo's independence the hard-line KLA leadership should go on fighting in the hope (if not expectation) that NATO would intervene in the absence of Serb agreement. Thaci remained adamant in his opposition throughout the last days of negotiations and resisted the extreme pressure applied by the U.S. government. A flabbergasted U.S. official at the talks commented, "Here we had the secretary of state being stiffed by someone no one has ever heard of. I guess he decided that since he had stood up to [Belgrade], he could say no [to Albright]."[58] Since the Kosovo delegation agreed to work on the basis of consensus, Thaci's refusal meant that the Kosovars could not sign the draft agreement. However, at the last-minute suggestion of one of the delegation members, Veton Surroi, the delegation declared in writing to the co-chairmen of the Rambouillet conference that it had "voted in favor of [the] agreement" and it could "sign the agreement in two weeks after consultations with the people of Kosovo, political and military institutions."[59]

Faced with this situation, Contact Group foreign ministers were left in a quandary. Albright had hoped, indeed expected, to get at least the Kosovo delegation to sign the agreement at Rambouillet. At that point, an international consensus would have existed to pressure Belgrade by unleashing NATO airpower, if necessary. (However, Albright stated as late February 21 that if the Kosovars did not sign, "there will not be bombing of Serbia.")[60] But rather than signing, the Kosovars indicated their acceptance of the agreement and an intention to sign two weeks later. As a result, upon the expiration of the noon deadline on February 23, Contact Group ministers in effect agreed to extend the deadline for signing the agreement until March 15, when the conference would reconvene in Paris.[61]

The intervening weeks between Rambouillet and Paris were used to pressure both sides to accept the accords. The Kosovar leadership, including key KLA representatives, increasingly indicated that the agreement as written would be acceptable, and there was every expectation that the delegation arriving in Paris on March 15 would in fact sign the accords.[62] Efforts to convince Milosevic to agree were, if anything, even more intense. After Russian, OSCE, and European entreaties failed to convince Belgrade to give up its opposition to the stationing of foreign troops in Kosovo, Washington sent its chief Balkans troubleshooter, Richard Holbrooke, to try to work something out just days before the Paris meeting. Arriving in Belgrade on March 9, Holbrooke emphasized the seriousness of the situation: "We are only a few days away from a tragedy of even greater dimensions than what has occurred already. We might be on a collision course here between Yugoslavia and the Western authorities, including NATO."[63] Despite hours of tough talk, Milosevic did not budge. Instead, he issued a statement upon Holbrooke's departure indicating his continued defiance: "Attempts to condition a political agreement on our country's acceptance of foreign troops . . . are unacceptable."[64]

As the delegations arrived in Paris on March 15, the mood was somber, and expectations for a final resolution had dwindled to almost nothing. As expected, the Kosovars indicated that they accepted the accords and were prepared to sign at a time and place of the co-chairs' choosing. The Serbs, in contrast, remained intransigent, making clear that Belgrade could not accept either the details of the political agreement or its linkage to the deployment of foreign troops. Their suggested changes to the draft not only affected an estimated 70 percent of the text but also violated the principles that guided the talks from the start. They sought once again to break the link between the accords and their implementation with NATO troops on the ground in Kosovo.[65] When on March 18 the Kosovars signed the agreement and the Serbs did not, the conference co-chairs adjourned the conference, stating that "the talks will not resume unless the Serbs express their acceptance of the Accords."[66]

Thus ended the diplomatic effort to reach a political solution to the latest Balkan crisis. Six days later, on March 24, 1999, NATO airplanes and cruise missiles bombed targets throughout Kosovo and Serbia. A dramatically new phase in the conflict had begun. NATO and Serbia were now, in effect, at war over Kosovo.

Rambouillet: Failure or Success?

The collapse of the Rambouillet conference led almost immediately to a lot of second-guessing. Some of this was personal, implying that Albright's purported desire to have "her own Dayton" failed because, in the end, she was no Holbrooke.[67] Most of it concerned the negotiations themselves. To some the negotiators were not sufficiently flexible in their approach, both eschewing additional carrots to bring the Serbs on board and refusing to wield any significant sticks against the Kosovars to persuade them to be more accommodating. To others the U.S. approach to the negotiations was not sufficiently forceful. Rather than leading the effort as Washington had done in Dayton, the administration deferred to allied and Russian sensitivities, thus weakening its ability to persuade Serbia and reassure the Kosovars to sign the accords. In that sense, Albright's failure to get the Albanians, if not the Serbs, to sign the accords in Rambouillet was emblematic of Washington's inability to lead the effort effectively.

While some (though not all) of the critics' points are well founded, the common assumption that a change in tactics could have produced a negotiated deal at Rambouillet does not stand up to closer scrutiny. The difference between Rambouillet and Dayton was not just the personality of the lead

U.S. negotiator. Dayton was convened only after the parties had exhausted themselves with three years of fighting; after they had negotiated and signed two basic agreements outlining the nature of a settlement; and after they had signed a countrywide cease-fire. In contrast, Rambouillet was convened when fighting had resumed, when evidence of a brutal massacre had been uncovered, when both sides were gearing up for a major escalation once the snows melted, and when neither side was prepared to compromise one inch. Moreover, whereas in Dayton the de facto partition of Bosnia offered an acceptable compromise, in Rambouillet fundamental differences separated the sides both over their rights and responsibilities and over how the conflict would finally be resolved. Finally, Milosevic's stake in Kosovo was much greater than in Bosnia, where he had been fully prepared to settle so as to get the sanctions that were crippling the Serb economy lifted. For all these reasons, while the prospects for success in Dayton were high when the talks began, the likelihood of agreement at Rambouillet was exceedingly small.

It was this realization that led the United States, the Contact Group, and NATO to issue an ultimatum before convening Rambouillet: accept an interim deal enforced by NATO troops or face the military consequences. For some in the Clinton administration, as indeed in key allied capitals like London, the purpose of Rambouillet was not so much to get a deal that few thought attainable. Rather it was to create a consensus in Washington and among the NATO allies that force would have to be used. While the talks failed to get agreement on an interim accord, they did succeed in convincing everyone that diplomacy without the use of force would not succeed in ending the conflict in Kosovo. From this perspective, Rambouillet could be viewed as successful.

Was Rambouillet conducted with poor negotiating tactics? A considerable body of criticism believes that it was, although many differ as to the specific reasons for the failure. One frequently heard criticism of Rambouillet was that the negotiators wielded sticks only against Serbs and provided carrots only for the Kosovars.[68] The implication is that a more balanced and judicious application of carrots and sticks would have made a difference. However, this is highly doubtful. While the principal threat issued by NATO before Rambouillet was directed against the Serbs, that did not mean that sticks were wielded only against one side. Before and during the negotiations, the Kosovars were repeatedly told that their refusal to sign the accords would render the NATO threat against Serbia mute. Indeed, Albright warned privately and publicly that the Kosovars would not receive NATO's support if they failed to sign the accords, the implication being that they would be left on their own to face a growing Serb security apparatus. Could the Kosovars have been threatened in other ways? Threatening to bomb the KLA made little sense, given their dispersed operation. Also, while the alliance agreed to examine ways to stop the arms flow into Kosovo,[69] it was never clear how this could be accomplished without deploying tens of thousands of troops along the Kosovo-Albanian border. Moreover, even if NATO did this, it is extremely doubtful that the Serbs would have then accepted Rambouillet, given that the task of destroying the KLA would thereby have been easier.

Others have suggested that more flexibility with regard to carrots might have achieved better results. For example, Michael Mandelbaum has argued that if the United States offered to place Kosovo under UN administration, rejected the Kosovar demand for a referendum, and deleted a provision in the security annex giving NATO a right of access throughout Serb and Yugoslav territory, a deal might have been possible.[70] This seems far-fetched. Quite apart from the fact that Serb behavior at Rambouillet conveyed no serious intent to negotiate a deal, these changes are hardly of a sort to have changed the fundamentals of the situation. For example, at no time during the negotiations did the Serbs indicate that they would accept UN administration for Kosovo, even when rejecting self-government for the local population. Belgrade's goal was to limit international involvement in Kosovo, not to expand it. Nor is it plausible that if the United Nations had been assigned the roles given to the OSCE in the Rambouillet accords that Belgrade's attitude would have been any different. Further, the Kosovars were never promised that the territory's future would be determined solely by a referendum on independence. Instead, the final text stated:

> Three years after the entry into force of this Agreement, an international meeting shall be convened to determine a mechanism for a final settlement for Kosovo, on the basis of the will of the people, opinions of relevant authorities, each Party's efforts regarding the implementation of this Agreement, and the Helsinki Final Act, and to undertake a comprehensive assessment of the implementation of this Agreement and to consider proposals by any Party for additional measures.[71]

Although it was generally acknowledged that the "will of the people" would be expressed by way of a vote—whose outcome, given the ethnic Albanian majority in Kosovo, was all but assured—this was to be only one element in determining the mechanism for a final settlement. Belgrade had good reason to be upset about the inclusion of this provision, but it was not unreasonable to give the local population, whose future was at stake, some say in that future.

Finally, in regard to NATO's right of access to all of Yugoslavia, this provision was included in the security annex to ease logistical support for KFOR. The language, which was drawn from a standard status-of-forces agreement that the alliance signs with any country hosting NATO troops, was similar to the agreement Croatia signed in 1995 as part of the Bosnia peace implementation process.[72] Had the Serbs complained about this provision in the context of accepting the accords, there is every reason to believe that NATO would have abandoned it. As State Department spokesman James Rubin declared one year after the war had started, "had President Milosevic been prepared to accept a NATO force in Kosovo, and had [he] been prepared to work out the kind of military-technical agreement that was worked out at the end of the air war—without the silver bullet clause, without the ability to deploy anywhere in Yugoslavia—we would have accepted it."[73] Confirms a senior British official, "You don't think we would have bombed Serbia for this reason alone, do you?"[74]

Milosevic's main objection to Rambouillet was to having NATO troops anywhere on Serb territory—and in particular, in Kosovo. He feared that once there, NATO would remain for a long time, effectively depriving him of control over Kosovo. Given that fact, and Belgrade's utter resistance to negotiating a comprehensive accord, it is extremely unlikely that concessions of the kind Mandelbaum suggests would have made a bit of difference in the outcome.

Another cadre of Rambouillet critics concurred with this conclusion but went even further. Rather than being too inflexible, the chief contention was that the absence of American leadership during the conference caused its failure.[75] The early signals about Washington's commitment to the process were all discouraging. The conference was to be convened in Europe rather than the United States. It was to be chaired by the British and French foreign ministers. There were to be three negotiators, giving the European Union and Russia equal billing with the United States. The contrast with Dayton—a conference convened at a U.S. Air Force base in the middle of America, with negotiations led from the outset by Richard Holbrooke, an assistant secretary of state who was also the president's chief Bosnia envoy—was both immediate and stark. Not that atmospherics alone guarantee success or even explain failure. But these early decisions did send mixed signals to the parties about America's seriousness of purpose and its commitment to effect a negotiated outcome.

atmospherics → same to question US commitment.

Aside from these more symbolic aspects, critics of the Clinton administration's policy at Rambouillet also point to more substantial indications of the U.S. failure to lead. First, they argue that the United States failed to secure the participation of Slobodan Milosevic, who alone could have made the Serb concessions necessary to arrive at an agreement. "The Rambouillet peace conference on Kosovo," Jim Hoagland charged in the *Washington Post*, "degenerated into a play lacking both a director and a main character."[76] However, Milosevic's absence was not for lack of trying. Hill traveled twice to Belgrade to meet with Milosevic (succeeding the first time but not the second), and in the final days Albright resorted to calling the Yugoslav president on the phone to find a way toward a deal. Moreover, Milosevic's absence was less an indication of the administration's lack of leadership than of the fact that the Serb leader had absolutely no intention of agreeing to a political solution to the conflict. Indeed, while he spurned Hill's and Albright's advances, Serb army and security police forces were massing by the thousands in and around Kosovo and deploying many hundreds of heavy weapons for good measure.[77] The problem, then, was not so much a lack of American leadership as it was Belgrade's evident desire to solve the Kosovo problem through force of arms and to face NATO down.

Second, critics of the Clinton administration note that it did little to reassure the Kosovars that the United States had its interests at heart. Not only did the chief American negotiators break the conference ground rules by flying semi-secretly to Belgrade to deal directly with Milosevic, but Washington did little until very late in the conference to reassure the Kosovars about security. Washington accepted the French decision to bar a NATO presence at Rambouillet, failed to provide the parties with a copy of the security annex until well into the second week of talks, and did not offer to brief the Kosovo delegation on what NATO planned to do until the eleventh hour. There was no reason that a senior U.S. military official could not have joined the American delegation in Rambouillet to provide a measure of reassurance.

Compounding these small mistakes was the much larger failure of deciding on possible U.S. participation in KFOR only a week after the talks started. Both in stressing that American troops would constitute just a small fraction of the total force and in delaying the timing of this decision, the administration conveyed a marked hesitation, which instilled little confidence in the extent of its commitment to implementing any peace agreement that might be arrived at during the talks. If nothing else, this perception was bound to feed any doubts the Kosovars might have had about the wisdom of placing their fate in U.S. and NATO hands or of giving up, at least temporarily, their aspirations for independence. Hence the difficulty in convincing the Kosovars to sign the draft accords.

However, even if the Kosovar delegation had not been split at Rambouillet and had signed the accords there (as it did three weeks later in Paris), the Serbs would not have gone along. The collapse of Rambouillet was not the result of the Kosovar refusal to sign, even if this refusal did contribute to the sense of doom surrounding the conclusion of the conference on February 23.[78] Rather, the lack of success was almost foreordained—the differences between the sides on key issues of policy were simply too great, their bitterness too deep, and their aspirations too distinct to be bridged by way of a political dialogue, however structured. There was very little if anything that the negotiators could have done to overcome these momentous obstacles, particularly absent a much more credible and foreboding NATO threat of force.

This raises a larger question: If the talks were bound to fail, what was the purpose of convening them in the first place? To be sure, everyone hoped, even if only a few expected, that the pressure cooker atmosphere of proximity talks undertaken under a tight deadline and in the face of an ultimatum would convince the parties to resolve their differences at the negotiating table. Much effort went into trying to turn that hope into reality. Even though the effort was likely to be for naught, it was important to try. Not only would Rambouillet give peace one last chance, its collapse would signal the end of the diplomatic road. Sending that signal was important to those, like Albright, who had long believed that the Kosovo problem could not be solved without the use of force against Serbia. It was only then that those reluctant to use force—in the White House, the Pentagon, and allied capitals—would come to see that this perspective was correct. As Sandy Berger recalled, if Milosevic "was playing a game with us at Rambouillet by building up his forces while pretending to negotiate seriously, so were we. We needed to demonstrate a real commitment to get a peaceful resolution in order to get the allies to go along with the use of significant force."[79] A close aide to Secretary Albright was even blunter. There was only one purpose in Rambouillet: "To get the war started with the Europeans locked in."[80] Rambouillet did just that and, viewed from that particular perspective, it was a success rather than a failure. *success*

A Strategic Blunder

If the purpose of convening the Rambouillet conference was to forge a consensus in favor of using force against Serbia, a final judgment about its success or failure depends upon an assessment of how this consensus was used to achieve the desired ends. Here the verdict is much more damning, because the consensus to bomb Belgrade was based on the presupposition that the alliance's goals would be achieved after only a few days of bombing. NATO neither expected nor prepared for an extended military confrontation. Although the alliance in the end achieved the fundamental objective that propelled the use of force in the first place, that achievement came at a very high cost for Kosovo and the people who lived there. It may not have been possible to have prevented this from happening, since Milosevic appears to have been bent on changing the ethnic balance in Kosovo through large-scale violence. But the strategy NATO adopted ensured that the allies would be in no position to prevent—or to deal with—the consequences of a Serb decision to accelerate the campaign against the Kosovar Albanians.

Ultimately, the success of the Rambouillet strategy depended on NATO's ability to achieve through force what the United States and its allies failed to achieve through negotiations. "Our objective in Kosovo," President Clinton proclaimed days before the NATO bombing, "remains clear: to stop the killing and achieve a durable peace that restores Kosovars to self-government."[81] To implement this resolution to the conflict, Serb security forces (both army and police) would have to be sharply reduced, if not withdrawn or eliminated altogether. A large, armed international security presence would need to be deployed in Kosovo to ensure the safety and security of the local population.

How was this outcome to be achieved militarily? According to NATO, the alliance would support international efforts to persuade Milosevic to agree to a political settlement by forcing an end to the Serb attacks against the population of Kosovo.[82] Left unstated was how these two elements of the strategy were linked. Even if NATO, in President Clinton's words, was able to "deter an even bloodier offensive against innocent civilians in Kosovo and, if necessary, to seriously damage the Serb military's capacity to harm the people of Kosovo,"[83] how would this lead Belgrade to accept the political and military essence of Rambouillet? The answer, though generally unstated at the time, was that NATO's use of force would achieve this outcome in one of two ways. Either the very act of using force would persuade Milosevic to do what the mere threat had not and convince him to sign Rambouillet, or the Serb military would be so extensively degraded that over time Belgrade would be forced to give up its control of Kosovo.

NATO leaders believed that airpower alone would be sufficient to bring the desired result about. As General Naumann confidently predicted before the war, the "bombing will go on as long as Milosevic wants us to continue;

he has to blink, and he has to give in and accept the interim settlement."[84] Reliance on airpower alone was based on two assumptions. First, policymakers assumed that NATO's use of significant force would quickly bring Milosevic to his senses. Rather than a prolonged military confrontation—a war, really—it was assumed that the fight between NATO and Serbia would be over in a matter of days; a few weeks, at most. Second, there was no military alternative to airpower. Any consideration of using ground forces to forcefully expel Serb forces from Kosovo was excluded because of political considerations at home and abroad. Of course, we now know that the first assumption was incorrect, disastrously so. The heart of the case for the success of the Rambouillet strategy thus rests on the presumed validity of the second assumption. Although no one will ever know, there are powerful reasons to doubt it as well.

The Quick-War Assumption

Although President Clinton and his national security adviser maintained after the war that they had judged the chances of the bombing succeeding in a matter of days to have been no better than fifty-fifty, all available evidence suggests that the betting was that Milosevic would soon capitulate.[85] As Secretary Albright said on national television the night the bombing started, "I don't see this as a long-term operation. I think that this is something . . . that is achievable within a relatively short period of time."[86] Nor was the expectation of a short campaign confined to Washington. It was, in fact, widely shared in Europe, among civilian and political leaders alike. Indeed, some in the British Ministry of Defence (including the defense minister and the chief of staff of the armed forces) were so convinced that a bit of bombing would do the trick that they proposed restricting the opening salvo to a limited air option, using just twenty to fifty cruise missiles against key targets in Serbia, before pausing to allow Milosevic to come back to the negotiating table.[87] Extensive interviews in Washington, in key allied capitals, and at NATO headquarters confirm not only that there was a widespread consensus that Milosevic would give in after just a few days of bombing but also that the likely upper bound on the duration of the air campaign was seen as two to three weeks.[88]

What was the basis for this alliance-wide consensus that the military confrontation would be over quickly? The primary reason was that most officials saw the Yugoslav leader as a bully, who in the words of Secretary Albright "understands only the language of force."[89] It followed quite naturally from that assumption that if threats to use force were not enough to compel a change of course in Belgrade, then its actual use would surely suffice. The consensus behind this conclusion was strengthened by NATO's previous experiences in dealing with Milosevic, including its decision to bomb Bosnian Serb forces in August 1995 and the air strikes threat of October 1998, which contributed to finalizing the Holbrooke-Milosevic agreement. As President Clinton stated a month into the NATO bombing campaign, "the reason we went forward with the air actions is because we thought there was some chance it would deter Mr. Milosevic based on two previous examples—number one, last October in Kosovo, when he was well poised to do the same thing; and number two, in Bosnia, where there were 12 days of NATO attacks over a 20-day period."[90]

As it turned out, these prior experiences did not prove to be indicative of what would happen. Rather than capitulate, Milosevic escalated exactly in the manner foreshadowed in Operation Horseshoe, the plan the Yugoslav leader hatched with his new chiefs of the army and secret police in late 1998 to defeat the KLA and forcefully expel a large portion of Kosovo's Albanian population. Why did so few American, allied, or NATO officials see this coming? Why assume the best case, rather than the worst, with someone with Milosevic's track record? The answers to these questions are twofold. First, there was a fundamental misreading of what happened in 1995 and even in the fall of 1998. Second, it was assumed, quite wrongly, that any demonstration of NATO's willingness to use force would be sufficient to convince Milosevic that the allies were united in their cause and would remain so until their objectives were achieved. Whereas the efforts expended to get to even this point may have been viewed as Herculean by those who achieved the task, Milosevic may well have calculated on that very basis that he could outlast NATO.

However strongly held, the belief that Milosevic would cave within days or, at most, about two weeks of sustained NATO bombing because he had done so in 1995 was based on two fundamentally flawed premises.[91] First, notwithstanding the obvious similarities between Kosovo and Bosnia, the two situations were in fact quite distinct. Kosovo was an integral part of Serbia and recognized as such by the international community, which has consistently opposed independence for the territory. In contrast, Bosnia was a separate republic within the former Yugoslavia, whose independence the United States and its allies recognized days after its declaration in April 1992. Moreover, Kosovo is the cradle of Serb nationalism: it is the site of Serbia's historic defeat by the Ottoman Empire, it is home to numerous important Serb monasteries, and it contains the seat of the patriarchate of the Serb

Orthodox-Christian Church. In the words of the last U.S. ambassador to Yugoslavia, Kosovo "is to Serbs what Jerusalem and the West Bank are to Israelis—a sacred ancestral homeland now inhabited largely by Muslims."[92] Bosnia shared none of these emotive ties to Serbia. If only for that reason, it ought not to have been surprising that the Serbs were more willing to fight for Kosovo than for Bosnia.

Second, policymakers misread what happened in 1995. Although Secretary Albright put it best, she was hardly alone among administration and NATO officials in believing that Milosevic "didn't see the light in Bosnia until the NATO bombing, and then he agreed to the Dayton Accords."[93] In fact the bombing in Bosnia commenced *after* Milosevic was committed to finding a diplomatic solution to the Bosnian war.[94] More than ten days before the NATO bombing began on August 30, Milosevic told Richard Holbrooke that he was willing to seize the negotiator's reins from Bosnian Serb hands. On the weekend before the Serb shelling of the Sarajevo market that would precipitate NATO's decision to bomb, Milosevic secured the Bosnian Serb leadership's acquiescence in his taking the lead role in negotiating a Bosnian peace. The NATO air campaign only reinforced the urgency of reaching such a solution.

What finally drove Milosevic to the negotiating table in 1995 was the Croatian offensive of early August, which created hundreds of thousands of Serb refugees, most of whom sought shelter in Serbia. A diplomatic settlement offered the best prospect of staving off a wider war pitting Bosnian Serb forces against Bosnian Croat and Muslim forces, which would likely have exacerbated the Serb refugee problem. In addition, the NATO bombing campaign in 1995 was assisted on the ground by substantial artillery fire from British, French, and Dutch troops that, weeks earlier, were deployed to the region as a rapid reaction force. Indeed, during the entire operation more ordnance was fired by ground forces than was dropped from the air. Finally, the objective of the NATO air operation was strictly limited to lifting the siege of Sarajevo—a goal that, in principle, could be achieved without completely undermining Bosnian Serb war aims, since the Serbs still held 51 percent of Bosnian territory.

Aside from misreading recent history, NATO leaders also misread Milosevic more generally. Although it is of course impossible to know why Milosevic decided to escalate rather than hunker down, let alone capitulate in the manner many expected he would, there were clear indications even before the fighting started that he was bent on achieving a military solution in Kosovo. Those who met with the Yugoslav leader in early 1999 reported that his demeanor was strikingly different from what it had been just a few months before. One senior State Department official indicated that during these meetings a "bunker mentality" was an apt description of Milosevic's attitude.[95] The reason for this change may have been partly the fact that Milosevic had begun to isolate himself from all but his most hard-line advisers. In late 1998 he fired those most critical of his campaign against the KLA (including the long-time head of the federal police forces and the chief of the Yugoslav army) and replaced them with hard-liners. Not only did this new set of advisers tell Milosevic not to trust the United States but they also suggested that the army and security forces could solve the KLA problem within a matter of days if given the go-ahead. It was a message that Milosevic took to heart and one he would repeat frequently to his Western interlocutors.[96]

The most important indicator of what was to come was how the Serbs approached Rambouillet. In stark contrast to Dayton, where Milosevic himself arrived to strike a deal—any reasonable deal, really—the Serbs sent to Rambouillet a minor delegation with little power to negotiate the fate of a territory deemed integral to Serbia itself. Not only did Milosevic not attend in person but neither, initially, did Serb President Milan Milutinovic, who before both Dayton (when he was Yugoslavia's foreign minister) and Rambouillet had negotiated on Milosevic's behalf. What is more, during the Rambouillet talks, Serb army and Interior Ministry police forces were preparing for a major military showdown. By the end of February, five Yugoslav army brigades were deployed in the region around Kosovo, and the overall total and disposition of Yugoslav army and Serb Interior Ministry troops in Kosovo exceeded that allowed by the agreement worked out between NATO and Milosevic in late October 1998.[97] None of this was done in secret; indeed the large movement of troops and materiel in Kosovo was reported in daily Kosovo Verification Mission reports and received prominent coverage in major newspapers.[98]

There was also reason to believe that Milosevic, who attempted a rapid military victory in Kosovo, thought he could outlast NATO with a duel of wills. As he told German Foreign Minister Joschka Fischer in March, "I can stand death—lots of it—but you can't."[99] To Milosevic, the validity of this assumption could have been underscored by two previous developments. First, although NATO had finally concluded that a decision to bomb could no longer be postponed, the route it traveled to that point was strewn with frequent threats, failed ultimatums, and feeble deadlines that were immediately reset once passed. There was, first of all, the 1992 Christmas warning, which was all but ignored once the event that would have triggered U.S. air strikes ("conflict in Kosovo caused by Serb action") came about in March 1998. Then, despite Secretary Albright's explicit admonition that the United States was "not going to stand by and watch Serb authorities do in Kosovo what they can no longer get away with doing in Bosnia,"[100] the Serbs escalated their attacks and forced one-sixth of the Albanian population from their homes without much of a response. In October 1998, NATO finally threatened air strikes and warned that it would respond to any violations of Milosevic's agreement with Holbrooke and NATO. But when these commitments were violated—when Serb army and police forces failed to withdraw from Kosovo and deployed outside of barracks, when villages were once again plundered, and when yet another massacre took place in Racak—NATO merely reiterated its threat and did nothing. It actually reduced its airpower in the region as well. Finally, at Rambouillet not one but two deadlines passed without a response. Given this record, it should not have been surprising that Milosevic might have come to believe NATO would not strike or, when it did, that the allies would not be able to sustain the effort for long.

There are additional reasons to believe that Milosevic thought NATO might bomb for a few days and then suspend operations. Not only did NATO generals and senior U.S. and allied officials say as much, but also American and British air strikes against Iraq the previous December suggested that the Clinton administration itself did not have the stomach for a sustained military effort. If anything, Operation Desert Fox demonstrated that air strikes designed to "degrade" an opponent's military capability—even that of an opponent as feared and loathed as Saddam Hussein, ruling a country in a region of critical interest to the United States, and possessing the capacity to produce weapons of mass destruction—would likely last only a few days. Then allied displeasure, increasingly frequent and audible murmurings from Russian and other diplomats in the UN Security Council, and an upcoming religious holiday combined to provide Washington with an excuse to claim success in having "degraded" the military capability and to suspend the bombing campaign. Indeed, this scenario might well have played out again in March or April against Serbia. Unease about NATO's bombing on the part of some allies, combined with vehement opposition from Moscow and the excuse of another impending religious holiday (Easter), could easily have forced a premature end to military action.

But then Milosevic decided that the bombing gave him the excuse he needed to implement his plan to rid Kosovo of a significant proportion of its Albanian population while destabilizing Serbia's neighbors. However much Washington or some other allies might have wanted to call it quits after a few days of bombing, these horrific acts fundamentally changed the stakes, thereby unifying NATO into demanding not only a halt in Serb actions but even a reversal of their consequences. In the end, the Yugoslav leader miscalculated even more badly than NATO had.

The No-Ground-Forces Assumption

From the start of the crisis, NATO leaders excluded the possibility of using ground forces in a "nonpermissive" environment, that is, to invade Kosovo. They did so even though it was clear that a presence on the ground in Kosovo would offer the best way to provide some degree of protection to the Kosovar Albanians and the only sure way to defeat the Serb security forces that were threatening Kosovo's civilian population. Without ground forces, NATO had to rely on what General Colin Powell called a strategy based on the "hope to win" and not on the certainty that, in the end, the alliance would prevail.[101]

Notwithstanding these broad strategic considerations, the ground force option never really was on the table. It was looked at briefly in the summer of 1998, and concepts of operations were developed for two different options: a concept for invading Kosovo using some 75,000 troops and a concept for subjugating Belgrade itself using about 200,000 NATO troops. But that is where matters ended. No operational plan was ever developed by NATO military authorities, and political leaders never requested that they devise one.[102] Once the notional force requirements for using ground forces in a nonpermissive environment were sent to Washington and other NATO capitals, the very idea of deploying ground forces was dismissed as a nonstarter.[103] In all the many hours that top administration officials spent discussing how to respond to the breakdown of negotiations in Rambouillet, the focus was squarely on the air campaign. Although senior military officials warned their civilian counterparts that airpower alone might not be sufficient to accomplish the stated political objectives, neither they nor anyone else suggested the need to rely on ground forces instead. As one senior official present at many of the meetings said, "We walked up to the ground force option many times and quickly walked back every time."[104]

Although opposition to the use of ground forces was centered in Washington, it was a sentiment shared by many U.S. allies in Europe. Even Britain worried about using ground forces. In January 1999, Prime Minister Tony Blair told President Clinton that "ground troops could not be used to fight a war."[105] Before the start of the bombing campaign on March 24, there was a clear allied consensus to rule out using ground forces for anything other than helping to implement an agreement reached by the Serbs and Albanians at the negotiating table. In his Oval Office address that evening, President Clinton accordingly announced that he did "not intend to put our troops in Kosovo to fight a war."[106]

But why rule out a key military option on the very day that combat operations were beginning? Even if the administration had no intention of using ground forces in combat, publicly ruling out their use only helped to reduce Milosevic's uncertainty regarding the likely scope of NATO's military actions, an uncertainty that silence would have preserved if not enhanced.[107] However, even after the war, key administration officials contend that the decision was right. Indeed, Sandy Berger, who authored the critical passage in the president's speech, maintains that "we would not have won the war without this sentence."[108] His reasoning was twofold. First, the only way in which NATO could lose the war with Serbia was if the alliance cracked. Publicly ruling out the use of ground forces at the outset was necessary, in administration eyes, to keep a fragile alliance consensus on the use of force intact, a consensus that would have shattered if Washington or anyone else had raised the possibility of having to go in on the ground. Second, the Clinton administration was convinced that the decision to use force in Kosovo, which was already controversial on Capitol Hill, would have precipitated a major public debate—including possibly a vote to cut off funding for the operation—if the ground force option had not been ruled out publicly by the president. As one official deeply involved in the planning for the war argued, "This administration was operating on the assumption ground troops would raise this to a new level, and we hadn't prepared [the] public for that or gotten the allies on board."[109]

It is of course impossible to know whether keeping the question of ground forces explicitly on the table would have proven as disastrous as administration officials contend, but there are good reasons to believe that a different strategy could have succeeded. A principal reason for assuming that the ground force issue would have been politically divisive at home was the administration's tortured experience during the preceding months for getting congressional support to deploy just 4,000 U.S. troops as part of a planned peacekeeping operation in Kosovo. As Secretary Cohen said some weeks into the war, "I saw no consensus or support for it in Congress. It was hard enough going up to the Hill even talking about a peacekeeping mission at that time."[110] If Congress balked at sending such a small U.S. force (which would have composed only 15 percent of the overall total) into a permissive security environment, then gaining support for a larger commitment of American troops to a far more risky operation would have been nigh impossible, or so the argument went.[111]

But this ignores the context in which the case for ground troops was made. From the start of the crisis—including well back in 1998—the Clinton administration acted on the presumption that Congress would not support the use of ground forces. It therefore consistently ruled out using combat troops until mid-February and then made the case for a mere token American combat presence in a peacekeeping force. If instead it had made the case for ground troops from the start, using the arguments the president and others employed regarding the strategic and humanitarian importance to act, the political case for both using force and relying on ground troops would have been much stronger. What weakened the administration's case was not only the innate opposition to its policy but also the tentativeness with which its key proponents had consistently approached the issue publicly and on the Hill.[112]

The same argument holds for the alliance. Sentiment in Europe for a ground force invasion was no more positive than in the United States. But then no one made the case for using ground forces, and persistent U.S. opposition even to planning for their use suggested that the option was ruled out on practical grounds. NATO could not go to war on the ground if the United States were to take no part. But private expressions of worry could have been overcome by concerted American leadership. Indeed, the allies were more forward leaning on the question of ground forces, at least in a noncombat capacity, than Washington was. Many expected that NATO would have to deploy combat troops to help implement the agreement that Richard Holbrooke negotiated with Milosevic in October 1998. Key allies deployed troops to Macedonia as part of the NATO Extraction Force in late 1998, even though the United States decided not to participate. Many allies made major commitments to deploying ground forces as part of a possible Kosovo Force (KFOR) to help implement an agreement if one were reached in Rambouillet, and all announced so publicly well before the United States announced its own participation. Finally, the major European allies decided in February to predeploy a large chunk of the forces that would have to go into Kosovo if peace were to break out—a total of 12,000 troops by the day the air war started.[113] What was missing, therefore, was less allied will than a demonstrated American ability and willingness to lead a joint effort. NATO works best when Washington knows what it wants done and leads the effort to get the alliance there. In the runup to the Kosovo war, both elements were tragically lacking.

Could a different strategy have been devised and sold both at home and abroad? Again, the answer cannot be known with any degree of certainty, but the answer is probably yes. One possibility would have been an early decision by the Clinton administration for U.S. forces not only to participate in KFOR but also to lead a robust deployment of some 50,000 NATO troops in case negotiations succeeded. Such a decision could have made a differences in two distinct ways. First, it would have indicated to the Kosovar Albanians that not just NATO but also the United States was preparing to deploy a strong security presence in Kosovo if they accepted the Rambouillet accords. Indeed, such a major presence would have been indicated by the difficulty of the peacekeeping operation even under the best of circumstances.

Most important, a major commitment to a robust NATO force could have provided the alliance with a ground presence in the region to back up the use of airpower. Indeed, if the force had been deployed to Macedonia just as the Rambouillet talks got under way in early February (as European units assigned to KFOR in fact did), there would have been a significant military presence on the ground by the time NATO planes took to the air at the start of the bombing campaign. To be sure, this force would not have been sufficient to launch an immediate invasion of Kosovo, but it would have laid the foundation for rapidly putting into place a capability that could have done so. At the very least, this ground presence would have given Milosevic reason to worry.

Instead of a forceful and robust strategy, the Clinton administration resorted to a policy based on political timidity. That policy was grounded in the dual assumption that any military confrontation with Milosevic was likely to be brief and that politics at home and abroad trumped any alternative strategy. As is evident now—as it was at the time—this is no way to go to war, even a war that one believes can be won with airpower alone. In deciding to use force, one must be prepared for the possible consequences and be willing to live with them. NATO, led by the United States, ignored this advice not because it was convinced of the soundness of its strategy, but because Washington and allied capitals were unprepared to face difficult choices head-on. Having rejected the alternatives—walking away from the conflict or relying on ground forces to ensure that their objectives would be achieved militarily—the allies hoped that what they saw as the least-bad strategy would somehow work. As President Clinton said some days into the air campaign, the chosen strategy was the best "among a bunch of bad options ... to maximize the possibility of achieving our mission."[114]

In arriving at this strategy, U.S. and allied officials were comforted by the hope—nay, the expectation—that a few days of bombing would suffice to bring Milosevic around to accepting NATO's point of view. Failing that, NATO would increase the pressure, moving from phase 1 attacks on air defense systems through phase 2 attacks on Serb forces in and around Kosovo to phase 3 attacks on military and strategic targets throughout Serbia, including Belgrade. No one seriously considered what would happen if this escalation failed to force Milosevic to halt Serb attacks on Kosovo's population and return to negotiations to restore autonomy for the ethnic Albanians. Asked what would happen then, one senior official admitted after one week of bombing, "There is no Phase 4."[115]

CHAPTER FOUR

Losing
the War

O N   W E D N E S D A Y ,   M A R C H   2 4 ,   1 9 9 9 , NATO unleashed a
set of air strikes against Serbia. It did so on the assumption
that this was not going to be a real military conflict but merely a way to
quickly convince Slobodan Milosevic to capitulate and accept the Rambouillet framework. It soon became apparent, however, that the alliance was not
simply engaged in a form of coercive diplomacy. It was at war.

NATO conducted Operation Allied Force primarily to protect the Kosovar
Albanian people. As President Bill Clinton stated on the day NATO's bombardment began, the alliance's goals were threefold: "To demonstrate the
seriousness of NATO's purpose so that the Serbian leaders understand the
imperative of reversing course, [to] deter an even bloodier offensive against
innocent civilians in Kosovo, and, if necessary, to seriously damage the Serb
military's capacity to harm the people of Kosovo."[1] NATO clearly failed to
achieve the last two of these objectives, and it made only limited progress
toward the first in the early weeks of the war. The Serb army, the Serb Interior Ministry police, and Serb paramilitary units in Kosovo acted largely
with impunity against the ethnic Albanians during much of the war.

Thankfully, most of the physical damage inflicted on the Kosovar Albanians by Serb forces was reversible and reparable. Serb leaders appear to
have decided that massacres like the 1995 killing of 7,000 men in ten days in
Srebrenica, Bosnia, were likely to harden NATO's resolve to act against them.
They used killing in Kosovo in a more limited way, principally to strike fear
among ethnic Albanians to make them flee the country. But NATO clearly
failed to stop the campaign of "ethnic cleansing" or to meaningfully limit
Serbia's ability to carry it out. Once it realized that its original objectives

were beyond reach, NATO established, and ultimately achieved, five different objectives for Kosovo:

—A verifiable stop to all Serb military action and the immediate ending of violence and repression.

—The withdrawal from Kosovo of all Serb military, police, and paramilitary forces.

—An agreement to the stationing in Kosovo of an international military presence.

—The acceptance of the unconditional and safe return of all refugees and displaced persons and unhindered access to them by humanitarian aid organizations.

—Credible assurances that Belgrade would work, on the basis of the Rambouillet accords, to establish a political framework agreement for Kosovo.[2]

In the end, NATO softened one of these conditions, promising to allow a small number of Serb security personnel to return to Kosovo to provide a presence at Serb patrimonial sites and border crossings, to mark and clear minefields, and to establish a liaison with the international civilian and security presence.[3] But the essence of the conditions remained. At war's end, NATO's key demands were satisfied. All Serb security forces withdrew, NATO took charge of Kosovo, and the territory became safe for the return of ethnic Albanians. However, during much of the conflict it was not at all clear that this would ultimately be the case. NATO did prevail eventually, but for the first month or more of hostilities, it was losing the war.

NATO went to war against Serbia without a UN Security Council resolution explicitly authorizing its attacks. It nonetheless based its actions on several UN decisions, principally UN Security Council Resolutions 1199 and 1203 of September and October 1998 (see appendix C). Those resolutions imposed restrictions on Serb military activities in Kosovo, including limits on the number of Serb personnel that could be there, and called for "full and prompt implementation of the agreements Milosevic had negotiated with the OSCE and NATO." As such, the international legal basis for NATO's actions was admittedly ambiguous—but certainly not altogether lacking.[4]

Yugoslavia—and more specifically, its Serb nationalist leader Slobodan Milosevic, Serb-dominated armed forces, and Serb paramilitary irregulars—failed to comply with the requirements spelled out in the 1998 Security Council resolutions. By November 1998, Belgrade had violated troop limits as well as restrictions on the disposition of the forces that were allowed to remain. Serb units massacred forty-five ethnic Albanians at Racak on January 15, 1999, after which Milosevic refused to allow experts from the International Criminal Tribunal for the former Yugoslavia to investigate. Other killings also occurred—and also went uninvestigated. Nor did the violations stop there. On March 24, just hours before bombing began, British Defence Minister George Robertson estimated that Yugoslavia had 16,000 police (Interior Ministry) and 20,000 army troops in Kosovo. NATO estimates were lower: some 15,000 Serb army troops and 14,000 Serb police in Kosovo. But even the lower estimates considerably exceeded the ceilings that President Milosevic and NATO military commanders had agreed on in October 1998 of 11,000 police and 12,000 troops.[5]

So NATO went to war. The world's most powerful alliance, with 4 million active-duty military personnel and combined annual defense spending of $450 billion, undertook hostilities against a small, impoverished country with an annual defense budget of perhaps $1.5 billion and total active-duty military forces of about 110,000 (plus thousands of internal police armed with heavy weapons).[6] Ultimately, those overwhelming advantages proved sufficient for NATO to prevail, though initially it was far from clear that this would be the case.

Stumbling into War

NATO did not expect a long war. Worse, it did not even prepare for the possibility. Many alliance leaders deny that assertion to this day, but the evidence is overwhelming. And the blame begins with Washington, ultimately the most important architect of the air campaign strategy.

NATO began Operation Allied Force with just 350 planes in range of Serbia. That was less than the 410 it had in the region in October 1998. It was only one-third the number ultimately necessary to win the war.[7] It was only about 10 percent of the number of coalition aircraft that participated in the air war against Iraq in 1991, and about one-fifth the number that the United States would plan to deploy in a major regional conflict today.[8] In size, the air armada most closely resembled that used for Operation Desert Fox, the four-day U.S.-British bombing of Iraq in December 1998.[9]

NATO's tepid enthusiasm for bombing manifested itself in other ways as well. For example, the United States had no aircraft carriers within bombing range of Serbia when the war began. In mid-March, the United States elected not to keep the carrier *Enterprise* in the Mediterranean-Adriatic region, where it could have contributed to the war. Instead, Washington sent it briefly to the Persian Gulf (on March 14) and then sent it home. It did so on the grounds, first, that it needed a carrier in the Persian Gulf at all times and, second, that crews had already spent their planned tours at sea and deserved to return to their ports and families on schedule. While the first concern is strategically valid, the navy ultimately deployed the *Kitty Hawk* from Japan to the Gulf, and could have done so earlier had planning been better. The second concern, while understandable at one level for the well-being of crews and their families, is hardly the type of action a country preparing for sustained military action would customarily undertake. Another carrier was not within bombing range of Serbia until April 5.[10] Once the *Theodore Roosevelt* did deploy, its crew performed very well during the war, as NATO military personnel did in general, but a fair amount of strategic damage was already done before its arrival.[11] By moving the *Enterprise* out of combat range before the war, the United States conveyed the impression that it was not planning a large military operation even if Milosevic remained unwilling to negotiate. Once the war started, NATO was unable to heavily strike Serb forces in Kosovo because it lacked sufficient aircraft.[12]

Indeed, in the days before the war many NATO officials worried not about causing too little damage to Serb forces in Kosovo but about causing too much. Their fear was that bombing would encourage and assist the Kosovo Liberation Army to achieve its preferred goal of independence. NATO's intention was to ensure an outcome that was "the war-making equivalent of the 'Goldilocks economy'—not too hot and not too cold."[13] Although understandable at one level, this smacked of an unwise surgical bombing philosophy, which alliance leaders should have been prescient enough not to rely on entirely.

Those still unconvinced that NATO got the war badly wrong in its early going should consult an unofficial, but widely circulated, postwar briefing by a straight-talking U.S. Navy officer, Admiral James Ellis, commander of NATO's southern forces during the war against Serbia (and thus situated directly below Supreme Allied Commander Wesley Clark in the chain of command). In Admiral Ellis's words, "We called this one *absolutely* wrong." He went on to say that NATO lacked not only a coherent campaign plan and target set but also the staff to generate a detailed plan when it was clear that one was needed.[14]

Another severe criticism of NATO's preparations was offered by German General Klaus Naumann, who headed the alliance's Military Committee before the war and in the conflict's early weeks. (The Military Committee consists of representatives of the top military officers of all member countries and is formally responsible for advising the North Atlantic Council on military matters.) Noting that NATO had applied a war plan that was devised in the fall of 1998 simply to get Milosevic back to the negotiating table, he observed that "we faced an opponent who had accepted war, whereas the NATO nations had accepted [just] an operation."[15]

In the early days of the bombing, NATO leaders did little to convey a commitment to prevail. Enunciating the objectives of the air campaign, both NATO officials and President Clinton stated that one of their goals was to "degrade" Serb capabilities to attack Kosovar civilians, reintroducing the same unfortunate term that had allowed the Clinton administration, in Desert Fox and other cases, to declare victory after virtually any military operation.[16] The possibility that NATO would, in effect, give it the old college try but then accept failure seemed more and more real as the first few days of the war unfolded. Toward the end of the first week of bombing, NATO Secretary-General Javier Solana said of the Serb campaign of violence, "We may not have the means to stop it, but we have shown we have the will to try."[17] During the second week, U.S. Defense Secretary William Cohen described the air campaign's goals as demonstrating "resolve on the part of the NATO alliance" or "to make him [Milosevic] pay a serious substantial price."[18] In other words, NATO sounded like it was prepared only to punish Milosevic while he attacked the Kosovar Albanians—and to deem that a success. The weakness inherent in such comments spoke for itself.

All of these tactical military failings can be summarized in one simple phrase: NATO had no "plan B."[19] The allies viewed force simply as a tool of diplomacy, intended to push negotiations one way or another. They were unprepared for the possibility that they might need to directly achieve a battlefield result. That was deeply regrettable. In the end, far from repudiating perhaps the key element of the so-called Powell doctrine—the notion of decisive force—NATO's war against Serbia was a vivid reminder that when using military power, one must be prepared for things to go wrong and be ready to escalate.[20]

Some Clinton administration officials and a number of members of Congress argued that the United States would have conducted a much more vigorous bombing campaign from the outset of the war if other NATO members had allowed it to do so. Secretary Cohen, for example, claimed that "if we were to carry out and act unilaterally, we would have a much more robust, aggressive, and decapitating type of campaign. . . . The difference here, of course, is that we're acting as an alliance."[21] However, such criticism ignores the fact that the basic philosophy of gradualism to change Milosevic's policy toward Kosovo was shared throughout the alliance, including by the United States. American officials drove the Rambouillet process, American military planners from General Clark on down devised much of the targeting strategy, and American assets were the most important in the war. U.S. concerns over casualties also dictated the policy of keeping aircraft at 15,000-feet altitude for most of the war and restricting their loiter time over the battlefield. France did exercise some restraining power on NATO planners, particularly after the first couple of weeks of the war, but the net effect was generally to push back the bombing of some specific targets at most a few days. Moreover, France was hardly the only country to scrutinize target sets in detail; reportedly, Joint Chiefs' Chairman General Henry Shelton was at the White House every day, seven days a week, for at least the first month and a half of the war requesting presidential approval to strike certain targets.[22] As a top British official aptly put it to us, choosing his words carefully, "No significant decision was significantly delayed" by the need to garner consensus during the conflict.[23] The United States cannot fairly blame the war's slow start on its allies.

Given its poor state of preparation, NATO could have lost this war. Ironically, Milosevic came to the alliance's rescue. In light of NATO's irresolute words and deeds just before and after March 24, he had a fairly promising strategy: hunker down, tolerate the bombing, and wait for Russian pressure or NATO internal dissension to weaken the alliance's resolve. A logical strategy for Milosevic would have been to drive a wedge in the alliance.[24] His decision to escalate and wreak havoc throughout Kosovo was hardly the most propitious way to achieve that end, however, and his actual strategy was focused more on attempting to change the internal ethnic balance in Kosovo in a short period of time. Had Milosevic not thoroughly "cleansed" Kosovo of its ethnic Albanian population, outraging virtually all NATO governments and peoples, a hunker-down strategy might well have succeeded, as a number of NATO officials with whom we spoke acknowledged.

Convinced that a little bombing would force Milosevic to accept NATO's terms, the allies failed to envision what might happen on the ground in Kosovo as it began to bomb from high altitudes. Remarkably, some officials appear to have ignored the basic fact that NATO airpower would simply not be physically able to stop Milosevic's onslaught against the Kosovars. NATO leaders collectively ignored the distinct possibility that Milosevic might actually intensify his efforts once NATO bombs began to fall. Having watched Milosevic act with some restraint the previous summer and fall, NATO failed to anticipate that he might be much more brutal in method, and much more comprehensive in scope, if under outside attack. Given the history of wholesale ethnic expulsion in the Balkans in the 1990s, U.S. and allied officials should have realized that Milosevic might try to forcibly change the ethnic balance in Kosovo to reclaim the purported cradle of Serb civilization and to make room for Serbs displaced by fighting in Croatia. But apparently they did not.[25] As General Clark put it, "We thought the Serbs were preparing for a spring offensive that would target KLA strongholds, which had also been reinforced in previous months. But we never expected the Serbs would push ahead with the wholesale deportation of the ethnic Albanian population."[26]

NATO's bombing lifted a constraint on the Serb leader that may have been operative until that point. Before the bombs began to fall, he had an incentive to keep NATO from attacking him. Once the attack was under way, however, he no longer had that same reason to hold back. General Clark recognized this dynamic—but alas, like other top Western officials, only well after the war was over.[27] President Clinton's insistence that the ground force option was not on the table, made in his speech to the nation on March 24, only made matters worse. It took away a large amount of intrawar deterrent power the United States and NATO might have otherwise had over Milosevic.

The intelligence community also failed to foresee any of these possible developments. Some were admittedly more predictable than others, but none should have been truly surprising. The CIA does appear to have expected that, partly because of growing KLA strength and assertiveness, Milosevic would resume his campaign of violence in 1999—and with greater intensity than in 1998. That assessment was a key element in convincing the Clinton administration to convene the Rambouillet negotiations and then use force against Milosevic. But the intelligence community does not appear to have predicted—or even to have prominently raised the possibility—that Milosevic would drastically intensify attacks on Kosovo's civilian population, let alone expel ethnic Albanians systematically. Rather, it appears to have promoted the view that a few days of bombing would likely restrain Milosevic. For example, a National Intelligence Estimate in November 1998 clearly stated: "The October agreement indicates Milosevic is susceptible to outside pressure."[28] As for the Defense Intelligence Agency, its February 1999 survey of the world's trouble spots did not even mention Kosovo.[29]

The initial bombing strategy of gradualism can be defended as a reasonable gamble, even if we now know it did not work. But it was wrong to hinge everything on it. At a bare minimum, NATO could have left its future plans ambiguous, and U.S. officials could have consistently underscored that they intended to conduct whatever strikes were needed to achieve their goals. There was a wide range of options between planning to carry out a small number of air strikes, on the one hand, and immediately preparing for the admittedly difficult task of a ground invasion, on the other.

NATO's chosen approach was a dangerous and sloppy way to use force. Few if any government strategists appear to have anticipated what proved necessary in April and beyond. In that sense, the alliance was simply lucky: lucky that it turned out to have sufficient escalatory capability to win the war when that was needed, lucky that Milosevic did not for the most part slaughter the ethnic Albanians but only "cleansed" Kosovo of them in a manner that was reversible, and lucky that the internally displaced ethnic Albanians who were driven from their homes but unable to leave the country had enough food to survive during the three-month period when NATO could bring them no relief. It would have been better not to use force at all than to bomb, fail, worsen the plight of the Kosovar Albanians in the process, and then have to concede defeat.

Serbia's War against the Kosovar Albanians

In military terms, the simplest way to understand the first month of Operation Allied Force—and indeed a fair amount of the second month as well—is to think of the conflict as two wars, which had little to do with each other. Serbia waged war against the Kosovar Albanian people and the KLA; NATO waged war against Serbia. In its official report on the war, the U.S. Department of Defense essentially accepted this characterization of the conflict, but explained it by arguing that Milosevic elected to use asymmetric tactics against NATO rather than fighting it directly.[30] We disagree. It was NATO that chose asymmetric means—high-altitude airpower—rather than engage Serb forces at the level where they could be directly prevented from committing their atrocities.[31] Milosevic certainly did further intensify his ethnic expulsion operation once NATO bombs began to fall, but these operations were fundamentally what he intended to do all along, on one scale or another. Indeed, the Serb operation reflected the very essence of what the conflict in Kosovo was about in the first place.

By the time of the NATO summit in late April, the Serb military, the Serb Interior Ministry police, and irregular Serb units had forced nearly 1 million ethnic Albanians to leave their homes in Kosovo. The vast majority were forcibly driven out, in contrast to the situation in 1998, when some 300,000 ethnic Albanians were displaced by violence but largely by choice, so as to ensure their own safety. Those ultimately driven from their homes in 1999 represented nearly three-fourths of the prewar population of roughly 1.8

Figure 4-1. Refugees from Kosovo, March 1999 to August 1999, by Country of Destination

Thousands

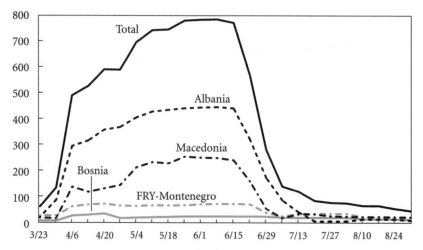

Source: UN High Commissioner for Refugees, "Kosovo Crisis Update," March 31, 1999, to July 14, 1999 (www.reliefweb.int [accessed March 2000]).

million ethnic Albanians, making Milosevic's ethnic expulsion campaign one of the most comprehensive of the post–World War II era. Of this total, 800,000 Kosovar Albanians were forced out of the country, primarily for destinations in Albania and Macedonia (see figure 4-1). Another 500,000 people were believed to be internally displaced within Kosovo, many hiding outdoors, though the absence of international monitors in the province made it difficult to be precise.[32] According to one NATO official, a reexamination of data and interviews with ethnic Albanians after the war suggests that far fewer displaced persons may actually have been homeless and living in the hills for extensive periods during the war. But NATO did not know that at the time.[33]

Serbia's attacks in Kosovo took a number of forms. Many of the forced expulsions were done at gunpoint and door-to-door. But heavy weapons including tanks, artillery, helicopters, and fixed-wing aircraft such as the low-flying Super Galeb were also in frequent use, even against unarmed refugees.

The death toll of Serbia's campaign in Kosovo remains unknown. At the end of 1999, before grave excavations were halted for the winter, some 2,100 bodies had been found in about one-third of the known major burial sites. Death toll estimates of Kosovar Albanians now range from 5,000 to 11,000, suggesting that the rough estimate of about 10,000 frequently used in the war's early aftermath is not far wrong though perhaps (one hopes) a bit high.[34] At least half of all victims were probably killed in the war's first month. Reports of summary executions were frequent, detailed, and generally consistent from witness to witness, leaving NATO officials in little doubt as to their veracity. Many members of the Kosovar Albanian intelligentsia were singled out for summary execution. Sometimes those ethnic Albanians who could not produce enough cash were killed by Serb forces. Looting was commonplace, and monetary motives seem to have driven many of the irregulars. Militia members were apparently paid wages for their work and allowed to keep a share of the spoils. According to some reports, they were sometimes guided to the homes of wealthy Kosovar Albanians by local Serb officials; their barbaric activities were directed by higher-ranking militia officials, leaving little doubt that the campaign of terror was carefully orchestrated.[35] Widespread destruction of property was clearly visible to NATO intelligence authorities, and on a growing scale, from the first few days of the war onward.[36] More than 100,000 homes in some 500 cities, towns, and villages were damaged or destroyed, often after being looted.

Women were frequently forced to watch their sons and husbands be killed, sometimes meeting the same fate themselves and sometimes being left in their agony. Many were raped. Families were deported by train, bus, automobile convoy, or forced march, often after being split up. Bodies of many victims and many dead animals were deposited in wells to contaminate drinking water, further jeopardizing Kosovar Albanian lives and discouraging those left alive from remaining in their towns and villages. Tear gas was used against refugees. (Yugoslavia possessed lethal chemical agents as well, but did not use them; President Clinton had promised a "swift and overwhelming response" if they had.)[37] Kosovar Albanians were pressed into work details, sometimes digging mass graves for their compatriots. They were also used as human shields around tanks and other Yugoslav military assets.[38]

A few specific examples that appear representative of the Serb reign of terror against the ethnic Albanians give the character of what went on. In the city of Djakovica, eleven Kosovar Albanian men were killed, then their bodies were cut up and left on the street. A woman was made to watch her two daughters murdered and was then shot herself. Her six-year-old granddaughter, who ran away and hid in a closet during the killings, was chased down, shot, and set on fire. Next door, eighteen people were shot in the back of the head, and a two-year-old was burned alive when Serb forces set fire to her house. Elsewhere, a fifty-year-old woman had her nipples hacked off. A two-year-old had his arm amputated by a masked Serb because the child's parents had no more hard currency to give the barbaric soldier.[39]

These specific acts may not have been directed from high command levels, and atrocities certainly occur in any war. But the campaign of ethnic killing and terror, and the idea of using undisciplined Serb irregulars to carry it out, were devised in Belgrade. Even before the May 27 indictment of Slobodan Milosevic by the International Criminal Tribunal for the former Yugoslavia at the Hague, the United States stated that it had clear evidence implicating nine Yugoslav military officers in crimes against humanity.[40] Ultranationalist militia leader Zeljko Raznatovic, better known as Arkan, who was apparently assassinated in Belgrade after the war, revealed that his "tigers" had routinely conducted ethnic killing and expulsion operations during earlier wars in Croatia and Bosnia under central government command. That left little reason to doubt that Belgrade exercised similar control over paramilitary forces in Kosovo.[41]

During the early weeks, Serb troops sometimes organized forced marches of Kosovar Albanians out of the province or loaded, and overloaded, them like cattle onto train cars to ship them out of the country. At other times, Serb forces closed Kosovo's borders with neighboring countries. It is not clear if they did so to ensure that adequate hostages remained within the country to serve as a deterrent to a possible NATO ground invasion, to reduce the apparent magnitude of their atrocities and thereby lower the odds of a ground invasion, to prevent the KLA from resupplying its units within Kosovo, or to bar KLA soldiers from fleeing Kosovo at certain times, when they were thought likely to try to cross the border.[42]

The violence against ethnic Albanians, most of them civilians, was on such a scale that the Department of State explicitly raised the possibility from the very first week of the war that genocide was under way in Kosovo. So did German Defense Minister Rudolf Scharping. In fact, on April 18, the Clinton administration's ambassador at large for war crimes, David Scheffer, emphasized the possibility that tens of thousands of Kosovar Albanians were already dead, even as the State Department and NATO officially continued to speak of no more than a few thousand estimated fatalities.[43] However, no NATO country formally made the charge of genocide, or invoked the 1948 UN convention against genocide, at any time during the war. To meet the formal definition of genocide, which is the effort to annihilate "in whole or in part" a given national, ethnic, racial, or religious group, ethnic killings need not reach any specific quantitative threshold. Nonetheless, NATO probably handled this issue correctly during the conflict over Kosovo, raising its concerns about the possibility of genocide without in the end invoking that weighty term to describe killings that, although ruthless, were not on a scale to compare with the century's—or even the decade's—worst massacres.[44]

The condition of the half million Kosovars who were believed to be internally displaced persons could not be ascertained. Many were feared to be without food and at risk of attack. Indeed, some 200,000 men of military age were believed missing; thankfully the vast majority later turned up alive, but in the war's early weeks the possibility that multiple Srebrenica-type massacres had occurred could not be ruled out.[45]

According to a NATO briefing on April 1, Milosevic had planned his ethnic "clean-and-sweep" operations in Kosovo for months and began them before peace talks in France had even concluded.[46] His forces conducted them with brutal efficiency and speed once NATO bombs began to fall. Refugee reports and other intelligence indicated that the majority of Kosovar Albanians were driven from their homes within the first week of the war. The pace at which Kosovar Albanians left their homes was at least ten times greater than during the worst of the events in 1998. As NATO's spokesman Jamie Shea put it on March 28, only five days into the conflict, "We are on the brink of a major humanitarian disaster in Kosovo, the likes of which have not been seen in Europe since the closing stages of World War II." He claimed that there was "a campaign under way to ethnically re-engineer the makeup of Kosovo."[47] NATO commander General Clark said that Milosevic was "working very, very fast, trying to present the world with a fait accompli, to change the demographics of Kosovo."[48] Unlike the situation before March 24, many of the displaced were being driven from locales where KLA rebels had not previously been active, meaning that the Serb ethnic expulsion operations could not in any way be justified on counterinsurgency grounds.[49]

Those leaving the country were deprived of their identification papers and told not to expect to return. By April 5, there were half a million Kosovar Albanian refugees in Macedonia, Albania, and Montenegro—some as a result of events before March 24, but most as a result of the preceding two weeks of fighting. On April 6, Milosevic declared a cease-fire—a phony gesture, since fighting against the KLA continued, and in any case it occurred only after most Kosovar Albanians had been forced from their homes. The only good that came from his duplicitous proposal was that it forced NATO to establish clear conditions for accepting any true cease-fire, conditions that the alliance held to thereafter throughout the war. Working day and night,

NATO ambassadors spent the first week of April agreeing on what their governments' demands on Belgrade would be, coming up with five in the end: an end to violence, complete withdrawal of all Serb forces from Kosovo, entry of an international armed presence, return to Kosovo of all refugees who wished to go home, and establishment of a dialogue leading to autonomy for Kosovo.

Serb forces in Kosovo, though doubled in size from their 1998 levels and much more synchronized in their operations from the year before, were not overwhelmingly large. Numbering some 40,000, including military personnel, Interior Ministry, and civilian militia led by the likes of the infamous Arkan, they outnumbered the KLA by a ratio of perhaps five to one at the outset of the war. Serb units in Kosovo drew in part upon the 110,000 active-duty troops in Yugoslavia's military. (There are another 400,000 reservists in Yugoslavia's armed forces.)[50] But that was not necessarily the core of the force. Almost as many gun-wielding Serbs in Kosovo in the spring of 1999 were from the smaller Interior Ministry ranks, of the type that had conducted the bulk of the 1998 counterinsurgency operations in Kosovo. Milosevic may have felt more comfortable entrusting much of the mission to the Interior Ministry police forces, which had been key to his rise to power in earlier years.[51] He also attempted to ensure the loyalty of regular army forces by replacing the top-level leadership of the Yugoslav military before the war, turning out General Momcilo Perisic in favor of his loyalist and crony General Dragoljub Ojdanic.[52]

According to classic counterinsurgency doctrine, which typically calls for an advantage of at least ten to one for government forces, the size of these Serb units in aggregate was not overwhelming. The exact force requirements for counterinsurgency war can be debated, and no rule of thumb is precise. But it is still easy to see why government forces may require a large advantage. Generally in counterinsurgency wars rebels hide themselves within civilian populations that are either at least partially sympathetic to the rebel cause or too afraid of retribution to inform on them. They also conduct hit-and-run attacks, using surprise and ambush to maximum effect, avoiding pitched battle as much as possible.[53]

There were elements of what might be termed proper counterinsurgent warfare in Serb operations throughout Kosovo. Initially, battles were heaviest in the northeast of Kosovo, notably along the transportation corridor between Podujevo and Pristina, as Serb units apparently sought to secure supply lines into the province. Serb units also concentrated their early efforts in the rebels' stronghold of the Drenica region, west of Pristina, in the center of the province. (In a rough approximation, it is possible to think of Kosovo's geography as consisting of concentric circles: a nearly continuous ring of mountains along its edges, within which is a circle of some half dozen major towns, including the regional capital Pristina; within this circle of towns is the central plateau, the Drenica region, where rebel forces controlled as much as 25–30 percent of Kosovo's land in 1998.)[54] Serb units also drove away civilian populations in villages along the Albanian border in order to interrupt KLA supply lines. As the war went on, moreover, Yugoslav units continued to try to interdict KLA supply lines, sometimes firing artillery into Albania in the process. They also succeeded in dismantling the KLA's seven principal headquarters, denying it control over any terrain to speak of and forcing the insurgents to return to hit-and-run warfare tactics.[55]

But in reality Serbia did not have any intention of fighting a humane counterinsurgency campaign, at least not once NATO's bombs started to fall (and probably not before, given what had happened in the summer of 1998). Rather, following Mao's dictum, it sought to drain the sea in which the rebel fish swam by forcibly removing the local population in ways similar to what had been done elsewhere during the decade's previous Balkan wars. That helps explain why it brought along at least 1,000 heavy weapons with the 40,000 troops—weapons that would have had relatively little purpose in standard, and discriminate, counterinsurgency operations.[56]

Some regions of Kosovo appear to have been ethnically "cleansed" in order to create a path for mass expulsions of ethnic Albanians from other parts of the province. Forced civilian evacuations in cities like Pristina and the western town of Pec were extremely organized, and on a massive scale, leaving little doubt about the Serbs' true desires to radically change the province's overall demographic mix. Army forces would surround the towns, relaxing their cordon only to permit Kosovar Albanians to flee, which they would typically do after being intimidated by Interior Ministry and paramilitary forces. What happened was certainly not just a counterinsurgency operation—even if one makes allowances for heavy-handed Serb tactics and human rights abuses—but was a carefully planned and orchestrated process of ethnic intimidation and relocation.[57]

Why did Milosevic resort to these tactics? Perhaps his military was too cowardly to fight a type of war in which considerable numbers of its troops would certainly have died. More likely, he may have come to doubt that he could win the war with traditional counterinsurgency methods. That was especially likely to be the case if the KLA ranks grew, as indeed they did in the course of the spring, roughly doubling in size, by NATO estimates, to some 17,000 fighters by war's end, taking advantage of the global Albanian diaspora for recruits as well as for funds.[58] Milosevic's forces were limited in both size and competence; even more to the point, the Kosovar Albanians were increasingly willing to use violence and risk their lives in fighting him, and they benefited from an increasingly sympathetic civilian population base, leaving less and less hope that the insurgency could be contained through judicious methods.[59]

Finally, there is little doubt that Milosevic saw this situation as not only a problem but also an opportunity to ethnically reengineer Kosovo. Ironically, as noted, he no longer saw any reason not to do so once the air war began, especially since alliance leaders were emphatically stating that they would not escalate to a ground war.

Largely out of its conviction that Milosevic would bow quickly in the face of bombing—and because of its desire not to encourage secessionism on the part of the Kosovar Albanians—the United States declined a KLA request to provide rebel forces with antitank weapons. In fact, NATO chose not to help the KLA in any substantial material way throughout the war.[60] The State Department, for example, actively discouraged Albanian Americans from joining the ranks of the KLA.[61] Confusingly, General Shelton and Secretary Cohen were at roughly the same time telling Congress that the KLA might ultimately be able to play the role of a ground force, allowing NATO to avoid any such role itself, even while the Pentagon was concluding that the small KLA was being badly hurt in battle.[62]

So in the course of late March and April, Serbia depopulated most of Kosovo of its ethnic Albanian population, making it very hard for the KLA to operate as a classic insurgent organization by blending into a friendly civilian population base. Further, Serb forces absorbed very few tactical losses from either NATO airpower or KLA units; Serbia also suffered only limited damage to its strategic military and economic assets from NATO bombs, as noted below. Pockets of KLA resistance remained, and these would prove troublesome to Serbia over time, as would the effects of the air war. But in the early going, Milosevic was succeeding.

NATO's War against Serbia

From the start of the war, NATO sought to use air strikes to weaken the Yugoslav military's ability to wreak destruction on the Kosovar Albanians. In his March 24 Oval Office address, President Clinton said that one of

NATO's three main goals was, if necessary, "to seriously damage the Serb military's capacity to harm the people of Kosovo."[63] Pentagon spokesman Kenneth Bacon stated, just before the war, that, "the primary goal of the air strikes would be to arrest the ability of the Serbs to brutally attack the Kosovar Albanians."[64] A NATO official said that "the purpose of air strikes is to remove his capacity to commit atrocities and remove his ability to use heavy artillery."[65] And British Defence Secretary Robertson told the House of Commons, "Our military objective—our clear, simple military objective—will be to reduce the Serbs' capacity to repress the Albanian population and thus to avert a humanitarian disaster."[66]

These aspirations were extremely optimistic—even verging on irresponsible. Whatever the odds that Milosevic might have buckled for strategic or psychological reasons, there was very little reason to believe that air strikes could make a quick and meaningful difference on the battlefield, as one of ·is pointed out before the war had begun[67] and as the U.S. Air Force general n charge of the air war claimed that he had known all along.[68] More sober than some, but still optimistic, was General Clark, who described NATO's goals in the air campaign as trying to "disrupt, degrade, devastate, and ultimately destroy" Yugoslav military forces as well as the facilities and infrastructure that supported them.[69] Clark was surely right that NATO needed to attack Serb forces in the field, undoubtedly a "center of gravity" and cherished asset of Milosevic, to weaken them as much as possible.[70] But what was particularly notable—and entirely predictable—about the first month of Operation Allied Force was how much more practical it was for NATO to achieve that goal for some subsets of military targets than for others.

To argue that NATO was ineffective in protecting ethnic Albanians is not to claim—as many have—that NATO somehow bears responsibility for the Kosovars' suffering.[71] Clearly, the pace and intensity of Serb atrocities increased significantly once bombing became a certainty after the failed peace talks in Paris. But it was Yugoslav forces that were driving the Kosovar Albanians from their homes, often killing, raping, and looting in the process. As Secretary Cohen later rightly put it, "The notion that NATO is in some moral equivalence with Milosevic is sheer, patent nonsense."[72] But in a broader sense, NATO's bombing clearly lifted a constraint on Milosevic, who no longer saw reason for restraint. He may even have felt an incentive to expel Kosovo's ethnic Albanian population as quickly as possible in case NATO attacks ultimately prevented him from continuing with the cowardly campaign. NATO was not to blame for what was happening in Kosovo. On the other hand, it was too involved to ignore it. Yet for the first few weeks of the conflict, its military operation almost seemed to do just that.

The Course of the Air War

NATO's military campaign followed, in large measure, the three-stage plan developed in the fall of 1998.[73] In the opening days of the war, NATO's phase 1 air attacks focused primarily on Yugoslavia's integrated air defense system and to a lesser extent on command and control and other military sites. About 160 cruise missiles were fired, 100 of them Tomahawks (U.S. Navy as well as British missiles) and the remainder conventional air-launched cruise missiles.[74] Some 350 NATO aircraft, about 220 of them American, participated in the opening night of conflict. That was roughly one-third of NATO's ultimate force, consisting of some 740 U.S. aircraft (and 50,000 personnel, all told) as well as more than 300 planes from the allies.[75]

In the war's early going, most aircraft flew out of nearby bases, largely in Italy; some flew from more distant bases in the United Kingdom and even the United States. Thirteen NATO countries were involved in the initial attacks; fourteen of the nineteen members would ultimately participate. NATO typically flew thirty to fifty strike sorties a day in the war's first few days.[76] Yet it did not take down Serbia's air defenses, which remained generally unused—and hence generally untargetable, since air defense radars that are not turned on are difficult to locate. In fact, they were never truly put out of action throughout the entire conflict.

U.S. and other NATO officials expected phase 1 strikes to change Milosevic's calculus and return him to the negotiation table. They did not. At the outset of hostilities, commanders had only three days' worth of targets, about ninety in all.[77] But officials soon began to rethink their optimism about an early and easy end to what were envisioned as essentially symbolic air strikes.[78]

By March 27 NATO had entered phase 2, allowing attacks against a wider set of military targets below the forty-fourth parallel, which roughly bisects Yugoslavia, with Belgrade and Novi Sad above it, Montenegro and Kosovo as well as cities such as Nis below it. In a sense, moving to phase 2 at that point deviated from traditional air force doctrine, since the latter called for first taking down the Yugoslav military's integrated air defense system before doing anything else. But basic logic, as well as exigencies on the ground, argued against such a rigid adherence to doctrine and to NATO's original battle plan.[79] Phase 2 targets included military infrastructure such as depots and airfields as well as Yugoslav forces in the field. In the words of NATO Air Commodore David Wilby, "in Phase Two of our operations, the major weight of our efforts focused on operations and installations supporting the paramilitary, military, and MUP [Interior Ministry] forces in Kosovo."[80]

The alliance lost a U.S. F-117 stealth fighter to enemy fire on the night of March 27–28, NATO's first aircraft loss of the war.[81] The plane may have been detected and tracked while dropping ordnance (with its bomb doors open), making the plane temporarily "unstealthy." Some reports suggest it may have been brought down by antiaircraft artillery or even machine-gun fire, though other reports claim unambiguously that an SA-3 missile was the culprit.[82] Even though there reportedly were some security lapses in NATO's handling of air-tasking orders in the war's early going, they do not appear to have contributed to the loss of the F-117.[83] Thankfully the pilot was rescued by U.S. special forces using Pave Low and Pave Hawk helicopters painted black and flying without lights.[84] There were some reports that the wreckage may have been sold to a country such as Russia or China. Air force officials tended to downplay their worries, emphasizing that F-117 stealth technology is not as modern as that on B-2 or F-22 aircraft. But the fact remains that Russia and China do not have stealth systems even as capable as the F-117, so the wreckage might be somewhat useful to them nonetheless.[85]

In the last days of March, alliance aircraft began to conduct some daylight attacks as they achieved air superiority, even if they had not yet achieved—and in fact never would achieve—what the U.S. military terms "air supremacy," in which aircraft can fly at most altitudes with virtually no risk of being shot down.[86] By March 30 NATO had entered what it termed phase 2-plus. It expanded considerably the set of targets attacked above the forty-fourth parallel in places such as Belgrade. Civilian infrastructure with military applications such as television and radio transmitters, as well as various leadership targets and eventually even a residence of Milosevic, were beginning to be fair game. Originally, the alliance's plan had been to go after such targets only after the formal adoption of phase 3 by the North Atlantic Council. However, several NATO countries, including Germany, Greece, Italy, and France, were reportedly unwilling to authorize phase 3. Rather than engage in a rancorous and divisive debate on the subject at the official level of the council, the allies compromised. As alliance officials later explained to us, without fully authorizing phase 3, they gave Secretary-General Solana the role of approving or disapproving specific categories of targets that were technically within phase 3. They only asked that he informally consult those countries with particular concerns before making his decisions and that he and General Clark also solicit input on particularly sensitive individual targets before attacking them.

During April (and also in May), more categories of civilian targets were approved for bombing in these ways. The broadening of the air campaign occurred somewhat more slowly than the United States and certain other countries might have preferred—but not radically so. After all, the strategy of gradualism was firmly supported in Washington, since the Clinton administration expected Milosevic to capitulate quickly. It thus had its own reservations about attacking civilian targets early in the conflict. In the end, most targets were approved, even from the phase 3 list, as the alliance collectively realized that the gloves would have to come off if Milosevic was to be defeated. Even though phase 3 was never formally adopted in the course of the war, in many ways it did not matter.[87]

On March 31, three U.S. soldiers along the Kosovo-Macedonia border were captured by Yugoslav forces, introducing a major new dimension to the conflict. They would be released a few weeks later, but the incident raised questions about whether Milosevic would use NATO soldiers as hostages, similar to what the Serbs had done in Bosnia when air strikes were threatened in 1995. Concerns grew in light of the fact that Yugoslavia's treatment of the prisoners, while generally humane, violated the Geneva Convention by denying the International Red Cross access to them and hastily putting them on trial. The capture of the American soldiers also raised worries about the security of Albania and the former Yugoslav republic of Macedonia, as well as the safety of the 12,000 or so Western forces based in those countries. Sent as the vanguard for a possible peacekeeping force in case of the successful conclusion of the Rambouillet negotiations, these troops had by late March 1999 essentially become a refugee relief force as well as a deterrent against Yugoslav attacks to the south. They were gradually augmented by contributions from individual NATO members during the war, becoming a possible nucleus for any eventual invasion force and an actual nucleus in the end for KFOR.

At the eve of the NATO summit on April 23, NATO had 690 aircraft in the theater of operations around Yugoslavia, as well as twenty ships in the vicinity, roughly twice as many of each as at the war's beginning. It had carried out about 2,700 strike sorties, roughly one-fourth of the total it would conduct by June 10.[88] Principal targets were air defenses, command and control assets, military-related infrastructure including transportation routes, and to the extent possible, Serb forces in the field in Kosovo.[89] (See figure 4-2.) NATO was now going after bunkers used by Milosevic, his party headquarters in Belgrade, one of his official residences, more bridges in major cities, and other sensitive targets. Finally, it was examining ways to tighten its oil embargo, without however forcibly stopping noncompliant ships headed to Yugloslavia.[90]

Figure 4-2. Average Number of Daily Targets in the NATO Air Campaign, by Type

Number

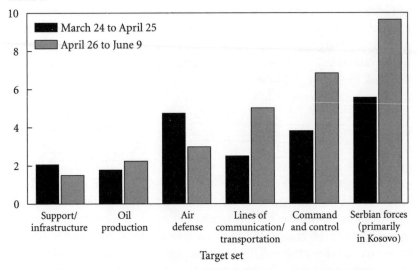

Source: NATO briefings, various dates (www.nato.int/kosovo [accessed March 2000]).

NATO's Effectiveness in the Bombing Campaign

NATO brought impressive technology to bear in Operation Allied Force. It marshaled stealth and electronic jamming aircraft; sophisticated reconnaissance and command and control planes; and a multicontinental, real-time planning process. Most bombs used in the early going were precision guided. Frequently pilots used night-vision goggles to find and confirm their targets during the night sorties.[91] Yet these advantages did not translate into battlefield success. Weather presented considerable problems for NATO's weapons and tactics, although that could hardly have been a surprise in Europe at that time of year.[92] Certain target sets were hit hard, notably fixed infrastructure such as fuel and ammunition facilities. NATO also estimated that it had damaged or destroyed some thirty Yugoslav aircraft by March 31.[93] But other categories of targets, most notably Serb forces in the field, went generally unscathed.

After twenty-one days of the campaign, General Clark estimated that NATO had had only seven days of good weather. On ten days, more than 50 percent of all strikes were canceled. The slow start may have had some advantages for managing intra-alliance relations, since it gave Milosevic the chance to display the depths of his depravity before NATO bombs could cause much collateral damage of their own. Allies who may have been skittish about the air war at first had time to see what Serb forces were doing in Kosovo and to steel their resolve. Nonetheless, on balance the slow start was unfortunate, for it reinforced the impression that NATO was powerless to stop Milosevic and gave him no reason to reconsider his basic strategy.

As April unfolded, alliance aircraft began to benefit from improving weather as well as growing confidence that they could operate fairly safely in Yugoslav skies. NATO continued attacks against major infrastructure and increasingly hit bridges with critical military uses; petroleum facilities, including Yugoslavia's two main refining plants at Pancevo and Novi Sad; telephone exchanges and other communications infrastructure; and military production facilities. The alliance estimated that it had hit about 150 major targets by April 10, including two of three major military headquarters and about 50 percent of Yugoslavia's fuel stocks. By April 13 General Clark estimated that 70 percent of all petroleum stocks had been destroyed; Pentagon briefer General Charles Wald stated that 100 percent of Milosevic's ability to produce finished petroleum products had been eliminated.[94] By the end of the war's first month, NATO had destroyed seventy Yugoslav aircraft, including five shot down in air-to-air engagements. The alliance also destroyed 40 percent of the country's SAM-3 facilities and 30 percent of SAM-6 missile systems. Many Serb antiaircraft missiles had been launched, though often only with generally ineffective optical guidance.[95]

In contrast, airpower's effectiveness against forces in the field remained modest. For example, as of April 17 NATO estimated it had destroyed only about a dozen Serb tanks.[96] On April 27, General Clark suggested that Serbia might even have strengthened its forces inside Kosovo since the war began. For these and other reasons, in mid-April General Clark requested nearly 400 additional aircraft to increase the intensity of attacks (he asked for another 200 or so in early May).[97]

Controversial Tactics and Target Sets

More than is often appreciated, NATO allies stuck together through thick and thin during Operation Allied Force. Most agreed on how to wage the war, at least in broad terms. That said, controversies did occasionally arise over what to target and how high to fly aircraft. Some allies appear to have been somewhat piqued by the independence with which a number of U.S. aircraft operated, though the fact that these aircraft never conducted attacks on targets vetoed by other allies limited the dissension.

Consider first the issue of how high to fly aircraft or, to put it differently, what risks to accept for NATO pilots. Alliance aircraft flew primarily at medium altitudes, generally around 15,000 feet above sea level (with a few exceptions), to avoid air defenses. That practice grew out of the experience of Operation Desert Storm in 1991; in that war, the U.S.-led coalition initially flew many low-altitude flights, but partly as a result twenty-seven aircraft were lost or damaged on the first three nights of the war, mostly due to antiaircraft artillery and infrared-guided surface-to-air missiles. Once higher-altitude tactics were adopted, the coalition's loss rates went down by about a factor of five (with fifty-nine more aircraft lost or damaged during the war's remaining forty days).[98] Thus there was a proven military logic to NATO's decision.

Nonetheless, the decision reinforced the alliance's sense of impotence at being able to affect developments on the ground with its attack aircraft, particularly in the war's early weeks. Some NATO allies were prepared to fly lower, ˌven at the risk of casualties; as a French official told us, "Dans la guerre, il faut des morts" (in war, there must be deaths), and there is no wisdom in pretending otherwise. But U.S. aversion to casualties prohibited such a policy for much of the conflict. It is not clear that flying below 15,000 feet woula have made an appreciable difference in the course of the war, given how little heavy weaponry was needed to forcibly expel a generally defenseless population. But the French were probably right, that it should have been attempted, at least in certain local settings where Serb forces were fighting the KLA.

By flying at medium altitude, NATO may have reduced risks to its own pilots, but it sometimes increased dangers for people on the ground, not only because it remained impotent against Serb murderers terrorizing the ethnic Albanian people but also because it sometimes hit innocents. While on the whole waging a careful war, in which every effort was made to minimize civilian casualties through the careful selection of targets and ordnance, NATO occasionally made mistakes (see appendix B).[99] Among its notable errors were, on April 12, striking a bridge in southern Serbia while a passenger train was crossing, killing mostly Serb civilians; and on April 14 hitting a convoy of Kosovar Albanian refugees that it apparently mistook for an armored column. Over the course of the entire war some 500 Serb and ethnic Albanian citizens may have died (in roughly equal numbers between the two groups) as a result of NATO bombing. That estimate was ultimately backed up by a Human Rights Watch report, though the report claimed that the civilian casualties occurred in a total of ninety attacks, while NATO estimated twenty to thirty such tragic incidents. Human Rights Watch also estimated that about half of the fatalities could have been prevented by more discriminate attacks, such as a reduced use of cluster bombs, which in fact the United States is reported to have stopped using, but only in May.[100] (Some have also criticized NATO for using depleted-uranium weapons, but any harmful effects from their modest radioactivity are unproven at this point.)[101] NATO introduced some changes into its aerial operations as a result of the tragedies. For example, pilots were allowed to descend below 15,000 feet to check targets with binoculars before returning to a higher and safer altitude to fire their weapons (since the firing process generally leaves them vulnerable, particularly when a laser beam must be maintained on a target for a period of time).[102]

However, even at lower altitudes pilots could not easily tell civilians from infantry soldiers. Moreover, manned airplanes did not always need to descend to low altitudes for NATO to have reliable targeting information, since unmanned aerial vehicles could sometimes conduct adequate low-altitude surveillance and transmit the data back to bomb-dispensing aircraft. (Assuming targets are correctly selected, dropping precision bombs from high altitudes does not usually reduce their accuracy, given the way in which such weapons function.) Nonetheless, there were occasions in which NATO's flight ceiling of 15,000 feet above sea level (which in practice usually meant 10,000–14,000 feet above ground level) did contribute to the risk of causing civilian casualties—and of conducting less effective bombing more generally.[103]

Concern over casualties—to NATO airmen, Kosovar Albanian civilians, and Serb civilians—influenced the air campaign throughout its course. It occasionally led to disagreements among the allies over what targets to hit. As noted, the allies officially delegated their role in scrubbing target sets to Secretary-General Solana, who in turn allowed informal input from countries with particular interests and concerns in the targeting process, most notably the United States, Britain, and France. Of particular concern were sites housing civilians (such as media centers) or those located near apartment buildings and hospitals and schools. London had special concerns about targets struck by B-52 bombers operating from British bases. Paris had special concerns about targets in Montenegro as well as bridges in Belgrade. More generally, France was worried that bombing the wrong set of targets might strengthen rather than weaken Milosevic, so it viewed many discussions over targeting with a careful strategic eye.

One high-ranking British official with whom we spoke offered both praise and criticism for the French role in preventing attacks against certain targets during the war. He argued that the French were right to think in political, rather than solely military, terms about the effects of bombing various assets but that, having made that conceptual leap, they then made exactly the wrong judgments about the likely political effects of various attacks.[104] Specifically, France argued against striking dual-use targets of particular importance to the civilian population, such as bridges and electricity grids, on the grounds that doing so would be inhumane and cause the Serb people to rally around Milosevic. In fact, however, NATO's decision to strike such targets with increasing conviction late in the war may have helped convince Milosevic to capitulate.

As a final, if lesser, matter of contention, France also noted that many U.S. aircraft operated outside of the main NATO daily war plan (or air tasking order). For example, bombers based in Britain and the United States and cruise missiles fired from navy ships were not integrated into the rest of the campaign because they did not need to coordinate use of runways with other aircraft and because dedicated corridors could be reserved for their ingresses and egresses. Other allies did not even know what the United States would do on a given day with its nonintegrated assets. As a senior NATO official told us, he was once surprised during the war when, knowing that official NATO air strikes had been suspended due to poor weather, he then saw TV pictures of buildings in Belgrade just set ablaze by allied bombing. That was his first indication that the United States had not chosen to take the day off.[105]

As the French pointed out, some U.S. military assets were not integrated because the United States had the option of not integrating them, given its overwhelmingly important political and military power and the fact that American generals effectively ran the NATO war. (The United States did not bomb targets that Paris or London or any other NATO capital vetoed, but it did choose the time and nature of many of the attacks without consultation or coordination.)[106] The French claimed to be not so much complaining as observing that, like them, the United States was not truly a fully integrated NATO member, either. In French eyes, this validated Paris's preference for a stronger, and perhaps more independent, European arm in the future.[107]

NATO's Humanitarian Relief Efforts

NATO's humanitarian relief role for refugees was considerable. At the request of the UN High Commissioner for Refugees, Sadako Ogata, NATO agreed in early April to coordinate the humanitarian relief operation for Kosovar refugees. It continued to provide much of the physical capacity for delivering food and giving shelter to them as well. For example, on one typical day—April 6—NATO delivered 300,000 meal-sized food rations as well as 180 tons of tents for refugees. It also flew refugees from border regions in Albania to safer "inland" camps. By the end of May, NATO had flown more than 4,500 tons of food and water to refugees from Kosovo and another 8,500 tons of other materials, including large quantities of medical supplies and tents. Largely as a result of NATO's prompt relief efforts, epidemics in the camps were avoided, and few refugees lost their lives.[108]

NATO considered the idea of airdrops to internally displaced Kosovar Albanians, but concerns about whether Serb forces would reach the supplies first, about risks to NATO pilots, and about the sheer scale of a comprehensive effort convinced it not to take action.[109] During the war only one particularly courageous nongovernmental organization, the International Rescue Committee, undertook airdrops, though they were of a quite modest scale.[110]

The Apache Saga

The first month of the war also witnessed the difficult deployment of twenty-four U.S. Apache helicopters to Albania. General Clark requested the deployment of the tank-killing helicopters forty-eight hours after the war began, in part to give him more options to take on the heavy weapons the Serb army was employing with virtual impunity against Kosovar civilians.[111] President Clinton approved Clark's request on April 4, after a week's delay. However, the deployment of the helicopters took far longer than expected, partly because basing the helicopters in Macedonia as originally planned proved infeasible, partly because Albania's airfield capacities were severely limited, and partly because the army was structurally not well prepared for such a deployment. The first Apaches arrived on April 21 and the last on April 26. More than 5,000 troops were sent as part of the deployment to provide engineering and maintenance support, protection for the helicopters and their crews, and advance fire using ATACMS (army tactical missiles) and MLRS (multiple-launch rocket system) rockets in any combat use of the Apaches. The total cost for deploying these forces to Albania, building a base for them, and training crews during the war amounted to about $500 million, perhaps as much as 20–25 percent of the total U.S. war cost.[112] The overall cost of Operation Allied Force was otherwise quite modest in budgetary terms (about 1 percent of the U.S. defense budget for 1999).

The Apache deployment never led to the actual combat use of the attack helicopters in the war. The reasons were many. There were worries that loss rates for the helicopters might be 5 percent per sortie or even higher, given that they would have to fly through difficult mountain passes and do so without the traditional ground troop support. (By contrast, loss rates for fixed-wing aircraft were less than a hundredth of a percent.) The absence of friendly ground troops also meant that the Apaches would not have their traditional means of acquiring targets; unmanned aerial vehicles and other such means would have to be relied upon. That fact, plus doubts about how many Serb armored vehicles would be in the open and vulnerable to Apache fire in any case, raised questions about whether the likely effectiveness of the attack helicopters justified the risk of losing pilots. In addition, improving weather in May made it more realistic to attack Serb targets in Kosovo from jets flying at medium altitudes.[113]

In one sense, these concerns were all reasonable—with the possible exception of the expected loss rates, given that the Pentagon often overestimates losses before a conflict and that the Apache attrition estimates were reportedly made with little rigor.[114] In further defense of the decision not to use the helicopters in combat, as one U.S. official argued to us, the mere fact of deploying the Apaches to Albania gave the Serbs an extra worry. It may have forced them to concentrate many of their man-portable surface-to-air missiles near Kosovo's border with Albania, thereby taking them away from places where they could have threatened low-flying NATO jets.[115] And it made NATO's later talk of a possible invasion more real and menacing to Milosevic than the veiled threats would otherwise have been.

Yet the saga of the Apache force, known as Task Force Hawk, was a disappointing one for the U.S. Army and for NATO, particularly in April and most of May. The highly visible fact that the helicopters were not used, despite public discussion of their impressive capabilities by the Pentagon (which touted the Apaches as providing NATO with the capability to "get up close and personal"), was a telling symbol of NATO's lack of resolve—and of its unwillingness to risk Western lives even as Kosovar lives were lost by the thousands in the war's early going.[116] Tragically, the Apache deployment also led to two helicopter crashes on training missions. The second, probably caused by mechanical failure (though the difficult flying conditions may have contributed as well), took the lives of two American pilots, the only NATO losses during the entire conflict.[117]

The International Politics of NATO's Air Campaign

The consequences of Operation Allied Force extended far beyond the battlefield. Perhaps most important was the negative impact of the war on relations between Russia and the United States as well as other NATO countries. There was also important political fallout in other countries, ranging from Serbia to NATO countries like Greece, in the war's first month.

NATO's bombing of Yugoslavia provoked a major crisis with Russia. On March 23, Prime Minister Yevgeny Primakov, en route to Washington, turned his plane around and returned to Moscow when Vice President Al Gore called to inform him that NATO military action against Yugoslavia was imminent. Shortly after bombs began to fall on March 24, Russian UN Ambassador Sergei Lavrov demanded "an immediate cessation of this unacceptable aggression" at an emergency UN Security Council meeting. Russian President Boris Yeltsin also condemned the action: "This is in fact NATO's attempt to enter the twenty-first century as global policeman. Russia will never agree to it."[118] Within a few weeks, public opinion polls in Russia showed anti-American sentiment doubling from 23 to 49 percent of the population and the favorable rating of the United States declining from 67 to 39 percent.[119]

On March 26 Russia introduced a draft UN resolution, cosponsored by non-Security Council members Belarus and India, calling for a halt to the NATO attacks and resumption of negotiations. China and Namibia also supported the motion, but the other twelve members opposed it: the United States, Britain, France, Argentina, Bahrain, Brazil, Canada, Gabon, Gambia, Malaysia, the Netherlands, and Slovenia.[120] For his part, UN Secretary-General Kofi Annan straddled these opposing positions adroitly, in effect supporting NATO when he said at the beginning of the war that "there are times when the use of force may be legitimate in the pursuit of peace," but hedging his statement by also observing that the UN Security Council retained "primary responsibility" for maintaining international stability and that it "should be involved in any decision to resort to [the use of] force."[121]

Even though the United States tried to contain the damage to U.S.-Russian relations, things got worse before they got better. During the last days of March, Russia sent several ships into the Mediterranean, from where they could enter the Adriatic. The naval action caused considerable tension between the alliance and Moscow and led to worries that Serb forces might receive information on NATO flight operations from the Russian ships.[122] Meanwhile, several days into April, Russian President Boris Yeltsin warned that NATO's air campaign against Yugoslavia could lead to world war, a threat that was later softened—but only after it caused considerable anxiety and further tension.[123]

Yet even in the war's early phases, Russia and NATO maintained an uneasy partnership. For example, Russian Prime Minister Primakov, with NATO's support, went to Belgrade in late March to attempt to find a solution (though his proposed solution was rejected by the allies).[124] Over time, as described in more detail in the next chapter, these collaborative diplomatic efforts would intensify, culminating in a joint U.S., Russian, and European effort that finally confronted Milosevic with a united front that he found impossible to ignore.

In Yugoslavia, NATO bombing initially rallied most Serbs around the flag—and hence around Slobodan Milosevic. Serb armed forces reportedly felt a new sense of purpose and began to have an easier time recruiting; many officers forgave Milosevic for rifts that had characterized their relationship over the previous decade and supported him more strongly. Public open-air rock concerts were held in Belgrade as an expression of patriotism and of defiance against the Western alliance. The symbol of Serb resistance became a patch or design on clothing in the shape of a target, in effect a taunting of NATO. Even anti-Milosevic politicians tended to condemn NATO's attacks and, by implication at least, to defend the Yugoslav president.[125] Most Serb leaders—not only Milosevic and other hypernationalists—were unwilling to criticize or even acknowledge the atrocities being committed against Kosovar Albanians.[126] Indeed, many if not most Serb citizens were equally unwilling to acknowledge what was really happening; as President Clinton said about them after the war, "The Serb people . . . are going to have to get out of denial; they're going to have to come to grips with [what Mr. Milosevic ordered in Kosovo]."[127]

Milosevic managed to silence much of what criticism the independent media attempted. He did so not only in Serbia but also in neighboring Montenegro, the other constituent republic of Yugoslavia, which with its 600,000 inhabitants is dwarfed by Serbia's 10 million.[128] Yugoslavia also tried to seize control of Interior Ministry troops within Montenegro. But Montenegrin President Djukanovic rejected the idea, just as he resisted other Serb pressure throughout the war. Formerly a Milosevic crony, Djukanovic had won the October 1997 election by defeating Milosevic's candidate and since then had increasingly become the Yugoslav leader's nemesis. He was fearful that Milosevic would drag Montenegro down with Serbia in pursuit of his foolish ambitions; he also worried that Milosevic might extend his Serb nationalist agenda into Montenegro or, at a minimum, treat any and all opposition there with the same strong-arm tactics he was using against fellow Serbs who opposed him at home. Although Djukanovic did call on NATO to end air strikes, he also criticized Serbia for its role in the war and for the atrocities being committed in Kosovo.[129] Worries grew that Milosevic might, in retaliation, undertake a coup against the government of Montenegro.[130] To deter such an eventuality, NATO made the extraordinary decision to give Montenegro an effective, if temporary, security guarantee.

NATO's military campaign also produced some challenges within the Balkan region and the alliance. In the war's early going, there were riots by ethnic Serbs in front of the U.S. embassy in the former Yugoslav republic of Macedonia. Macedonia also expressed concern about the number of ethnic Albanian refugees it was asked to accept, since their presence would drastically alter its demographic mix (about 25 percent ethnic Albanian before the war, of a population of about 2 million) if they were to remain in the country for the long term.

The non-NATO countries surrounding Yugoslavia were otherwise generally cooperative with the alliance's war effort. To shore up their resolve, NATO provided security assurances to Albania, the former Yugoslav republic of Macedonia, Bulgaria, Romania, and Slovenia, stating that "we will not tolerate threats by the Belgrade regime to the security of its neighbors. We will respond to such challenges by Belgrade to its neighbors resulting from the presence of NATO forces or their activities on their territory during this crisis."[131] Bulgaria, Romania, and Slovenia provided NATO access to their airspace. All of the neighboring states imposed economic sanctions on Yugoslavia, cutting off oil supplies and other trade, at no small cost to their own economies. (The bombing of bridges also closed the Danube, the region's main economic artery, to river traffic.)[132]

There were demonstrations against the war in NATO-member Greece. In fact, the Greek population remained strongly opposed to Operation Allied Force throughout its course. Greeks felt solidarity with their fellow Orthodox Christians in Serbia, with whom they shared not only a religion but also a history of struggle against Muslims in the region. Greek leaders, by contrast, tended to think more of the interests of the country, which involved being a good ally within NATO and casting its lot with the West in general.[133] They stuck by the war effort despite popular resistance.

The new NATO members—Poland, Hungary, and the Czech Republic—joined what had been one of the world's most peaceful alliances ever in March 1999, only to find themselves at war two weeks later. The Czech government was divided on the desirability of the war: President Vaclav Havel supporting it, Prime Minister Milos Zeman dissociating his government from it, and only 35 percent of Czech citizens endorsing the air strikes. Poland generally supported Operation Allied Force, with 60 percent of the public approving the campaign. Hungary, with 300,000 ethnic kin living in Serbia in the Vojvodina province, was divided: its government ruled out participating in any eventual ground offensive and pressed NATO to avoid bombing in Vojvodina, but it did open the country's airspace, military bases, and transportation routes for alliance use.[134] It also prevented a Russian aid convoy, headed to Yugoslavia with fuel and other supplies with potential military uses, from proceeding.

The U.S. Debate over Ground Forces

From the first day of the war, the Clinton administration ruled out the possible use of ground forces to fight their way into Kosovo, stating that it would only consider their deployment in a "permissive environment," meaning with Milosevic's approval. President Clinton stated on March 24: "I do not intend to put our troops in Kosovo to fight a war."[135] This position would remain unchanged for many weeks. Some officials occasionally intimated that an invasion option remained alive; for example, Deputy Secretary of State Strobe Talbott said that NATO plans for an invasion of Kosovo could be taken "off the shelf" and updated quickly any time the alliance chose. Secretary Cohen made a similar point on one or two occasions.[136] For the most part, however, the Clinton administration and other NATO officials left little doubt that their intention was to avoid the use, threat, or deployment of a ground invasion capability to the region.[137] Vice President Gore put it most bluntly on April 9: "That option is not under consideration."[138]

In addition to noting political pressures at home and abroad for putting aside the issue of using ground forces, Clinton administration officials have also defended the decision on strategic grounds. For example, in an interview after the war, Sandy Berger argued that NATO's advantage in the air gave the alliance an asymmetric advantage over Milosevic that it would effectively surrender with an invasion, since its ground force superiority over Yugoslavia was less overwhelming than its aerial dominance. As a result, Berger concluded that it was "not at all evident that not having the ground force option in our rhetorical quiver affected Milosevic's behavior."[139]

This logic is unconvincing. First, NATO would clearly have continued to bomb during an invasion, as it did in Desert Storm; in fact, the synergy between ground forces and airpower would have made bombing more effective (just as NATO's tactical air campaign improved once the KLA began to go on the offensive in late May). Second, the United States has an impressive track record in ground combat. It has abandoned missions in recent decades only when facing an insurgent or terrorist threat, as in Vietnam, Lebanon, and Somalia. When focused on liberating territory from an occupying army—as in the invasions of Grenada and Panama and the liberation of Kuwait—it has been overwhelmingly effective and surely would have been in this case too, as the Clinton administration recognized by war's end, when it invoked the invasion threat to intensify the pressure on Milosevic.

In retrospect, and in fairness to Berger and the administration, it is true that NATO ultimately prevailed without a ground invasion, proving most wartime critics, including ourselves, wrong on that crucial point. However, the public debate in the United States and elsewhere turned quickly to the ground forces issue because of the clear failure of the air war to achieve NATO's first two key goals: to deter a worse humanitarian crisis and, if necessary, to impede Serbia's ability to cause harm to the Kosovar Albanian people.[140] The basic moral character of the intervention seemed increasingly flawed. In the tradition of just war theory, some critics argued that it was unethical to choose tactics that effectively valued the lives of NATO troops—not to mention the political well-being of Western leaders—as far more important than the lives of the ethnic Albanians on whose behalf the air campaign was purportedly being fought.[141] In our view, the question was not whether NATO pilots were dying—it was certainly best that they were not—but whether NATO's chosen tactics were effectively accomplishing their mission. Clearly, they were failing to do so.

Even if no NATO ground force could have been deployed quickly enough to stop the ethnic expulsion campaign as it unfolded, there were other important reasons to consider preparing an invasion from the war's early going. One was the possibility that Serbia would, at some point, start slaughtering large numbers of Kosovars, with NATO unable to do anything to prevent it. A second concern was that displaced ethnic Albanians would lack food and would starve to death in large numbers. Serb forces had been taking steps to reduce food stocks in Kosovo since the summer of 1998, and it was not clear that the international community would find a reasonably safe way to get food to the internally displaced.[142] Indeed, it was concern over these internally displaced persons that motivated much of the rethinking of ground options that occurred toward the war's end. Critics also thought that clearly being prepared to undertake a ground invasion might coerce Milosevic into an early end to the war, sparing some of the damage to Kosovo and its population that would otherwise result. Finally, by keeping the ground force option viable, NATO would have signaled its unwavering intention to win the war, which was not otherwise obvious to observers in Western countries or, quite likely, in Serbia.

Within the first week or so of NATO's bombing campaign, many members of the Congress, former officials, and scholars began to argue that the United States and its allies should seriously consider an invasion of Kosovo.

Some advocated simply planning for such a possibility—and saying so publicly; others argued for promptly beginning deployments to countries bordering Serbia.[143] Proponents of a ground option covered the political landscape. Notable were former national security advisers Brent Scowcroft, Zbigniew Brzezinski, and Henry Kissinger as well as former NATO supreme commander General George Joulwan.[144] On Capitol Hill, Republican Senators John McCain, Richard Lugar, and Chuck Hagel joined their Democratic colleagues Chuck Robb, Joseph Biden, Joseph Lieberman, and John Kerry to make a similar pitch in the war's early going. All emphasized that NATO had to succeed now that it was committed to the conflict—and thus that no option could be taken off the table.[145]

Similar thinking even seeped out of the Clinton administration. According to senior State Department officials, Madeleine Albright also argued for a credible threat of ground invasion. Failing that, she advocated preparing to deploy NATO ground units into a "semipermissive environment," in which Serb forces would have partially but not fully withdrawn from Kosovo.[146] On March 28, Air Force Chief of Staff General Michael Ryan was quoted in the *New York Times* as saying, "I don't know if we can do it without ground troops."[147]

By early to mid-April, the British government was also advocating a ground invasion. After a visit to Brussels, where he received a detailed briefing from General Clark, Prime Minister Tony Blair became a strong voice in favor of using ground forces in Kosovo, at least once Serb forces there had been sufficiently weakened by sustained aerial bombardment. The rest of the British government was unified around this position as well and never wavered thereafter. This British resolve may have resulted in part from the fact that Blair was politically more secure than any other alliance leader. His party's 179-seat majority gave Blair control over parliament, and his popularity was so great that he had a virtual free hand in setting official U.K. policy.

Some also argue that Britain is generally more willing to accept combat losses than the United States at this point in history. Both countries ran risks in Desert Storm, but their experiences diverged in the early 1990s. In Bosnia Britain lost eighteen soldiers as part of a feckless UNPROFOR operation yet sustained its role in the operation.[148] At roughly the same time, the United States ended its participation in the 1992–93 Somalia mission after suffering similar numbers of losses. Still the U.S. aversion to combat casualties can be exaggerated.[149] When fully engaged in a conflict, confident of its leaders, and convinced that important interests are at stake, Americans do not shirk from combat or the casualties that may result from it, as not only Desert

Storm but also the Grenada and Panama invasions of the 1980s demonstrate. The United States lost 19 people in Grenada, 23 in Panama, and almost 400 in Desert Shield and Desert Storm; it also lost 43 people in Somalia, most of them not even in the fateful October 3, 1993, firefight.[150]

There were those who advocated a general invasion of Yugoslavia, either to simplify logistics, since NATO could have built up forces in Hungary more easily than in Albania or Macedonia, or to overthrow the Milosevic regime. In 1998 NATO military authorities estimated that 200,000 allied troops might be required to achieve that objective. The option was again considered officially in the course of the war in 1999 before being rejected. Most proponents of ground forces, however, favored a limited intervention confined to the territory of Kosovo. Proposals ranged from carving out safe havens to forcibly partitioning Kosovo into Serb and ethnic Albanian sectors (the latter presumably larger and allowed to become independent) to what was probably the most common position of ground force advocates: liberating the entire province but stopping the invasion at the northern and eastern edges of Kosovo rather than entering into Serbia proper.[151] Some invasion advocates would have tried to improve the odds of coercing Milosevic into capitulation by telling him that an invasion would mean Kosovo's independence but that a negotiated settlement would leave it as part of Serbia.

The Pentagon initially suggested that roughly 100,000 troops would be needed for the mission of entering Kosovo from the south and liberating most or all of it.[152] However, official estimates would grow in the course of the war, partly because Serb forces in Kosovo increased substantially from their 1998 levels and partly because the 1999 plans were made with a greater degree of caution and a larger margin for error. But general principles of defense planning suggest that the original figures were not unreasonable, especially in light of NATO's control of the skies. Had NATO limited its aims to the creation of safe havens within Kosovo, it could have gotten by using fewer forces. However, troop numbers would have had to be substantial nonetheless—probably at least 50,000. Even the creation of safe havens would have required a forcible entry operation over the mountains of southern or western Kosovo; moreover, NATO would have had to assume that Serb forces might concentrate their strength where the alliance was trying to establish a safe area.[153]

Despite the groundswell of support for a more robust military campaign, up to and including the use of NATO ground forces in a combat role, it would be wrong to suggest that the Clinton administration was alone in its opposition to such an approach. Many in the Congress remained against using ground forces, just as they were frequently opposed to the scale of U.S. military involvement in the Balkans throughout much of the decade. Senator Pat Roberts (R-Kans.) stated on CNN that the deployment of ground forces was "a political judgment the president is not willing to take, and I must say there's not any support for that in Congress." Senator Kay Bailey Hutchison (R-Tex.) argued that any ground forces should be sent by the European allies.[154] After visiting the region, House Armed Services Committee Chairman Floyd Spence (R-Fla.) released a statement declaring, "I do not support the deployment of American combat troops in Kosovo, and I do not believe the American people are prepared for the inevitable consequences of a ground war in the Balkans if it comes to pass."[155] Congressman Sonny Callahan (R-Ala.) said he was "opposed to ground troops in Kosovo under any circumstances."[156] Public opinion polls showed majority support for the ground force option even if U.S. casualties resulted—but only as a last resort and in percentages that declined somewhat over the course of the conflict.[157]

Given the Balkan geography, a ground invasion of Kosovo would not have been easy. Some analysts argued that, even though Serbia only had about 40,000 troops in the province and limited capacity for reinforcement in the face of NATO airpower, the dearth of good ports and roads in countries such as Albania meant that NATO would have required a three-month buildup before launching the actual invasion—as well as, ideally, access to deepwater ports in Greece.[158] This analysis was essentially correct if one envisioned a NATO force of some 175,000—as plans developed in 1999 would have required—using heavy ground units from the U.S. military as well as some 50,000 British forces and 15,000–20,000 French troops.

Other analysts argued that there were simpler ways to defeat the relatively poorly armed and small Serb military—which, depending on the unit of measure, deployed only about one-tenth the strength of forces in Kosovo that Saddam Hussein sent into Kuwait in 1990. The keys to their proposed operation might have been NATO's helicopter-mobile and airborne forces—such as the U.S. 101st Air Assault Division and Marine Corps forces, Britain's Sixteenth Parachute Brigade, and France's Eleventh Parachute Division—in addition to medium-weight units such as those of the U.S. Marine Corps. The invasion force might have also included some of the nearly 20,000 NATO forces already in Macedonia and Albania, including Task Force Hawk.[159] In fact, the *Wall Street Journal* reported in early May that NATO planners had developed just such a plan.[160]

The helicopters employed by most of these units gave NATO a way to circumvent the minefields and entrenched Serb positions in southern Kosovo as well as the congested roads and underdeveloped airports in Albania, albeit at some danger of losing helicopters to accidents or Serb fire on their way into Kosovo. Air-mobile units could have set up bases by air, built them up, reinforced them with successive flights of their various helicopters, and then leapfrogged across a battlefield as desired.[161] The danger to their movement would have been real, but limited: Serb forces could not have confidently anticipated the flight corridors and landing zones that the helicopter-mobile units would have employed. NATO would have needed to have some tanks in Kosovo, in part for their psychological value and in part for protection against Serb antitank weapons, recoilless rifles, and antiaircraft guns in certain combat settings.[162] It would not have needed a huge force, however, and it might have been able to fly its heavy equipment into a Kosovo airfield after seizing it. Some troops and equipment might also have been moved by land through Hungary, Romania, Bulgaria, and then to Macedonia. With such a game plan, NATO might have conducted this operation within six to eight weeks of deciding to do so—admittedly at higher risk of casualties than in a large and armor-heavy operation.

As an alternative to a NATO ground war against Serbia, some argued for arming the KLA. Such an operation, perhaps emphasizing antitank weapons and mortars, could have been begun within days. It might well have made a major battlefield difference within a couple weeks. Senators Joseph Lieberman (D-Conn.) and Mitch McConnell (R-Ky.) introduced legislation that would have authorized such an effort. The White House resisted the idea (though it did once suggest that, in the war's final stages, ethnic Albanian refugees returning to Kosovo might be armed to protect themselves against fleeing Serb forces).[163] The idea of arming the KLA was rejected because it might have furthered Kosovar Albanian proclivities to seek independence, conflicting with NATO's position that Kosovo was an intrinsic part of Serbia. Those political risks were not necessarily as great as the human risks to the Kosovar Albanians of continuing to face a far stronger and ruthless Serb killing machine without an ability to properly defend themselves.[164]

Yet in the end, arming the KLA would have been a poor surrogate for a muscular NATO military strategy up to and including the threat of a ground invasion. Even a KLA armed by NATO would have remained outnumbered and outgunned by Serbia and thus incapable of controlling much land in Kosovo. In the interim, the humanitarian crisis would have persisted and could easily have intensified, particularly as the winter of 1999–2000 approached. Moreover, as the United States learned in Afghanistan and elsewhere during the cold war, arming friendly insurgents is a better way of bleeding and punishing enemies than of bringing conflicts to a close. In a war fought largely to save lives, hinging too much on such an approach would have been counter to the basic rationale of the mission.

A Bad Beginning

During the first month of Operation Allied Force, there were really two separate wars in the Balkans, which had little to do with each other. NATO was clearly losing the first; in fact it was barely a participant in the struggle between Serb forces and the Kosovar Albanian people. It was doing better in the second, in the sense of turning up the pain and pressure on Slobodan Milosevic, but it was hardly winning that conflict either.

Through late April, NATO was clearly failing to achieve its principal goals of alleviating violence against Kosovar Albanians and weakening Serbia's ability to perpetrate that violence. The monthly death rate among Kosovar Albanians was up at least twentyfold over the fifteen-month period before NATO's bombardment; the magnitude of the forced expulsions was at least five times that of the summer and fall of 1998. Serbia's military had lost no more than a few percent of its heavy equipment in Kosovo; its supply lines were under stress but were certainly more than adequate to sustain the actions of troops, police, and paramilitary forces within the contested province. NATO was achieving neither its humanitarian goals of saving lives and preventing ethnic expulsions nor its strategic goals of stopping aggression and stabilizing the region. The alliance showed unity and determination, but these together with its air campaign were insufficient to accomplish the desired ends. And hanging together in a losing effort was no great virtue.

Taking events up to March 24 as a given, adopting a more muscular policy early in the war was unlikely to have guaranteed a better outcome. It should have been tried nonetheless. Military and political preparations for an open-ended and intensive bombing campaign would have increased the odds that Milosevic would have buckled before or shortly after March 24. Even if the alliance resisted committing to a long air war in advance, every effort should have been made to keep the option public and prominent. That certainly could have been done, both before the war and in its early going. Other subtle ways of raising at least a veiled threat could have helped as well—for example, predeploying a larger and more robust ground force to Macedonia (perhaps on the valid pretext of preparing for a peacekeeping operation), sending necessary supplies for a ground invasion to Italy, and sailing several U.S. ships carrying heavy combat equipment into the Adriatic. NATO should have tried such measures. But in the war's first few weeks, it was not yet serious enough about winning to do so.

CHAPTER FIVE

Winning
the War

O N WEDNESDAY, APRIL 21, two days before the start of
NATO's fiftieth anniversary summit, British Prime Minister Tony Blair arrived in Washington to propose an invasion of Kosovo to
President Bill Clinton. This summit before the summit was among the most
momentous tête-à-têtes of the war.

In the most immediate sense, Blair failed in his mission. He made a strong
case for deploying ground forces and for using the NATO summit as an
opportunity for Washington and London to convince the other allies to support an invasion of Kosovo, but he was rebuffed by the American president.
At about the same time, Secretary of State Madeleine Albright, who had also
concluded by early April that ground troops might well be needed, was
broaching the subject within the administration, only to lose out to the Pentagon and the White House, neither of which was prepared to concede that
airpower would fail to do the job.

There was no reason for the president to be swayed immediately by the
counsel of either Prime Minister Blair or Secretary Albright. Albright in particular had been among the most confident officials, within both the administration and NATO, to predict that bombing would quickly convince
Milosevic to capitulate to NATO's terms. She had been proven wrong.
Clinton's other advisers, including Secretary of Defense William Cohen and
National Security Adviser Samuel ("Sandy") Berger, had reportedly been at
least somewhat less sure Milosevic would buckle, and they remained less
than convinced that ground forces would be necessary. Moreover, U.S. officials were convinced that a ground war debate could be divisive, preventing
the NATO summit from sending a clear message of resolve and unity, and

that an expanded air campaign might still prove capable of coercing Milosevic back to the negotiating table on NATO's terms.

Yet those talks just before the summit may have planted a seed in President Clinton's mind. As Blair pointed out, failure was not an option for NATO, and airpower was hardly guaranteed to work. Having heard the arguments, Clinton would have much to reflect on in the coming weeks. Ultimately, what he heard that April evening, together with a building frustration with the course of the air campaign and a keen awareness that NATO could not allow itself to lose the war against Serbia, convinced the president that he needed to do what it would take to win—including, it appears, a ground force invasion of Kosovo, if necessary.

The actual NATO summit itself also succeeded, if only because it did not fail. Major protests against the air campaign on the part of one or more allies were absent. No NATO leader forced a showdown with his colleagues over the bombing campaign; no one insisted on a rapid termination to the conflict or a radical change in strategy. Implicitly, if not vocally and visibly, NATO conveyed the impression that the war would have to be won, no matter what it would take. In fact, a number of NATO officials who attended the summit, including Sandy Berger, told us after the war that they had been struck by the cohesion and dedication of the alliance and never doubted the war's outcome from that point on (if they had before).[1]

This political momentum and resolve had more tangible manifestations as well. In the early days of the air campaign, most NATO leaders considered it a limited coercive action, likely to last anywhere from a couple of days to at most two or three weeks. Accordingly, attack plans were quite limited and short-term. By the time of the summit, however, NATO shifted to a rolling thirty-day war plan and braced itself for the long haul.

Part of the reason for the alliance's success in showing resolve during the fiftieth anniversary summit was the fact that the Blair-Clinton discussion about ground forces occurred before the formal convocation of heads of state, and the subject was then dropped for the rest of the weekend. As a compromise, just before the summit began, it was agreed that NATO Secretary-General Javier Solana could use his personal authority to ask General Wesley Clark to reassess the plans for a ground war that had been drawn up the summer before. In one sense, that decision had only limited significance. Planning, after all, is something military organizations do as a matter of course; it is not the same as taking steps to prepare for implementing the plans. Moreover, as noted, the planning proceeded on the basis of Secretary-General Solana's own authority and thus lacked the political significance of a directive from the North Atlantic Council. In fact, formally he had authorized only an updated reassessment of previous plans and not any new planning exercise. As a NATO spokesman, Peter Daniel, said on May 1 in response to a reporter's question about the ground force planning, "I think you are reading too much into it. Contingency planning is a normal occupation in this organization. . . . There is no plan for ground troops."[2]

But Daniel's comment was misleading. The Solana decision was significant. Within NATO, this compromise prevented disputes over the ground option from contaminating the spirit of solidarity at the summit. It gave both sides in the debate something to grasp onto. NATO countries were clearly willing to tolerate keeping the ground force option somewhere on the table, even if far from a prominent position. That said something. As it turned out, it reflected thinking that would strengthen greatly by the war's end. In the broader scheme of things, even though President Clinton turned down Prime Minister Blair's suggestion for an immediate decision to prepare a ground option in April, seeds were planted that would eventually begin to grow.

One can overstate the degree to which the events of April 23–25 constituted the war's chief turning point or the degree to which there was any crystal clear turning point. After all, NATO had started to increase the pressure on Serbia before the summit, expanding its air armada and its target sets within Yugoslavia throughout late March and April. It clarified its conditions for ending hostilities in early April and remained firm to them thereafter. The alliance had also declared its intention to impose a naval blockade on Yugoslavia and to pursue war crimes investigations against Serbia's top leaders.

That increasing pressure on Serbia, however, was countered in large part by the chorus of voices, including President Clinton's, that continued to insist that a ground invasion option was not on the table. Making matters even worse was uncertainty about how long the alliance could sustain the air campaign, how well it could withstand pressure to desist from Moscow, Beijing, and other key capitals, and how successfully it could impose a blockade and otherwise turn up the economic pressure on Milosevic. Meanwhile, Serbs were in control of Kosovo, and most ethnic Albanians remained out of their homes, if not the country. It was not until the summit that momentum began to shift in NATO's favor, and even then, the shift became only gradually apparent over several more weeks.

The NATO summit also marked a definite turning point in U.S.-Russian relations. Russian President Boris Yeltsin, perhaps aware that NATO was going to hold together after all, called Clinton from Moscow on the last day of the summit to urge a dialogue on how to bring peace to the Balkans. Yeltsin was intent on finding a way to end the war rapidly and on making sure that Russia would play a key role in bringing that about. His feelings were so intense and his focus so clear that he reportedly dominated the conversation with Clinton, talking for most of the seventy-minute conversation.[3] The Yeltsin government appeared to have realized that its interests lay not in opposing the war outright but in helping Milosevic get as good a deal as he possibly could: continued Serb sovereignty over Kosovo, a UN role in Kosovo's administration, a Serb sector of Kosovo if possible, and a balancing role by Russia and other non-NATO countries to any NATO troop presence that might ultimately deploy to the territory. Supported by European (especially German) efforts, the U.S.-Russian discussions led to a statement by the G-8 countries (Britain, Canada, France, Germany, Italy, Japan, Russia, and the United States) two weeks later and a month of intense diplomacy between Deputy Secretary of State Strobe Talbott, Russian special envoy Viktor Chernomyrdin, and Finnish President Martti Ahtisaari, who represented the European Union. The world was increasingly providing a united front against Milosevic, something that probably contributed to his surrender as much as any NATO bomb or the incipient threat of an invasion.

Victory was by no means assured by April 25. Amid misery in the Balkans, and for an alliance that was losing its first major war, the fiftieth birthday party was in many ways an unbecoming fête. But beneath the surface, at least, the tide was beginning to turn.

The Path to Victory

From the NATO summit through early June 1999, the Western alliance turned the war against Serbia around. Losing the struggle for a month or so, it then over the next month and a half decisively won the war, achieving an outcome that amounted to a clear—even if imperfect and tainted—victory.

The key to NATO's success was simple: alliance leaders decided that they could not afford to lose this war, even at the cost of a considerable expenditure of effort and blood if necessary. With its 35-to-1 superiority in military manpower, its 300-to-1 superiority in defense spending, and its clearly defined political and military goals limited to Kosovo, NATO was virtually assured of victory if it was prepared to devote adequate means to that end. Unlike wars in places like Vietnam, where Western powers also enjoyed tremendous advantages in materiel, NATO would have fought amid a supportive population had it intervened in a more muscular way in Kosovo. Also unlike the situation in the cold war in Southeast Asia, NATO was fighting a country cut off from international diplomatic and material support and one less prepared to suffer punishment than was North Vietnam.[4] Unlike the situation in the U.S. struggle against Islamic fundamentalism, or Britain's fight in Northern Ireland, or Russia's conflict with Chechnya, there also appeared to be relatively little reason to worry about Serb terrorist attacks against Western civilian targets.

The story of the second, and victorious, part of the war is primarily a story of the evolution in American and Russian thinking. Prime Minister Blair's continued steadfast support of a more muscular strategy, and his patient and dogged lobbying of Clinton to join him in promoting and pursuing that strategy, were important. But by itself Britain could not win the war, and its position was clear from the conflict's early going. What changed in the war's second half, what tilted the balance from a strategy that was producing failure to one that became sufficiently muscular to produce success, took place primarily in Washington and Moscow.

Immediately after the NATO summit, the Clinton administration put in place an integrated strategic campaign plan that combined military, economic, diplomatic, and other means to achieve core U.S. objectives. These objectives, as President Clinton was to state in the *New York Times* in late May, were three: victory in the war against Serbia (defined as ensuring that Serb forces were out of Kosovo, to be replaced by an international military presence with "NATO at its core"), holding the alliance together, and making sure the U.S. relationship with Russia was not undermined completely by these efforts.[5] Increasingly over time, the first goal became paramount. The military dimension of this campaign plan consisted of an intensification of the air war and accelerated planning for a possible ground campaign. Economically, the plan sought to enhance pressure on Serbia as well, partly by trying to enforce an oil embargo and partly by targeting the economic assets of Milosevic's cronies (both militarily and otherwise). Diplomatically, the strategy sought to find a way to convince Russia to endorse NATO's core demands and to pressure Milosevic to accept these as the best way to end the war. By early May, the National Security Council staff was given the task of pulling together these various policy strands into a thirty-day campaign plan, which could be rolled over for additional thirty-day periods as necessary.[6]

In Moscow, too, policy toward the Kosovo conflict changed markedly—and with positive results. Russia had reacted with particular vehemence to the start of NATO bombing in late March. Prime Minister Yevgeny Primakov had pointedly underscored Moscow's opposition by turning around his airplane in midflight as he was en route to the United States for his semiannual meeting with Vice President Al Gore. Rhetorical condemnation was followed by disturbing military maneuvers, including sending part of the Russian fleet into the Aegean and suspending Russia's link with NATO. Yet a Russian draft UN Security Council resolution demanding an end to NATO action garnered the support of just three countries, with twelve in opposition.

Realizing that Russian opposition was falling on deaf ears in NATO, President Yeltsin decided in mid-April to change tack, appointing his former prime minister Viktor Chernomyrdin as his special envoy for the Balkans. In contrast to the obstreperous Primakov, Chernomyrdin was interested in finding a way out Russia's self-imposed isolation by forging a compromise that would end NATO's bombing of Serbia. It would take another seven weeks of intense diplomacy to bring this about, but the effort proved crucial to the eventual success.[7]

NATO's military hammer was strengthening just as the anvil of its political cohesion, and its international legitimacy, was hardening. By early June, Milosevic was facing a true crisis. In Belgrade and other major cities, NATO was starting to physically destroy electricity plants, putting them out of action for days and thereby affecting water supplies as well. Alliance bombs were also striking more targets of immediate interest to Milosevic's chief associates and cronies, adding to the pressure of previous actions that had curtailed their access to offshore property and bank accounts. That escalation in the strategic air campaign came on top of earlier attacks against bridges, petroleum refineries, and other key infrastructure, which in turn came on top of years of sanctions against Yugoslavia. In Kosovo, better weather and more reinforcements for NATO airpower, combined with a militarily stronger Kosovo Liberation Army, were apparently starting to inflict Serb loss rates as much as five to ten times higher than in the war's earlier going. The alliance was talking more and more about a ground invasion of Kosovo, had committed to double its troop presence in Albania and Macedonia, and seemed just days away from making a decision to prepare for a ground war.

In the face of all of this pressure, Milosevic was confronted by Russia's decision to join the alliance in urging him to accept NATO's core demands: an end to the violence, all Serb forces to leave Kosovo, an international force to enter the territory, the refugees to return, and a political process to restore autonomy for the ethnic Albanians. Probably fearing that time would only work against him strategically from that point on—and that in the mean-

Figure 5-1. NATO Aircraft Committed against Serbia, January 1, 1999, to June 10, 1999

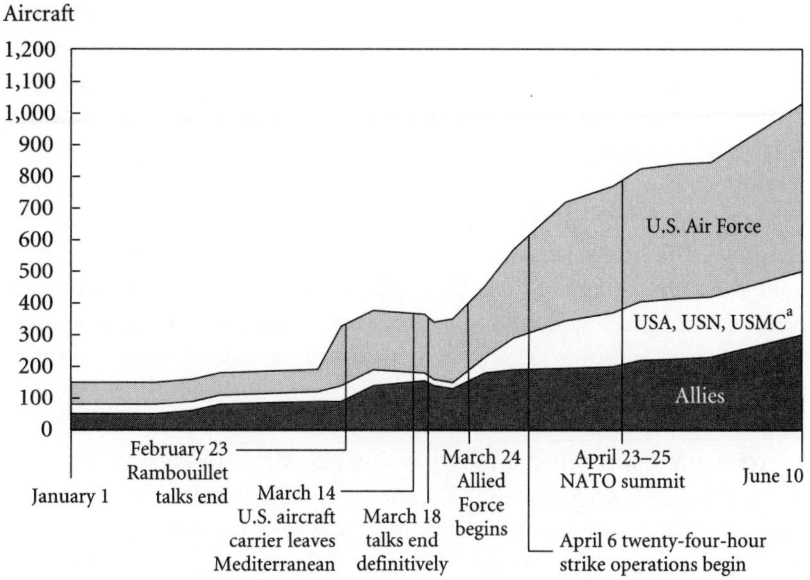

Aircraft

Source: Rebecca Grant, "The Kosovo Campaign, Aerospace Power Made It Work" (Arlington, Va.: Air Force Association, October 1999), p. 20; *Report to Congress: Kosovo/Operation Allied Force After-Action Report* (U.S. Department of Defense, 2000), pp. 31–32.
a. U.S. Army, U.S. Navy, and U.S. Marine Corps.

time he would endure more punishment from the bombing campaign in Serbia's cities and also on the battlefield—Milosevic relented.

NATO's Military Campaign Intensifies

Shortly after the NATO summit, many of the airplanes that General Clark had requested in mid-April arrived in theater. Authorization for an additional 176 U.S. aircraft was given on May 6.[8] (See figure 5-1.)

NATO's expanded air armada translated into an increase in sortie rates. The alliance averaged somewhat more than 300 total sorties a day, about 100 of them strike sorties, in the war's first month (and just 30–50 strike sorties daily in the first week). Thereafter, NATO typically flew more than 500 sorties a day, almost 150 of them strike sorties. Daily sortie rates were often in the range of 600–700 by the end of May and beginning of June;

indeed on some days the alliance exceeded 300 strike sorties, roughly a ten-fold increase over the war's first week. By late May planes were based in Hungary and Turkey (and benefited from overflight rights from Bulgaria and Romania), as well as Italy, Germany, France, Britain, and the United States. Support sorties were also being flown out of Greece and Spain.[9]

Weather improved as well, although it was poor again in early May. The Pentagon estimates that weather was a major factor on fifty-four days of the seventy-eight-day war. (To put it differently, cloud cover was greater than 50 percent more than 70 percent of the time.)[10] The majority of NATO's direct-attack precision munitions in Operation Allied Force were laser-guided bombs, underscoring the need for good weather, since laser light does not penetrate clouds.[11] Against fixed targets, there was often little harm in waiting a day or two for the skies to clear, so that laser-guided bombs could be used. In addition, the semiprecise joint direct attack munition (JDAM), guided by the global positioning system (GPS) satellite constellation and accurate enough to hit many targets but not small or mobile ones like tanks, could be dropped from B-2 bombers even in bad weather. But clouds did in large measure provide a sanctuary for Serb heavy weapons, which could concentrate their efforts (and thus their exposure in the open) on overcast days.

By late May aircraft were frequently flying below 15,000 feet to identify targets before returning to higher altitudes to deliver their ordnance. (Some missions, but not many, were flown at lower altitudes as early as April.)[12] Aircraft flew as low as 6,000 feet altitude. That was a reasonably safe height by that point in the war, judging by the fact that no planes were lost after May 2 (and it was certainly safer than the low altitudes at which Apaches would have flown).[13]

Military targets generally included the integrated air defense network; infrastructure such as barracks, ammunition storage facilities, command centers, and airfields; military industry such as ammunition production facilities; and Serb forces in the field in Kosovo. Several main Yugoslav Army units were hit particularly hard, including the 243d, 125th, 252d, and 211th Brigades.[14] By May 20 or so, NATO had destroyed about 100 Yugoslav airplanes, hit Yugoslavia's nine main airfields hard enough to reduce their operational capability by about two-thirds, and destroyed about 75 percent of the country's fixed surface-to-air missile sites.[15] NATO also attacked dual-purpose targets such as bridges, communications infrastructure, and petroleum-related assets, as well as political targets including Socialist Party headquarters.

Beginning in late April, NATO took Serb TV off the air in large parts of the country for long periods of time. The alliance also temporarily blacked out much of Serbia as early as May 3, using new CBU-94 munitions, which are essentially parachute-delivered canisters of carbon-graphite thread. These munitions short out power switching stations and transformers (but not electricity production facilities themselves). By the end of May, NATO launched more severe attacks against the electricity infrastructure, which disabled it for days and disrupted water supplies in several cities as well. (Serbia was known to have hundreds of backup generators, which could supply hospitals and other critical facilities with electricity even during general blackouts, although doing so could have required Serb armed forces to do without power in key command and air defense sites.)[16] Eventually, NATO was striking virtually all target subcategories that appeared on its original phase 3 list. The most prominent exceptions were bridges over the Danube in Belgrade and most targets in Montenegro. In addition, NATO spared the Serb cell telephone network. According to William Arkin, that may have been because NATO wanted to eavesdrop on conversations of the Serb elite. Or perhaps it felt that keeping the Serb elite interconnected would increase the odds of a coup against Milosevic, a goal the United States reportedly had sought since December 1998, with its so-called Operation Matrix.[17]

The tactical air effort also became much more effective toward the war's end. Late in May and early in June, NATO reported that it was striking two to four dozen heavy weapons a day, including artillery, tanks, armored personnel carriers, mortars, and air defense infrastructure.[18] As we discuss below, these numbers may not have been accurate, but there is little doubt that attrition increased considerably toward the war's end. Over the course of the war, mobile tactical assets made up about one-third of the total target set (NATO attacked 7,600 fixed targets and 3,400 mobile ones).[19]

One of the more noteworthy performances of the war was that of the B-2 bomber, which made its combat debut in Operation Allied Force. Crews flew all the way from home base in Missouri, given the difficulty of maintaining the aircraft at other locations, and dropped 656 JDAM, nearly 10 percent of all NATO precision ordnance used during the war. They did this in less than 1 percent of the war's total strike sorties. However, those sorties were rather expensive, given the length of the voyage, size of the plane, and maintenance requirements for its stealth surfaces. Also, and more important, the special radar that permitted JDAM to be delivered more accurately from the B-2 than from other planes could certainly be installed on other, nonstealthy (and hence cheaper) aircraft; the B-2's stealth shapes and coatings were not important to the use of these munitions. NATO's mastery of the skies meant that high-altitude bombers could fly over Serbia even if they were not stealthy, at least in all but the most heavily defended regions. In fact, though generally unsung, the nonstealthy B-1 bomber also performed quite well in Operation Allied Force. Its towed decoy confused defenses, as intended, and if it had been equipped with the same radar, it could have done essentially as well as the B-2. So Operation Allied Force does not prove the case for buying more B-2s, as some allege, even though the plane and its crews clearly did an excellent job.[20]

NATO's losses in the war were remarkably low, even by those conditioned to low losses from Operation Desert Storm, and even though Serbia frequently fired up to 30 missiles a day at alliance aircraft (some 700 were fired over the course of the war).[21] An F-16 went down in Serbia on May 2, making it the second and last fixed-wing aircraft combat loss of the war and the first since the F-117 loss on the night of March 27–28. Also, a marine Harrier jet malfunctioned and crashed in the Adriatic. Additional aircraft were hit by enemy fire, but all returned safely to base. Two army Apache helicopters crashed on training missions in Albania, the second accident tragically killing the two American crew members.[22] Those were the only two NATO deaths of the war, in contrast to nearly 400 U.S. deaths in the 1991 Persian Gulf War.[23] (The three U.S. POWs seized on March 31 were released to Reverend Jesse Jackson on May 2. On May 16, President Clinton authorized the release of two Yugoslav POWs.)[24]

The alliance pledged to impose a binding naval embargo against Yugoslavia in late April, and the European Union approved the decision effective May 1. That became a somewhat hollow promise, however, when NATO decided it would not physically enforce the embargo through a blockade at Montenegro's two main ports, Bar and Kotor Bay. But all was not lost. It did go into effect and was joined by a number of non-EU and non-NATO countries. In addition, the voluntary "visit and search" scheme at least had the benefit of preventing profiteers using ships flagged in cooperating countries from shipping oil into Montenegro.[25] NATO was also able to use its influence and its SFOR troops in Bosnia to clamp down on oil flowing from Bosnia to Serbia.[26]

NATO considered employing cyber warfare, but in the end carried out attacks against air defense computers only from jamming aircraft. Partly out of fear of the legal ramifications—NATO lawyers were worried about war crimes charges, if computers caused major damage to the civilian infrastructure—and partly due to the limited interconnectedness of many Serb computer systems, NATO reportedly did not carry out any hacking activities. The relatively rudimentary state of U.S. cyber warfare capabilities was apparently also a factor in this decision.[27]

NATO's Bombing of the Chinese Embassy

Despite the most careful efforts, NATO continued to make occasional mistakes in its targeting, sometimes killing civilians as a result. Its most politically and strategically important bombing mistake was the accidental strike against the People's Republic of China embassy in Belgrade on May 7. In that strike, three Chinese lost their lives due to a CIA mistake in identifying a building holding Serb military communications facilities, an error for which one employee later lost his job (and for which several others were disciplined). The tragedy led to reprisal vandalism against the U.S. embassy compound in Beijing and other American interests in China. More important, it was yet another major problem disrupting U.S.-Chinese relations.[28] Those relations did not improve until late 1999 (after a U.S. reparations payment), when efforts to bring China into the World Trade Organization got back on track and U.S.-PRC military-to-military contacts resumed. Even thereafter, U.S. relations with China remained tense over a host of issues.

Many Chinese and some Western journalists (most notably in Britain) continue to assert that the attack was not accidental, questioning how the world's best intelligence capability could make a mistake that the average citizen on the street of Belgrade would not have made.[29] However, a mistake it almost surely was. The best proof is that the attack's predictable damage—not only to U.S.-PRC relations but even to NATO solidarity—was far too great to justify the military benefit of silencing any Chinese military or intelligence assistance to Serbia that could theoretically have been provided from that building. Had the building housed a Serb weapon of mass destruction being prepared for use against NATO troops, for example, it is conceivable that the United States might have run the risk of hurting third-party neutrals to destroy it. Under the circumstances that prevailed, however, it is implausible that the attack was intentional.[30]

The Military Role of the NATO Allies

The European NATO allies played an important military role in the war, although not as important as their military role in the postwar KFOR operation, for which they have supplied roughly 80 percent of all NATO troops. In concrete military terms, the role played by bases in Italy cannot be overstressed: they were absolutely critical to the mission and were more impor-

Figure 5-2. Basing of NATO Aircraft for Operation Allied Force, as of June 1, 1999

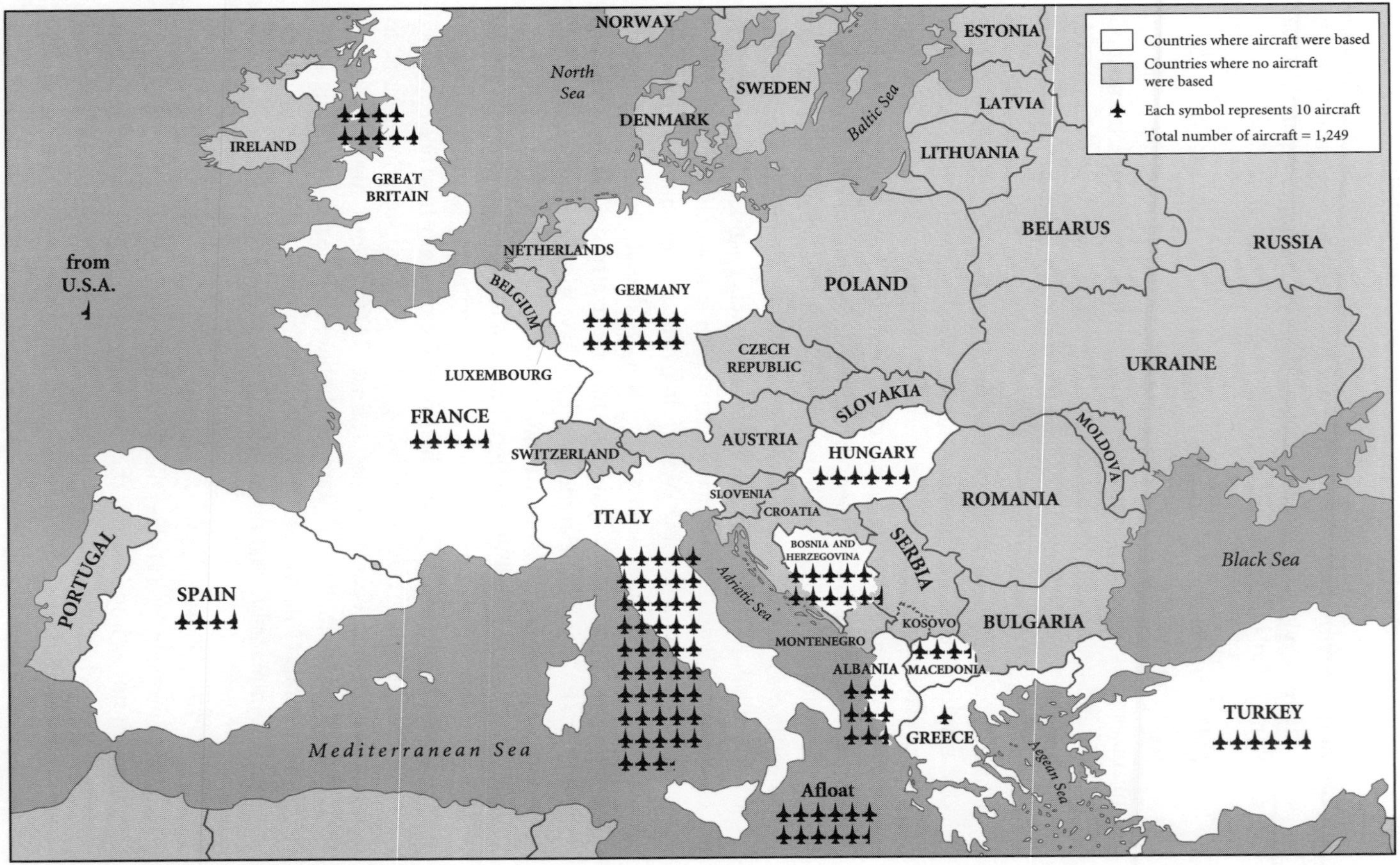

Note: Not all aircraft shown were actually employed.

tant than the aircraft contributions of any individual European ally. NATO based nearly half of its aircraft—about 500 planes, including helicopters—at sixteen bases in Italy; without them, NATO's tactical air campaign would not have been nearly as effective or ambitious. Of the remaining aircraft, at war's end nearly 10 percent were based in Britain (mostly bombers and tankers), about 10 percent in Germany (mostly fighters, tankers, transport aircraft, and AWACS), almost 10 percent on a U.S. carrier in the Adriatic, roughly 10 percent in Albania, almost 5 percent in Macedonia (mostly helicopters), about 5 percent in France (fighters and tankers), another 5 percent in Turkey (mostly fighters and jammers), and smaller numbers in Hungary, Spain, and Greece.[31] (See figure 5-2. For full details, see appendix table B-1.)

Counting both manned and unmanned aircraft, thirteen non-U.S. allies provided a total of 327 planes. According to the Pentagon's final report on the war, France marshaled 84, Italy 58, the United Kingdom 39, Germany 33, the Netherlands 22, Turkey 21, Canada 18, Belgium 14, Denmark 8, Spain 7, Norway 6, Hungary 4, Portugal 3, and NATO's common asset pool another 10.[32] They contributed nearly 40 percent of all sorties and about 47 percent of all strike sorties. Several European countries dropped laser-guided bombs; France and Germany operated unmanned aerial vehicles; Germany, among others, dropped antiradiation missiles on air defense sites. However, the European allies and Canada dropped only 20 percent of all bombs and 20 percent of the precision-guided bombs used in the war. They conducted less than 10 percent of the reconnaissance and electronic warfare effort.[33] (See table 5-1.)

Given that the European NATO allies account for about 40 percent of the alliance's total defense spending burden, these proportions are not entirely surprising. Together, however, the allies have an aggregate gross domestic product slightly larger than the GDP of the United States, so one might expect their aggregate defense spending to at least equal that of the United States, making possible a greater contribution. In addition, although they did have greater responsibilities than the U.S. armed forces in Bosnia, European militaries were far less committed globally than U.S. forces, which had substantial, long-standing deployments in East Asia and the Persian Gulf. So this level of burden sharing was less than ideal.[34] Also of concern was the fact that not all allies shared common secure communications technologies, forcing some air traffic control to be done on open lines—meaning that Serbs could listen in on discussions of when and where NATO fighters were operating.[35] The allies also lacked sufficient electronic warfare aircraft and other specialized assets.[36]

Table 5-1. U.S. Participation in Operation Allied Force, as Percent of
NATO Total

U.S. contribution	Percent
Sorties	60
Support (all types)	71
Strike	53
Electronic warfare	90
Intelligence/reconnaissance	90
Ordnance	
Precision guided munitions	80
Cruise missiles	95

Source: "Prepared Statement of the Honorable William S. Cohen, to the Senate Armed Services Committee," Hearing, *U.S. Policy and Military Operations Regarding Kosovo,* Senate Committee on Armed Services, 106 Cong. 2 sess. (July 20, 1999), pp. 5–6.

On the whole, Operation Allied Force certainly revealed what many already realized or suspected before: that European NATO members are not, on balance, contributing their share of the transatlantic security bargain. To quote German General Klaus Naumann, NATO's top military official during much of the war, in his capacity as chairman of the alliance's Military Committee, "There is a totally unacceptable imbalance of military capabilities between the U.S. and its allies, notably the Europeans. With no corrective action taken as a matter of urgency, there will be increasing difficulties to ensure interoperability of allied forces, and operational security could be compromised. Moreover, it cannot be tolerated that one ally has to carry on average some 70%, in some areas up to 95%, of the burden."[37]

The War on the Ground

Just as the air war was beginning to inflict real pain on Serbia, the war on the ground in Kosovo was intensifying. Serb forces concentrated much of their effort in the second half of the war in western Kosovo, near the border with Albania. In an attempt to cut off KLA supply lines, the Yugoslav military laid extensive minefields along the border, shelled suspected KLA strongholds in both Kosovo and Albania, and undertook numerous ground operations.[38] Some of these efforts also served to prepare their defense against any possible NATO invasion.

Even though most ethnic Albanians had already been forcibly expelled from their homes by Serb forces within the first month of the war, intense humanitarian concerns continued to arise. Important Kosovar individuals continued to be killed, such as the Rambouillet negotiator Fehmi Agani, who was murdered by Serbs in early May.[39] On May 22, nearly 600 Kosovar Albanian men who had been incarcerated, put on a near-starvation diet, and beaten were released from prison and allowed to leave the country. Their physical condition was appalling.[40]

More generally, Serb units continued to shell groups of internally displaced ethnic Albanians.[41] U.S. officials, including Defense Secretary Cohen and the State Department's ambassador for war crimes, David Scheffer, estimated that 100,000–200,000 Kosovar Albanian men were missing and raised the possibility that many might be dead. Concerns over hunger grew for the half million ethnic Albanians internally displaced within Kosovo. Yet only toward the very end of the war did NATO begin to seriously consider the option—risky to pilots and admittedly difficult to execute properly—of airdropping supplies into Kosovo's hills.[42] Thankfully, despite worries of mass starvation, the final death toll of the war appears to have been limited to no more than 10,000 or so Kosovar Albanians.[43] KLA Commander Agim Ceku estimated that perhaps 1,500 KLA fighters were among the dead (his tally included cumulative losses over fifteen months, however).[44] These numbers constitute a tragically high toll but are far less than were feared at the time.

NATO, and the international community more broadly, continued relief efforts in Albania and Macedonia, where the overwhelming majority of refugees remained. At war's end, there were roughly 800,000 refugees, of whom more than 400,000 were in Albania, more than 300,000 in Macedonia, 22,000 in Bosnia, and 75,000 outside the immediate region. (More than 13,000 went to Germany, more than 7,000 to Turkey, and roughly 2,000–6,000 to each of the following: Norway, Italy, Canada, the United States, France, Austria, the Netherlands, Sweden, Australia, the United Kingdom, and Denmark.)[45] Some 70,000 Kosovars fled to Montenegro, officially making them not refugees but internally displaced.

THE GROWING KLA.   The KLA strengthened considerably over the war's second month. An ethnic Albanian who had been a general of the Croatian army, Agim Ceku, became its commander on May 3.[46] Later that month, Hashim Thaci, head of the Albanian delegation at Rambouillet, declared that the KLA had 30,000 troops. He also stated that it would fight until it achieved independence, which has for years been the overwhelming political preference of the Kosovar Albanian people.[47] At the end of May, an American admiral, Thomas Wilson, estimated that the KLA had 15,000–17,000 fighters in Kosovo and 5,000 more in Albania—huge increases over the March 24 numbers of 5,000 and 1,000–2,000, respectively. There were reports that the KLA was financed by drug smuggling and that it had ties to Islamic fundamentalists, although a CIA report after the war contested such claims.[48] But the most remarkable, and most credible, story of its growth was the manner in which the global Albanian diaspora came to its support, providing financial assistance and additional manpower. Some money and volunteers came from the United States and other Western countries.[49]

NATO's collaboration with the KLA also grew. That was not a step the alliance took lightly. Officially, operations were not coordinated; even in practice, there were limits to the degree of cooperation. NATO did not wish to align itself explicitly with the KLA, given its concerns about the nature and goals of that organization. Nor did alliance leaders wish to lose whatever remained of their semblance of a neutral stance in the conflict; while clearly on the ethnic Albanians' side on the battlefield, they still hoped to play a mediating role in subsequent discussions over Kosovo's political future, if and when negotiations resumed.

On the other hand, the immediate issue at hand was the defeat of Serbia or at least of Slobodan Milosevic's will to sustain the conflict. To reach this goal, a reasonable degree of KLA-NATO coordination was only sensible. It made no sense for NATO to accidentally bomb the KLA as a result of insufficiently close communications (as did happen). Nor did it make sense for NATO to bomb Serb troops only when they were hunkered down; it was more effective to combine NATO's airpower with the KLA's ground forces synergistically and simultaneously, profiting from whatever the KLA could do to force Serbs out of their protected defensive positions. Using intermediaries such as the Albanian military, and possibly working through the CIA rather than direct military channels, the alliance knew what the KLA's general patterns of operations were by war's end.[50]

One notable case of KLA-NATO collaboration arose on June 7, when a large battle between Serb and KLA forces took place near the Albanian border, and NATO sent two B-52s to bomb the Serb positions. Initial reports estimated Serb casualties at 800 dead. Subsequent analyses did not confirm such large losses, but even if Serb forces got away, they undoubtedly knew it had been a close call. Not only were their armored movements constrained by NATO's ability to conduct "tank-plinking," at least in good weather, but even their infantry units now appeared vulnerable.[51]

Overall, it is not clear how effective the KLA became on the battlefield or how good the synergy was between KLA ground forces and NATO airpower (partly because the overall tactical effectiveness of airpower still cannot be discerned). But it does appear that the KLA was, at a minimum, growing in overall strength and remaining active in some geographic zones. Early battles generally went Serbia's way, but it was not clear that its forces in Kosovo would be able to consolidate their gains against the ethnic Albanian insurgents, particularly as NATO airpower was providing increasingly effective support for the KLA.

ESTIMATING SERB LOSSES.   What were the effects of the tactical battle on Serb forces in Kosovo? NATO officially estimates that about one-third of Serbia's initial holdings of heavy weapons there were destroyed by June 10. But there is a great deal of uncertainty surrounding these estimates, and they should be understood as rough—in fact, very rough. They may well be substantial overestimates.

Immediately after the war, the Pentagon and NATO both reported that the alliance had destroyed nearly 800 heavy Serb weapons. According to the Department of Defense, that total included 450 artillery tubes and mortars, 220 armored combat vehicles, and 120 tanks, with 80 percent of the damage done in the final two and a half weeks, after the KLA had begun its offensive operations.[52] Assuming these losses were mostly in Kosovo, they represented at least 30 to 40 percent of Serbia's initial armored strength there, given NATO's estimates that the March 24 totals were around 350 tanks, 430–450 armored combat vehicles, and 750 artillery tubes, mortars, and antiaircraft artillery. Depending on how many weapons in the last category are counted as heavy, that means that Serbia had 1,000–1,500 large armored weapons in Kosovo. However, the Pentagon and NATO estimate that Serbia managed to replace much of what it lost, so its overall firepower in the province declined little in the course of the war, even by these estimates.[53]

A sense of NATO's uncertainty over its "bomb damage assessment" can be gained by comparing the alliance's estimates made during the war with the figures released after the war. For example, on May 23 President Clinton claimed that NATO had destroyed one-third to one-half of Milosevic's heavy weapons in Kosovo. However, postwar Pentagon and NATO estimates suggest that the real damage at that point was no more than 7–10 percent (as an upper bound).[54]

Over the summer months, as NATO troops—together with many Western reporters—gained access to the Kosovo battlefield, cumulative estimates for the entire war declined as well. No more than a few dozen carcasses of heavy equipment were found on the battlefield. In testimony before the Senate Armed Services Committee in July, Defense Secretary William Cohen repeated a number of statistics on what NATO had destroyed in Yugoslavia, but estimates of armored losses were conspicuously absent.[55]

By mid-September, NATO had revised its original June 10 numbers downward some 20 percent. General Clark, together with Air Force Brigadier General John Corley, who led a NATO bomb damage assessment team, claimed that the alliance had badly damaged or destroyed 93 tanks, 153 armored combat vehicles, and a total of 389 artillery pieces and mortars.[56] Serb decoys explain some of the discrepancy of about 160 weapons between initial and final results. But only 33 decoys were actually found in Kosovo.[57] (By contrast, NATO's original estimates that Serbia lost about 100 aircraft were less in need of revision.) Still a downward revision of 20 percent in the number of heavy weapons destroyed is unsurprising. It is comparable, for example, to the revision that U.S. intelligence made in its initial estimates of how much Iraqi weaponry it destroyed in Operation Desert Storm.[58]

However, even the revised Serb loss estimates may not be accurate. NATO's methodology for estimating Serb losses was based not just on hard evidence but also on correlating the impressions of air crews with flight footage (generally taken at least several miles from the target, given the 15,000-foot altitude floor on most attack missions) as well as photos from spy satellites and other methods. In the end, in its January 2000 report, the Pentagon chose not to estimate actual numbers of Serb weapons destroyed or even just damaged but only the number of "successful strikes" against mobile targets, a vaguer formulation reflecting the uncertainty behind the estimates.[59] Finally, had losses been as great as claimed, one would have expected more evidence on the ground in Kosovo. Even if damaged equipment had been removed by Serbia for future cannibalization, one would have expected to find shards of metal, oil stains, and other remnants of major damage from explosives. Such evidence was reportedly absent in most cases.

Troop casualties are even harder to pin down. At one time, NATO estimated that it might have killed or wounded 10,000 Serb soldiers, police, and militia forces, or nearly 25 percent of their total wartime strength in Kosovo (assuming that most of the casualties were there).[60] But it failed to provide quantitative estimates for troop attrition in its briefing in September, and most evidence collected during the summer of 1999 suggests numbers lower than initially believed, even if greater than the 576 military losses that Serbia itself acknowledged. One investigative reporter, Michael Dobbs of the *Washington Post*, estimated that Serbia lost 1,000 military personnel.[61]

In the end, one thing seems clear: Serb losses in Kosovo, while perhaps not great enough to be decisive in the conflict, did become substantial by war's end. Moreover, they were almost certainly accumulating at a much more rapid pace at the end than was the case in the beginning, promising much more destruction in the weeks and months ahead, if the war were to continue that long. As General Wes Clark convincingly argues, given Milosevic's obvious reliance on his security forces, this trend must have been of major concern to him.[62]

THE IMPACT IN BELGRADE AND OTHER PARTS OF SERBIA.   Milosevic, whose armed forces were formed primarily by conscripts, banned foreign travel by military-aged men early in the war in an effort to mobilize extra personnel. Nonetheless, he had trouble raising extra troops, even after taking the extreme measure of mobilizing men over fifty years of age and stopping buses near Serb borders to make sure that draft-eligible men were not fleeing. During May, his problems increased. Reports surfaced of Serb men protesting their calls to military duty in Kosovo and of a number of actual desertions by forces in the field. Protests unfolded in certain towns, particularly where Milosevic was not especially popular and where reservists had been called up for duty in large numbers; as many as 2,000 people protested at Krusevac, in southern Serbia, for example. Protests also took place in Montenegro against the presence of increased numbers of Yugoslav army forces.[63]

This is not to say that NATO was becoming popular in Serbia. Most Serbs seemed unapologetic for their nation's basic policy of fighting for Kosovo. Some were savvy and thoughtful enough to distrust official Belgrade news accounts of the conflict and to worry and regret that reports of widespread atrocities against ethnic Albanians were true. But the general mood remained one of anti-Western diffidence, even as outright defiance declined and people became tired of the conflict.[64]

NATO's Implicit Invasion Threat

Even though NATO never explicitly threatened a ground invasion to liberate Kosovo, and never formally considered the option in the North Atlantic Council after the war had started, key allies signaled a growing interest in the idea as the war's second half unfolded—and did so in a way that no careful observer, including Milosevic, could fail to notice.

The basis for this speculation about a possible ground invasion was in part a set of plans that General Clark had quietly begun to draw up at SHAPE headquarters in Belgium.[65] At the urging of the U.S. government, NATO Secretary-General Solana asked General Clark, just days before the Washington summit, to take another look at the ground force options that the military authorities had pulled together in the summer of 1998. Although the purpose of the U.S. request and of Solana's endorsement was to provide an excuse for not having to discuss the possibility of a ground invasion at the summit, the effect was to give General Clark a virtual carte blanche to plan for such an eventuality.[66] The initial results of these efforts were briefed by General Naumann to the North Atlantic Council on May 4 and to President Clinton a day later, when the president visited NATO headquarters.[67]

General Clark's multinational staff examined a variety of options, including different invasion routes (coming in from the north, through Hungary, from the west through Bosnia and Montenegro, and from the south through Albania and Macedonia) and diverse goals (including forcing the removal of Serb forces from Kosovo, setting up safe havens for internally displaced Kosovars, and creating a safe corridor for their passage out of Kosovo). In the end, Clark settled on what one senior U.S. official called a "fail-proof force" of 175,000 troops that would enter mainly from the south through Albania with the purpose of driving the Serb security forces out.[68] Clark estimated that it would take about three months to deploy the force to the region and as much as one month of offensive operations in Kosovo to create a secure environment for refugees to return.[69] Assuming that it would be prudent to complete operations before the onset of winter, which could come as soon as mid-October, a decision on whether to begin preparations for a ground invasion would ideally be reached no later than mid-June.[70]

As Clark's people pulled together the plans for an invasion, the Clinton administration began to move gradually but unmistakably toward embracing the ground option. On May 18, in response to a reporter's question, President Clinton stated that NATO "will not take any option off the table."[71] Administration officials denied any contradiction with earlier statements from the president and vice president that they had no intention of using ground forces and that the ground invasion option was not under consideration. But after nearly two months in which the administration defended its air-only strategy, the shift in position was real. In fact, it was deliberate: a meeting of top-level officials on May 10 had explicitly decided that the administration's rhetoric about the possibility of a ground invasion should be changed.[72] President Clinton, who had publicly made the case in mid-May that the political costs of failure were greater than the political costs of casualties to American troops, braced himself for what might be necessary— and made it increasingly clear to the world where he was headed.[73] To emphasize that his May 18 statement was not a fluke or a mistake, President Clinton wrote in a May 23 New York Times op-ed that he did not rule out other (ground) options, though he argued for continuing the air campaign in the short term.[74]

On May 20, President Clinton met with his main advisers, including General Clark, to discuss the timelines for an invasion. Clark briefed the president on the various invasion scenarios he had presented to the Joint Chiefs of Staff at a session in the Pentagon's "tank" the previous day. Clark's preference was for the maximum force: 175,000 troops to take Kosovo, using Albania as the primary invasion route. Given limited allied capabilities, the United States would have to contribute upward of 100,000 soldiers to the effort. In view of the magnitude of the task and troop commitment, neither the president nor any of his advisers was at that point prepared to endorse this option. All realized, however, that the time for making a decision was running short.[75]

Meanwhile, NATO continued to build up troops in the region. Task Force Hawk, featuring twenty-four Apache attack helicopters, eighteen multiple launch rocket systems, fourteen Bradley fighting vehicles, and more than 5,000 soldiers, was in place by late April. The task force's deployment took seventeen days, after an initial expectation that ten days would suffice. It also remained unused in an offensive mode thereafter, though some of its radars were employed to track Serb artillery.[76] These setbacks aside, NATO's ground troop presence just to the south of Kosovo was growing in size and capability substantially. Having begun as roughly a 12,000-strong presence in Macedonia as the vanguard of a possible peacekeeping force at the outset of the war, NATO forces in Macedonia and Albania increased gradually for the next month and a half, reaching 20,000 by April 27 and 25,000 by May 12.[77] At that point in mid-May, Britain had roughly 6,400 troops in Albania and Macedonia, the United States roughly the same number (plus another 2,200 marines afloat in the Adriatic), the Germans 3,500–4,000, the Italians 3,300, and the French 2,800.[78]

Rather than immediately accepting General Clark's plan for a ground invasion, the president agreed at the meeting of his advisers with Clark on May 20 to support his request to increase NATO's troop strength along the Kosovo border to numbers approaching 45,000–50,000. Although ostensibly meant to prepare for the rapid deployment of KFOR into Kosovo once Milosevic had relented, Clark had advocated this buildup partly for its effect as an implicit invasion threat and also to speed the deployment of any such ground combat force should it ultimately be agreed on.[79] The North Atlantic Council approved the idea on May 25.

On May 27, defense ministers from the United States, Britain, France, Germany, and Italy met secretly in Cologne, Germany, for seven hours to discuss a possible ground war. At the meeting, Britain pressed its case for beginning immediate preparations for a ground invasion. To underscore Britain's seriousness, Defence Minister George Robertson told his colleagues that London would contribute 54,000 troops to the effort. And to underscore the seriousness of this commitment, the Defence Ministry prepared 30,000 letters, which it planned to send out in early June, calling up reservists.[80] Although neither France nor Italy was prepared to make a commitment on a par with Britain's, the defense ministers of both countries indicated that their forces would participate if an invasion was approved (albeit with substantially smaller numbers of troops). Only Germany and the United States remained noncommittal.[81]

By early June, pressure for a decision to prepare a ground invasion was becoming strong. Military commanders in Brussels had hoped for a decision by May 31 in order to have enough time to deploy the necessary forces to the region. Instead of a U.S. or NATO commitment, however, all General Clark received that day was approval to begin improving roads in Albania for possible use by heavy ground combat vehicles.[82]

It is doubtful that NATO had the engineering capacity on hand to build up roads, ports, and airfields quickly. Transporting additional engineering units to Albania from the United States would have required either a sealift—which is rather slow—or a large airlift operation.[83] Such logistical challenges, particularly severe in Albania, would have argued strongly for using the more capable Greek infrastructure as much as possible, thus placing a high premium on getting Athens' support for the operation, as well as Skopje's. NATO might have also made use of land routes through Hungary, Romania, and Bulgaria, and then Macedonia in any preparation for a ground invasion.[84]

But policymakers were still focused on more basic questions. On June 2, Berger called in a group of outsiders (including Daalder) who, while supportive of the administration's policy, had all in one way or another called for the deployment and possible use of ground forces.[85] Sitting around the large, oblong table in the Roosevelt Room, Berger told the assembled gathering that U.S. and NATO policy was based on four irreducible facts:

First, we will win. Period. Full stop. There is no alternative.

Second, winning means what we've said it means.

Third, the air campaign is having a serious impact.

Fourth, the president has said that he has not ruled out any options. Go back to 1: We will win.

Elaborating on each of these points, Berger noted that failure to win "would do serious, if not irreparable harm, to the U.S., NATO, and European stability." As for what winning meant, Berger reiterated NATO's long-standing demands for Serb forces to leave and an international military force "with NATO at its core" to deploy to Kosovo so that refugees could return home. He left no doubt that the phrase "NATO at its core" meant in fact that NATO would have to command the entire international military force in Kosovo; without this, there would be no political support for U.S. participation in the force.

On the third point, Berger noted that the air campaign was having a serious impact: "It is not dispositive, but it is real." Clear indications of its impact were not only the damage that bombing was inflicting on Milosevic's military and military-industrial complex but also changes throughout Serb society, including anti-Milosevic demonstrations, increasing desertions from army units, a greater willingness of opposition leaders to speak out, and a growing restiveness among Milosevic's cronies. On the last point, Berger mentioned that the United States and NATO were looking at a number of options for using ground forces. While he was not yet convinced the air campaign would fail to achieve its intended effect, the point at which one had to decide in favor of using ground forces was clearly approaching.

Immediately following the meeting, Berger retreated to the wood-paneled Situation Room in the White House to discuss the issue of ground forces in more detail with the president's other principal national security advisers. Before reviewing the ground force options, the principals addressed the question of whether a ground campaign could be avoided. Although no one was ready to give up on the air campaign, Clinton's national security team agreed that the war would need to be concluded in 1999. They rejected the possibility of the bombing campaign being extended into the following year, fearing for the well-being of the internally displaced within Kosovo and concerned that the alliance might not hold together that long. The remainder of the discussion focused on the ground options, which the president was scheduled to review with the Joint Chiefs of Staff the next day. [86]

In the evening of June 2, Berger sat down in his West Wing office to compose a memo to the president containing his recommendation on what needed to be done. Berger's memo laid out the president's options:

—Arm the Kosovars. But not only was it probably too late for this option to have a major impact, it would also mean another twenty years of conflict.

—Hold off until spring. But this option would leave tens, if not hundreds, of thousands of internally displaced Kosovars facing a brutal winter with neither food nor shelter. And if one were to create a safe corridor to allow them to get out of Kosovo, the military requirements would be little different than for a full-scale invasion;

—Go for a ground invasion. This was the only option left.[87]

In the end, the president apparently arrived at the same conclusion. As Berger told us, "He had made a decision that he was not going to lose and that he was prepared to go for a ground invasion." Indeed, Clinton himself said as much on the *Newshour with Jim Lehrer* the day after the bombing stopped.[88]

Privately, most NATO officials with whom we spoke in preparing this book also expressed the view that a ground war decision was close, based on their sense of where alliance thinking was headed, and that an invasion option would have elicited the unanimous approval of the alliance, assuming that the United States was prepared to join Britain in pushing for it. However, there is good reason to believe that President Clinton was willing to invade without formal NATO assent. As Berger told the group of outsiders on June 2, victory would be won "in or outside NATO," adding: "A consensus in NATO is valuable. But it is not a sine qua non. We want to move with NATO, but it can't prevent us from moving."[89] This raises the question of why, earlier in the war, the president felt unable to propose military options that some allies might resist. In effect, the president reversed himself on this point, just as he had on the basic notion of whether a ground war was a viable option. By this time he rightly realized that avoiding defeat was the overriding priority in the war and that all other considerations were secondary.

Milosevic probably did not know about all of these developments, but he knew of some. He may have had more sources of intelligence than a Western newspaper reader, and he may have suspected behind-the-scenes maneuvering within the alliance, given what NATO was saying and doing in plain view.[90] In any case, he was told about NATO's likely invasion plans by Viktor Chernomyrdin during the latter's first visit to Belgrade on May 27.[91]

In the end, it must be said that President Clinton never offered a binding, public commitment to deploy ground forces to Kosovo for a combat operation, and thus it would be presumptuous to claim that his mind was truly made up. Sending American troops to fight in a war of secondary importance to core American interests in a region legendary for its difficult combat conditions would have been one of the most important and risky decisions of Clinton's presidency. As Clinton undoubtedly realized, although public support for the war initially stood at about 60 percent in most polls, with more than 50 percent also supporting the use of ground forces in a

Table 5-2. European Public Opinion of NATO Intervention in Yugoslavia,
by Country, June 2, 1999[a]

Percent

Country	Approve	Disapprove
Britain	67	29
France	62	32
Germany	54	44
Italy	51	40
Belgium	42	45
Portugal	41	51
Spain	39	49
Greece	2	97

Source: Kosovo Task Force, "Kosovo Situation Reports" (Congressional Research Service, June 22, 1999), p. 6, based on polling by the French daily newspaper *Liberation*.

a. The question asked was, Do you approve or disapprove of NATO military intervention in Yugoslavia?

combat mode if necessary, the latter number declined somewhat over the course of the conflict and would certainly have declined much more had an invasion gone badly. (In fact, toward the end of the conflict, the American public became divided about the wisdom of even continuing air strikes, unlike most European publics, which remained generally supportive of the war; see table 5-2).[92] Those caveats noted, the evidence strongly suggests that Clinton was on the verge of making a decision to conduct a ground invasion, in which the likely American force would have constituted nearly two-thirds of NATO's total.

The Role of Congress

The Republican-led Congress, and particularly the House of Representatives, did not distinguish itself as a body in the war against Serbia. The Senate approved air strikes on March 23, before hostilities began. But the House got around to voting on the issue only a month later and then was as confusing and irresolute as possible about where it stood. On April 29, it voted not to allow ground forces into the Balkans without explicit prior congressional approval. It rejected a measure to require the president to end the conflict; then, in a tie vote, it also failed to signal its approval for the ongoing air campaign. Having refused to support both a ground war and the air war, the House next voted to approve the funds necessary to continue the war as planned! The best that can be said about these contradictory votes is that it would have been even worse to be consistent by both opposing the war *and* cutting off funding.[93]

Congress has understandable incentives to delay votes on the use of force and to send mixed messages when it does vote, but it cannot, in that event, expect to wield much policy influence.[94] It was undoubtedly this mixed voting record that contributed to the June decision of a federal judge to throw out a case charging that the president had violated the War Powers Resolution (which requires him to have explicit congressional support for war within sixty days of its initiation), on the grounds that Congress had not availed itself of its power to oppose the war with legislative measures and had not demonstrated a "sufficiently genuine impasse between the legislative and executive branches."[95]

Given that backdrop, what would Congress have done had a ground war been proposed and had the president requested congressional support for it? President Clinton pledged that he would seek Congress's support for a ground campaign, though that does not mean that he would, at that point, have recognized the constitutionality of the War Powers Resolution or otherwise have allowed Congress to prevent an invasion.[96] In the end, knowing that the president would probably go ahead with an invasion anyway, and knowing that many of its most distinguished and expert individual members (Democrats and Republicans) favored a robust strategy for victory, even a House of Representatives in which anti-Clinton sentiment was strong would have probably supported an invasion. It is unlikely that Congress would have voted to cut off funds, let alone overturn the president's inevitable veto of any such cutoff.

The Role of Key Allies

What were the views of other NATO countries, besides Britain and the United States, on a possible ground war? According to two senior French officials, some in Paris would have preferred to delay an invasion until 2000 in order to have more time to marshal France's forces. They wanted France to remain as central in any ground invasion as it had been in the air war, where its number of aircraft was first among European powers and nearly 10 percent of the NATO total.[97] France almost certainly would have lost this debate. Waiting until 2000 would have been unconscionable and unwise. It would have left internally displaced ethnic Albanians huddling—and possibly starving—in the hills of Kosovo throughout a long and cold winter, would have given Milosevic months to make false promises to NATO in an attempt to weaken the alliance's will, and would have likely led many Kosovar refugees to permanently settle elsewhere rather than retain hope for returning to their native land. Once it lost the argument over timing, however, France no doubt would have participated in an invasion, albeit with 15,000–20,000 troops at most.[98]

Italy, despite its leftist government, may have been ready both to support and to participate in a ground war. As the conflict continued, Italy appeared to come around to the view that the alliance had to do either more or less— and that the worst option was a drawn-out air campaign conducted for many months primarily from Italian soil.[99] Prime Minister Massimo D'Alema made statements to this effect in meetings at NATO headquarters in May. But Italy also sent out somewhat conflicting messages. Defense Minister Carlo Scognamiglio said that Italy would be a part of any ground war should NATO decide to wage one (a message he apparently also conveyed to his four NATO colleagues in Cologne on May 27); Foreign Minister Lamberto Dini disagreed.[100] In the end, D'Alema, as prime minister, probably could have carried the day, assuring Italian support and participation.

German Chancellor Gerhard Schröder publicly opposed the ground invasion option in May and suggested that Germany would block NATO authorization of any such proposal.[101] However, his position may have been more flexible than that, and in fact there is little chance that Germany would have thwarted a NATO consensus and even a reasonable chance that it may have participated with its own combat troops. As one senior German official put it, this war was a "coming of age" for a Germany ready and anxious to finally put the burdens of the past behind it, and participating in a ground war could have been the logical culmination of that progression.[102] Exactly what would have happened cannot be known, of course, but it is worth underscoring just how surprising Germany's strong role in the air war had already been. Not only did Germany have a Social Democratic–led government, but it included the pacifist Green Party as well. Foreign Minister Joschka Fischer, threatening to resign in a raucous party conference, somehow managed to keep his fellow Green Party members in line during the air war. It was the first time the German military undertook combat operations since World War II, and it did so in a particularly historic manner, dropping substantial numbers of air-to-ground munitions against radar sites in a country that had earlier been a victim of Nazi aggression. It is quite possible that Germany would have again done more than expected in any NATO ground invasion of Kosovo.

Greece, whose population overwhelmingly opposed the war, nevertheless had a political culture that recognized the country's core interests. Greece's solidarity with fellow Christian Orthodox Serbia made it understandably difficult for the country to embrace Operation Allied Force. On the other hand, its disputes with Turkey, its relative geographic isolation in Europe, and other factors made Athens value its NATO ties very dearly. It would have been hard-pressed to vote against a NATO resolution for invading Serbia and, according to most NATO hands with whom we spoke, would have been unlikely to deny the alliance the use of its ports, given how helpful they would have been in a ground operation.

No one can really know how NATO would have reacted to a strong U.S.-British push for a ground invasion of Kosovo, but there are, as noted, good reasons to think the alliance would have supported the proposal. It is important not to lose sight of how well the alliance performed as a body and an institution during this conflict. Individual governments worked to shore each other up; decisions were made only carefully and gradually, in the interest of maintaining solidarity, but once made, they tended to stick. Communication among governments was frequent and open and occurred at all levels—among heads of state, foreign and defense ministers, national security advisers, chiefs of defense staff, and even press spokesmen.[103] The purpose of these communications was both to shore up alliance unity and to head off potential problems before they threatened NATO's cohesion or undermined NATO's strategy. The overall impact was remarkable, if a bit unexpected. As President Clinton himself put it shortly after the war, "I was a little surprised that we had no more problems than we did in maintaining our allied unity, given the enormous pressures that were on some of our allies. And I think that gives you some indication about the depth of conviction people had that this was right."[104] It also gives an indication about how powerful and self-sustaining a politically unified NATO can be. Although the alliance was not yet unified around the ground war option, it was firmly resolved to win the war—meaning that it would likely do whatever it took to accomplish that end.

The lessons for the United States are threefold. First, it must respect its allies in order to ensure alliance cohesion. But second, there is no virtue in remaining united while losing; NATO must succeed in its major ventures. Therefore, third, the United States must be prepared to lead and do so resolutely and intelligently, in order to create a new consensus in situations where the existing one will not do. No other NATO country has the military muscle to do this in difficult circumstances that could involve sustained combat. For all of Britain's clearheaded thinking and resolve in Operation Allied Force, for example, the fact that it was supplying only about 4 percent of NATO's airpower in the conflict inherently limited its influence and its capacity for strategic leadership. Recognizing this power reality, London focused its pressure for a ground campaign not in Brussels but in Washington.

The Diplomatic Endgame

When, contrary to expectations, NATO's initial volley of air strikes failed to convince Milosevic to return to the bargaining table to resolve the issue of Kosovo's political future, the alliance was forced to consider what conditions Milosevic had to accept to end the bombing campaign. Fearing that he might soon offer to cease offensive operations (without withdrawing his forces from Kosovo) and propose a diplomatic initiative in an effort to persuade wavering allies to abandon their support for the air campaign, the NATO allies worked day and night to develop a set of conditions. That process proved to be exceedingly important in providing a precise bottom line—or what one NATO diplomat called "an irreversible commitment"—for the alliance as a whole to continue military action until Milosevic accepted all of its five conditions.[105] Specifically he had to

—ensure a verifiable stop to all military action and the immediate ending of violence and repression;

—ensure the withdrawal from Kosovo of Serb military, police, and paramilitary forces;

—agree to the stationing in Kosovo of an international military presence;

—agree to the unconditional and safe return of all refugees and displaced persons and unhindered access to them by humanitarian aid organizations;

—provide credible assurance of his willingness to work on the basis of the Rambouillet accords in the establishment of a political framework agreement for Kosovo in conformity with international law and the charter of the United Nations.[106]

With Milosevic showing little interest in accepting any of these conditions, it was becoming increasingly evident that the bombing campaign might continue for many weeks, if not months. This possibility created significant concern in key European capitals, notably in Berlin. There was, first of all, a deep-seated worry that domestic support for the bombing campaign would begin to falter over time, a particular concern for a German coalition government that included not only Social Democrats traditionally reluctant to sanction the use of force but also pacifist Greens. A second concern related to Russia, whose vociferous opposition was disquieting to many alliance members.

Fear of the domestic and international political fallout of a prolonged bombing campaign led the German government to try to involve Russia in a diplomatic initiative designed to end the war.[107] For Berlin, Moscow's inclusion in a diplomatic effort served multiple purposes. It was a sign to critics at home that Germany and NATO were attempting to resolve the crisis without having to bomb Belgrade into submission. Moscow was viewed as a major partner in the effort to create a stable Europe. And given Moscow's closeness to Belgrade, getting the Russians on board might actually help convince Milosevic to accept NATO's conditions.

After German Foreign Minister Joschka Fisher and Michael Steiner, Chancellor Schröder's national security adviser, traveled to Moscow for bilateral discussions, Germany presented its European Union colleagues with a six-point plan for ending the war on April 14.[108] Although the German initiative incorporated the key demands that NATO had publicly enunciated just days earlier, it went beyond the alliance position in at least four important respects: first, it proposed that a final settlement offer be negotiated by the G-8 countries; second, it called for the negotiation and passage of a UN Security Council resolution to incorporate NATO's demands and set forth the modalities of implementing a peace once Belgrade accepted these demands; third, it proposed that an interim administration of Kosovo be authorized and run by the United Nations; and fourth, it suggested that NATO agree to a twenty-four-hour bombing pause as soon as Serb military and other security forces commenced their withdrawal from Kosovo.

This final element of the German plan, the call for a bombing pause, led Washington to reject the initiative. For weeks before the start of the NATO air campaign, the United States had argued against proposals for a bombing pause after a set number of days. Recalling NATO's unhappy experience in Bosnia in 1995, when alliance military commanders suspended bombing after the first day, the Clinton administration was adamant that the bombing continue until Milosevic accepted NATO's five key demands and made substantial progress toward withdrawing its forces from Kosovo. The United States was supported in this position by other allies, especially Britain.[109]

Despite its rejection, the German initiative had two important consequences. First, Berlin had demonstrated the importance—if only for purely domestic political reasons—of engaging Moscow in a diplomatic initiative. Indeed Russia's interest in a more positive, diplomatic engagement was clearly boosted by the German initiative. That became clear when, on the same day that Germany floated the proposal, President Yeltsin appointed Viktor Chernomyrdin as his special envoy, a move that effectively pushed aside hardline oppositionists like Prime Minister Yevgeny Primakov (whom Yeltsin dismissed a month later). Second, the initiative contained a number of suggestions—including a role for the G-8, the need for a UN interim administration, and the importance of a UN Security Council resolution—that might make arriving at a diplomatic settlement less objectionable to Belgrade.

With Germany having greased the way, the Clinton administration sought to engage Russia in a dialogue. Washington's purposes for the attempted U.S.-Russian rapprochement were threefold. First, the German initiative demonstrated the importance of the United States and NATO being seen by their respective publics as trying to resolve the conflict diplomatically. Second, the vitriolic Russian reaction to the NATO bombing—with top officials, including President Yeltsin himself, warning of a new cold war and worse—made it vital for Washington to seek to reengage with Moscow in order at the very least to lower the temperature of the relationship among Russia, the United States, and NATO. Third, given Moscow's closeness with Belgrade, there was a sense that Russia could help to persuade Milosevic to give in. In what State Department officials termed the dual-magnet strategy, the idea was to attract Russia closer to NATO's position, and Russia in turn would attract Serbia closer to Russia's position.

Thus when President Yeltsin phoned President Clinton on the final day of the NATO summit, the United States was eager to seize the opening the phone call seemed to provide. Clinton proposed to send his top Russia hand, Deputy Secretary of State Strobe Talbott, to Moscow for immediate consultations with Chernomyrdin. In subsequent days, Vice President Gore also sought to use his long-standing relationship with the Russian envoy to ascertain Russia's seriousness in assisting in a diplomatic effort and to try to convince him to support NATO's position.

On May 2 Yeltsin again phoned Clinton suggesting that the time might be ripe for Chernomyrdin to meet with the U.S. president and others to see whether a common position could be worked out. The Russian envoy arrived in Washington the next day, carrying a letter from Yeltsin to Clinton outlining some of Moscow's ideas, including a proposal for the partial withdrawal of Yugoslav forces, the deployment of an international force carrying only side arms, and a bombing halt that would take effect before Serb forces would begin to withdraw.[110] Although none of these suggestions was acceptable, before meeting with Chernomyrdin President Clinton hinted that he would support a "bombing pause" if Milosevic accepted NATO's key principles and Serb forces started to withdraw. He also said there was room for negotiation on the composition of the international force to implement a settlement. "I think there's room for discussions—and I think there's room for discussion, within limits, about who's in this force and all of that.... [For example,] I personally think it's quite important that the Russians, perhaps the Ukraines, perhaps others who come from the Orthodox tradition, who have close ties to the Serbs, be a part of such a mission."[111]

The administration's heightened interest in engaging the Russians and its sudden support for a diplomatic solution appeared to suggest that the administration might consider compromising on its core demands in order to end the war. Even before Chernomyrdin arrived in Washington, rumors abounded about the content of possible compromises: leaving some Serb forces in Kosovo or agreeing to place the "international military presence" under UN rather than NATO command. Concern that the administration might be tempted to move in this direction increased when a senior administration official suggested that the president would find a way to sell any compromise. "Clinton is a better communicator than anyone else," this official told the *New York Times*. "Once Clinton decides that's what he's going to do, he'll sell it. If Nixon could sell the fall of Saigon as peace with honor [sic], Clinton can sell this."[112]

Concern about the administration's possible willingness to compromise was heightened on May 6, when the foreign ministers of the G-8 countries meeting in Bonn released a statement of principles that could serve as the potential basis for an end to the air campaign. Reflecting some of the ideas first contained in the April 14 German initiative, the G-8 statement appeared to weaken NATO's core demands in two key areas. First, the statement dropped the critical word "all" in front of the demand that Serb military and paramilitary forces be withdrawn from Kosovo, suggesting that some forces could remain. Second, the statement called for the "deployment in Kosovo of effective international civil and security presences, endorsed and adopted by the United Nations" as well as the "establishment of an interim administration for Kosovo to be decided by the Security Council."[113] Missing from these provisions was any mention of NATO; instead, the United Nations was to be accorded a key role in Kosovo after the war ended.

Although none of the provisions in the G-8 statement was inconsistent with NATO's five core demands, neither were they necessarily inconsistent with a softening of these demands.[114] This possibility was underscored when, on May 10, Milosevic told former UN envoy to Yugoslavia Yasushi Akashi that he would negotiate on the basis of the G-8 statement but only if no NATO troops from countries participating in the air campaign were allowed into Kosovo (which would have allowed the Czech Republic, Iceland, Greece, Luxembourg, and Poland as the only NATO countries to participate in the international force).[115]

The task of defining the actual terms of a final agreement fell to three individuals: Strobe Talbott, who represented NATO's interests, Viktor Chernomyrdin, who negotiated on Moscow's behalf, and Martti Ahtisaari, the Finnish president, who represented the European Union. The inclusion of Ahtisaari in the negotiations stemmed from an idea raised by Chernomyrdin at a breakfast meeting at Vice President Gore's residence on May 4 that was also attended by Albright, Berger, Talbott, and Leon Fuerth, the vice president's national security adviser. Over muffins, Chernomyrdin suggested that it might be useful if there was someone who could be the "bad cop," representing NATO's view (something a Russian representative could not and would not do), to balance his role as the "good cop." The UN Secretary-General Kofi Annan was proposed as a possibility, but Albright vetoed that idea. Instead, she suggested Ahtisaari, the leader of a neutral nation that nevertheless was supportive of the NATO action. Finland would take over the EU presidency in July, and Ahtisaari could therefore represent its interests well. Moreover, the Finnish president had considerable experience in dealing with nettlesome political issues and civil conflicts, including as a UN mediator in Namibia for thirteen years and as a UN representative during the Bosnian civil war. He was the right person for the job. "Voht!" Chernomyrdin replied when Albright suggested Ahtisaari. "That's it!"[116]

Ahtisaari was formally designated as the European Union's envoy for Kosovo on May 11.[117] He found himself almost immediately in a tug-of-war between NATO and Russia. Talbott, supported by the Europeans in NATO, wanted Ahtisaari to go to Belgrade alone and deliver NATO's demands in person to Milosevic. Chernomyrdin wanted the Finn to accompany him to Belgrade in the hope that he could get Ahtisaari to support the Russian position. Wisely, the Finnish president would have none of this back-and-forth. Instead, he insisted that he would travel to Belgrade only when the United States and Russia reached a common position on what Milosevic had to agree to for the bombing to stop. He would mediate between them, rather than among Milosevic, NATO, and Russia.[118] It was the right strategy. Rather than contesting it, Talbott, Chernomyrdin, and Ahtisaari set to work out common language.

From mid-May to early June, the three negotiators met four times, once in Helsinki, twice in Moscow, and once in Bonn. They quickly agreed on the least contentious issues: Yugoslavia's territorial integrity and sovereignty were not in question, an interim administration would be established by the United Nations, refugees would be allowed to return, international humanitarian agencies and relief would be allowed into the area, and the entire package would have to be endorsed by the UN Security Council.

But there were still four key sticking points. First, Talbott insisted that *all* Serb military, paramilitary, and police forces be withdrawn. Chernomyrdin insisted that Serbia have the right to maintain a considerable security presence on territory that all acknowledged was legally its own. Initially, he suggested that as many as 24,000 Serb troops remain to guard 8,000 Serb religious sites in Kosovo, but by the end he acknowledged that the level could be as low as 800–1,000. That was still more than the 200–300 Serb forces the Clinton administration believed could return to Kosovo after a secure environment had been established. Their role would be limited to monitoring border posts and guarding key religious and cultural sites.[119]

Second, Chernomyrdin insisted that NATO agree to halt the bombing campaign as soon as Milosevic accepted the basic principles of a settlement. Talbott dissented, insisting that the NATO-agreed language had to prevail. As the allies had said during the Washington summit, "NATO is prepared to suspend its air strikes once Belgrade has unequivocally accepted the [five core] conditions and demonstrably begun to withdraw its forces from Kosovo according to a precise and rapid timetable."[120]

Third, Talbott insisted that the international military force to be deployed in Kosovo have "NATO at its core," meaning a unified command structure under which the commander of KFOR would report directly to NATO's Supreme Allied Commander Europe, and, through him, to the North Atlantic Council. Chernomyrdin objected on two counts. First, he sought a UN rather than a NATO force as the basis of the military presence in Kosovo. Second, he insisted that Russian participation in the international force be separate from the NATO command structure. The United States objected to both these ideas, arguing that while the international presence could be endorsed or even authorized by the UN, it had to be run by NATO, an organization that had proven its competence in Bosnia. Moreover, it was clear that disparate chains of command were no way to run a military operation. The NATO-led operation in Bosnia had also shown that NATO command was in fact no impediment for Russia's participation.

Finally, there was the question of who could participate in the international force and where those forces would be deployed. Whereas Talbott made it clear that any country should in principle be allowed to contribute forces as long as it accepted the principle of unity of command, Chernomyrdin had different ideas. First, he suggested that Belgrade would not accept the deployment of soldiers from countries that had participated in the NATO bombing campaign. Second, he proposed that Russia contribute troops to the force but that these be deployed not only under separate UN command but also in the northern zone of Kosovo, where no NATO troops would be deployed. Talbott rejected both ideas; NATO would not make national distinctions when it deployed its forces, and the idea of a Russian sector in Kosovo was unacceptable, given the risk that this might in effect become a Serb zone that could one day be partitioned from the territory.[121]

Each of these issues was discussed in detail during trilateral conversations in Helsinki and Moscow, although there was little progress in narrowing the differences. The first breakthrough came during the third set of meetings, which took place in late May at Stalin's Kuntsevo retreat outside of Moscow. When the delegations sat down at a three-sided table, it became clear that the most important party was not present. All agreed that the real issue was how to get Milosevic to accept the terms necessary for the bombing to stop rather than for the three delegations to come to an agreement. The decisive element was what Talbott called "the man in the empty chair"— Milosevic. To emphasize his importance, Talbott at one point got up and placed an empty chair at a corner of the table. As various issues came under discussion, someone would point to the chair and wonder, "Yes, but what about that guy?"[122]

The talks in Stalin's dacha appeared to crystallize two things in Chernomyrdin's mind. First, it was clear that NATO would not back down from its key demands—which Talbott called "the family jewels"[123]—that all Serb forces would have to leave Kosovo (even if a few might eventually be allowed to return) and that the international peacekeeping force would have to have a unified command structure with NATO at its core. Second, it was evident that there was no gap dividing the Europeans and the Americans that Russia could exploit to its advantage. Therefore, if there was to be agreement, it would have to be mostly, if not wholly, on NATO's terms.[124]

Chernomyrdin traveled to Belgrade on May 27 in an effort to convince Milosevic that NATO's basic terms—particularly the need to withdraw all forces and the deployment of an international force with NATO at its core— were likely the best he could get. To pressure the Serb leader, the Russian indicated that it was Moscow's belief that NATO would be prepared to launch a ground invasion rather than settle for less and that, if NATO did so, there was little Moscow could or would do about it.[125] Milosevic remained unpersuaded. He was prepared to accept some NATO presence in Kosovo but only under three conditions. First, NATO forces in Kosovo were to be staffed by countries that had not participated in the air campaign (any NATO forces from countries that had participated in the air campaign could only be deployed outside Kosovo, in Macedonia or Albania). Second, Russian and other non-NATO forces were to be deployed in the northern half of Kosovo. And third, while NATO forces could be under NATO command, non-NATO forces were to be under a separate, UN command.[126]

Although this proposal suited Moscow fine (and likely originated there), it was clearly unacceptable to the United States and its European allies. Fearing an impasse and concerned that the war might escalate before the G-8 summit meeting scheduled to convene in Cologne in mid-June, President Yeltsin at this point appeared to have decided that a U.S.-Russian agreement to end the war had to be found. On May 30, Yeltsin's new Prime Minister Sergei Stepashin phoned President Clinton to say that Moscow wanted to find a way to settle all differences with the United States as soon as possible—and certainly before the Cologne summit.[127]

And so it was that Ahtisaari, Chernomyrdin, and Talbott arrived at the guesthouse on the Petersberg, outside Bonn, on June 1 to try to clinch the deal. All day and most of the night the negotiations remained stuck on two key issues: whether all or just most of the Serb forces would have to leave Kosovo and whether the international force entering Kosovo would have a unified command with NATO at its core. By the time the negotiators retreated to their bedrooms at 4:00 a.m., there was agreed text for all but those two points. The talks appeared on the brink of failure, and Talbott was not surprised to be awoken at 7:00 a.m. on June 2 by a CNN reporter asking for his comments on the apparent Russian decision to return home.

The report of Chernomyrdin's impending departure turned out to be mistaken, and when negotiations resumed, Chernomyrdin provided Talbott with a new draft agreement, this one containing the word "all" before the clause that Serb forces that had to be withdrawn. The text also stipulated that "an agreed number of Yugoslav and Serbian personnel will be permitted to return" to perform such functions as conducting liaisons with the international civilian and security presence, marking and clearing minefields, and maintaining a presence at Serb patrimonial sites and key border crossings. The text further noted that the agreed number of personnel that could return after the complete withdrawal of all Serb forces was small—"hundreds, not thousands"—and that details of their return would be negotiated in a subsequent military-technical agreement.[128]

Finally, the two sides resolved to shelve their disagreement on the composition and command of the international force. The actual text of the agreement to be presented to Milosevic stated that "the international security presence with substantial North Atlantic Treaty Organization participation must be deployed under unified command and control," but it did not refer to Russia's participation in the force. That issue was addressed in an elaborate footnote to the agreement presented to Milosevic, but which did not require Serbia's assent. As Talbott explained,

One way we were able to justify doing it in a footnote is that, in a very real sense, this was not Milosevic's business. Milosevic's business was to get out of Kosovo, to let the international community come in and run the place. Our business, including with the Russians, was who exactly was going to come in and what the relationship was going to be between NATO, as an institution, and the non-NATO participants, who were contributors to the Kosovo force.[129]

With that, the United States and Russia had a single, agreed text of ten principles, Milosevic's full acceptance of which would result in an end to the bombing. As soon as agreement was reached, Chernomyrdin and Ahtisaari departed in separate aircraft for Belgrade and a meeting with Milosevic. They met the Yugoslav leader for more than four hours, starting at 5:00 p.m. on June 2. Ahtisaari read aloud the entire document—informally known as the "ten commandments"[130]—while Chernomyrdin sat in silence (see appendix C). The key points of the document were

—an immediate and verifiable end to violence and repression in Kosovo;

—verifiable withdrawal from Kosovo of all Serb military, police, and paramilitary forces according to a rapid timetable (defined in a footnote as, for example, seven days to complete withdrawal);

—deployment in Kosovo under United Nations auspices of effective international civil and security presences, acting under Chapter VII of the UN Charter;

—safe and free return of all refugees and displaced persons and unimpeded access to Kosovo by humanitarian aid organizations;

—a political process toward the establishment of an interim political framework agreement providing for substantial self-government for Kosovo, taking full account of the Rambouillet accords, the principles of sovereignty and territorial integrity of the Federal Republic of Yugoslavia and the other countries of the region, and the demilitarization of KLA;

—a comprehensive approach to the economic development and stabilization of the crisis region.[131]

Milosevic carefully listened to Ahtisaari's recitation and then asked whether there could be any revisions. "No," Ahtisaari answered. They were not in Belgrade to negotiate, only to amplify the document. Milosevic then sought further clarifications. Would the UN be the authority in Kosovo rather than NATO? Ahtisaari answered yes, but NATO would have operational command of the international security force. Was the Rambouillet text still operative? Ahtisaari said no, noting that the G-8 agreement had superseded it.[132]

Having failed to open negotiations on the text and having exhausted his questions, Milosevic turned to Chernomyrdin and asked, "Is this what I have to do to get the bombing stopped?" Chernomyrdin said yes. He then asked the same thing of Ahtisaari, who responded "This is the best you can get. It's only going to get worse for you." Milosevic responded, "Clearly I accept this position."[133] Milosevic agreed to recommend the document's acceptance by the Serb parliament, which on June 3 dutifully voted 136 to 74 to approve the plan.[134]

Milosevic met again with Ahtisaari and Chernomyrdin at 1:00 p.m. that same day and was provided with the telephone numbers of General Clark and other NATO commanders, whom the Yugoslav military authorities were to call to begin military negotiations. That evening, as Talbott was briefing the North Atlantic Council on the details of the accord, General Clark entered the room announcing that the Yugoslav military had just called him proposing a first meeting on Sunday, June 6. When Clark reminded them that the bombing would continue until their force had begun to withdraw, they quickly agreed to begin talks on Saturday morning.[135]

In the technical military talks that took place over the next few days, Yugoslav generals resisted NATO's more specific suggestions about how to translate the broad principles that Milosevic and the Yugoslav parliament had accepted on June 3 into a concrete implementation plan. For example, they demanded fifteen days to withdraw forces rather than the seven that NATO offered. In the end they effectively got their way, since they were given eleven days to withdraw effective from a date several days after negotiations on the subject had begun.[136] The Yugoslav military was also successful in convincing NATO to reduce the military buffer zone within Serbia proper from fifteen miles to three miles in width, a decision that came back to haunt the 100,000 or so ethnic Albanians who live in that border region, since some suffered repression from Serb forces after the war (though Serbia's action was at times provoked by former KLA extremists).[137]

The exact details of the Serb withdrawal and KFOR deployment were spelled out in a military-technical agreement signed by the Yugoslav military and NATO military representatives on June 9 (see appendix C). The next day, NATO Secretary-General Javier Solana declared the cessation of the bombing campaign, though reconnaissance and patrol flights continued. The UN Security Council then approved a Chapter VII resolution spelling out the peace accord and implementation procedures for the force in Kosovo.[138] Despite some unhappiness with the resolution, Beijing could take some solace from the fact that the United Nations gained considerable influence over the ultimate political settlement in Kosovo. The open-ended KFOR mission will thus remain until another Security Council resolution is adopted, and all Security Council members will be able to play a role in the passing of such a resolution.

As Serb forces withdrew from Kosovo and NATO troops began to enter, one issue remained to be resolved: the question of Russian force participation in KFOR. Although Moscow accepted that the international military force would have a unified command structure, it had never agreed to placing Russian forces under NATO command. Nor did it accept the division of Kosovo into five military sectors—British, French, German, Italian, and U.S.—that excluded the possibility of a Russian sector (any Russian sector might be expected to revert to Serbia in the event that the rest of Kosovo ultimately gained its independence).[139] Indeed, to preempt NATO, on June 11—before NATO troops even entered Kosovo—some 200 Russian troops participating in the NATO mission in Bosnia left their posts and, with apparent Serb complicity, moved rapidly through Serbia into Pristina, deploying to the airport.[140] There were indications that Moscow decided on the airport so as to be able to send thousands of troop reinforcements from Russia by air and then to establish a de facto Russian sector in northern Kosovo—with forces not subject to NATO command or control. If that was the intention, the effort was thwarted by the refusal of Serbia's neighbors to grant Russian planes overflight rights.[141]

Russia then negotiated with the United States regarding its participation in KFOR. After thirty-three hours of intense discussions between the two countries' defense ministers, an agreement was reached on June 18 allowing the deployment of nearly 4,000 Russian troops into Kosovo.[142] Under the agreement, Russian forces would be distributed among the U.S., French, and German sectors rather than have a sector of their own. Although Russian forces would remain under Russian tactical command (with Russian officers placed in liaison functions at all levels of the command chain), Moscow agreed to place the forces under the general operational control of the NATO sector and force commanders. A similar arrangement prevailed in Bosnia and had worked quite well since early 1996, when Russian forces were deployed there. As a result, Russian forces began to arrive in mid-July.

After the War

Serb forces withdrew from Kosovo essentially as demanded. No major incidents occurred as they moved out and NATO forces moved in. The process followed the time deadlines set out for it: Serbia's air defense equipment was removed from the province within forty-eight hours, and its ground forces were gone within ten days.

More troublesome was the role of Russia. As mentioned, Russian troops left their posts in Bosnia on June 11, and on June 12 Russian tanks began moving into Kosovo without authorization from or coordination with NATO commander General Clark or the British KFOR commander Lieutenant General Mike Jackson. General Clark then demanded that General Jackson use helicopters to block the Russian path to the airport. Jackson, seeing the potential for a major international incident and believing that the Russian move could be reversed diplomatically, demurred, reportedly stating, "I'm not going to start World War III." He was later criticized for this alleged insubordination, particularly by U.S. Senator John Warner (R-Va.) and Joint Chiefs Chairman General Henry Shelton.[143] But, in fact, it was not insubordination, since NATO procedures allow for such decisions to be "bumped up" to higher-ranking military and political leaders, and British officials backed Jackson—as did the Clinton administration.[144] Moreover, it was wise policy; Russia had conceded to NATO on almost every major point, and some frustration among its military leadership was understandable. Smart money suggested that, once diplomacy had its chance to let cooler heads prevail, Russia would relent on this as it had on other matters. And so it did, albeit with some help from countries like Romania and Bulgaria, which denied Russia access to their airspace to fly in reinforcements.[145]

NATO moved into Kosovo in force, although the full process took a couple of months. By early September, there were 49,000 peacekeepers for the Kosovo mission, nearly the goal of 50,000. From the very beginning KFOR accomplished its mandate admirably. As outlined by UN Security Council Resolution 1244, the mandate included preserving the cease-fire, demilitarizing the KLA, creating a secure environment for refugees and the internally displaced to return to their homes, ensuring public safety, and providing support for the international civil presence. As a result of its successful deployment and also as an expression of Albanian confidence in NATO, virtually all ethnic Albanian refugees were home by the end of June. Indeed, this reverse exodus occurred at an even faster pace than the forced expulsions of late March and April.

If KFOR carried out its missions as intended, the same could not be said of international police forces that were to take over much of the public order functions from KFOR. In September, the number of international police was only slightly more than 1,000, and even in early 2000 the total remained less than 2,000. These totals contrasted with the initial goal for the force of 3,000, later increased to nearly 5,000.[146] (Even that latter goal is modest, translating to 2.5 police for every 1,000 inhabitants of Kosovo, which is below the U.S. rate of 4 law enforcement officials per 1,000 people.)[147] It is regrettable that they have been deployed so slowly, and the experience argues for steps to make police units more rapidly deployable. In February 2000, the Clinton administration released a presidential directive designed precisely for that purpose.[148] However, one should not overstate what police forces are capable of doing in a former combat zone like Kosovo. Significant numbers of NATO troops will remain necessary indefinitely. Even at full strength, the police force will remain modest in size. Its role will remain limited to ensuring public safety, leaving the task of deterring larger-scale violence, including possible threatening action by Serbia, to KFOR.

Unfortunately a considerable number of revenge attacks by ethnic Albanians against local Serbs took place after the war, leaving hundreds of Serbs dead.[149] Many appear to have been politically motivated, reflecting a KLA desire to uproot Serbs so as to consolidate the Kosovar Albanians' hold on the province.[150] Fearing further violence, a large number of Serbs fled Kosovo, cutting the prewar Serb population of at least 200,000 to no more than 100,000 by early 2000.[151] Even those who remained in Kosovo segregated themselves largely in three enclaves, with most settling in the northern part of the territory stretching from the town of Mitrovica to the border with Serbia.[152]

These developments were unfortunate and may even have helped Milosevic by allowing him to benefit from Serbs' resentment at their compatriots' treatment in Kosovo.[153] Yet they must be kept in perspective, something the Western media frequently failed to accomplish in the aftermath of the conflict.[154] The number of Serbs killed after the war—roughly 200–300 in the first nine months, for example—was high in a minority population that declined to 100,000 over that period. But it was not at all akin to what happened to the Kosovar Albanians during the war. Moreover, by early 2000, the annual murder rate was down to five a week, ten times less than in the summer of 1999 and about a quarter of the per capita rate in Washington, D.C. That is still too high but is not particularly surprising for a country recently at war. By early 2000 a Serb in Kosovo was no more likely to be killed than an ethnic Albanian, moreover.[155]

There is a silver lining to the ethnic segregation that occurred in Kosovo after June 1999. It has reduced the likelihood of interethnic violence by physically separating those who would commit it from their potential victims. Kosovo is a land that was at war a short time ago, and it would be unrealistic to expect passions to cool quickly. The violence that erupted in the divided city of Mitrovica in February and March 2000 shows what can happen when the two ethnic communities interact. The better part of wisdom in this case is not to expect them to interact peacefully in the foreseeable future. If the self-segregation of Serbs within Kosovo leads to a partitioning of the province, with a modest swath of the land to rejoin Serbia and the remainder to become an independent state (perhaps joined by small swaths of southeast Serbia outside Kosovo that are predominantly ethnic Albanian), there is no reason to consider that a bad outcome in and of itself, let alone a failure for NATO's war, as some would have it. Partition would not satisfy the noble Western vision of multiethnic tolerance and harmony, but it might keep people alive, allow them to rebuild their lives, and hold out hope for a future era in which hatreds would be dampened and ties between the different communities restored.

As for the KLA, it resisted complete demobilization, but ultimately was amenable to a form of demilitarization.[156] It missed its main disarmament deadlines by only days and ultimately voluntarily handed over more than 36,000 weapons to KFOR, compared to fewer than 2,000 that KFOR had to confiscate.[157] Among the KLA weapons handed over were 173 mortars and 300 antitank weapons; the vast majority (27,000) consisted of grenades. The KLA agreed to disband and create in its stead a Kosovo Protection Corps, of 3,000 individuals, that would focus on natural disasters and emergencies. Critics rightly saw this as camouflage for the KLA's real intention of retaining some type of military organization and, in addition, of establishing political control in Kosovo.[158] The commander of the KPC, former KLA battlefield commander Agim Ceku, acknowledged as much after its formation and also stated that many individuals who trained to join the KPC would promptly resign to allow more individuals to be trained.[159]

Still these concerns should be kept in perspective. First, the KLA had just watched virtually the entire ethnic Albanian population uprooted from their homes and seen thousands of friends and fellow soldiers killed. Although NATO provided assurances in the near term, the duration of its stay is uncertain, and Serbia retained the right of sovereign control over Kosovo in the longer term. Second, this small force—allowed to keep just 200 weapons and to carry only side arms—represented a reduction of perhaps 80 percent in the KLA's wartime manpower.[160] Finally, to the extent that the former KLA organization helps provide administrative functions and even some law and order in Kosovo, it should be welcome. How can the international community, slow to provide funding and personnel for security and administration in Kosovo itself, resent a local organization able to provide such necessities?[161] If the former KLA becomes further implicated in organized violence and crime, that would be deeply regrettable; and indeed there are still rogue elements among the former KLA.[162] But if it can help prevent violence and crime, we should welcome its role, even while moving quickly to make such a role unnecessary. It is the international community, not the former KLA, that currently bears responsibility for the slow development of Kosovo's own police, judicial, and administrative institutions.

Economically, the news from Kosovo has been mixed. Relief supplies moved into the region relatively quickly, in fact much more quickly than in many crisis and disaster areas in places such as Africa.[163] Reconstruction efforts began fairly quickly, too, and the large international Albanian community pumped vast amounts of dollars, marks, and lira into the economy. Thankfully, the actual price tag for reconstruction appears likely to be much less than had been feared: just over $1 billion.[164]

However, the NATO and UN presence also skewed the Kosovar marketplace. Many qualified citizens have been lured into working for this enormous international presence instead of working to build a sustainable local economy. In addition, funds for administration—notably, the salaries of Kosovar Albanian administrators—were not made available quickly, leaving many of these workers frustrated and impoverished (and allowing, if not encouraging, the former KLA to gain political strength). As a result, the atmosphere in Kosovo is more chaotic, and the economy less recovered, than might otherwise be the case.[165]

Not all of the economic challenges resulted from the war: Kosovo's communist economic system left it among the poorest parts of the former Yugoslavia.[166] Making matters worse, transforming that communist system to a market economy is difficult, since the international community still recognizes Serb sovereignty over Kosovo, impeding the privatization of many assets and the establishment of laws governing business transactions. Further, the donor community's focus is on infrastructure and other large-scale projects, which are prone to corruption and mismanagement (as in Bosnia), rather than on helping small businesses get established.[167] Taken together, these problems mean that it will take time—many years rather than months—before Kosovo can become a functioning market economy.

Kosovo's long-term political future remains undecided. Kosovar Albanian and Serb views are unchanged; if anything, they have hardened. Virtually all ethnic Albanians saw the accord ending the NATO bombing campaign as an interim measure on the path to complete separation from Serbia, even if Milosevic leaves office soon, as Yugoslavia's constitution requires that he do in the spring of 2001. Other Serb leaders are also, in general, quite nationalist and not sympathetic to the ethnic Albanian cause.[168]

When the war ended, there was a consensus that the issue of Kosovo's future was probably better left to the future. There were, of course, voices that suggested that it was unreasonable and impractical to expect a people that had been systematically attacked by a strongly nationalist regime to continue to submit to its jurisdiction.[169] But the magnitude of the postwar task and the certainty of widespread international opposition to any move toward Kosovo's independence led the United States and NATO officials to conclude that this was not the time to raise the status question. Instead, a decision on the territory's political future would be made only once the Kosovar Albanians began to rebuild their lives and political institutions, the former KLA had further distanced itself from its military ways, Bosnia's future had come closer to being resolved on its own merits, and Milosevic had left office, being replaced by someone the international community could negotiate with.[170]

By early 2000 prominent voices were beginning to question the desirability of deferring decisions on Kosovo's political future. The UN administrator in Kosovo, Bernard Kouchner, suggested that without greater clarity about what "substantial autonomy" for Kosovo meant—including the extent, if any, of Belgrade's remaining authority over the territory—it was impossible to administer the area effectively. Kouchner urged the Security Council to empower the UN administration by, in effect, allowing it to run Kosovo as if the United Nations rather than Yugoslavia were sovereign.[171]

Kouchner's plea suggests that it is no longer desirable to postpone the issue of Kosovo's status for future consideration. At the very least, the UN interim administration in Kosovo must be given the right to act on key questions as if it were sovereign so that critical legal, constitutional, and economic decisions need no longer be delayed. But even this step provides only an interim solution. Ultimately, the question of Kosovo's political status must be resolved. The key to a resolution must be recognition that any solution has to conform with the desires of the vast majority of Kosovo's local population. For now, these desires point invariably to independence—a fact that is unlikely to be changed even if the political leadership in Belgrade improves.

It is likely that Kosovo will one day be independent. The question for U.S. policy is not whether to support its independence, but how. Given strong European and Russian opposition, this is not the time to champion an immediate move to independence. Instead, Washington should work with its Contact Group partners to devise a series of steps—benchmarks, really—that Kosovo must take before it can expect international support for independence.[172] These steps could include abandonment of violence as a means of settling disputes or furthering political goals, full guarantees for minority rights, establishment of municipal, local, and Kosovo-wide administrations through free and fair elections, a functioning local police and judicial system, sustainable economic activity, and eventually a referendum on Kosovo's future status. By setting clear goals, the United States and its Contact Group partners would set forth an agreed path for Kosovo to earn its independence. There would be nothing automatic in this process; instead, the territory's future fate would depend on the behavior of its population.

A NATO Victory

Although there is some chance that war over Kosovo could have been prevented by a better diplomatic strategy, and there is much to criticize in the cavalier way that NATO began its war against Serbia, the alliance prevailed in the end. In this David versus Goliath struggle, Goliath just had too many advantages, even if that was not apparent during the war's first few weeks.

The real accomplishment of Operation Allied Force was achieved by the strength of the Western alliance. Possessing nearly two-thirds of the world's economic strength and military might, enough international political credibility to wage war even without a UN Security Council mandate, and the support of the Kosovar Albanian population, NATO had several fundamental advantages over an atavistic tin-pot communist dictator and his bands of criminal militias. Nor did the alliance shrink from standing up to Russia and China when they were wrong on the substance of the conflict and opposed the war without offering a serious alternative to stopping the humanitarian catastrophe. Nor did the West show quite the aversion to battle casualties that pundits had been claiming to detect, in the American political system in particular, since the conflict in Somalia in 1993. To their credit, politicians like Tony Blair and, in the end, Bill Clinton recognized that they could raise the possibility of a NATO ground invasion without dooming their political futures.

There is much to debate over how the Kosovo conflict was undertaken and conducted, but it would be wrong to lose sight of the broader message, and broader lesson, of the conflict. The world's greatest alliance in history, described by many as due to recede or dissolve after the demise of the Soviet Union, proved its capabilities and its continued relevance in Kosovo. It demonstrated that Western peoples, whatever their self-indulgences and flaws, do care enough about suffering in the world to support efforts to reduce or end it. That they do so selectively, unevenly, and imperfectly does not invalidate their accomplishments in a place like Kosovo. But it inevitably raises the question about what the war over Kosovo should teach us for handling other conflicts.

CHAPTER SIX

Conclusions and Policy Implications

T HE STORY OF WHY and how NATO went to war over Kosovo raises at least three important questions. First, was it possible to prevent the war without giving Slobodan Milosevic and his security forces free rein in Kosovo to wreak the havoc that occurred there in the spring of 1999? Second, did NATO win the war, or were the costs of the conflict so high, and the problems remaining in Kosovo after hostilities so severe, as to make any claim of victory a hollow one? Finally, how did NATO win? After enduring an attack by a vastly superior military force for seventy-eight days, why did Milosevic decide to capitulate?

These questions are of considerable historical interest. They also must be answered if we are to learn the diplomatic and military lessons of the Kosovo conflict. Based in part on our answers to these three central policy questions, we then offer specific lessons for U.S. policy about how similar crises might be addressed better in the future.

Key Conclusions

Could war in Kosovo have been prevented? The answer, we believe, is maybe. Although NATO could—and should—have crafted a policy that was more likely to avert war, doing so would not have been sufficient to guarantee success. It would have needed to combine a much more robust and credible military threat—at a minimum, the threat of substantial and sustained aerial bombardment and more likely an evident willingness to consider using ground combat forces to achieve its objectives—with an insistence that NATO be allowed to send a large, armed peacekeeping force into the province to demilitarize the Kosovo Liberation Army and protect the ethnic Albanian people from Serbia. In the end, of course, that is exactly what NATO did, but only after waging war for nearly three months.

We do not push this argument to the point of claiming that war was definitely avoidable. Crafting a credible military strategy would have been very challenging, given likely resistance from Congress and several allies. Even if NATO had backed its threats with muscular military preparations, it might still have failed to prevent war. Milosevic might have doubted the alliance's credibility and proceeded with his plan anyway. Thus we strongly disagree with those who argue that tactical changes in the way the United States approached the negotiating efforts at Rambouillet, and a somewhat different proposal for the modalities of a peace accord, could by themselves have produced a peaceful resolution. By the time of Rambouillet, Milosevic was firmly set on the use of force. Different tactics—including the willingness to deploy NATO ground forces to implement an agreement that might be reached—could possibly have proven effective earlier on, even as late as October 1998. But that was not tried. By the time the alliance was prepared to move in this direction, it was too late to convince Milosevic of the benefits of such a strategy. By that time, only a far more credible use of coercive diplomacy by NATO would have stood a chance of averting the war.

Second, did NATO win? We believe that, on balance, it clearly did—not just on the battlefield but also in terms of its broader policy and the achievement of its major aims in Kosovo. Kosovo is a much better place today than it would have been absent NATO intervention. To be sure, the alliance prevailed at a considerable price and only after it badly mishandled the war's early going. Still, even though NATO did not have an adequate strategy for the situation it confronted on March 24, 1999, a critique of its strategy should not be confused with a judgment about the war's final outcome. That outcome was not bad, at least by the reasonable standards against which such a conflict ought to be evaluated. Had war been easily preventable and the cause of justice served without resorting to violence, it would not be possible to argue that NATO won, for even victory in war is far worse than the avoidance of war. But as argued above, even though steps could have been taken to make war less likely, there is no assurance that these would have succeeded. By the same token, while a successful outcome provides no vindication for NATO's overall strategy, neither does a flawed strategy necessarily mean that the outcome was poor. The two issues are at least partly separate and must be evaluated as such.

Third, how did NATO win? We argue that there were probably several reasons for Milosevic's decision to give in, including the threat of a ground war and Russia's diplomatic role in the endgame. The NATO air campaign was the most fundamental factor, including both tactical strikes against Serb forces in Kosovo and the strategic campaign against Belgrade and other cities. But we caution against describing other factors as inherently less important. Airpower might best be thought of as the force driving Milosevic into a dead-end corridor and threatening to crush him against the far wall. But had NATO not remained unified, Russia not joined hands with NATO in the diplomatic endgame, and the alliance not begun to develop a credible threat of a ground invasion, Milosevic might have found doors through which to escape from the corridor despite the aerial punishment. The fact that each of these possible escape doors closed in late May and early June proved absolutely critical to the outcome. In other words, the role of the various explanatory factors can only be understood, we argue, in combination with each other.

Was War Preventable?

NATO's wartime success would, in the broader perspective, be no success at all if a different policy could have prevented war in the first place, on just and fair terms to the ethnic Albanian people, whom Milosevic had oppressed for years. On balance, we do not believe one can make a convincing case that war was clearly avoidable. The fundamental political dilemma in Kosovo became severe by 1998: both Serbs and ethnic Albanians wanted political and physical control of the province and were prepared to fight for it. Sufficient NATO threats, and a sufficiently adroit diplomatic approach, might have staved off that conflict. But NATO was dealing with a part of the world beyond the scope of its Article V security guarantees that an attack on one is an attack on all. Nor could it easily take sides in the looming conflict, since it harbored grave reservations about the nature of the KLA and, understandably, did not wish to countenance any further ethnic splintering of the Balkans. It also faced the traditional dilemma of undertaking preventive action: although conflicts are often easiest to stop when outside powers intervene early, before violence and extremism have developed self-perpetuating momentum, policymakers are unlikely to focus on problems that are not yet acute. Given this basic situation, not to mention long-standing congressional skepticism about U.S. military involvement in the Balkans and the equally ambivalent views of other key countries such as Russia, Germany, and Greece, it would have been quite difficult to prevent war.

We cannot, however, exonerate the Clinton administration and the alliance for their overall policy toward Kosovo. Even if war was not demonstrably preventable, there were many measures that could have been attempted to make war less likely, and some of these should have been evident to policymakers at the time, even without the benefit of the twenty-twenty hindsight we enjoy. Just as it would be wrong to claim that war was demonstrably preventable, it would also be incorrect to claim that it was inevitable. NATO had opportunities to make war less likely but generally failed to make use of them. In the most basic terms, had it coupled more convincing threats of extensive aerial bombardment with a demand that Yugoslavia allow armed NATO forces into Kosovo to ensure security and control the KLA, it might have convinced Milosevic to accept its demands.

There was a small chance that concerted preventive action immediately after the conclusion of the Dayton Accords ending the Bosnian war, coupled with the threat to reimpose sanctions if Milosevic refused to compromise on restoring autonomy to the Kosovars, might have led to a resolution of the conflict short of war.[1] Regrettably, that chance was missed. The complications of securing the implementation of the Dayton Accords overwhelmed Western governments, while the sheer exhaustion of negotiating an end to the Bosnian war meant that no one was prepared to devote the energy necessary to addressing a Kosovo problem that, at least to the outside world, had yet to reach crisis proportions. With time and energy in limited supply, governments deal with those issues most evident on their radar screens. Until early 1998 the problems in Kosovo did not reach that level.[2] Clearly, in retrospect, they should have. Even with the knowledge they had at the time, policymakers should have done more, for Kosovo had been a festering problem for years in what had become the most dangerous part of Europe.

The greatest obstacle to early action on Kosovo was the Clinton administration's decision—strongly supported by the European allies—to continue to rely on Slobodan Milosevic (as well as Croat President Franjo Tudjman) to secure the implementation of the Dayton Accords. In substituting for the recalcitrant Bosnian Serb leadership at Dayton, Milosevic had been the key to getting an agreement ending the Bosnian war in 1995. Thereafter Washington continued to look toward Belgrade for assistance in forcing the Bosnian Serbs to implement the terms of the Dayton Accords, which, with Western pressure, Milosevic more or less delivered. But the Yugoslav president's assistance came at a considerable price. Washington no longer had much leverage over Belgrade on issues unrelated to Bosnia. Thus the Clinton administration largely stood on the sidelines during opposition demonstrations in 1996–97 in Belgrade, and it never seriously pressed Milosevic to make concessions in Kosovo that could have forestalled the emergence of a violent opposition. It is clear now—as it was to many at the time—that this was a price too high to pay. Even on the merits, continued reliance on Milosevic for securing peace in Bosnia had serious drawbacks, not least because it undermined the notion that Bosnia was a single, fully sovereign state that with time might come to stand on its own feet. Moreover, Bosnia's essential stability from 1996 on was ensured by NATO troops, not Milosevic's goodwill, meaning that the United States overestimated its dependence on Milosevic for the most critical dimension of the Bosnia operation. It also meant that the Clinton administration never really explored whatever opportunity may have existed to use its leverage—diplomatic and economic, in the first instance—to persuade Milosevic to offer an acceptable deal to the Kosovars before the eruption of violence in early 1998.

Once tensions mounted and violence escalated, international attention to the Kosovo problem correspondingly increased. In January 1998 Contact Group countries set forth principles for resolving the conflict and the following month reiterated the need for maximum restraint and pursuit of a political dialogue.[3] However, the United States did not repeat the Christmas warning it first conveyed privately to Belgrade in December 1992 and that was reiterated twice by the Clinton administration in 1993—namely that "in the event of conflict in Kosovo caused by Serbian action, the United States will be prepared to employ military force against the Serbs in Kosovo and in Serbia proper."[4] By 1998 Washington feared the potentially negative repercussions of the threat for the Bosnia peace process and also believed that, given the large number of NATO troops in the region, Balkan policy was now fundamentally an alliance matter. Convinced that the allies would not back a serious threat, the Clinton administration backed off from reiterating the warning.

The question thus remains whether a stern warning of military action issued at that time or, at the least, shortly after Serb forces massacred more than eighty Kosovar Albanians in the first week of March 1998 could have stopped the conflict from escalating over the next year. The answer is perhaps. At that time, deescalation remained a very real possibility. Despite the tragic massacre, Kosovo was a long way from the humanitarian disaster it would become in only a few months' time. The local population still supported its elected "president," Ibrahim Rugova, including his nonviolent policies of civil disobedience. The KLA was little more than a small, unorganized, ragtag band of rebels that would most likely have disappeared once a serious political dialogue aimed at granting greater autonomy had started. Therefore a solution well short of independence may still have been possible and would have satisfied most of Milosevic's immediate concerns. Missing from the equation was an incentive on the part of Milosevic to settle. A credible threat of significant NATO military action could have been exactly what was needed to push the situation toward a solution.[5]

Of course, there is no guarantee that such a threat would have succeeded. Therefore, NATO would have had to be prepared to carry out the threat—and bomb for an extended period if necessary. Because military force is a blunt instrument of policy, it should never be invoked lightly and generally should not be threatened or used to settle low-intensity civil conflicts, such as the one developing in Kosovo in early 1998. However, by that point NATO already knew Milosevic, and what he was capable of—given the experiences of Croatia and Bosnia, as well as the history of conflict between Serbs and ethnic Albanians in Kosovo. The allies had ample reason to fear, and indeed to predict, a worsening crisis. In addition, the United States was committed to Kosovo's security by virtue of the Christmas warning. Under these circumstances, the case for early action was strong.

The reasons this threat did not materialize are familiar and not without some foundation: some allies might not have gone along, relations between the president and the Congress were poor, the potential impact on Bosnia was real (if overestimated), and there were legitimate questions about the prospects for a successful use of military force. However, even though the allies might have preferred inaction to threats and the possible use of force, a U.S. decision to issue threats could well have convinced them otherwise. While domestic politics militated against foreign adventurism, key Republican leaders had spoken out forcefully on Kosovo and would likely have supported a reiteration of the Christmas warning (issued originally by President George Bush).[6] If Bosnia's stability stood or fell on what Milosevic was prepared to do to support the Dayton process, then the vitality of the Bosnian peace process itself had to be addressed rather than avoiding the issue through the appeasement of Milosevic. In any case, Bosnia's stability was guaranteed principally by NATO, not by what Milosevic might do to moderate the Bosnian Serb leadership.[7]

Spring 1998 was likely one of the last moments that Western action might have influenced the course of events in Kosovo at relatively little cost.[8] By summer, the conflict in Kosovo had escalated as Serb forces responded to KLA advances by terrorizing the civilian population, forcing one-sixth of all Kosovar Albanians to flee their homes for urban areas or the mountains. As a result, the Albanian population became more radical in its demands; the KLA became stronger politically, financially, and militarily; and the Serb desire to take drastic measures in Kosovo correspondingly intensified. Under these circumstances, negotiations—never mind a negotiated solution—became increasingly unlikely. The differences dividing the two sides on the question of Kosovo's future status and the role to be accorded to Serbs and Albanians in running the territory were simply too large to bridge diplomatically. This was underscored by the fact that at no time until the Rambouillet conference in February 1999 did the two sides actually sit in the same room to discuss the issues dividing them, and even at Rambouillet they did so only a few times.

A policy that relied primarily on promoting a political dialogue between the parties was therefore bound to fail. By the summer of 1998, and certainly by early fall, it was clear that there were only three real options for Western policy. First, the United States and its allies could have acquiesced in what Milosevic and the Serb forces were doing and accepted the humanitarian consequences that this implied. Second, they could have supported Kosovo's independence and assisted the KLA in its attempts to wrest all or most of the territory from Serbia. Third, they could have imposed an international protectorate to prevent the inevitable violence and instability of the first two options.

The basic reason for this stark set of choices is clear: by late 1998, most Kosovar Albanians were more determined than ever to achieve outright independence from Serbia, and an increasing number were prepared to fight for it. Meanwhile, Milosevic could not countenance independence, given Kosovo's importance to the Serbian nation and to his own rise to power. The intermingling of Serbian security forces and KLA partisans was a volatile and deadly mix, which had to be defused if conflict were to be contained. Only a military victory of one side over the other, or a situation in which NATO ensured the ethnic Albanians' safety as well as the KLA's demilitarization, could have staved off escalating warfare. Partitioning Kosovo was not a promising option either; any partition would have had to give a far larger share of territory to the Kosovar Albanians than Milosevic would have accepted without a fight. At that time partition was for him tantamount to defeat.

It was not until early 1999 that the Clinton administration and its European allies decided that only the third option—an international protectorate—was acceptable. After Bosnia, NATO could not again ignore a humanitarian crisis of the dimensions that Milosevic's forces had indicated in the summer of 1998 that they were quite prepared (and by February 1999 were evidently planning) to inflict. Similarly, there was widespread agreement that Kosovo's independence would be destabilizing for the neighboring countries and the region as a whole. Therefore, the United States and its allies came to accept, as much by default as through analytical rigor, that imposing a de facto international protectorate in Kosovo was the only acceptable solution.

The Clinton administration came to this conclusion very late in the game. Had it decided sooner that an international protectorate was necessary for Kosovo, there may have been a chance to prevent war. (In an August 1998 cable to Washington, Alexander Vershbow, the U.S. ambassador to NATO, suggested this option. Although the cable was widely read, his recommendation was not heeded.) NATO's confrontation with Serbia in October 1998 provided an opportunity to persuade Milosevic to accept a de facto protectorate in a Kosovo that legally would still be an integral part of Yugoslavia. The United States, however, rejected a NATO ground presence under any circumstances. Instead of armed forces capable of separating the sides and enforcing both Serb and KLA compliance with the international community's demands, an unarmed monitoring force was deployed, which proved helpless in preventing an escalation of violence and effectively undermined NATO's threat to respond to violations from the air.

The Clinton administration not only was too late in deciding that an international protectorate for Kosovo was needed, it also was never really prepared to do what was necessary to impose this solution. Until the very end, the administration and its NATO allies clung to the hope that a deal would somehow emerge, that the threat of limited air strikes and, failing that, a few days of bombing would suffice to create the necessary incentives for both sides to accept a deal establishing a protectorate. The credibility of this threat was fatally undermined, however, by the administration's previous record as well as by the tentativeness with which it was issued. The Clinton administration had repeatedly failed to follow through on its threats to use force in Kosovo: it ignored the Christmas warning when violence first erupted in March 1998, failed to bomb when Milosevic violated the October agreement, and let three-plus deadlines pass unanswered at Rambouillet. Its track record on the use of force was also severely damaged by the tentativeness of the four-day bombing campaign against Iraq the previous December. Worse still, as the Rambouillet deadlines came and went, it failed to prepare for a sustained, hard-hitting air campaign against Serbia.

What is more, the administration consistently and openly ruled out the possibility of deploying ground forces in Kosovo to support the de facto protectorate that needed to be established. There was no way—not in October 1998 and not in February 1999—that anything less than a large and heavily armed NATO force operating with robust rules of engagement could have created the security environment in Kosovo necessary to stabilize the situation. At least 50,000 troops, as in the ultimate KFOR, rather than the 28,000 troops that NATO was prepared to deploy in February 1999, would have been required. It also would certainly have required a significant U.S. combat presence, if not actually an American lead. Yet only after the Rambouillet talks had been going on for over a week did the Clinton administration publicly accept the need for some U.S. troops. The president made the announcement in the peculiar forum of a Saturday morning radio address; furthermore, he minimized the U.S. contribution and ruled out its deployment in anything but a nonthreatening environment.

This reluctance to lead and to make the decisions necessary for policy to succeed has been explained by administration officials as the result of three factors. First, there was a belief that Congress would not support the deployment of yet more troops to the Balkans, even in a peacekeeping capacity.[9] Indeed some officials feared that even suggesting that ground forces might be part of the equation could have led Congress to cut off funding for U.S. participation in the NATO air campaign. However incredible the idea, such was the political atmosphere in Washington. Although the administration's reluctance to make a case for intervention under these circumstances is understandable, it provides no excuse. What is more, the White House undoubtedly overestimated the degree of congressional and, especially, public opposition to a well-argued case for intervention in Kosovo. The interests at stake were clear, including a fundamental interest in extending eastward and southward the security and stability that Western Europe has long enjoyed and in upholding the rule of law and protecting human rights throughout Europe.[10] Congress rarely opposes presidential leadership on major foreign policy issues, and when it does the opposition is more likely to be rhetorical than substantial. Although the current Congress may have been more likely to oppose Bill Clinton than most Congresses have been to challenge presidents, that reality is largely countered by the fact that the U.S. commitment to Kosovo's security began under a Republican president. Finally, public opinion data revealed a reservoir of potential support for the operation, provided the president made his case, the objectives were clear, and the likelihood of success was great. Indeed latent public support for the war (including the use of ground forces) was consistently greater than administration officials assumed.[11]

Second, the administration consistently argued that the prospect of using ground forces in a combat role would have created major fissures within the NATO alliance and posed particular problems for key allies like Germany and Italy. There clearly was no allied consensus on the use of ground forces, and it would have been difficult to create one. But in this type of situation, American leadership matters. Had Washington made it clear that it believed ground forces (including substantial numbers of U.S. troops) would have to be part of the equation, most if not all allies would have followed. Britain surely would have, France almost as surely so, and together with American forces these constituted the vast bulk of what was required. If necessary, they could even have conducted an invasion as a coalition of the willing rather than a formal NATO force.[12]

Third, the administration argued that Russia consistently opposed the use of force under any circumstances and would have reacted very negatively if U.S. and NATO troops entered Yugoslavia without Belgrade's consent. The administration worked assiduously to assuage Moscow's concerns and to gain Russian support for the basic goals of the military operation. Russia certainly would not have condoned an invasion, but it could not oppose the move militarily. More to the point, it is highly probable that the prospect of a ground invasion energized Russian diplomacy in late May; in his last meeting alone with Milosevic, Viktor Chernomyrdin reportedly warned him that Washington was about to decide to build up for a ground invasion and that Belgrade could not expect any assistance from Moscow.[13] In the end, Moscow's estrangement from NATO was not deepened by the growing plausibility of an invasion. If anything, the contrary was true; once it saw that the alliance was intent on victory, Moscow realized that it had no option but to work hard to convince Milosevic to accept NATO's basic terms, and it got increasingly serious about doing so.

So NATO's initial strategy left much to be desired, and was hardly optimized for reducing the odds of war. That said, even if the Clinton administration had been able to overcome congressional opposition, allied squeamishness, and Russian fears there is no guarantee that a more robust and forceful threat of military action would have convinced Milosevic to accept NATO's demands for establishing a de facto protectorate in Kosovo. There are many reasons to assert he might not have, not least his apparent belief that, if he could solve the Kosovo problem through force in a matter of days, he would confront the allies with a fait accompli. Moreover, he probably suspected that once NATO troops entered Kosovo, regardless of the specific auspices, they would not leave for many years—effectively depriving him of the territory.

Nonetheless, a robust Western strategy, promising sustained air strikes at a minimum and, better yet, the threat of a ground invasion if necessary was advisable. It would have enhanced the chances of success short of war. Failing that, it would have provided the alliance with a better chance of ending the war quickly.

Did NATO Win?

In the aftermath of Operation Allied Force, a number of policy analysts argued that NATO did not prevail in the 1999 war against Serbia. One went so far as to describe the war as a "perfect failure."[14] Is there a fair basis for these claims?

The answer, in our judgment, is unambiguously no. The vast majority of Kosovars are far better off today—and their future is much more promising—than would be true had NATO not intervened in Kosovo. Even if NATO's victory was not cost-free or absolute, it was real in this very important relative sense.

Milosevic unquestionably lost the war, and his defeat was overwhelming. He had to relinquish control over all of Kosovo and remove all of his troops and other security personnel. NATO-led forces established firm control over the territory, with an open-ended mandate that should allow them to stay as long as necessary—which the alliance can now afford, since the need to base huge numbers of forces in Germany ended with the dissolution of the Soviet threat. All Kosovar refugees were allowed to return, and nearly all did within just a few weeks, a powerful testament to their faith in NATO and their desire to return to their homeland. The principle that the Kosovar Albanians would, at a bare minimum, regain substantial political autonomy within Yugoslavia was firmly established by the UN Security Council.

Milosevic did salvage something out of his defeat. He protected the principle that Kosovo was part of Yugoslavia, at least for the short term. He kept NATO troops off the territory of Serbia proper (that is, non-Kosovar parts of the republic). He convinced NATO to reduce the size of the demilitarized zone within Serbia just north and east of Kosovo. He managed to have the mandate for KFOR placed under UN auspices, making sure that Russia and China would have some ultimate say over the terms of its withdrawal (and thus reducing the odds of an independent Kosovo). And he made sure that Russia would be part of KFOR; in fact he may have expected that Moscow would have its own sector, making it likely that even if Kosovo did someday become independent, at least a small part of it might remain part of Serbia.

Milosevic could view these as important consolations; he could also portray them that way to his domestic audiences. However, the most important among them—that Kosovo would remain part of the Yugoslav federation—was unsurprising in light of the fact that NATO itself insisted on such an outcome throughout prewar diplomacy and the conflict. Whatever Kosovo's formal relationship with Yugoslavia ultimately may be, the odds that the United States and like-minded NATO countries will ever again leave its people at the mercy of Milosevic or any other nationalist Serb are now very small. Russia did not obtain its own KFOR sector. If Kosovo is ultimately partitioned, with the ethnic Albanian element becoming independent or joining with Albania, the overwhelming bulk of the province's territory will surely remain under ethnic Albanian control. Those who described the war's outcome as a failure—perfect or otherwise—lost sight of the fact that Milosevic capitulated on every one of NATO's major demands. Where NATO softened its terms or offered concessions to Milosevic and to Russia (as in allowing the return of "hundreds" of Serb personnel to Kosovo), it was simply exercising good discretion in the effort to end the war quickly and successfully, since the drawbacks of these concessions were insignificant.

As for the war's effects on the lives of the Kosovar Albanians, one need only ask them: the vast majority are overwhelmingly appreciative of NATO's efforts and are happy to again live in their homes in peace and security. Refugees and the internally displaced have returned home—and in safety. The June 9 accords between NATO and Milosevic achieved the core conditions needed to protect the ethnic Albanians in Kosovo: specifically, keeping Serb military, police, and paramilitary forces out of the territory and placing a large NATO-led force with robust rules of engagement within it for what is likely to be a long stay.

None of this is to say that the NATO victory was absolute. Most important, as many as 10,000 people may have lost their lives in the conflict, and countless others were raped, robbed, and terrorized. Less important—but significant—was the tremendous damage to property. Moreover, in the aftermath of the war, half of the 200,000 or so Serbs who lived in Kosovo before the events of 1999 left the territory, some of them intimidated into leaving by ethnic Albanians operating with the encouragement of former KLA elements. Further, many Serbs who stayed in Kosovo left their original homes and resettled in Serb-dominated sectors, such as the northern part of the city of Mitrovica and the region around the Trepca mines. Thus the war was hardly low cost, nor has it made possible a harmonious multiethnic society within Kosovo.

But to see shortcomings in NATO's victory is not to diagnose success as failure. As bad as the war over Kosovo eventually became, it was not particularly bloody by comparative measures.[15] The death toll, while tragic, was far

Table 6-1. Humanitarian Emergencies due to Ongoing Conflict,
by Country, 1999

Country	People in need[a] (millions)
Sudan	4.4
Afghanistan	4.0
Angola	3.0
Ethiopia	2.0
Yugoslavia	1.6
Sierra Leone	1.0
Burundi	0.9
Colombia	0.7
Democratic Republic of Congo	0.6
Sri Lanka	0.5
Uganda	0.5
Eritrea	0.4

Source: National Intelligence Council, "Global Humanitarian Emergencies: Trends and Projections, 1999–2000" (August 1999), pp. ix–xii.

a. "People in need" is defined by the National Intelligence Council as total refugees from the country, internally displaced persons, and those requiring humanitarian aid in their home locations.

less than those of about two dozen civil wars around the world in the 1990s. It was about ten times less than the death toll of the Bosnian civil war (roughly five times less in per capita terms). Those who died numbered less than 1 percent of the total driven from their homes by Milosevic's forces—and that action could be, and was, reversed (see table 6-1, which is also relevant to the general lessons that we offer below).

A revealing perspective on the casualty issue can be conjured up by recalling that hundreds of thousands of displaced Kosovars were feared to be at risk of death from starvation or exposure during the war. These fears were not realized; nor were those of David Scheffer, the State Department's ambassador for war crimes, who worried that as many as 200,000 Kosovar men might have been killed. Had these possibilities come to pass, NATO's war would have clearly failed to save lives in Kosovo, and its battlefield success would have come at too high a price to be described as a victory in broad political or strategic terms.

One does not, of course, know what would have happened absent NATO's decision to bomb. Perhaps fewer people would have died, since Milosevic might have hoped that limiting the scale of atrocities during his already-planned Operation Horseshoe would minimize the chances of Western military intervention.[16] However, hundreds of thousands of Kosovar Albanians would surely have been expelled, without any possibility of returning. Some of these might have ended up in refugee camps, others unwelcome and un-employed in neighboring countries unable to absorb them. A major politi-cal injustice would have been done to the Kosovar Albanian people and to the principles of the European community of nations. Moreover, it is just as possible that Milosevic—who had already contributed to the killing of tens of thousands of Bosnians and Croats in other wars and who had driven 300,000 Kosovar Albanians out of their homes on the verge of the 1998–99 winter—would have caused far more deaths if left to his own devices. If he thought that NATO had no stomach for intervention, he might have used lethal force against many more Kosovar Albanians. Seen in this perspective, the loss of life that resulted in Kosovo and other parts of Yugoslavia from March 24 through June 10, 1999, while highly regrettable, seems relatively modest.

The NATO alliance—with help from other parties, including the Russian government and Finnish President Martti Ahtisaari—achieved all five goals it worked toward for the bulk of the war: Serb forces stopped their killing, they left Kosovo, NATO forces entered the province in large numbers, refu-gees were allowed home as humanitarian aid entered the province freely, and conditions for Kosovar self-government were firmly established.

NATO failed to achieve two of its three initial goals, as articulated by Presi-dent Clinton on March 24: to stop attacks on the Kosovar people and, if necessary, to limit Serbia's ability to carry them out. Some observers have concluded that, for these reasons, the outcome of the war was at best a draw for NATO. But the alliance achieved its final goal of making Milosevic re-verse course, and in the end that goal mattered far more than the others. This is especially true since the amount of irreversible damage done during the conflict—notably, the numbers of Kosovars killed—was modest by the standards of such wars.

NATO reversed a horrendous campaign of mass expulsion, contained a massive risk to innocent lives, preserved dignity and political rights for the Kosovar Albanian people, and upheld important international principles at the cost of up to 10,000 dead ethnic Albanians and perhaps 1,000–2,000 Serbs. That, by the standards of war, is a very good outcome.

If what happened during the war makes it difficult to argue that NATO did not win, others base their criticism on the war's aftermath. They assert that the reverse "ethnic cleansing" of Serbs by Albanians since June 10, 1999, undercuts the humanitarian and political underpinnings of Operation Al-lied Force. If NATO made Kosovo safe for ethnic Albanians only to make it unsafe for Serbs, this argument goes, how can it claim to have accomplished anything of note?[17]

This argument is fair on one level, since NATO and the international community must do everything possible to curb the forceful expulsion of Serbs and other minorities from Kosovo as well as to more generally stem violence in the territory. But it is starry-eyed at another level. The victims of the worst ethnic expulsions in Europe in two generations cannot be expected to forgive and forget overnight. It is simply not within the capacity of most human hearts to do so. That may be unfortunate, but it is reality. Moreover, the scale of postwar violence was far less than that in the spring of 1999. About 200–300 Serbs were killed in Kosovo in the first nine months after the war, in contrast to 5,000–10,000 Kosovar Albanian deaths during the conflict. As for ethnic self-separation, although an affront to Western ideals of multiculturalism and tolerance, it has served to make Kosovo a safer place since the summer of 1999. Per capita murder rates, for example, declined by a factor of ten from the summer of 1999 to the winter of 1999–2000. They are now below those of Washington, D.C., and the rate of Albanian-on-Albanian violence now equals the rate of Albanian-on-Serb attacks (when adjusted for the respective sizes of the populations). Although Kosovo in early 2000 was still a violent, ethnically tense place, Kosovo in the spring of 1999 was a land at war. This distinction cannot be forgotten. Surprisingly, it sometimes has been by people who should know better.

Had the war been preventable, NATO's Kosovo policy would have to be judged by different standards and would be difficult to declare a success. Indeed, as we argue above, there is some chance that a better NATO strategy—and in particular a stronger and more credible threat, certainly of a sustained air campaign and ideally even of a ground invasion—might have prevented the war without a bomb being dropped. But we do not, in the end, think that the odds of success would have been particularly high even for such a strategy. Moreover, it would have been extremely difficult, even for a U.S. administration less tainted on Capitol Hill than the Clinton administration, to rally the country and the alliance behind a ground war in the Balkans to resolve a crisis in a small place like Kosovo. The Clinton administration and NATO cannot claim to have achieved an overwhelming victory, since that term would only apply had they prevented war in the first place. Nor is it correct to claim—as the president and others in the administration have done repeatedly—that NATO did the right thing in the right way.[18] But the crisis was resolved reasonably well nonetheless, given the practical difficulties and challenges of the situation.

What about the broader geopolitics of the war? Most important are the relationships between Russia and NATO countries. These were certainly damaged by the experience, despite the fact that all parties ultimately worked together in pursuit of their common interest in ending the conflict. The war truly did worry Russian officials. They now see that NATO has become not only bigger but also more ambitious in its geographic scope and less apt to be constrained by UN Security Council procedures than they had believed before. These facts will reinforce Russia's concerns about a dominant West and a purportedly hegemonic United States. These concerns are now reflected officially in Russia's January 2000 document, "Concept of National Security," which takes a critical stance on the U.S. and NATO role in the world and particularly on Operation Allied Force.[19]

Russia's concerns should not be overblown, however—as they often are by critics.[20] Russia's reaction to Operation Allied Force probably has more to do with wounded Russian pride and a realization that its veto power at the UN Security Council will not always grant it a decisive voice in major international decisionmaking than with a heightened perception of a real security threat from NATO. Russia's recent decision to emphasize nuclear weapons more prominently in its national military policy is a natural response to the decay of its conventional military forces and its economy. Kosovo was not the main provocation, even if it may have provided a convenient public explanation for the change.

Some would argue that Russia's 1999–2000 war against Chechen rebels had much of its strategic origin in the Kosovo war. Moscow in fact did frequently refer to NATO's war against Serbia in defending its subsequent attacks against Chechen rebels (a conflict that probably produced thousands of civilian casualties as well).[21] However, it would be wrong to argue that it was a fundamental cause of the latter conflict, which involved core Russian security concerns and would not have been undertaken simply out of pique at the West.[22] It is possible that pro-Western voices in the Russian political debate were weakened by the legacy of Kosovo and had less of a restraining influence on subsequent Russian actions in Chechnya than they would have otherwise, but the absence of any real debate over that war in Russian politics throughout 1999 and into 2000 suggests that voices of restraint would have been few and far between in any event. Compared with issues such as economic reform, crime, and corruption, moreover, NATO's war against Serbia seems unlikely to be a dominant force in future Russian politics. Nor will it turn Russia back toward a communist or imperialistic form of government or even lead Russians to decide that they can cut their country's economic and political ties to the West.[23]

No Western official and few if any independent individuals in the West proposed using force to stop Russia's attacks against Chechnya in the months that followed Operation Allied Force. That fact should put an end to Russian worries that Kosovo would be a precedent for a more general doctrine of NATO interventionism that could even apply to their territory. In the words of Russian Foreign Minister Igor Ivanov, spoken in February 2000 after Russian President Vladimir Putin agreed to restore formal Russian relations with NATO, "What happened happened. Let us leave it for history. . . . We must move forward."[24] Operation Allied Force will not soon be forgotten in Russia, but it is fair to conclude that its long-term impact on U.S./NATO-Russian relations will be modest.

How Did NATO Win?

What does the available evidence suggest about the cause of NATO's victory? The answer to this question could be important for determining how to approach similar crises and conduct similar interventions in the future. In fact, the debate over how NATO would win began even before the war was over, with NATO Supreme Commander General Wesley Clark believing that Serb forces in Kosovo would need to be directly defeated, while the head of the air campaign, Lieutenant General Michael Short, argued that Milosevic's "center of gravity" was Belgrade.[25] Given the closed nature of the Yugoslav government and the inaccessibility of archives on the war, all that can be said with complete confidence is that a combination of NATO airpower, the prospect of a NATO ground invasion, and international diplomacy forced Slobodan Milosevic to accept NATO's terms for ending Operation Allied Force on June 10, 1999.

The conclusion that it was NATO's military effort and U.S.-Russian-EU diplomacy that led Milosevic to finally give in has been challenged by those who argue that the real reason for the Yugoslav leader's decision is that he got a better deal in June than was available to him in February or March. In particular, Milosevic is said to have gained in three ways: the administration of Kosovo by the United Nations rather than a western organization, the elimination of a referendum on Kosovo's independence, and restrictions on NATO's access to just Kosovo rather than all of Yugoslavia.[26] This argument is wrong in its main thrust and incorrect on most details as well.

First, whatever the specifics of the agreements that ended the war, one fundamental fact is unassailable: Serbia has no formal control over any part of Kosovo's territory and, with the exception of a small enclave in the north, Belgrade does not control anything that goes on there. Nor is it likely to regain control of the territory. Either Kosovo will remain a de facto protectorate for years to come or it will come under the effective (if not de jure) control of ethnic Albanians, who now constitute 95 percent of Kosovo's population. None of this would have been the case had Milosevic signed the Rambouillet accords. That agreement would have ensured the Serbs a role in the local governance of Kosovo and Belgrade a continuing stake in the territory as a whole. In accepting a political solution, Milosevic would also have gained the goodwill of the international community and perhaps a lifting of sanctions. He irretrievably lost that hope by instead resorting to massive violence against the Kosovar population—for which he and other key leaders were indicted by the Internation War Crimes Tribunal in The Hague.

Second, those who suggest that Milosevic got a better deal in the final settlement are also incorrect on the details. NATO's role in Kosovo today is far greater than it would have been under Rambouillet in terms of not only the size of its presence but also its mandate, which is more far-reaching because of the war (including in particular its requirement that all Serb forces be removed from Kosovo). The decision to anoint the United Nations rather than the Organization for Security and Cooperation in Europe (OSCE) as the principal institution for administering Kosovo was politically expedient but has no real import as far as Serbia is concerned. While Russia and China retain a say over the final status of Kosovo by virtue of their Security Council membership, the day-to-day task of administering the territory is in no way controlled by them—and their ability to exercise any influence over Kosovo's future is subject to the approval of the other permanent members of the Security Council, including the United States. As for a referendum, while it is true that there is no promise of a vote to determine the "will of the people," as Rambouillet would have allowed, there can be no doubt that the Kosovar Albanians are in a far better position to determine the territory's political future than they would have been if Milosevic had decided to deal before the war. NATO will not desert them now that it has seen what harm Milosevic in particular, and Serbian nationalists more generally, are willing to inflict on the ethnic Albanians. Finally, although NATO does not have a right to enter Yugoslav territory at will, its real interest was always Kosovo. Moreover, NATO's commander does retain the right, as part of the so-called silver bullet clause, to use force against anyone—including forces not deployed in Kosovo—whom he believes constitutes a threat to NATO and its mission or to any other party.[27] These robust rules of engagement give international forces more control in Kosovo than they requested at Rambouillet, and it is Kosovo that has always been the heart of the issue.

In short, Milosevic's diplomatic acumen cannot be regarded as the key to his decision to accept NATO's terms. The real explanation is far simpler: the combination of NATO airpower and a possible ground invasion confronted

Table 6-2. NATO Damage to Yugoslavia

Percent

Target	Damaged or destroyed
Defense industry	
Petroleum refining	100
Aviation equipment assembly and repair	70
Armored vehicle production and repair	40
Explosive production	50
Ammunition production	65
Lines of communication	
Danube road bridges	70
Danube rail bridges	50
Rail lines to Montenegro	100
Kosovo rail corridors	100
Kosovo road corridors	50
Army infrastructure	
First Army	35
Second Army	20
Third Army	60

Source: William S. Cohen, "DoD News Briefing" (U.S. Department of Defense, June 10, 1999).

Serbia with certain defeat, a defeat that neither Russia nor anyone else would save him from. As soon as that became apparent to him, Milosevic accepted the loss of Kosovo and concentrated on strengthening his power base at home.

THE AIR CAMPAIGN.   NATO's air war had two main thrusts. The strategic campaign against the Serbian heartland, featuring an effort to destroy military, dual-use, and some principally civilian assets, was complemented by a tactical war against Serbian forces in Kosovo, in particular the heavy weapons, logistical support, and supply routes that were sustaining operations throughout the territory. Over time, NATO airpower was able to inflict major damage in both these areas.

NATO's bombardment of civilian and economic assets throughout Belgrade and other parts of Serbia was undoubtedly an important factor in forcing Milosevic's ultimate capitulation (see table 6-2). The Serb war industry was largely destroyed, typically by 50 percent or more. Assets important for both military and civilian purposes—such as bridges, television and radio towers, oil refineries, and factories making vehicles or certain other types of dual-use machinery—were attacked from the war's early weeks. As time went on, NATO's gloves came off. Civilian assets with no more than indirect or secondary military purposes began to be hit. For example, electricity grids and transformers were taken down in much of the country toward the end of May and remained out of action long enough to disrupt water supplies. Cigarette factories, fertilizer plants, and the chemical industry were also attacked. Petroleum refining facilities remained out of action, as they had been since April, meaning that petroleum reserves dwindled. NATO also showed that it was willing to turn up the heat on Milosevic's inner circle, attacking his cronies' residences and businesses as well as party headquarters. These attacks came on top of a decade of sanctions and stagnation, which had dropped Yugoslavia's per capita gross domestic product roughly in half (to about $1,400 a year) and driven up World Bank estimates of the unemployment rate to about 50 percent.[28]

NATO airpower also did a considerable amount of damage to the Yugoslav military machine. Most of this campaign occurred in Kosovo, and most of that in the war's final weeks, when a fielded KLA force of nearly 20,000 fighters undertook tactical offensives in southern Kosovo. The air campaign also encompassed other attacks against the Yugoslav military infrastructure in Serbia (and occasionally in Montenegro).

The effects of the tactical air campaign are even more difficult to measure than those of the strategic bombardment effort. As discussed in chapter 5, it remains unclear how much Yugoslav equipment NATO destroyed and even less clear how many Yugoslav troops NATO and the KLA killed or wounded. The evidence suggests that the effects were considerable. NATO estimates that some 30 percent of Serbia's initial armored holdings may have been struck. Even if that figure is too high by a factor of two or three, it could still have been significant in Milosevic's eyes, particularly in light of the rapidly accelerating effectiveness of the tactical air strikes and the disconcerting prospect of a summer of such attacks. As General Clark put it:

> As the campaign progressed, Allied forces closed in on Serb forces on the ground in Kosovo—the campaign's top priority. In favorable weather, these forces felt the full weight of NATO air power. Serb forces were relegated to hiding during the day and maneuvering at night. When they formed up to fight the UCK, the Kosovar armed elements [KLA], they greatly risked NATO strikes. They dispersed into smaller units, which made them more vulnerable to the UCK, whom, after a year of continuous operations, the Serbs could not defeat. This was an army in decline; an army that knew it was losing.[29]

How should we judge the overall impact of the strategic and tactical air war on Milosevic's thinking? It seems doubtful that losses in Kosovo were the deciding factor. Historically, armies often fight until they are depleted 30–50 percent or even more.[30] Given the importance of Kosovo to Serbia, it seems dubious that this war would have been a glaring exception to that rule. KLA strength was growing considerably, but Serbia had tens of thousands of additional troops that it could have called upon to reinforce its forces if necessary, and there is little reason to think that NATO bombs could have prevented such reinforcements. Even if Yugoslavia lost one-third of its initial armored holdings in Kosovo, as NATO claims, many appear to have been replaced in the course of the war. Nonetheless, Serbia was probably frustrated by the slow pace of consolidating its gains on the Kosovo battlefield. It had to acknowledge that the KLA was growing stronger and must have recognized that NATO aircraft were becoming much more effective against Serb forces in the field. With armored attrition becoming nontrivial, and with his highly valued security forces starting to suffer real personnel losses, Milosevic probably recognized that the tactical tide was turning against him and factored this into his calculations.[31]

The strategic air campaign was likely at least as decisive. The mounting damage undoubtedly raised questions in Milosevic's mind about what NATO airpower would strike next. He may even have worried that NATO would bomb a building while he was in it. Good weather over the Balkans promised a summer of heavy pounding ahead, and alliance leaders like Bill Clinton were indicating that such a summer might well be in store.[32]

In reaching this judgment about the effectiveness of the air campaign, we acknowledge that during the war our frequently voiced skepticism about the wisdom of relying solely on airpower was excessive and that some of our predictions were wrong. Airpower did not by itself produce victory, but it does, in our judgment, deserve principal military credit for the outcome. It made Operation Allied Force different from most other wars, including Vietnam and World War II. (Although Japan did capitulate after a campaign of strategic bombardment in World War II, it did so only after enormous damage was inflicted, obviously making it a far different case than anything NATO contemplated in its war against Serbia.)

Opinions that the strategic bombing campaign alone was responsible for NATO's success became common in the summer of 1999. Typical, if pithier than most, was *New York Times* columnist Thomas Friedman's statement that "the war was won on the power grids of Belgrade, not in the trenches of Kosovo." *Washington Post* columnist Charles Krauthammer was no less categorical: "In the end it was the massive attack on civilian infrastructure in

Serbia proper that forced Milosevic's surrender." The commander of NATO's air war, American Lieutenant General Michael Short, stated that he never felt Serbian forces in Kosovo to be "a center of gravity" and argued that destroying assets that kept Serb leaders in power and in comfort was NATO's key to victory.[33]

However, the strategic airpower absolutists have no direct evidence—such as statements from top Yugoslav officials—on which to base their case. Their arguments fly in the face of the historical evidence that countries bombed much more severely than Yugoslavia rarely gave in for that reason alone. They ignore the fact that dissension within the alliance over bombing could have been expected to intensify as NATO started causing more pain to civilians in Serbia.[34] Indeed, our interviews suggest that Italy in particular—a critical and irreplaceable country for the air war—was making clear to its allies that it would not support an indefinite bombing campaign and was pushing for either escalation or negotiations to end the war.[35] Strategic air champions are also dismissive about other factors, such as the likelihood that Serb forces had suffered significant damage in Kosovo by the end of the war and the fact that the odds of an eventual NATO ground invasion of Kosovo were becoming substantial by late May and early June. Their arguments are difficult to disprove directly, but they are not compelling either.

THE THREAT OF A GROUND WAR.   What about NATO's increasingly frequent and convincing suggestions that it would consider an invasion of Kosovo after all? In our judgment, that was a critical factor in Milosevic's thinking as well, and it is doubtful that the war could have been won without it.

By early June, Milosevic would have seen several signs pointing to a growing likelihood of a NATO invasion. He knew that NATO was building up its ground forces in Macedonia and Albania, officially not for the purpose of preparing an invasion but nonetheless in numbers that would soon equal the combined strength of all of his forces in Kosovo. He knew that President Clinton was talking about the need for victory in far less nuanced and far more determined tones than earlier in the war; Prime Minister Tony Blair continued to do the same. Milosevic would have read reports of Clinton's meetings with his military advisers to discuss ground war options, including a major session scheduled for the day after the Russian and Finnish envoys first presented Milosevic with the terms for ending NATO's bombing. He apparently had also been told by Chernomyrdin that a ground war was likely if he continued to reject a settlement on NATO's terms and that Russia could not stop it.

However, were the possibility of invasion Milosevic's main fear, he probably would have tested NATO further to make sure it had the gumption to undertake a ground war before relenting. Given Bill Clinton's frequent wavering on the subject, his general reluctance to use ground forces throughout his presidency (continuing an American aversion to casualties that had been recognized, even if often exaggerated, since Vietnam), the possibility that NATO would not approve such a mission, and the challenging terrain in Kosovo that would have required as many as three months to prepare the type of ground war NATO was contemplating, Milosevic had ample reason to doubt whether he should worry about a ground war—or at least whether he had to worry about it right away.

Germany remained opposed to a ground war option, and Italian Prime Minister Massimo D'Alema strongly preferred trying to secure a UN Security Council resolution authorizing any such campaign. Italy's private position appears to have been more sympathetic toward ground forces, but Milosevic might not have known that. Key Balkan countries, notably Greece, Hungary, and Macedonia, continued to oppose the use of their territories as staging bases for an invasion.[36] Knowing all this, Milosevic presumably would have looked for hard evidence of an impending ground war, such as a formal NATO resolution authorizing ground troops, U.S. and British officials courting Athens for access to a deep-water port in Thessaloniki, preparations for the loading of armored equipment onto ships, a speech to the nation on the subject by President Clinton, and perhaps a congressional debate in the United States on a measure authorizing the use of ground forces. None of these occurred; most would have been necessary, or at least highly desirable, were a ground invasion to take place. Modest upgrades that NATO forces made of a road between Tirana and Kukes in Albania, which could have served as a major transportation corridor for armored forces, may have given Milosevic some reason to worry that more was coming, but these were by themselves far from definitive indications of a looming invasion.[37]

All that said, in our judgment, Milosevic was probably right. A ground war had become a decided likelihood, even if not a certainty, by June 1999.[38] Given the punishment of airpower, and the closing of the diplomatic noose around his neck, Milosevic made what was undoubtedly a wise decision not to push his luck any further.

THE DIPLOMATIC NOOSE.   As if the punishment of NATO airpower and the intensifying talk of a possible ground invasion were not bad enough for Milosevic, the politics of the situation worked increasingly against him as well. Nineteen countries, ranging from the world's top military power, to independent-minded France, to pacifist-leaning Germany, to pro-Serb Greece, to former communist states such as the Czech Republic, Poland, and neighboring Hungary, supported the decision to bomb Serbia and stayed with the war through thick and thin. Countries such as Germany and Italy, which at various times called for cease-fires and bombing pauses, did not waver in their basic support for Operation Allied Force. They may not have been prepared to support a NATO ground war in late May and early June, but they also seemed increasingly unlikely to countenance defeat as the war went on, meaning that the odds that they would ultimately support an invasion of Kosovo were probably greater than the odds that they would obstruct the continuation of the war. Other countries were also signing up to host NATO aircraft much faster than those already part of the coalition were losing their will to sustain the effort.[39] As *Washington Post* reporter Michael Dobbs insightfully wrote, "While it is true that Western leaders underestimated Belgrade's staying power, it is also true that Mr. Milosevic made an equally serious miscalculation of the staying power of NATO."[40]

By late May, Chernomyrdin was also telling Milosevic that in his estimation NATO would escalate to a ground war if necessary—and that Russia could not and would not do anything to prevent such an eventuality. More generally, the decision by Russia to work in accord with NATO was of absolutely critical importance. Together, these developments probably took away much of whatever hope the Yugoslav leader may have still had that he could outlast the alliance.

Milosevic may also have taken some solace in the possibility that Russia would establish and maintain its own sector in Kosovo. That plan, if realized, would have improved the odds that a swath of the province would remain populated by Serbs—and an integral part of Serbia politically—regardless of the ultimate fate of the rest of Kosovo, which Milosevic probably recognized would be largely beyond his control.[41] The fact that Russia proved unable to carve out such a sector—stymied by NATO and more directly by the refusal of Romania and Bulgaria to allow overflights of reinforcements to the airport in Pristina—was unknown to Milosevic when he decided to give up the fight. As the diplomatic pressure increased around Milosevic, NATO and Russia also offered modest and prudent concessions, adding a few small carrots to the alliance's big stick and further improving the odds of a successful outcome.

It is difficult to determine if Slobodan Milosevic's indictment by the International Criminal Tribunal for the former Yugoslavia affected his decision to relent. Thankfully, the worry of many that the indictment would steel his resistance and make it more difficult to negotiate with him was not realized.[42] It is possible that the indictment, and the silence from Moscow and Beijing that followed, increased pressure on Milosevic to deal while the world was still willing to talk to him—and still willing to cut a deal that did not demand his immediate removal from power. In the end it is hard to deduce the effects of the war crimes process on Milosevic's decisionmaking, but it does not appear to have worked at crosspurposes with NATO's broader goals.

So the effects of NATO airpower were intensifying on Milosevic and his cronies, as talk of an alliance invasion grew more common and credible. Just as important perhaps, it became less and less probable that someone would intervene to save the Serbs by cutting the hangman's rope. Undoubtedly realizing that trends were working against him, Milosevic cut his losses and accepted the core of NATO's terms.

In broader terms, Milosevic appears to have acted rationally—at least in a narrow tactical sense—throughout this crisis, even if his behavior was also thoroughly reprehensible and immoral. He tested NATO (which seemed in the prewar period and the war's early going as bent on saying what it would *not* do militarily as on making credible threats) until it became clear that neither dissension within the alliance nor an outside party like Russia would emerge to save him. He relented in time to give himself a reasonable chance to remain in power, the ultimate motivation for an autocrat like Milosevic. Relative to Rambouillet, he gambled, and lost; but the gamble was not a foolish one in light of all the information he had available to him in March 1999.

Implications for Policy

What are the implications of this assessment of Operation Allied Force for future U.S. and Western policy? The following lessons, while admittedly reflecting our other foreign policy views and other experiences, draw on the course, conduct, and consequences of NATO's 1999 war against Serbia to lay out suggestions for future approaches to the use of force. Some lessons relate to the specifics of how a given crisis should be handled or a war conducted; others are more general and range from issues such as the future of NATO to the nature of current U.S. global leadership.[43]

Lessons for International Intervention

INTERVENTIONS SHOULD OCCUR AS EARLY AS POSSIBLE. Policymakers considering humanitarian interventions face an uncomfortable paradox: to save the most lives and stop a war in its early phases when it may not yet have developed full momentum, it is desirable to intervene as early as possible. Yet to avoid intervening in countless conflicts, it is often necessary to wait in the hope that a war will be halted by a negotiated settlement or simply fester at a low level that does not risk destabilizing an entire region or creating a humanitarian debacle. For busy policymakers and politicians, who recognize that humanitarian interventions tend to carry few political rewards but many risks, the incentive to wait is especially great.

These contradictory pressures are innate to most conflicts. Yet policymakers must understand and try to overcome them whenever possible. In the case of Kosovo, U.S. and allied leaders had a major advantage in that they knew whom they were dealing with. Even though levels of violence in Kosovo throughout 1998 and early 1999 were not particularly severe, the international community had seen what Milosevic was capable of in Bosnia, and by the summer and early fall of 1998 it had also witnessed the forcible displacement of 300,000 Kosovar Albanians. These facts made an otherwise complex situation rather simple. Intervention was the only real option. The alternative of standing by and seeing what Milosevic would do in Kosovo was simply unacceptable. That made relatively early action possible, with the result that, in Kosovo, ten times fewer people died than in Bosnia, where the West's response had been far slower.

Some critics of NATO's war argue that the relatively low death toll of ethnic Albanians in Kosovo invalidated the justification for a humanitarian intervention there.[44] They are missing the point. It is extremely fortunate that NATO could intervene quickly and decisively enough for the death toll to remain modest in a war in which, absent outside intervention, there was very good reason to think it might not.

That is not to say that NATO acted early enough. Had it intervened diplomatically and economically before 1998—threatening Milosevic with sanctions unless he restored autonomy to the Kosovar Albanians—there is a chance, albeit modest, that the conflict could have been averted. Had it threatened air strikes in the first half of 1998, before Milosevic's massive "ethnic cleansing" operation, it might have been possible to keep the two parties off their path to war, although it would only have made sense to do so if NATO was prepared to escalate to a prolonged air campaign, and possibly a ground intervention, as it ultimately did in 1999. Such a military commitment would admittedly have been difficult to undertake in early 1998, since the conflict had not yet become severe. But in retrospect it appears to have been the best last chance to avoid a drastically deteriorating situation. Milosevic might have been more easily influenced then, since he could have still held out hope that ethnic Albanians would accept a restoration of autonomy rather than push for independence. The ethnic Albanian population was not yet as radicalized as it would later become, and the KLA was not yet a major force. Under these circumstances, it might have been possible to reach an agreement with Milosevic under which Kosovo could enjoy autonomy with a modest international peacekeeping force to protect its inhabitants. NATO troops could have entered the province as genuine peacekeepers. Instead, all the international community could ultimately produce that year was the Holbrooke-Milosevic agreement and the small unarmed OSCE monitoring mission it created. That did little more than put off the conflict (though in light of the coming winter, buying a few months' extra time may have been an acceptable interim policy on humanitarian grounds, provided it was recognized as being no more than that).

These latter ideas for earlier action would have been smart to try, though we recognize that they would have run into the dilemma of early action: in their early phases it is hard to know which conflicts warrant the commitment of major Western military resources, even though it is in these early phases that one would like to act. It is also difficult to generate public and congressional support for military operations in conflicts that few citizens have yet heard about. Even if early intervention had been tried, it might not have worked, given Milosevic's evident opposition to either restoring autonomy to the ethnic Albanians or allowing NATO troops on Serbian soil.

In the end, NATO acted fairly promptly, and future interventions would do well to get under way when a conflict has claimed no more than 2,000 victims if the risk of escalation is as evident as it was in this case. If NATO's timing was adequate, the amount of military power it initially brought to the effort was wholly insufficient—and that, as argued below, was a major flaw.

COERCIVE DIPLOMACY REQUIRES A CREDIBLE THREAT OF FORCE.   NATO's 1999 war against Serbia began as a foreign ministers' battle. It was less a military operation than a last-gasp exercise in coercive diplomacy. Only after thousands of aircraft sorties had been flown did the alliance begin to recognize that it was at war. Some would argue that this gradual escalation from limited force, aimed principally at inducing a negotiated settlement, to full-fledged combat operations was inevitable, given the nature of the negotiation process and the diversity of the NATO alliance. We disagree. NATO badly harmed its prospects for success at the negotiating table by threatening an amount of force that carried little weight in Belgrade. Even if it made sense to hope that a limited dose of bombing might change Milosevic's thinking, it was wrong to count on that hope—and to signal to Belgrade that the alliance had no backup plan if the initial attacks failed. Military compellence—that is, using force to try to change an adversary's behavior rather than to directly achieve a battlefield outcome—is always difficult when an adversary cares a great deal about the stakes involved in a conflict, as Milosevic did in Kosovo; it is also difficult when the military forces immediately available to make the threat are modest in capability.[45]

The belief that a few days of bombardment would make a major difference in Milosevic's eyes came out of an unfortunate habit of the Clinton administration to use small amounts of force and declare success virtually irrespective of the outcome. It had done so with cruise missile strikes against Saddam Hussein in President Clinton's first term, in response to Iraq's attempted assassination of former President George Bush and its oppression of the Kurds in northern Iraq. During its second term, the Clinton administration again relied on this strategy when it conducted the four-day bombing raids against Iraq in December 1998. The administration subsequently claimed success on the grounds that it had "degraded" Iraq's weapons of mass destruction, even though its main accomplishment was to set back the ballistic missile program for no more than a year.[46] Using force in small amounts to send messages, deflect domestic political pressure, or attempt to affect the course of a difficult negotiation process is generally ill advised. It conveys weakness rather than strength—a sense that the use of force is based more on the *hope* that it will be effective rather than on the *certainty*.

Bomb-and-pray strategies, as well as the tendency to be satisfied with "degrading" the military capacity of an opponent in vague and limited ways, generally have little if any strategic impact on those we seek to influence. Indeed, the reliance on such strategies eventually undermines the credibility of threatening force. As a result, the need actually to use force increases, as does the amount ultimately necessary to achieve the intended objective. This is exactly what appears to have happened in Kosovo. Not only was Milosevic unaffected by NATO's initial threat, but it took eleven weeks of bombing, nearly 40,000 aircraft sorties, and the serious threat of a ground invasion to bring home to him that NATO meant business.

Sometimes, force can be threatened even when it is not adequate to the task of preventing or reversing the event that precipitated its use. In such cases, the amount of force threatened or used should be fairly large. That is the best way to maximize the odds of causing the adversary to change its behavior or to make it pay a strategically significant price for not doing so. In other words, coercive diplomacy, and coercive uses of force, are not always wrongheaded. But they are risky. And coercive diplomacy based only on weak threats is never a good idea.

WHEN FORCE IS USED, MILITARY MEANS MUST RELATE TO POLITICAL ENDS. The alliance's broad political objectives in going to war against Serbia were simple and clear-cut, as President Clinton stated the day before military operations were authorized. "Our objective in Kosovo remains clear: to stop the killing and achieve a durable peace that restores Kosovars to self-government."[47] The allies, however, chose a military strategy that could not prevent Milosevic's forces from continuing—or even accelerating—the killing. Nor could it force him to accept a political settlement guaranteeing self-government to the Kosovars and a stable peace. The stated goals of the bombing campaign were limited to what the Clinton administration referred to as the three Ds: demonstrating NATO resolve, deterring attacks on Kosovar civilians, and failing that, degrading the Serb capacity to inflict harm on the Kosovars. But these *military* objectives of the bombing campaign were only indirectly related to the overriding *political* objective of achieving "a durable peace."

This shift in objectives was problematic. It was possible for the alliance to achieve its military objectives but not its political one. For example, rather than returning to the negotiating table, Milosevic could have decided to wait NATO out by simply hunkering down. Under such circumstances, how long would the alliance have remained united behind a bombing campaign? How long would Milosevic have restrained himself from further atrocities after the bombing had ended? Although General Klaus Naumann, the chairman of NATO's Military Committee, confidently predicted before the war that the "bombing will go on as long as Milosevic wants us to continue; he has to blink, and he has to give in and accept the interim settlement,"[48] consensus within the alliance would likely not have lasted long if Milosevic had just tried to wait NATO out.

There was also no guarantee that any of the military objectives were even achievable by using force. A strategy relying solely on airpower could not prevent a determined adversary from inflicting massive harm on a civilian population in Kosovo. Although the Yugoslav army and its heavy weapons participated in the expulsion campaign, much of the damage was inflicted by paramilitary forces operating in small groups using machine guns and other small-caliber weapons. There was very little that airpower could do to prevent this form of terror, particularly airplanes that flew above the clouds, at 15,000 feet above sea level.

What explains the mismatch between military and political means? On one level it clearly was the result of the prevailing assumption among NATO leaders that in Kosovo a little bombing could go a long way. That was a political error. It also appears that there were military errors. Although U.S. and allied senior officers did warn that airpower alone might not achieve NATO's objectives, they do not appear to have taken the argument to the next logical step and discussed what military tools would in fact ensure success. There is no indication that U.S. or NATO military leaders counseled that alternative means—that is, ground forces—would be needed to make sure the alliance's political goals could be achieved. To the contrary, U.S. military leaders, at least, never seriously considered recommending the use of ground forces before the war. Indeed, even after the war had started most of them doubted whether the use of force was justified, questioned what national interests were being served by using force, and suggested that non-military means might be preferable.[49]

When it became clear that force would be required, the military's counsel was to divorce its use from the stated political objectives and instead to focus on military goals that were achievable by definition—at least as they could be spun by administration officials. Any successful hit against any part of Serbia's military machine would "degrade" Serbia's capacity to repress civilians in Kosovo. But that degradation might have only semantic meaning. Unless doing so could also stop the killing and achieve a durable peace, even the severe degradation of Serb forces would not be enough to achieve NATO's stated objective for going to war.

The lesson for future military operations is clear: military means must relate to political objectives. In drawing up a viable strategy, the role of senior military officers is to advise their leaders on how the stated political objectives can best be achieved militarily. In the end, that is their greatest responsibility. They can weigh in on whether chosen objectives are prudent and on what kinds of military capabilities ought to be ruled out, but they should not make those subjects the focus of their counsel or avoid debate on military options they find unattractive. The costs and consequences of employing the right military forces must of course be made plain, but the ultimate choice has to be left to the political leaders who were elected to make precisely those judgments.

AIRPOWER ALONE USUALLY CANNOT STOP THE KILLING IN CIVIL WARS. Operation Allied Force was in the end a remarkable success for NATO airpower, but that does not mean we should now adopt a paradigm of immaculate intervention from high altitude. NATO's war against Serbia underscored the limits of airpower as well as its great potential. Moreover, in most wars of this type, airpower will be even harder to use to good effect.

The first point is the most obvious: airpower was in fact powerless to physically prevent Milosevic's atrocities against the ethnic Albanians. Alas, the fact that it is obvious now does not mean that it was obvious to most NATO governments before the war. Recall that in his March 24, 1999, speech to the nation, President Clinton stated that one of the three goals of the air campaign was to prevent Serbian forces from conducting operations against Kosovo's civilians. Most of the population in Kosovo was uprooted before NATO's bombing campaign succeeded. By then it was too late to save 10,000 ethnic Albanians killed by Serbs or to prevent the thousands of rapes, maimings, and robberies that tragically occurred in the meantime. Were it not for the relative restraint of Serb forces—who used murder fairly sparingly, by the standards of many civil and ethnic wars—far more could have died before NATO was in any position to save them.

The limits of airpower are even starker in most other ethnic conflicts. Serbia did have a large amount of armored weaponry in Kosovo as well as a relatively advanced economic infrastructure it did not wish to sacrifice. Militias in Mogadishu, *genocidaires* in Rwanda, drugged marauders in Liberia, hardened insurgents in Angola, or intoxicated Bosnian Serbs laying siege to Sarajevo in the early 1990s could not have been so easily targeted at either the tactical or the strategic level.

There are exceptions to the contention that airpower cannot do much on its own in civil conflicts. In Rwanda in 1994, attacks against radio transmitters used by the Hutu extremists to rally their supporters might have slowed the momentum toward all-out genocide and perhaps reduced the ultimate scale of the tragedy. A government marching on a rebel stronghold with a mechanized formation might be stopped by airpower. If that could save a large number of lives, and possibly even change the tide of war in a desirable direction, it might be worth the effort. In general, however, civil wars today take place in rather undeveloped countries and are conducted by small units of soldiers and rebels using relatively light weaponry. These characteristics limit the potential of modern airpower, and little about the so-called revolution in military affairs will change that fact any time soon.[50]

THE POWELL DOCTRINE FOR THE USE OF FORCE REMAINS VALID. NATO's success in using (relatively) limited means to achieve victory in Kosovo led some to welcome the demise of the so-called Powell doctrine: the notion that the United States should use military force only after exhausting all other alternatives and then only decisively, to achieve clearly defined political objectives. One White House official claimed that NATO's Kosovo strategy was the "anti-Powell doctrine." Another said, "You won't see Colin Powell on TV today talking about the Powell doctrine."[51] We disagree with these arguments. In the most fundamental sense, Operation Allied Force does more to confirm than to refute the Powell doctrine, since it underscores the need for decisive force. But there is more to it than that.

First, a clarification on definitions. The Powell doctrine is often confused with the Weinberger doctrine, which in reality is quite different. Both emphasize the need to use force only as a last resort and to employ force decisively to accomplish clear objectives, but they differ in other, important ways. Caspar Weinberger, secretary of defense under President Ronald Reagan, insisted that force should be used only in defense of vital U.S. interests.[52] Powell, by contrast, was less concerned with limiting objectives than with defining them carefully and using whatever force was required to achieve them decisively. He defended the Bush administration's use of force to remove Manuel Noriega from power in Panama and to protect democracy against coup attempts in the Philippines. He also supported humanitarian relief missions in Bangladesh, Bosnia, Iraq, Russia, and Somalia, as well as the Clinton administration's intervention in Haiti.[53]

However, as noted, Powell agreed with Weinberger in rejecting the use of force for vague purposes or in insufficient doses to achieve key objectives. As he put it,

> Decisive means and results are always to be preferred, even if they are not always possible. We should always be skeptical when so-called experts suggest that all a particular crisis calls for is a little surgical bombing or a limited attack. When the "surgery" is over and the desired result is not obtained, a new set of experts then comes forward with talk of just a little escalation. . . . History has not been kind to this approach to war-making.[54]

In other words, Powell generally objected to the coercive use of force; he preferred using enough military power to directly achieve clearly defined U.S. battlefield objectives. Powell argued that military strategies should ensure victory rather than simply hope to achieve it.

The Powell doctrine has also frequently been mistaken for advocating an all-or-nothing approach to the use of force. For example, in explaining the difficulty of gaining the military's backing for using force in Kosovo, Madeleine Albright pointed to the existence of the "Gulf War syndrome," which argues for getting involved only with "half a million Marines" to guarantee victory.[55] But while the military generally prefers using overwhelming force both to improve the odds of success and to minimize the risk of casualties, the key idea is using *decisive force*, that is, enough force to achieve the agreed objectives militarily. What this concept warns against is threatening or using force in quantities insufficient to achieve those objectives. And that warning, as Kosovo shows, is wholly appropriate.

Opposition to the Powell doctrine comes largely from those who believe that the American public will not tolerate casualties in war—meaning that insisting on decisive force is tantamount to ensuring inaction, since the United States will not accept the risks of a large military operation. The modern origin of the problem is of course the Vietnam experience, but the Beirut barracks tragedy of 1983 and the Mogadishu debacle of 1993 reaffirmed the belief that Americans have a low tolerance for casualties, particularly in humanitarian or peacekeeping missions. This belief is, however, generally exaggerated. While it is true that Americans expect low casualties, they do not insist on bloodless wars. Even after the October 1993 Mogadishu firefight, in which eighteen U.S. troops died, as many Americans wanted to escalate as to withdraw from battle. The public also supported the Bush administration's 1989 invasion of Panama, even though twenty troops lost their lives (the goal of the invasion was more to foster democracy and human rights and to curtail the drug trade than to respond to a traditional challenge to American security). When military operations are clearly explained, well handled, and successful, Americans tend to support them.[56]

More to the point, the Kosovo experience does not refute the Powell doctrine's emphasis on using decisive force. NATO prevailed in Kosovo only when it tripled its air armada, ultimately deploying about two-thirds as many airplanes as the United States would now envision sending to a major war against Iraq or North Korea. NATO bombed for eleven weeks, flying one-third as many combat sorties as in Desert Storm. It began to build up ground forces near Kosovo while talking increasingly credibly about an invasion scenario. At that point—once its strategy became decisive—it finally won the war. Operation Allied Force may not be a textbook case of the Powell doctrine in action, but it is hardly its antithesis.

Our qualms with Powell's views are two. First, as other critics of the Powell doctrine frequently assert, there may be times when a robust strategy of coercive diplomacy, or even of punitive strikes, makes sense. For example, if Iraq continues to refuse the return of international weapons inspectors, the United States and its partners may be faced with the choices of doing nothing militarily, invading, or making Iraq pay a significant price for its refusal.

Depending on circumstances, the latter option may be best, even if it cannot guarantee the return of the weapons inspectors. But General Powell was surely right to suggest that such punitive actions be conducted only infrequently and judiciously.

Second, the United States should not always wait to use force until all other (nonviolent) means have been tried. That may be true in many cases; in others, patience can cost lives. By conveying irresoluteness, it can also increase the odds that threats of force will fail and that force will have to be used in larger doses. Of course, conceptually speaking, one should always ask if a crisis can be resolved without force—and employ military power only if the answer is unequivocally no. That does not mean that, chronologically speaking, one should take the time to sequentially attempt several nonviolent means of handling a crisis if the problem is likely to worsen as a result.

HUMANITARIAN INTERVENTIONS NEED REALISTIC GOALS. Much of the attention to Kosovo after the war has emphasized the shortcomings of postwar life there. It is true that the situation in Kosovo is far from ideal and that the actions of Western policymakers, the UN system, NATO forces, and extremists on all sides have sometimes exacerbated the problems. But it would be a mistake to conclude that NATO's victory in Kosovo is therefore hollow. As a result of outside intervention, life is immeasurably improved for the ethnic Albanians, many of whom would otherwise have been driven out of the province for good. There has been a regrettable degree of reverse "ethnic cleansing" of Serbs by ethnic Albanians since June 10, 1999, but it is neither surprising in the aftermath of this type of conflict nor realistically preventable. Nor is it comparable to what happened to the ethnic Albanians in the spring of 1999—or for that matter in 1998. The ethnic separation and separatism prevalent in Kosovo today conflict with American ideals. But ethnic separatism is far less heinous than ethnic violence or open warfare.

In violent civil wars, stopping the killing and then restoring some degree of social and economic normalcy must be the paramount goals of policymakers. Rebuilding harmonious, nondiscriminatory, multiethnic societies is often a worthy goal and in some cases may even contribute to improving the long-term prospects for peace, but the immediate objective must be to create and then maintain a secure environment so that the killing will not resume. In many cases, that will be accomplishment enough.

EXIT STRATEGIES ARE DESIRABLE BUT ARE NOT ALWAYS ESSENTIAL. In the mid-1990s, U.S. policymakers tended to insist that future humanitarian or peacekeeping missions have clear exit strategies before being initiated.[57] This view seemed a logical extension of Powell and Weinberger's insistence on establishing clear objectives for military operations. It also reflected a reaction to the Somalia experience—and to the Vietnam and Lebanon conflicts—in which large numbers of U.S. soldiers ultimately lost their lives conducting operations characterized by "mission creep."

For a time, policymakers thought that the United States needed not only an exit strategy but an exit schedule. Thus the initial Bosnia peacekeeping mission was sold to Congress with the promise that it would last only a year. Congress felt deceived when that proved not to be the case, but it also recognized that pulling out to conform to an arbitrary schedule made no sense either. That experience led to the demise of the exit schedule concept, especially when the second deadline for withdrawing U.S. troops from Bosnia came and went without an end to the operation. In the past, the United States deployed forces without an exit schedule—for example, to counter the Soviet, North Korean, and Iraqi threats (the latter two deployments of course continue) or to help stabilize the peace in regions of critical U.S. concern (as in the Sinai). In Bosnia, Washington also came to learn that such schedules were counterproductive.[58]

Kosovo may now have shattered the exit strategy concept. Powell and Weinberger are surely still right that military missions need clear goals. But in cases where violence becomes extreme and the humanitarian argument for intervention is convincing, there may be times when it is better to act first and figure out long-term political-military exit strategies later. That would have been appropriate in Rwanda in 1994; it was appropriate in Kosovo in 1999.

Not only is it impossible to say when NATO troops will leave Kosovo, it is also impossible to specify under what circumstances they will do so. When there is a truly democratic Serbia led by someone besides Slobodan Milosevic? When there is an independent Kosovo, whether partitioned or whole? When there is an independent Kosovo with NATO membership or at least NATO security guarantees? One cannot say; it would be unwise at this point even to try.

Lessons for Multilateral Operations

OTHER COUNTRIES NEED BETTER, MORE DEPLOYABLE MILITARIES. The United States routinely bases or deploys about 260,000 troops in other parts of the world; more than a third of them are in Northeast Asia, more than 10 percent are in the Persian Gulf region, and large numbers are in Europe. By contrast, all other NATO countries, with aggregate military strength twice that of the United States, base or deploy only half as many forces in other countries (counting their presence in Germany as well as deployments in former colonies).[59] That reflects poor military burden sharing. Although we support U.S. involvement in humanitarian missions, other Americans, including many in the Congress, do not, at least partly out of a sense of this unequal burden sharing. In any case, if these missions are to be done, and done well, other countries and multilateral organizations need to contribute more. Moreover, a glance around the world suggests that the need for such efforts will endure (see table 6-1).

The magnitude of the problem should not be overstated. Countries besides the United States already do a great deal in international peace operations. European countries provide more than three-fourths of the NATO-led forces in Bosnia and Kosovo. Beyond NATO, Australia is leading the UN mission in East Timor. In Sierra Leone, Nigeria took primary responsibility for keeping a lid on that country's tragic civil war. Almost none of the world's UN peacekeepers, typically numbering in the tens of thousands at any point in the 1990s, are American. But while the contributions of other countries to traditional peacekeeping and peace implementation are substantial, few of these countries are capable of mounting forcible interventions in distant places. Moreover, even those capable of traditional peacekeeping are often severely limited in how well they can respond to large-scale violations of a cease-fire in peacekeeping missions gone awry—and such violations are far from uncommon, as experiences in Angola and Rwanda underscore.[60]

Among the major western European countries, the United Kingdom should be the model for improving peace operations and forcible intervention capabilities. Its all-professional military is actually smaller and less expensive than France's or Germany's, but it is much more useful beyond its own borders. It is capable of deploying perhaps 50,000 combat troops, with air support, well beyond its territory within three to four months. Britain is also acquiring more sealift and airlift capabilities in order to move these forces more rapidly. It spends just over 10 percent as much as the United States on defense and has at least 5 percent as much deployable military force as the U.S. military—a much better ratio of relative expenditures to relative deployability than any other European country can muster.[61] Whether European countries wish to make their militaries more deployable either individually, under EU auspices, or through some other framework matters much less than that they do so in some way. (In this regard, the December 1999 decision of the European Union to create by 2003 a modest rapid-reaction force of 50,000–60,000 troops that can be deployed within two months and remain abroad for at least one year is welcome.)[62]

What about developing countries? Expensive hardware, such as airlift capabilities, helicopters, and fighter aircraft, will generally be beyond their means in large numbers. It is more realistic for these countries to develop well-trained and capable soldiers, proficient in basic combat and basic peace-keeping skills, and equipped with serviceable small arms, body armor, vehicles for transport, some night-vision devices, and logistics support for sustained operations abroad.[63] Many countries—including those that have sent forces to UN peace operations—do not now possess such troops or capabilities.[64] Even if these countries cannot be reasonably expected to lead forcible interventions, they can still provide credible combat forces capable of upholding cease-fires and peace accords.[65]

To aid such countries, programs like the African Crisis Response Initiative, created by the Clinton administration, should be expanded in size and scope. At present the ACRI funds only occasional training rotations for regional troops and costs the United States $20 million a year. It should do more, expanding its reach beyond the several thousand foreign troops now participating annually, helping to provide them better equipment, conducting more rigorous training, and assisting them financially when they deploy to places like Sierra Leone and Angola when conditions so warrant.[66] Others besides the United States should also assist in similar training and equipping programs.

UN AUTHORIZATION FOR INTERVENTION IS HIGHLY DESIRABLE, EVEN IF IT IS NOT REQUIRED. NATO went to war in March 1999 against a sovereign country. It did not do so to uphold the inherent right of individual or collective self-defense or with explicit authorization from the UN Security Council. This does not make NATO's action illegitimate. During 1998, the Security Council voted three times to identify the crisis in Kosovo as a threat to international peace and security. The only reason NATO countries did not request the council's authorization to use force in 1999 was the stated position of Russia (quietly supported by China) that it would veto any such resolution. The NATO countries were thus confronted with a choice between not responding to an internationally recognized humanitarian emergency, with potential implications for the broader region's stability, or acting without the Security Council's explicit backing. After much debate, the allies chose the latter, arguing that the emergency represented sufficient cause to act.

Did NATO's action set a precedent that a UN imprimatur on intervention for humanitarian ends is desirable but not necessary? Perhaps. But those who think the issue is now fully settled—that NATO or any other regional organization can easily arrogate the right to intervene—are mistaken. Kosovo exposed the fissures in views regarding humanitarian intervention that exist around the world. As UN Secretary-General Kofi Annan argued after the war,

> NATO's intervention cast in stark relief the dilemma of humanitarian intervention. On the one hand, is it legitimate for a regional organization to use force without a UN mandate? On the other, is it permissible to let gross and systematic violations of human rights, with grave humanitarian consequences, continue unchecked? The inability of the international community to reconcile these two compelling interests in the case of Kosovo can be viewed only as a tragedy.[67]

Given the wide disparities of views within the UN system in general and on the Security Council in particular, this dilemma is unlikely to be resolved any time soon. However, that does not give license to those who would want to intervene for humanitarian purposes without regard to the UN framework. Such interventions should always be the exception rather than the rule, and their legitimacy will require a consensus on a par with that formed in the Kosovo case. There, NATO countries agreed to threaten force in 1998 only after months of difficult diplomacy to secure passage of UN Security Council Resolution 1199, which identified developments inside Kosovo as a threat to international peace and security and demanded specific actions by the Milosevic government to rectify the situation.

Moreover, even though NATO eventually used force without explicit UN backing, the allies returned to the UN system as part of the diplomatic effort to end the war. A UN administration was given political control of Kosovo and was charged with managing and coordinating the mammoth task of building a stable, peaceful, and, one hopes, a democratic Kosovo. The UN's administration of Kosovo is open-ended, thus granting the Security Council the decisive role in determining the territory's political future. On the whole, NATO's intervention in Kosovo did not weaken the UN's role in such situations; indeed, in some ways it strengthened that role.

RUSSIA'S SUPPORT IS VALUABLE IN THESE TYPES OF OPERATION. The official and popular Russian reactions to NATO's bombing campaign were strident condemnation. Not only did NATO attack Slavic brethren, but the use of the recently enlarged Atlantic alliance in offensive military operations seemed to confirm some of Russia's worst fears about U.S. and NATO intentions.

Yet contrary to its critics, the Clinton administration did not embark on this venture in disregard of Russian interests or Moscow's likely reaction.[68]

Rather, from the start of the Kosovo crisis, the administration enlisted Moscow's assistance in trying to resolve the conflict without the use of force. The Kosovo issue was raised in the Contact Group in late 1997, and diplomatic efforts were handled within this framework (in which Russia was a full member) once violence erupted in March 1998. Even when the Western allies decided to impose sanctions on Yugoslavia in May 1998, Russia opted out but persisted in the joint effort to find a solution. In early 1999, Secretary Albright traveled to Moscow before going to allied capitals to seek Russia's input in and support for the Rambouillet strategy. Russia endorsed the negotiating framework for the Rambouillet conference, including the principles for negotiations, the text of the interim agreement, and the two-week deadline for talks. It did not join NATO in issuing an ultimatum but indicated that the threat of force might have a beneficial effect, even if Moscow would neither participate in nor condone its implementation.

Having gone down this road, should the United States have abandoned the strategy that Russia supported up to the final point and forgone bombing after the impasse at Rambouillet? To us, the answer is clearly no. Moscow could not have expected that it would have the right to veto U.S. and NATO policy on so crucial a matter in the former Yugoslavia, which borders three NATO states and is in close proximity to several others. Moscow's subsequent protestations can therefore be taken with a grain of salt—even though they should not be, and were not, ignored or trivialized.

The assiduous way in which the Clinton administration sought to keep Russia on board before the war paid off once the bombing began. Within weeks, a serious U.S.-Russian dialogue developed, in part to forestall a worsening of relations and in part to see how Moscow might assist in finding a way out of the crisis. With the appointment of Viktor Chernomyrdin in mid-April as President Yeltsin's special envoy, diplomatic efforts took a serious turn for the better. Ultimately, they proved to be a major reason for Milosevic's decision to accept NATO's demands. Had Washington dismissed Russian interests and efforts as cavalierly as critics suggest, such cooperation in forging an agreed diplomatic strategy would not have occurred. The lesson here is that the United States needs to make the effort to engage Russia, without however weakening U.S. or Western freedom of action.

NATO WORKS WELL IN PEACE AND IN WAR BUT ONLY IF THE UNITED STATES LEADS. A common criticism both during and after the war was that, however effective the Atlantic alliance was at deterring conflict throughout its half-century history, Kosovo proved it was ill suited as a war-fighting organization. The main concern was the supposed squeamishness of U.S. allies about hitting Milosevic hard in the war's early going. Moreover, word that Paris used its right to veto the bombing of certain targets—including, for a time, two television towers in Belgrade and key bridges crossing the Danube in the Yugoslav capital—led to accusations that political interference in the running of the war undermined NATO's efforts and might even have exposed U.S. and NATO pilots to unacceptable risks.[69] For example, Lieutenant General Short, the U.S. Air Force general in charge of executing the air war, maintained that political interference by the NATO states was "counterproductive" to military goals. "I hope the alliance will learn that before you drop the first bomb, or fire the first shot, we need to lock the political leaders up in a room and have them decide what the rules of engagement will be so they can provide the military with the proper guidance and latitude needed to prosecute the war," Short said in an interview with the *Washington Post*.[70]

This criticism of NATO's effectiveness as a war-fighting instrument is inaccurate. For one, it ignores the fact that, in General Naumann's words, "the gradualism of the air campaign was much more caused by the political objectives . . . than it was influenced by politically motivated interference."[71] In other words, at least at first, the slow start to the war reflected the fact that NATO was engaged in an exercise in coercive diplomacy, which all allies, including the United States, supported for good reasons.

For another, the strategy of gradual escalation and the decision to publicly rule out the deployment of ground forces came out of Washington. Reflecting a conviction on the part of President Clinton, Secretary Albright, and others that Milosevic was bound to give up quickly, NATO planners generated only three days' worth of targets for the bombing campaign. Fear of casualties also drove the strategy toward minimalism, especially by restricting NATO aircraft to fly above 15,000 feet to reduce the risk to pilots— a decision made primarily by Americans. British attempts in April to persuade Washington to consider the use of ground forces went for naught.

It is indisputable that the United States could have wielded a more intimidating air threat over Milosevic, even given whatever restrictions the allies might have placed on it. Just before and just after the war began, Washington went out of its way to suggest that it envisioned nothing more than a short period of limited air strikes. It sent an aircraft carrier out of the Mediterranean on March 14, meaning that it had none there until April 5. It based only a modest air armada within combat range of Serbia in the days just before and just after March 24. It gave Milosevic ample reason to think that the air campaign would be limited and brief—not only by using short, largely symbolic, military strikes against Osama bin Laden and Iraq in previous months but also by stating that the operation against Serbia would be over quickly. Even if the NATO allies were unwilling to approve a massive use of force in advance, none would have insisted that the United States demonstrate irresoluteness or seem to rule out the possibility of escalation.

NATO as an institution, as well as individual NATO countries, did have some influence over the details of the air war, but that hardly constituted interference, and it was modest in scope and significance. The North Atlantic Council, NATO's central decisionmaking body, placed the decision to start the bombing campaign in the hands of the secretary-general on January 30, 1999. Once the bombing started and it became clear that limited air strikes were not effective in persuading Milosevic to abandon his attacks, the council quickly met and approved moving to phase 2 of the air campaign. Within six days of the war's commencement, moreover, the council approved the targeting of military assets throughout Yugoslavia—thus in effect approving implementation of much of phase 3 of the campaign plan. At no other time did the NAC interfere with, let alone veto specific target sets in, the bombing campaign. Besides the United States, that right was reserved to two U.S. allies only: Britain and France. Prime Minister Blair insisted that London have the right to veto targets to be hit by American B-52 bombers flying from British soil. President Jacques Chirac requested the right to review possible targets in Montenegro. Together with President Clinton, the two European leaders demanded the right to veto targets that could cause high casualties or could affect large numbers of civilians, principally in Belgrade.[72] As the political leaders most responsible for the conduct of a war, it was entirely appropriate that they be accorded a role in the decisionmaking process. No war should ever be fought without clear political guidance provided by those who are ultimately accountable for its conduct. Moreover, in these decisions they affected the war plan in its details, not in its basic course.

Some maintain that the United States would have preferred a more robust strategy from the war's outset but knew that the allies would not have agreed. The same people assert that a NATO consensus on using ground forces became possible only in early June, after it seemed that a ten-week-plus bombing campaign was not likely to dislodge Milosevic. Although it is impossible to know whether the allies would have gone along with a more robust strategy, including early use of ground forces, the United States never made the case. U.S. policy presumed the allies' rejection, just as it presumed congressional opposition to the use of ground forces. No one tested the validity of these presumptions, which instead proved a convenient excuse for not making tough strategic choices. It was easier to blame NATO than to make the case for a war-winning strategy.

In fact, it is quite possible that a concerted American effort to persuade the allies to go along would have been successful. Among the key NATO countries, Britain was certainly prepared to escalate early in the conflict; France would probably not have been far behind. That left Germany and Italy. Convincing Berlin would have been a tall order, given both Germany's reluctance to use force outside its national territory and a government led by Social Democrats and Greens who traditionally oppose the use of force. Rome also faced considerable domestic pressures, although its prime minister seemed more inclined to support a winning strategy (eventually including, it appears, the use of ground forces) than accept defeat. If the choice was between joining the United States, Britain, and France on the one hand and sitting on the sidelines or vetoing a NATO decision on the other, it is unlikely that they would have chosen the latter—especially since, for better or worse, their troops would not have played a major role in an invasion. This suggests that NATO's effectiveness in both peace and war remains today, as it has always been, a function primarily of U.S. leadership.

Lessons for U.S. Policy

AN EFFECTIVE FOREIGN POLICY REQUIRES THAT THE PRESIDENT LEAD WITH CONFIDENCE. The underlying problem in the Clinton administration's Kosovo policy was its presumption that Congress and the American public would not support a more decisive approach to dealing with the conflict. As a result, in October 1998 the administration ruled out on an a priori basis any consideration of deploying U.S. ground forces in Kosovo, even simply to implement a deal negotiated by Milosevic and Richard Holbrooke. This fatally undermined the ensuing agreement by making it impossible for the resulting, small international force either to protect the ethnic Albanian population or to subdue the KLA. The Clinton administration deferred to the last minute a decision on whether American troops would participate as part of the promised NATO force to assist in the implementation of the accords that were being negotiated at Rambouillet. By the time the president finally did decide to contribute a small percentage of the force, the Kosovar Albanians—who were supposed to be reassured by the U.S. presence on the ground—had begun to doubt the administration's commitment to their people's safety and balked at signing the final text negotiated in Rambouillet. More important, Milosevic could not have failed to notice Washington's tentativeness. Finally, once the NATO bombing began, the administration not only deferred a decision on the possible use of ground forces but also publicly announced that it had no intention of ever sending troops to the region for combat purposes. Even as late as May, administration officials worked tirelessly to convince the Senate not to vote on a resolution authorizing the use of "all necessary force" to accomplish NATO's objectives in Kosovo.

The administration compounded these mistakes by failing to make the case publicly for intervention. Until a week before the bombing began, President Clinton had raised the Kosovo conflict only sporadically in a few speeches, press conferences, statements, and a radio address. Not until his Oval Office address to the nation on the night the bombing started did the president devote an entire speech to the issue. Nor, with the exception of Secretary Albright's address on Rambouillet on February 4, had any of his security advisers done so. When an issue involves the possible use of U.S. military power, there is no substitute for the president using the bully pulpit to make a public case forcefully and frequently. It is not only good politics, it is also a prerequisite for good policy.

Of course, matters were not helped by the political circumstances dominating at the time. The first six weeks of 1999 were taken up by the president's trial in the Senate following his impeachment by the House on December 19, 1998. Nor were they helped by reflexive opposition in the Congress to the use of U.S. military power in the Balkans—an opposition that, at least in the House, persisted into the war itself.[73] This state of affairs, however, made it more, not less, important for the president to state his case to the American people. He had to convince them and their elected representatives not only that the use of force was warranted in this case, and that the objectives were both worthwhile and militarily achievable, but also that his goals were driven by the requirements on the ground in Kosovo, as opposed to his possible political needs at home. That case could be—and eventually was—made, notably in his address at the National Defense University on May 13, in which Clinton underscored the stakes involved. But these efforts came too late to get the kind of backing for a robust, war-winning strategy that would have been necessary to minimize Milosevic's ability to inflict massive harm on the Kosovo people—or to have any chance of avoiding war in the first place.

Having failed to make a public case for the use of force, the Clinton administration opted for a minimalist strategy. Its hope was that a bit of bombing would work. This was the military equivalent of the "Hail Mary" play in football. Not only was this an irresponsible way to go to war, it also was unnecessary. A case for decisive military action—at a minimum, a robust air campaign from the war's outset—could have been made. The American public would probably have supported such a strategy given its disdain for Milosevic and memories of the Bosnian war. The tragedy of this case is that, in fearing the absence of public and congressional support, the administration embarked on the use of force lacking both. That is no basis for taking the tremendous risks that the use of force necessarily implies.

THE UNITED STATES IS NO HEGEMON OR HYPERPOWER; IT IS A SUPERPOWER MORE PRONE TO UNDERACHIEVEMENT THAN TO IMPERIAL AMBITION. Many foreign observers of the United States—as well as many Americans themselves—describe the United States as more than a superpower today. Given its dominance in military, economic, technological, and cultural realms, they often describe it in even more sweeping and grandiose terms: as either a hegemon or, to use French Foreign Minister Hubert Védrine's term, a "hyperpower."

These terms misrepresent the nature of current American leadership, as Operation Allied Force demonstrated. To be sure, with a defense budget five or six times larger than those of the world's next powers, an economy nearly the size of the European Union, and the best economic growth rate in the world among the modern industrial states in the 1990s, the United States enters the twenty-first century in a position of considerable strength and influence. In the post-Soviet period, it certainly is fair to describe it as the sole surviving superpower. No other country, be it Germany or Japan or China, shows any real potential to challenge its position any time soon.[74] This, to be sure, is a unipolar moment if not a unipolar era.

However, in Operation Allied Force, the United States displayed a number of limitations regarding what it can and will do with its power in these post–cold war days. Some of the limitations are desirable, others less so, but all are real—and frequently underappreciated. In the desirable category is the fact that the United States went to war only with the support of its major allies in the region. During that war it depended heavily on the military bases of Italy in particular (without which it could have conducted this type of air campaign only by deploying most of its fleet of aircraft carriers to the Mediterranean Sea, a rather unthinkable proposition). In the less desirable category of limitations was President Clinton's evident reluctance to lead, either at home or abroad. Domestic politics rather than strategic requirements dominated American policymaking to an unfortunate degree. President Clinton was so worried about casualties that, for most of the war, he eschewed the use of ground forces or even the use of Apache helicopters and low-flying combat jets. He sought to minimize the risks of using force by adopting a bomb-and-pray strategy in the war's early going and even preferred not to view the confrontation as a war at all. It was hardly a problem unique to the president: he faced a Congress that was even less willing to countenance the use of American power abroad to stabilize the politics and help the peoples of the Balkans. Further, he had to worry about a military that is both reluctant to get involved in nontraditional operations and somewhat overtaxed because of its long-standing missions and responsibilities in places like the Persian Gulf and Korea.

Some would claim that U.S. overseas commitments in places such as the Gulf and Korea underscore the hegemony of the United States. If so, it is a strange and ahistorical form of hegemony. The U.S. goals in those regions are to defend traditional allies, prevent proliferation of weapons of mass destruction, and ensure access to oil not for the benefit of the United States alone but for the world economy as a whole. Hegemons of yesteryear, though sometimes serving the broader interests of the international community, were generally much more bent on expanding their own possessions and wealth.

We do not pretend that the United States ignores its national self-interest when employing military force; far from it. But it does not generally pursue benefits that are exclusive to itself. Whatever modest benefits it may occasionally gain from arms or airplane sales to Persian Gulf and East Asian countries grateful for U.S. military protection, for example, are outweighed by the costs of maintaining military vigilance in those theaters. U.S. allies and nonallies can (and should) question American policy in places such as the Persian Gulf and the Korean peninsula; this policy is sometimes flawed and is often unilateralist. But even when U.S. policies are wrongheaded, basic U.S. motives generally are not.

At a time when the domestic political debate favors doing less rather than more overseas, concerns about American hegemony or hyperpower behavior are overstated. Better to worry about the opposite possibility: American disengagement. The United States is more likely to underuse than to overuse its power, to the detriment of most.

Chronology

1998

January 8   The Contact Group calls on both the Yugoslav and Kosovar Albanian leadership to begin a political dialogue.

February 28   In their first major offensive, in Qirez and Likosane, Serbian forces kill twenty-four people.

March 5–7   A second large-scale offensive by the Serb military in the Drenica Valley region leads to the deaths of over sixty more Kosovar Albanians.

March 9   The Contact Group condemns the use of force against Kosovar civilians and gives Slobodan Milosevic ten days to withdraw special units, allow humanitarian groups into Kosovo, commit to a dialogue with the Kosovar Albanians, and cooperate with other Contact Group demands.

March 25   The Contact Group insists on unconditional dialogue between Serbs and Kosovar Albanians but delays concrete action on sanctions.

March 31   The UN Security Council passes Resolution 1160, which places an arms embargo on the Federal Republic of Yugoslavia. It is to remain in effect until the Federal Republic of Yugoslavia and the Kosovar Albanians begin a substantive political dialogue, the Serbs remove their troops from Kosovo, and international organizations are allowed entry into Kosovo.

April 29   Contact Group members (less Russia) impose sanctions on Serbia for failure to comply with previous demands regarding initiation of a political dialogue and cessation of hostilities. Sanctions include a freeze on the international assets of the Federal Republic of Yugoslavia and Serbia.

May 15	Milosevic and Ibrahim Rugova meet face-to-face for the first time but without the international mediation demanded by the Contact Group.
May 18	The Contact Group agrees to review the freeze on international assets, given that Milosevic began talks with the Kosovar Albanians.
May 28	At a North Atlantic Council meeting in Luxembourg, NATO commissions studies for a possible preventive deployment near Kosovo and preparation for NATO exercises in the region.
June 11	NATO defense ministers agree to conduct air exercises in Albania and Macedonia to demonstrate the alliance's ability to project power in the region. They also issue instructions for NATO to begin planning a range of military options for ending the violence in Kosovo.
June 12	The Contact Group bans commercial air flights to and from the Federal Republic of Yugoslavia and implements the freeze on international assets and an investment ban.
June 15	NATO conducts Operation Determined Falcon, involving eighty-five warplanes from thirteen NATO countries, over Albanian and Macedonian airspace and within fifteen miles of the Serbian border.
June 23	Richard Holbrooke begins a series of shuttles between Belgrade and Pristina; Milosevic agrees to a very small diplomatic observer mission.
July 18–21	Serb forces launch a counteroffensive in and around Orahovac, forcing up to 12,000 Kosovars to flee. The offensive serves as a harbinger of the violence of that summer, which forces up to 300,000 Kosovar Albanians out of their homes.
September 23	The UN Security Council passes Resolution 1199 demanding the end of hostilities by Serb security forces, the withdrawal of security units used for civilian repression, international monitoring in Kosovo, the safe return of refugees and displaced persons, and progress on a timetable for talks with the Kosovar Albanian leadership.
September 24	NATO issues its activation warning (ACTWARN) for a "limited air option and a phased air campaign," thus opening the door for increased preparation for military operations.

September 30	At a meeting in Washington, the NSC's Principals Committee agrees to send Holbrooke to Belgrade to find a settlement.
October 3	UN Secretary-General Kofi Annan submits a report to the Security Council on the situation in Kosovo and the status of Yugoslav compliance with Security Council Resolutions 1160 and 1199. The report finds the Federal Republic of Yugoslavia in substantial noncompliance.
October 5	Holbrooke holds the first of an extended set of meetings with Milosevic.
October 8	NATO ambassadors approve an operation plan for air strikes but do not yet issue an activation order.
October 13	NATO issues activation orders (ACTORDS) for limited air strikes and a phased air campaign in Yugoslavia to begin in approximately ninety-six hours. Holbrooke then reaches agreement with Milosevic, who agrees to comply with UNSC Resolution 1199, and withdraw special police and combat forces and engage in a political dialogue with the Kosovar Albanians. He also accepts NATO reconnaissance flights over Kosovo and the deployment of 2,000 unarmed monitors under the auspices of the Organization for Security and Cooperation in Europe to verify the agreement.
October 16	NATO extends its threat of air strikes for an additional ten days to give Milosevic's forces time to come into compliance with the agreement and give the OSCE monitors more time to enter Kosovo and gather verification data.
October 24	The UN Security Council adopts Resolution 1203 endorsing the Holbrooke-Milosevic agreement and calling on both sides to fully cooperate with its implementation.
October 26	General Wesley Clark and General Klaus Naumann reach an agreement with the Yugoslav military on a list of specific police and military units to be withdrawn.
October 27	NATO forgoes launching air strikes after more than 4,000 members of the Yugoslav special police leave Kosovo.
November 11	William Walker arrives in Pristina, marking the establishment of the OSCE Kosovo Verification Mission (KVM).
December 24	Yugoslav and Serbs forces lead an assault near Podujevo, effectively ending the makeshift cease-fire in Kosovo.

1999

January 15	A massacre in Racak kills forty-five Kosovar Albanians, including three women, a twelve-year-old boy, and several elderly men.
January 19	President Clinton's top national security advisers agree to a new strategy for Kosovo, comprising a last-ditch negotiating effort with a clear threat of air strikes in case Milosevic refuses to endorse a settlement.
January 26	A joint U.S.-Russia statement on Kosovo demands that both sides cease hostilities; that Serbia cooperate with the KVM and meet the demands of the Security Council, the International Criminal Tribunal for the former Yugoslavia, and the Holbrooke-Milosevic agreement; that Serbia punish those responsible for Racak; and that both sides reach an agreement on autonomy and engage in negotiations.
January 29	The Contact Group outlines steps needed for a political solution: both sides must agree to negotiate a settlement based on Contact Group principles and use the framework agreement drafted by the Contact Group during the previous months; negotiations are set to begin in Rambouillet, France, on February 6 and end within seven days, with a one-week extension possible.
January 30	NATO announces specific measures if either side fails to comply with Contact Group demands, including the use of force to compel compliance.
February 6	Peace negotiations open at Rambouillet.
February 20	Negotiations at Rambouillet are extended to February 23.
February 23	Kosovar Albanians agree in principle to a peace plan and agree to sign after they consult with advisers in Kosovo.
March 15	Paris peace conference opens.
March 18	Kosovar Albanians sign peace agreement.
March 23	After his final attempt to reach an agreement fails, Holbrooke leaves Belgrade.
	—NATO Secretary-General Javier Solana directs Clark to begin air operations.
	—Russian Prime Minister Yevgeny Primakov, on a previously scheduled trip to Washington, orders his plane back to Moscow when notified by Vice President Al Gore that NATO bombing against Yugoslavia is imminent.

—By a vote of fifty-eight to forty-one the U.S. Senate authorizes U.S. bombing attacks as part of NATO's campaign.

March 24   NATO initiates phase 1 of the Operation Allied Force air campaign.

March 26   In the UN Security Council, Russia introduces a draft resolution calling for an immediate end to NATO bombing of Yugoslavia. It is defeated by a vote of three to twelve.

March 27   Phase 2 of the air campaign begins, targeting Serbian military infrastructure and Serbian forces in Kosovo.

—A U.S. F-117 stealth fighter is shot down in Serbia; the pilot is rescued six hours later.

March 30   Phase 2+ of the air campaign begins. It expands NATO target sets above the forty-fourth parallel and includes civilian infrastructure.

March 31   Three U.S. soldiers patrolling Macedonia's border with Kosovo are captured by Yugoslav forces.

April 4   President Bill Clinton orders twenty-four U.S. Apache gunships to Albania.

April 5   The *Roosevelt* carrier group arrives in the Adriatic Sea, marking the first time that a U.S. aircraft carrier has been within combat range of Serbia since mid-March.

April 6   Milosevic announces an immediate unilateral halt to all military activities in Kosovo for Orthodox Easter.

April 7   NATO dismisses Milosevic's cease-fire announcement and states that only complete compliance with NATO conditions, featuring a full withdrawal of Serb forces from Kosovo and Belgrade's permission for a NATO-led force to enter the territory, will end the bombing campaign.

April 12   Clark requests nearly 400 additional aircraft for the air campaign.

—A NATO bomber strikes a passenger train crossing the Juzna Morava River in Serbia, killing twenty civilians.

April 14   NATO bombs a convoy of Kosovar Albanian refugees in southern Kosovo, killing seventy-three civilians.

April 21   The first Apache gunships arrive in Albania.

April 22   British Prime Minister Tony Blair unsuccessfully presses Clinton to make a U.K.-U.S. proposal for ground troops to the rest of the NATO allies.

April 23–25	NATO's fiftieth anniversary summit takes place in Washington.
April 25	Russian President Boris Yeltsin and Clinton agree over the phone to open a diplomatic channel between Vice President Al Gore and Viktor Chernomyrdin.
April 27	Clinton authorizes a call-up of 33,102 reservists to serve up to nine months' active duty in southeastern Europe.
April 29	By a vote of 249 to 180, the U.S. House of Representatives votes to bar Clinton from sending ground troops to Yugoslavia without congressional approval. In a tie vote of 213 to 213, the House fails to pass a resolution supporting NATO air strikes in Yugoslavia.
May 1	The European Union agrees to impose a naval embargo against Yugoslavia for ships from countries that agree to participate in the blockade. The U.S. imposes sanctions to ban oil sales and freeze Belgrade's assets in the U.S.
May 2	The Yugoslav government releases the three U.S. prisoners of war to the Reverend Jesse Jackson.
May 3	Yeltsin sends Chernomyrdin to Washington to devise a diplomatic strategy for ending the war.
	—NATO for the first time uses CBU-94 munitions, which are able to short out power-switching stations.
May 5	An Apache gunship crashes on a training mission in Albania, killing two Americans (the only U.S. and NATO fatal casualties of the war).
May 6	The foreign ministers of the G-8 adopt principles for a solution to the crisis, mirroring NATO's earlier demands. These include withdrawal of Serb military, police, and paramilitary forces from Kosovo, deployment of an international civil and military presence endorsed by the UN into the territory, and the start of a process to find an interim political framework agreement for Kosovo.
	—Clark's request for 176 additional U.S. aircraft is approved by Clinton.
May 7	The Chinese Embassy in Belgrade is bombed.
May 10	At a high-level meeting, U.S. administration officials decide to publicly employ language suggesting that NATO ground troops might invade Kosovo.
	—Milosevic tells UN envoy to Yugoslavia Yasushi Akashi that he will negotiate on the basis of the G-8 principles.

May 11	The European Union appoints Finnish President Martti Ahtisaari as its special representative for Kosovo.
May 12	NATO ground forces in Macedonia and Albania reach a wartime high of 25,000.
May 16	Clinton authorizes the release of two Yugoslav prisoners of war taken by the Kosovo Liberation Army in April.
May 18	For the first time during the war, Clinton publicly says no options are off the table, implying that a ground invasion is possible.
May 19	Milosevic tells Chernomyrdin that he will agree to a peace plan based in general on the G-8 principles.
May 20	U.S. administration officials, in an internal meeting, discuss possible timelines for a ground invasion.
May 21	The U.S. administration announces it will push its NATO allies to deploy up to 50,000 troops in the countries south of Yugoslavia.
May 25	The North Atlantic Council approves a proposal to expand the Kosovo Force (KFOR) to 48,000 troops.
May 26	The KLA begins concerted offensive operations against Yugoslav forces in Kosovo.
May 27	Defense ministers of five NATO countries meet secretly in Cologne, Germany, where they discuss the possibility of a ground invasion.
	—The International Criminal Tribunal for the Former Yugoslavia indicts Milosevic, Serbian President Milan Milutinovic, and three other senior Federal Republic of Yugoslavia officials for murder, persecution, and deportation in Kosovo.
June 2	Chernomyrdin and Ahtisaari dictate NATO's demands to Milosevic.
June 3	Milosevic and the Serbian parliament approve the peace plan.
June 9	NATO Lieutenant General Mike Jackson and Yugoslav General Svetozar Marjanovic sign the Military-Technical Agreement, which calls for the withdrawal of all Serb forces from Kosovo and entry of an international security force to monitor the agreement and facilitate the return of refugees.
June 10	Solana instructs Clark to suspend NATO's air operations. The UN Security Council then adopts Resolution 1244

welcoming an end to the war, calling on all Federal Republic of Yugoslavia forces to leave Kosovo, and authorizing the immediate deployment of international security and civilian presences into Kosovo for an indefinite period.

June 12   A Russian column of fifty vehicles from Bosnia enters Kosovo and seizes the Pristina airport. NATO's first deployment of KFOR troops enters Kosovo three hours later.

June 16   U.S. and Russia agree on modalities of Russian participation in KFOR, including Russian troops at Pristina airport.

June 20   The Yugoslav military completes its withdrawal from Kosovo.

August 4   The United Nations High Commissioner for Refugees estimates that more than 765,000 refugees have returned to Kosovo; they numbered 800,000 by early June.

Military
Issues in
Operation
Allied Force

S EVERAL DIMENSIONS OF Operation Allied Force, less
than central to an understanding of the main course of
NATO's war against Serbia, were nevertheless important in other ways. A
number of military technologies and weapons saw their first use, or first
major use, in this war. In broader terms, an important question is whether a
superpower like the United States, with global security interests, can afford
to wage a significant war in a place like the Balkans. That issue is considered
here—as well as two others. One is the budgetary costs of the war for the
United States. The other is a more tactical military question that achieved
some prominence during the conflict: the degree to which NATO airpower
might have been able to cut off and isolate Serbian forces in Kosovo.

Notable Military Developments in Operation Allied Force

The B-2 stealth bomber, operating out of Whiteman Air Force Base in Missouri, made its combat debut in the war. Its precise radar allowed global
positioning system (GPS) guided bombs, known as joint direct attack munitions (JDAM), to strike within roughly six meters of their aim points even
in poor weather (when dropped from other aircraft, JDAM typically has twice
as great a miss distance, at least at present).[1] B-2 attacks, as well as certain

other missions such as cruise missile strikes, were planned independently by the United States and were not part of NATO's integrated air-tasking orders for most fighter aircraft. Non-U.S. allies often did not know what targets had been hit until well after attacks were carried out. Part of the reason was to preserve operational secrecy for these sensitive strikes, but this practice may nonetheless have engendered some resentment. (If the end result is to give greater impetus to European countries to develop more military capability, however, it may improve military burden sharing within NATO and thus be positive for the long-term health of the alliance.)

Unmanned aerial vehicles were used extensively for basic reconnaissance during the war. These helped keep losses of manned aircraft low without forgoing all the benefits of loitering or of low-altitude flights. The United States alone lost fifteen unmanned aerial vehicles during the war, most apparently to enemy action.[2] In other notable developments, NATO also made use of video teleconferencing among commanders as well as secure web sites and e-mail for sharing information. These practices allowed many data processing capabilities to remain in the United States or at other allied home bases in a technique termed "reachback." Finally, the Pentagon could keep individual track of many of its supplies as they were in transit overseas, allowing commanders to know when they would arrive—and to reroute some shipments while they were in transit if plans changed.[3]

There were some problems with these new information technologies. Expanded use of web sites and e-mail sometimes led to overloading the systems with less-than-essential information (even though total bandwidth was twice that available in Operation Desert Storm). Tactical military communications systems were still too slow and uncoordinated, making difficult real-time data dissemination "between sensor and shooter," so targets could often escape after being detected but before being fired upon. The U.S. armed forces, and those of other NATO countries, still have a long way to go in creating efficient, fast information networks. Finally, some U.S. classification systems prevented sufficiently rapid sharing of data between allies, as the Pentagon now acknowledges.[4] On the whole, however, data networking made important strides in Operation Allied Force.

Many other types of NATO military assets performed impressively during the conflict. The U.S. Navy, for example, played an important role with its Tomahawk cruise missiles and airpower from the *Theodore Roosevelt* battle group, which arrived in the Adriatic around April 5.[5] The Tomahawks were fired from nine different platforms and were especially important in the war's early going, when poor weather limited the effectiveness of airpower. The carrier battle group arrived in the Adriatic two weeks into the war and possessed only about 8 percent of the alliance's total airpower strength at war's end. Yet it reportedly contributed to 30 percent of the estimated kills against Serb forces in Kosovo. It also staged important raids on short order (most air force and other NATO assets were assigned missions up to three days in advance of flying them and hence were not generally available for quick-reaction strikes). For example, the *Roosevelt's* air wing attacked the Yugoslav military's airfield in Podgorica, Montenegro, to ensure that no attack could be mounted from there against the nearby Apache helicopter assets in Albania—and did so on half a day's notice.[6]

The War in Kosovo and U.S. Global Military Preparedness

Could the United States have led a NATO ground invasion of Kosovo without letting down its guard in other parts of the world? A prominent air force general, Richard Hawley, commander of the Air Combat Command, suggested during the war that the answer was no.[7] Some opponents of a ground war also highlighted this issue. They noted that, under the Pentagon's 1997 Quadrennial Defense Review, the nation is supposed to have the capacity to fight two regional wars beginning nearly simultaneously and overlapping chronologically. In practical terms the two-war strategy is focused largely on Iraq and North Korea—and on the fear that they could both stir up trouble at the same time.

In short, the answer to this complicated question is that the country could not have easily fought three full-scale wars at once and probably would have elected not to try, in the highly improbable event that it had to contemplate doing so. More likely, it would have fought two to conclusion at once and then turned to the last—quite likely the war against Serbia, which might have been essentially turned over to the allies in the interim. However, for the more likely (though still quite improbable) scenario in which a single major war coincided with Operation Allied Force, the United States could probably have handled both and still had something left to mount a deterrent effort in the remaining theater if necessary.

In other words, the United States could have conducted three operations at once, including a possible ground war against Serbia over Kosovo, if only one of the other wars had approached Desert Storm proportions. To give a concrete example, of its thirteen active-duty ground divisions (ten army and three marine), the United States might have sent two to Kosovo, seven or eight to the Persian Gulf in the event of another major war there, and three or four for a more limited role in another war, such as in Korea.[8]

The capability to muster such forces for other theaters would probably have been adequate to deter aggressors even during a NATO ground war in Kosovo, but clearly this is conjectural.

It must be acknowledged that if all three wars had broken out nearly at once, U.S. strategic transport assets would have been incapable of handling the surge requirements properly.[9] In addition, combat planes would have been in short supply, since almost a full major-war equivalent of airpower was ultimately deployed to Operation Allied Force in some categories of aircraft (though airplanes can be redeployed quickly if necessary, so this concern was not as severe as for ground or even naval forces).[10] So in the end the United States did assume some real risks to its other interests by going to war against Serbia, even if they were less than some critics claimed.

The Budgetary Costs of the Conflict

The overall U.S. cost of Operation Allied Force was estimated by Steve Kosiak of the Center on Strategic and Budgetary Assessments at $2 billion to $3 billion, with expenditures dominated by the costs of aircraft flights (for fuel and maintenance), ordnance, and transportation to and from the region. Kosiak estimated that the costs for non-U.S. NATO allies may have reached $1 billion.[11] After the war, the Pentagon estimated that it had spent about $2 billion on the conflict, and another $1 billion by September 30, 1999, on the KFOR mission, with future KFOR expenses estimated at roughly $2 billion a year. It is possible that costs will eventually prove somewhat greater, if equipment used heavily in the war has suffered long-term damage from the higher pace of operations that is not yet apparent. However, total costs of the actual war are unlikely to exceed $5 billion even in that event.

The Pentagon also specified $3.6 billion to expand its capabilities in realms of EA-6B jamming aircraft, advanced munitions, unmanned aerial vehicles, and other assets that were either particularly useful in Operation Allied Force or revealed to be in short supply.[12] But these should not be viewed as costs of the conflict; indeed, the fact that the Pentagon could identify and then address these concerns is actually a benefit of the war against Serbia.

What if a ground war had been undertaken? The Congressional Budget Office estimated that, for a ground invasion of Kosovo by 100,000 troops, costs would have totaled about $7 billion over a six-month period of buildup, war, and builddown. That estimate may be too low, however; after all, the United States spent well over $10 billion for every 100,000 troops deployed to Operation Desert Storm.[13]

In mid-May 1999, Congress approved and the president signed a $13 billion supplemental funding bill for the war, which was certainly far beyond the total 1999 costs of the air campaign and the KFOR mission combined. Much of it was devoted to easing other readiness strains in the force, which had become an object of acute political debate in September 1998, leading to proposals by both the Congress and the executive branch for increased defense spending between 2000 to 2005.[14]

The Attempt to Cut off Serbian Supply Lines into Kosovo

NATO spent a good deal of effort attempting to weaken supply lines linking Serbian forces in Kosovo with the rest of Serbia. In fact, by April 8 the Pentagon was arguing that Kosovo had been largely cut off from the rest of the country.[15] These claims were not convincing at the time and proved not to be right later, given that the Pentagon admitted it had stopped traffic on only half the roads into Kosovo by the end of the war.[16] Indeed on April 27 General Wesley Clark acknowledged that Yugoslav forces in Kosovo might even have grown in size and strength since the war's beginning.[17]

In places where bridge or road access was locally impeded, Serbian forces could still resort to use of boats or helicopters—the latter only occasionally being shot down. By one estimate, Serbian forces in Kosovo would have needed only a few hundred tons of supplies a week, corresponding to no more than a few dozen small truckloads of supplies a day, on average, from Serbia into Kosovo. In addition, Serbian forces had had months of warning that an air attack was possible and were believed to have built up weeks of supplies in Kosovo in advance of March 24, just in case.[18]

There may have been some hope that, if NATO eventually brought down the entire Serbian economy, it could bring down Serbia's military too. If NATO had been able to choke off those oil supplies still reaching Serbia from the outside world while keeping Serbia's own oil refineries out of commission, fuel supplies may eventually have gotten so low that shortages would have affected forces in Kosovo as well. But this strategy faced long odds. For example, Serbia imported about 50,000 metric tons of petroleum products (many already refined) in the first month of the war—perhaps twenty to fifty times what its forces in Kosovo needed over the same time period.[19] Even with a tight embargo in place, therefore, it would probably have been able to smuggle in enough supplies to sustain its forces indefinitely.

Clearly, if NATO could not interdict supply lines carrying thousands of gallons of fuel into Kosovo, it could not expect to prevent communications between Belgrade and its forces in the field either. Not that these forces required much in the way of instructions; in the words of one U.S. official, "The Serbs in the field are just thugs on a rampage. They don't need guidance on how to knock down doors and kill people."[20] In that sense, it was unrealistic to expect that attacks against leadership and communications targets would stop the "ethnic cleansing" in Kosovo. Indeed, even in Iraq and Kuwait in 1991, where distances were greater, terrain more exposed, and the enemy's need for coordination of military operations greater, given the nature of the fighting, the Iraqi military maintained communications with forces in the field throughout the war. In fact Iraq was able to order the launching of SCUD missiles, as well as a synchronized retreat from Kuwait, even at war's end. Given this experience, it was never realistic to think that NATO could cut off the Belgrade military command from the murderous units in Kosovo, as some NATO officials appear to have hoped.[21]

"Collateral Damage" in Yugoslavia

The events listed below are some of the prominent incidents during the air war, from April 5, 1999, to May 31, 1999, in which innocents were inadvertently harmed and killed by NATO.[22] In the course of their field investigation, Human Rights Watch found a total of ninety separate incidents of collateral bombing damage in Yugoslavia as compared with a Pentagon estimate of twenty to thirty incidents. The total estimated civilian toll of these attacks, using either NATO or Human Rights Watch estimates, is approximately 500 persons killed. Yugoslav government estimates range from 1,200 to 5,700 persons.

April 5	A 550-pound NATO bomb aimed at Yugoslav army barracks in Aleksinac in southern Serbia misses its target and lands in a residential area. Serbs put death toll at seventeen. Human Rights Watch later concluded that ten civilians were killed.
April 7	NATO hits homes near a telephone exchange in Pristina. NATO said civilian casualties were possible, but neither side has provided a death toll.
April 12	A NATO pilot inadvertently fires two missiles into a train crossing a bridge at Grdelicka Klisura in southern Serbia, killing about twenty people.
April 14	NATO bombs refugee convoys in the Djakovica region of south-east Kosovo along a twelve-mile stretch of road, leav-

ing seventy-five dead, according to Belgrade. NATO, without confirming the civilian toll, said it was targeting military vehicles but admitted hitting two refugee convoys.

April 27 NATO, aiming for an army barracks in the Serb village of Surdulica, bombs a residential area, leaving at least eleven civilians dead.

May 1 NATO bombs a bridge at Luzane near Pristina, killing thirty-nine people aboard a passenger bus, according to Human Rights Watch. NATO, without confirming the figure, admitted the following day having targeted the bridge without the intention of causing civilian casualties.

May 7 A NATO air raid hits central Nis in southeast Serbia, leaving at least fifteen dead and seventy injured. NATO said its planes were aiming for a landing strip and a radio transmitter but that a cluster bomb had opened immediately upon release, instead of over its target.

 —NATO mistakenly attacks the Chinese embassy in Belgrade, killing three Chinese citizens. The United States and NATO said the intended target was a Yugoslav building with military use but that U.S. maps used in the planning of the operation were old and marked the embassy at a previous address.

May 13 NATO bombs the village of Korisa, leaving eighty-seven civilians dead, according to the Serbs. Human Rights Watch later stated that at least forty-eight, and as many as eighty-seven, were killed. The allies claimed that the civilians were being used as human shields and that Korisa was a legitimate military target.

May 20 The Dragisa Misovic Clinical and Hospital Center in Belgrade is hit by a NATO missile at around 1:00 a.m., killing four patients. NATO attributed the accident to a missile that went astray during an attack on a military barracks 1,500 feet away.

May 21 NATO bombs Istok prison in northwest Kosovo. Alliance officials insisted that the prison was being used as an assembly point for Serb forces in the province. Serbs said that at least a hundred inmates and a prison officer were killed. Human Rights Watch estimated at least nineteen people dead.

May 22 NATO bombs positions of the Kosovo Liberation Army at

Kosare near the Albanian border, by mistake. Sources close to the KLA said that seven guerillas were killed and fifteen were injured.

May 30   NATO bombs a highway bridge at Varvarin in a daytime raid in central Serbia. The Serbs claimed that nine people died while attempting to cross the bridge in their cars. NATO has not confirmed whether there were cars on the bridge and insisted that the bridge was a legitimate military target.

—Missiles strike a sanatorium at Surdulica in southern Serbia, killing at least twenty people, according to the Serb authorities. NATO said it successfully attacked a military barracks in the town but refused to confirm, or categorically deny, hitting the hospital.

May 31   A NATO bomb intended for a radio relay station lands in a residential neighborhood in the Serbian town of Novi Pazar.

Source: Federation of American Scientists, "Collateral Damage Incidents," Washington, D.C. (www.fas.org/man/dod-101/ops/allied_force.htm [accessed March 2000]); Human Rights Watch, "Incidents Involving Civilian Deaths in Operation Allied Force," February 2000 (www.hrw.org/reports/2000/nato/natbm200-02.htm#P440_116432 [accessed April 2000]); and Lord Robertson of Port Ellen, "Kosovo One Year on: Achievement and Challenge," March 21, 2000 (www.nato.int/kosovo/repo2000/index.htm [accessed April 2000]).

Table B-1. Basing of NATO Aircraft Devoted to Balkans Operations, June 1, 1999

Countries Providing Basing and Aircraft	Type of Aircraft	Number
Albania[a]		87
Austria[a]	AB212	4
France	Puma	6
Greece	CH-47	1
ICRC[a]	Puma	1
Italy	HH-3F	3
	A109	1
Netherlands	CH-47D	2
Switzerland[a]	Super Puma	2
Ukraine[a]	Mi-8	1
United Arab Emirates[a]	Puma	4
United States	AH-64A	36
	UH-60	15
	CH-47D	11
	OH-58D	n.a.
Bosnia and Herzegovina (SFOR)[a]		117
Czech Republic	Mil Mi-8	2
France	AS532UL Cougar	3
	SA341 Gazelle	4
	SA530 Puma	2
Germany	CH-53G Sea Stallion	7
Italy	AB205A-1	2
	AB212	2
Netherlands	MBB Bo105	2
Spain	AS532UL Cougar	3
United Kingdom	Gazelle AH.1	4
	Chinook HC.2	3
	Sea King HC.4	2
	Lynx AH.7	11
United States	UH-60L	2
	C-12	1
	AH-64A	24
	UH-60 A/L	39
	EH-60A	4
	RQ-1A Predator	n.a.
France		47
France	KC-135FR	3
	Mirage F1CR	2
	Mirage IV	2
	E-3F	1
United Kingdom	Tornado GR.1	12

Countries Providing Basing and Aircraft	Type of Aircraft	Number
United States	U-2S	2
	KC-135	25
Germany		120
NATO	E-3A	13
United States	F-117A	12
	F-16CJ	24
	E-3B/C	5
	KC-10A/KC-135R	40
	E-8C	2
	C-130E	18
	C-17A	6
Greece		10
United States	KC-135E	10
Hungary		58
United States	KC-135R	10 (?)
	A-10A	3
	F/A-18D	24
	AC-130U	2
	MC-130P	4
	MH-53J	10
	MH-60G	2
	EC-130E	2
Italy		483
Belgium	F-16A/AM	20
Canada	CF-18	18
Czech Republic	An-26	1
Denmark	F-16A/B	6
France	Mirage 2000C	8
	Jaguar	12
	Mirage 2000D	15
	Mirage F1CT	10
	C-160	1
Germany	Tornado ECR/IDS	20
Italy	G.222	1
	F-104ASA	10
	Tornado IDS/ECR	12
	Tornado IDS	4
	B.707/T	1
NATO	E-3A	4
Netherlands	F-16A/F-16AM	16
	KDC-10	2
Norway	F-16A/B	6
	C-130H	1
Portugal	F-16A/B	7
	C-130	1

Countries Providing Basing and Aircraft	Type of Aircraft	Number
Spain	EF-18	6
	KC-130H	1
	CASA 212	1
Turkey	F-16C/D	12
United Kingdom	E-3D	2
	Harrier GR.7	16
	VC-10	5
	Tristar K.1	2
	Nimrod R.2	1
United States	EA-6B	25
	F-117A	12
	F-15C	25
	F-15E	20
	F16-CJ	84
	EC-130H	2
	EC-130E ABCCC	5
	KC-135	12
	KC-130F/R	2
	CH-53E	2
	P-3C-III(AIP)	13
	CH-53E	3
	VP-3A	1
	C-2A	4
	U-2S	2
	C-9	1
	A/OA-10A	24
	A-10A	18
	C-21	2
	RC12	2
	C-130	2
Macedonia[a]		34
France	Puma	2
	Gazelle	4
	Crecerelle	n.a.
	CL-289 UAV	n.a.
Germany	CL-289 UAV	n.a.
Italy	A-129	15
	AB-412	2
	Mirach (UAV)	n.a.
Netherlands	CH-47D	1
United Kingdom	Puma	2
	Lynx AH0	2
United States	Hunter UAV	6
Spain		37
United States	KC-135R/KC-10A	35
	EP-3E	2

Countries Providing Basing and Aircraft	Type of Aircraft	Number
Turkey		58
United States	F-15E	36
	F-16CJ	18
	C-130	4
United Kingdom		88
United States	B-52H	12
	B-1B	5
	KC-135R	20
	KC-135R	45
	RC-135V/	5
United Kingdom	Canberra PR.9	1
United States		6
United States	B-2A	6
Afloat		
USS *Inchon*		8
United States	MH-53E	8
USS *Kearsage*		30
United States	AV-8	8
	CH-46E	12
	CH-53E	4
	AH-1W	4
	UH-1N	2
USS *Theodore Roosevelt*/CVW-8		77
United States	F-14A	28
	F/A-18C	24
	EA-6B	4
	S-3B	8
	E-2C	5
	C-2A	2
	SH-60F/HH-60H	6
Total		1,241

Source: Tim Ripley, "Operations Allied Force/Allied Harbour/Joint Forge—Order of Battle/Basing," June 1, 1999 (www.janes.com/defence/features/kosovo/airassets.html [accessed March 2000]). Number of aircraft based on USS *Inchon* found at www.spear.navy.mil/ships/mcs12/missionp.html (accessed March 2000).

Note: Table includes all NATO aircraft based near Serbia or involved in the war. Some aircraft, such as those in Bosnia, were not used in the operation, however, and others are not combat aircraft.

n.a. Not available.

a. Not a member of NATO.

Documents

UN Resolution Calling for End to Violence in Kosovo

United Nations Resolution 1199 (1998), S/RES/1199,
23 September 1998

Adopted by the Security Council at its 3930th meeting on 23 September 1998

The Security Council,

Recalling its resolution 1160 (1998) of 31 March 1998,

Having considered the reports of the Secretary-General pursuant to that resolution, and in particular his report of 4 September 1998 (S/1998/834 and Add.1),

Noting with appreciation the statement of the Foreign Ministers of France, Germany, Italy, the Russian Federation, the United Kingdom of Great Britain and Northern Ireland and the United States of America (the Contact Group) of 12 June 1998 at the conclusion of the Contact Group's meeting with the Foreign Ministers of Canada and Japan (S/1998/567, annex), and the further statement of the Contact Group made in Bonn on 8 July 1998 (S/1998/657),

Noting also with appreciation the joint statement by the Presidents of the Russian Federation and the Federal Republic of Yugoslavia of 16 June 1998 (S/1998/526),

Noting further the communication by the Prosecutor of the International Tribunal for the Former Yugoslavia to the Contact Group on 7 July 1998,

See www.un.org/docs/scres/1998/sres1199.htm (accessed April 2000).

expressing the view that the situation in Kosovo represents an armed conflict within the terms of the mandate of the Tribunal,

Gravely concerned at the recent intense fighting in Kosovo and in particular the excessive and indiscriminate use of force by Serbian security forces and the Yugoslav Army which have resulted in numerous civilian casualties and, according to the estimate of the Secretary-General, the displacement of over 230,000 persons from their homes,

Deeply concerned by the flow of refugees into northern Albania, Bosnia and Herzegovina and other European countries as a result of the use of force in Kosovo, as well as by the increasing numbers of displaced persons within Kosovo, and other parts of the Federal Republic of Yugoslavia, up to 50,000 of whom the United Nations High Commissioner for Refugees has estimated are without shelter and other basic necessities,

Reaffirming the right of all refugees and displaced persons to return to their homes in safety, and *underlining* the responsibility of the Federal Republic of Yugoslavia for creating the conditions which allow them to do so,

Condemning all acts of violence by any party, as well as terrorism in pursuit of political goals by any group or individual, and all external support for such activities in Kosovo, including the supply of arms and training for terrorist activities in Kosovo and *expressing concern* at the reports of continuing violations of the prohibitions imposed by resolution 1160 (1998),

Deeply concerned by the rapid deterioration in the humanitarian situation throughout Kosovo, *alarmed* at the impending humanitarian catastrophe as described in the report of the Secretary-General, and *emphasizing* the need to prevent this from happening,

Deeply concerned also by reports of increasing violations of human rights and of international humanitarian law, and *emphasizing* the need to ensure that the rights of all inhabitants of Kosovo are respected,

Reaffirming the objectives of resolution 1160 (1998), in which the Council expressed support for a peaceful resolution of the Kosovo problem which would include an enhanced status for Kosovo, a substantially greater degree of autonomy, and meaningful self-administration,

Reaffirming also the commitment of all Member States to the sovereignty and territorial integrity of the Federal Republic of Yugoslavia,

Affirming that the deterioration of the situation in Kosovo, Federal Republic of Yugoslavia, constitutes a threat to peace and security in the region,

Acting under Chapter VII of the Charter of the United Nations,

1. *Demands* that all parties, groups and individuals immediately cease hostilities and maintain a ceasefire in Kosovo, Federal Republic of Yugosla-

via, which would enhance the prospects for a meaningful dialogue between the authorities of the Federal Republic of Yugoslavia and the Kosovo Albanian leadership and reduce the risks of a humanitarian catastrophe;

2. *Demands also* that the authorities of the Federal Republic of Yugoslavia and the Kosovo Albanian leadership take immediate steps to improve the humanitarian situation and to avert the impending humanitarian catastrophe;

3. *Calls upon* the authorities in the Federal Republic of Yugoslavia and the Kosovo Albanian leadership to enter immediately into a meaningful dialogue without preconditions and with international involvement, and to a clear timetable, leading to an end of the crisis and to a negotiated political solution to the issue of Kosovo, and *welcomes* the current efforts aimed at facilitating such a dialogue;

4. *Demands further* that the Federal Republic of Yugoslavia, in addition to the measures called for under resolution 1160 (1998), implement immediately the following concrete measures towards achieving a political solution to the situation in Kosovo as contained in the Contact Group statement of 12 June 1998:

(a) cease all action by the security forces affecting the civilian population and order the withdrawal of security units used for civilian repression;

(b) enable effective and continuous international monitoring in Kosovo by the European Community Monitoring Mission and diplomatic missions accredited to the Federal Republic of Yugoslavia, including access and complete freedom of movement of such monitors to, from and within Kosovo unimpeded by government authorities, and expeditious issuance of appropriate travel documents to international personnel contributing to the monitoring;

(c) facilitate, in agreement with the UNHCR and the International Committee of the Red Cross (ICRC), the safe return of refugees and displaced persons to their homes and allow free and unimpeded access for humanitarian organizations and supplies to Kosovo;

(d) make rapid progress to a clear timetable, in the dialogue referred to in paragraph 3 with the Kosovo Albanian community called for in resolution 1160 (1998), with the aim of agreeing confidence-building measures and finding a political solution to the problems of Kosovo;

5. *Notes*, in this connection, the commitments of the President of the Federal Republic of Yugoslavia, in his joint statement with the President of the Russian Federation of 16 June 1998:

(a) to resolve existing problems by political means on the basis of equality for all citizens and ethnic communities in Kosovo;

(b) not to carry out any repressive actions against the peaceful population;

(c) to provide full freedom of movement for and ensure that there will be no restrictions on representatives of foreign States and international institutions accredited to the Federal Republic of Yugoslavia monitoring the situation in Kosovo;

(d) to ensure full and unimpeded access for humanitarian organizations, the ICRC and the UNHCR, and delivery of humanitarian supplies;

(e) to facilitate the unimpeded return of refugees and displaced persons under programmes agreed with the UNHCR and the ICRC, providing State aid for the reconstruction of destroyed homes,

and *calls for* the full implementation of these commitments;

6. *Insists* that the Kosovo Albanian leadership condemn all terrorist action, and *emphasizes* that all elements in the Kosovo Albanian community should pursue their goals by peaceful means only;

7. *Recalls* the obligations of all States to implement fully the prohibitions imposed by resolution 1160 (1998);

8. *Endorses* the steps taken to establish effective international monitoring of the situation in Kosovo, and in this connection welcomes the establishment of the Kosovo Diplomatic Observer Mission;

9. *Urges* States and international organizations represented in the Federal Republic of Yugoslavia to make available personnel to fulfil the responsibility of carrying out effective and continuous international monitoring in Kosovo until the objectives of this resolution and those of resolution 1160 (1998) are achieved;

10. *Reminds* the Federal Republic of Yugoslavia that it has the primary responsibility for the security of all diplomatic personnel accredited to the Federal Republic of Yugoslavia as well as the safety and security of all international and non-governmental humanitarian personnel in the Federal Republic of Yugoslavia and *calls upon* the authorities of the Federal Republic of Yugoslavia and all others concerned in the Federal Republic of Yugoslavia to take all appropriate steps to ensure that monitoring personnel performing functions under this resolution are not subject to the threat or use of force or interference of any kind;

11. *Requests* States to pursue all means consistent with their domestic legislation and relevant international law to prevent funds collected on their territory being used to contravene resolution 1160 (1998);

12. *Calls upon* Member States and others concerned to provide adequate resources for humanitarian assistance in the region and to respond promptly and generously to the United Nations Consolidated Inter-Agency Appeal for Humanitarian Assistance Related to the Kosovo Crisis;

13. *Calls upon* the authorities of the Federal Republic of Yugoslavia, the leaders of the Kosovo Albanian community and all others concerned to cooperate fully with the Prosecutor of the International Tribunal for the Former Yugoslavia in the investigation of possible violations within the jurisdiction of the Tribunal;

14. *Underlines* also the need for the authorities of the Federal Republic of Yugoslavia to bring to justice those members of the security forces who have been involved in the mistreatment of civilians and the deliberate destruction of property;

15. *Requests* the Secretary-General to provide regular reports to the Council as necessary on his assessment of compliance with this resolution by the authorities of the Federal Republic of Yugoslavia and all elements in the Kosovo Albanian community, including through his regular reports on compliance with resolution 1160 (1998);

16. *Decides*, should the concrete measures demanded in this resolution and resolution 1160 (1998) not be taken, to consider further action and additional measures to maintain or restore peace and stability in the region;

17. *Decides* to remain seized of the matter.

UN Endorsement of the Holbrooke-Milosevic Agreement

United Nations Resolution 1203 (1998), S/RES/1203, 24 October 1998

Adopted by the Security Council at its 3937th meeting, on 24 October 1998

The Security Council,
   Recalling its resolutions 1160 (1998) of 31 March 1998 and 1199 (1998) of 23 September 1998, and the importance of the peaceful resolution of the problem of Kosovo, Federal Republic of Yugoslavia,
   Having considered the reports of the Secretary-General pursuant to those resolutions, in particular his report of 5 October 1998 (S/1998/912),
   Welcoming the agreement signed in Belgrade on 16 October 1998 by the Minister of Foreign Affairs of the Federal Republic of Yugoslavia and the Chairman-in-Office of the Organization for Security and Cooperation in Europe (OSCE) providing for the OSCE to establish a verification mission in Kosovo (S/1998/978), including the undertaking of the Federal Republic of Yugoslavia to comply with resolutions 1160 (1998) and 1199 (1998),
   Welcoming also the agreement signed in Belgrade on 15 October 1998 by the Chief of General Staff of the Federal Republic of Yugoslavia and the Supreme Allied Commander, Europe, of the North Atlantic Treaty Organization (NATO) providing for the establishment of an air verification mission over Kosovo (S/1998/991, annex), complementing the OSCE Verification Mission,
   Welcoming also the decision of the Permanent Council of the OSCE of 15 October 1998 (S/1998/959, annex),
   Welcoming the decision of the Secretary-General to send a mission to the Federal Republic of Yugoslavia to establish a first-hand capacity to assess developments on the ground in Kosovo,
   Reaffirming that, under the Charter of the United Nations, primary responsibility for the maintenance of international peace and security is conferred on the Security Council,
   Recalling the objectives of resolution 1160 (1998), in which the Council expressed support for a peaceful resolution of the Kosovo problem which would include an enhanced status for Kosovo, a substantially greater degree of autonomy, and meaningful self-administration,

See www.un.org/docs/scres/1998/sres1203.htm (accessed April 2000).

Condemning all acts of violence by any party, as well as terrorism in pursuit of political goals by any group or individual, and all external support for such activities in Kosovo, including the supply of arms and training for terrorist activities in Kosovo, and *expressing* concern at the reports of continuing violations of the prohibitions imposed by resolution 1160 (1998),

Deeply concerned at the recent closure by the authorities of the Federal Republic of Yugoslavia of independent media outlets in the Federal Republic of Yugoslavia, and *emphasizing* the need for these to be allowed freely to resume their operations,

Deeply alarmed and concerned at the continuing grave humanitarian situation throughout Kosovo and the impending humanitarian catastrophe, and *re-emphasizing* the need to prevent this from happening,

Stressing the importance of proper coordination of humanitarian initiatives undertaken by States, the United Nations High Commissioner for Refugees and international organizations in Kosovo,

Emphasizing the need to ensure the safety and security of members of the Verification Mission in Kosovo and the Air Verification Mission over Kosovo,

Reaffirming the commitment of all Member States to the sovereignty and territorial integrity of the Federal Republic of Yugoslavia,

Affirming that the unresolved situation in Kosovo, Federal Republic of Yugoslavia, constitutes a continuing threat to peace and security in the region,

Acting under Chapter VII of the Charter of the United Nations,

1. *Endorses* and supports the agreements signed in Belgrade on 16 October 1998 between the Federal Republic of Yugoslavia and the OSCE, and on 15 October 1998 between the Federal Republic of Yugoslavia and NATO, concerning the verification of compliance by the Federal Republic of Yugoslavia and all others concerned in Kosovo with the requirements of its resolution 1199 (1998), and *demands* the full and prompt implementation of these agreements by the Federal Republic of Yugoslavia;

2. *Notes* the endorsement by the Government of Serbia of the accord reached by the President of the Federal Republic of Yugoslavia and the United States Special Envoy (S/1998/953, annex), and the public commitment of the Federal Republic of Yugoslavia to complete negotiations on a framework for a political settlement by 2 November 1998, and *calls* for the full implementation of these commitments;

3. *Demands* that the Federal Republic of Yugoslavia comply fully and swiftly with resolutions 1160 (1998) and 1199 (1998) and cooperate fully with the OSCE Verification Mission in Kosovo and the NATO Air Verifica-

tion Mission over Kosovo according to the terms of the agreements referred to in paragraph 1 above;

4. *Demands also* that the Kosovo Albanian leadership and all other elements of the Kosovo Albanian community comply fully and swiftly with resolutions 1160 (1998) and 1199 (1998) and cooperate fully with the OSCE Verification Mission in Kosovo;

5. *Stresses* the urgent need for the authorities in the Federal Republic of Yugoslavia and the Kosovo Albanian leadership to enter immediately into a meaningful dialogue without preconditions and with international involvement, and to a clear timetable, leading to an end of the crisis and to a negotiated political solution to the issue of Kosovo;

6. *Demands* that the authorities of the Federal Republic of Yugoslavia, the Kosovo Albanian leadership and all others concerned respect the freedom of movement of the OSCE Verification Mission and other international personnel;

7. *Urges* States and international organizations to make available personnel to the OSCE Verification Mission in Kosovo;

8. *Reminds* the Federal Republic of Yugoslavia that it has the primary responsibility for the safety and security of all diplomatic personnel accredited to the Federal Republic of Yugoslavia, including members of the OSCE Verification Mission, as well as the safety and security of all international and non-governmental humanitarian personnel in the Federal Republic of Yugoslavia, and *calls upon* the authorities of the Federal Republic of Yugoslavia, and all others concerned throughout the Federal Republic of Yugoslavia including the Kosovo Albanian leadership, to take all appropriate steps to ensure that personnel performing functions under this resolution and the agreements referred to in paragraph 1 above are not subject to the threat or use of force or interference of any kind;

9. *Welcomes* in this context the commitment of the Federal Republic of Yugoslavia to guarantee the safety and security of the Verification Missions as contained in the agreements referred to in paragraph 1 above, *notes* that, to this end, the OSCE is considering arrangements to be implemented in cooperation with other organizations, and *affirms* that, in the event of an emergency, action may be needed to ensure their safety and freedom of movement as envisaged in the agreements referred to in paragraph 1 above;

10. *Insists* that the Kosovo Albanian leadership condemn all terrorist actions, *demands* that such actions cease immediately and *emphasizes* that all elements in the Kosovo Albanian community should pursue their goals by peaceful means only;

11. *Demands* immediate action from the authorities of the Federal Republic of Yugoslavia and the Kosovo Albanian leadership to cooperate with international efforts to improve the humanitarian situation and to avert the impending humanitarian catastrophe;

12. *Reaffirms* the right of all refugees and displaced persons to return to their homes in safety, and *underlines* the responsibility of the Federal Republic of Yugoslavia for creating the conditions which allow them to do so;

13. *Urges* Member States and others concerned to provide adequate resources for humanitarian assistance in the region and to respond promptly and generously to the United Nations Consolidated Inter-Agency Appeal for Humanitarian Assistance Related to the Kosovo crisis;

14. *Calls* for prompt and complete investigation, including international supervision and participation, of all atrocities committed against civilians and full cooperation with the International Tribunal for the former Yugoslavia, including compliance with its orders, requests for information and investigations;

15. *Decides* that the prohibitions imposed by paragraph 8 of resolution 1160 (1998) shall not apply to relevant equipment for the sole use of the Verification Missions in accordance with the agreements referred to in paragraph 1 above;

16. *Requests* the Secretary-General, acting in consultation with the parties concerned with the agreements referred to in paragraph 1 above, to report regularly to the Council regarding implementation of this resolution;

17. *Decides* to remain seized of the matter.

Clark-Naumann Agreement with Serb and Yugoslav Authorities

Record of NATO-Serbia/FRY Meeting in Belgrade, 25 October 1998

1. The meeting was attended by Milan Milutinovic, President of the Republic of Serbia; Nikola Sainovic, Vice Prime Minister of the Federal Government of the FRY; Colonel General Momcilo Perisic, Chief of the General Staff of the Yugoslav Army; Colonel General Vlastimar Dordevic, Chief of Public Security of the Ministry of Interior of the Republic of Serbia; and their delegation. The NATO Military authorities were represented by General Naumann, Chairman of the Military Committee; General Clark, Supreme Allied Commander Europe; and their delegation.

2. The purpose of the meeting was to discuss specific steps to be taken to achieve full compliance by the FRY with the requirements of the United Nations Security Council Resolution 1199.

3. The position of the FRY and Serbian authorities is reflected in the attached statement. The NATO Military Representatives took note of the statement.

Attachment: Yugoslav Statement

Recognising UNSCR 1199 and proceeding from the fact that organised terrorism has been defeated in Kosmet and that all actions against terrorists have ceased as of September 29, 1998 the authorities of the Federal Republic of Yugoslavia have decided, among other measures, to undertake a series of actions that would help further confidence-building among citizens, members of all national communities living in Kosmet, as well as the resolution of all pending humanitarian problems, especially the speedy return to their homes of all displaced persons. These measures are undertaken with a clear view of ensuring the return to full normality of life as soon as possible throughout Kosmet, while continuing to secure the safety and well-being of all citizens, members of all national communities living in Kosovo and Metohija to carry on their everyday life free from any threat and constraint, which includes full freedom of movement for all citizens and state authorities representatives, as well as normal activity of all State organs.

In order to further encourage the return to peace and normality, the state authorities of the FRY will bring down the level of presence and the

---

See Marc Weller, *The Crisis in Kosovo 1989–1999* (Cambridge, England: Documents and Analysis, Ltd., 1999), p. 283.

equipment of security forces (MUP and VJ) throughout Kosmet to normal levels, i.e. to the levels preceding the outbreak of terrorist activities, with the clear intention of creating conditions that would help the speedy resumption of the political process and resolution of all outstanding political and humanitarian issues. In this process the State authorities of the FRY are counting on the assistance and support of the OSCE Verification Mission, KDOM and international humanitarian and other organisations. With these goals in mind, the State authorities of the FRY have announced the following measures:

1. Special police units deployed to Kosovo after February 1998 will be withdrawn from Kosovo. Combined police/special police strength in Kosovo will be reduced to their February 1998 duty level.

2. Any additional (that is, brought in or transferred after February 1998) heavy weapons (12.7mm or above) or equipment brought into Kosovo or transferred from the VJ to the police/special police will be withdrawn from Kosovo or returned to the VJ.

3. Police/special police will resume their normal peacetime activities. Heavy weapons and equipment remaining under MUP control in Kosovo will be returned to cantonments and police stations.

4. All VJ units and additional equipment brought into Kosovo after February 1998 will be withdrawn from Kosovo.

5. Except for those VJ currently augmenting border guards, all VJ elements remaining in Kosovo will return to garrison except for three company-sized teams which will remain deployed, each to protect lines of communications between a) PEC-LAPUSNIK-PRISTINA, b) DAKOVICA-KLINA, and c) PRIZREN-SUVA REKA-PRISTINA. These three company-sized teams will return to garrison not later than one week after signature of the Political Agreement.

6. VJ border guards will remain in position along the international border of FRY and conduct ongoing border security operations.

7. The withdrawals and deployments described above will be completed by 1200 hours, 27 October 1998, except for the three company-sized teams in paragraph 5 above. On commencement, movements will be notified to KDOM and the new structures and numbers will be given to KDOM not later than 1200 hours 29 October 1998.

8. In order to ensure verification of these provisions, VJ and MUP commanders will provide to KDOM/OSCE detailed weekly reports of manning, weapons, and activities of their forces and will provide immediate notification to KDOM/OSCE of any deployments contrary to these provisions and will explain the circumstances regarding such deployments.

The FRY intends to comply unconditionally with UNSCR 1199 and the actions described in Para. LI above. It calls on all other parties to also comply unconditionally with this Resolution. The FRY remains committed to seek solutions to all outstanding issues and problems peacefully and in consultation with the OSCE. However, as a last resort, and consistent with the right of self defense, the State authorities retain the right to respond adequately and proportionately to any form of terrorist activity or violation of law which could jeopardize the lives and safety of citizens and representatives of the State authorities.

Contact Group Statement Calling for Rambouillet Conference

Conclusions of the Contact Group, 29 January 1999

1. Contact Group Ministers met in London on 29 January to consider the critical situation in Kosovo, which remains a threat to peace and security in the region, raising the prospect of a humanitarian catastrophe.

2. Despite the intensive efforts of the international community, violence remains a daily occurrence in Kosovo. Ministers unreservedly condemned the massacre of Kosovo Albanians at Racak which resulted in several thousand people fleeing their homes. The escalation in violence—for which both Belgrade's security forces and the KLA are responsible—must be stopped. Repression of civilians by the security forces must end and those forces must be withdrawn. Ministers of the Contact Group deplore the failure of the parties to make progress towards a political settlement, and cannot accept that this should permit the crisis to continue. Time is of the essence in reaching a solution, and the Contact Group is therefore assuming its responsibility.

3. Ministers called on both sides to end the cycle of violence and to commit themselves to a process of negotiation leading to a political settlement. To that end, the Contact Group:

—insisted that the parties accept that the basis for a fair settlement must include the principles set out by the Contact Group;

—considered that the proposals drafted by the negotiators contained the elements for a substantial autonomy for Kosovo and asked the negotiators to refine them further to serve as the framework for agreement between the parties;

—recognised that the work done by the negotiators had identified the limited number of points which required final negotiation between the parties;

—agreed to summon representatives from the Federal Yugoslav and Serbian Governments and representatives of the Kosovo Albanians to Rambouillet by 6 February, under the co-Chairmanship of Hubert Vedrine and Robin Cook, to begin negotiations with the direct involvement of the Contact Group. The Contact Group recognised the legitimate rights of other communities within Kosovo. In the context of these negotiations, it will work to ensure their interests are fully reflected in a settlement;

See www.ohr.int/docu/d990129a.htm (accessed April 2000).

—agreed that the participants should work to conclude negotiations within seven days. The negotiators should then report to Contact Group Ministers who will assess whether the progress made justifies a further period of less than one week to bring the negotiations to a successful conclusion.

4. The Contact Group demanded that the parties seize this opportunity to reach a settlement offering peace to the people of Kosovo. The Contact Group praised the present role of the OSCE Kosovo Verification Mission in working to reduce tensions in Kosovo and create the conditions for political dialogue, and recognised the continuing role of KVM. The Contact Group recognised that continuing international engagement would be necessary to help the parties implement a settlement and rebuild the shattered province. It required that the parties accept the level and nature of international presence deemed appropriate by the international community.

5. In the meantime, the Contact Group demands that the FRY:

—stop all offensive actions/repression in Kosovo;

—comply fully with the OSCE/FRY and NATO/FRY agreements and relevant SCRs;

—promote the safe return of all those who have been forced to flee their homes as a result of the conflict. This includes full cooperation with humanitarian agencies and NGOs bringing much needed relief to Kosovo;

—cooperate fully with the OSCE and permit the KVM and its Chief of Mission to continue to carry out their responsibilities unhindered;

—cooperate fully with ICTY as required by relevant SCRs;

—conduct a full investigation of Racak with participation of ICTY, allowing the Chief Prosecutor and ICTY investigators to enter and work in Kosovo to participate in the investigation of the massacre;

—identify and suspend the VJ/MUP officers operating in Racak at the time of the massacre until the results of the investigation become available;

—mitigate the sentences of those imprisoned in connection with the conflict and provide due process to all detainees.

6. The Contact Group emphasised that compliance with SCRs 1160, 1199 and 1203 applied equally to the Kosovo Albanians. It condemned all provocations by the UCK which could only fuel the cycle of violence, and insisted that all hostages should be released. The Contact Group believes that the framework it has set out meets the legitimate aspirations of the Kosovo Albanians and demanded that their leaders rally behind negotiations to reach a settlement and end provocative actions which would impede the political process.

7. The Contact Group asked Robin Cook to travel to Belgrade and Pristina to transmit these messages to the parties.

8. The future of the people of Kosovo is in the hands of leaders in Belgrade and Kosovo. They must commit themselves now to complete the negotiations on a political Settlement within 21 days to bring peace to Kosovo. The Contact Group will hold both sides accountable if they fail to take the opportunity now offered to them, just as the Group stands ready to work with both sides to realise the benefits for them of a peaceful solution.

NATO Statement Setting Forth Demands on Kosovo

Statement on Kosovo by the North Atlantic Council, 23 April 1999

1. The crisis in Kosovo represents a fundamental challenge to the values for which NATO has stood since its foundation: democracy, human rights and the rule of law. It is the culmination of a deliberate policy of oppression, ethnic cleansing and violence pursued by the Belgrade regime under the direction of President Milosevic. We will not allow this campaign of terror to succeed. NATO is determined to prevail.

2. NATO's military action against the Federal Republic of Yugoslavia (FRY) supports the political aims of the international community, which were re-affirmed in recent statements by the UN Secretary-General and the European Union: a peaceful, multi-ethnic and democratic Kosovo where all its people can live in security and enjoy universal human rights and freedoms on an equal basis.

3. Our military actions are directed not at the Serb people but at the policies of the regime in Belgrade, which has repeatedly rejected all efforts to solve the crisis peacefully. President Milosevic must:

—Ensure a verifiable stop to all military action and the immediate ending of violence and repression in Kosovo;

—Withdraw from Kosovo his military, police and para-military forces;

—Agree to the stationing in Kosovo of an international military presence;

—Agree to the unconditional and safe return of all refugees and displaced persons, and unhindered access to them by humanitarian aid organisations; and

—Provide credible assurance of his willingness to work for the establishment of a political framework agreement based on the Rambouillet accords.

4. There can be no compromise on these conditions. As long as Belgrade fails to meet the legitimate demands of the international community and continues to inflict immense human suffering, Alliance air operations against the Yugoslav war machine will continue. We hold President Milosevic and the Belgrade leadership responsible for the safety of all Kosovar citizens. We will fulfill our promise to the Kosovar people that they can return to their homes and live in peace and security.

Issued by the heads of state and government participating in the North Atlantic Council meeting held in Washington, D.C., April 23–24, 1999. See Press Release S-1(99)62, April 23, 1999 (www.nato.int/docu/pr/1999/p99-062e.htm [accessed April 2000]).

5. We are intensifying NATO's military actions to increase the pressure on Belgrade. Allied governments are putting in place additional measures to tighten the constraints on the Belgrade regime. These include intensified implementation of economic sanctions, and an embargo on petroleum products on which we welcome the EU lead. We have directed our Defence Ministers to determine ways that NATO can contribute to halting the delivery of war material including by launching maritime operations, taking into account the possible consequences on Montenegro.

6. NATO is prepared to suspend its air strikes once Belgrade has unequivocally accepted the above mentioned conditions and demonstrably begun to withdraw its forces from Kosovo according to a precise and rapid timetable. This could follow the passage of a United Nations Security Council resolution, which we will seek, requiring the withdrawal of Serb forces and the demilitarisation of Kosovo and encompassing the deployment of an international military force to safeguard the swift return of all refugees and displaced persons as well as the establishment of an international provisional administration of Kosovo under which its people can enjoy substantial autonomy within the FRY. NATO remains ready to form the core of such an international military force. It would be multinational in character with contributions from non-NATO countries.

7. Russia has a particular responsibility in the United Nations and an important role to play in the search for a solution to the conflict in Kosovo. Such a solution must be based on the conditions of the international community as laid out above. President Milosevic's offers to date do not meet this test. We want to work constructively with Russia, in the spirit of the Founding Act.

8. The long-planned, unrestrained and continuing assault by Yugoslav military, police and paramilitary forces on Kosovars and the repression directed against other minorities of the FRY are aggravating the already massive humanitarian catastrophe. This threatens to destabilise the surrounding region.

9. NATO, its members and its Partners have responded to the humanitarian emergency and are intensifying their refugee and humanitarian relief operations in close cooperation with the UNHCR, the lead agency in this field, and with other relevant organisations. We will continue our assistance as long as necessary. NATO forces are making a major contribution to this task.

10. We pay tribute to the servicemen and women of NATO whose courage and dedication are ensuring the success of our military and humanitarian operations.

11. Atrocities against the people of Kosovo by FRY military, police and paramilitary forces represent a flagrant violation of international law. Our governments will co-operate with the International Criminal Tribunal for the former Yugoslavia (ICTY) to support investigation of all those, including at the highest levels, responsible for war crimes and crimes against humanity. NATO will support the ICTY in its efforts to secure relevant information. There can be no lasting peace without justice.

12. We acknowledge and welcome the courageous support that states in the region are providing to our efforts in Kosovo. The former Yugoslav Republic of Macedonia and Albania have played a particularly important role, not least in accepting hundreds of thousands of refugees from Kosovo. The states in the region are bearing substantial economic and social burdens stemming from the current conflict.

13. We will not tolerate threats by the Belgrade regime to the security of its neighbours. We will respond to such challenges by Belgrade to its neighbours resulting from the presence of NATO forces or their activities on their territory during this crisis.

14. We reaffirm our support for the territorial integrity and sovereignty of all countries in the region.

15. We reaffirm our strong support for the democratically elected government of Montenegro. Any move by Belgrade to undermine the government of President Djukanovic will have grave consequences. FRY forces should leave the demilitarised zone of Prevlaka immediately.

16. The objective of a free, prosperous, open and economically integrated Southeast Europe cannot be fully assured until the FRY embarks upon the transition to democracy. Accordingly, we express our support for the objective of a democratic FRY which protects the rights of all minorities, including those in Vojvodina and Sandjak, and promise to work for such change through and beyond the current conflict.

17. It is our aim to make stability in Southeast Europe a priority of our transatlantic agenda. Our governments will co-operate urgently through NATO as well as through the OSCE, and for those of us which are members, the European Union, to support the nations of Southeast Europe in forging a better future for their region—one based upon democracy, justice, economic integration, and security co-operation.

Ahtisaari-Chernomyrdin-Milosevic Agreement

Proposal Presented by Martti Ahtisaari and Victor Chernomyrdin to President Slobodan Milosevic, 2 June 1999, as Approved by the Yugoslav Parliament

Annex 2

Agreement should be reached on the following principles to move towards a resolution of the Kosovo crisis:

1. An immediate and verifiable end of violence and repression in Kosovo.

2. Verifiable withdrawal from Kosovo of all military, police and paramilitary forces according to a rapid timetable.

3. Deployment in Kosovo under United Nations auspices of effective international civil and security presences, acting as may be decided under Chapter VII of the Charter, capable of guaranteeing the achievement of common objectives.

4. The international security presence with substantial North Atlantic Treaty Organization participation must be deployed under unified command and control and authorized to establish a safe environment for all people in Kosovo and to facilitate the safe return to their homes of all displaced persons and refugees.

5. Establishment of an interim administration for Kosovo as a part of the international civil presence under which the people of Kosovo can enjoy substantial autonomy within the Federal Republic of Yugoslavia, to be decided by the Security Council of the United Nations. The interim administration to provide transitional administration while establishing and overseeing the development of provisional democratic self-governing institutions to ensure conditions for a peaceful and normal life for all inhabitants in Kosovo.

6. After withdrawal, an agreed number of Yugoslav and Serbian personnel will be permitted to return to perform the following functions:

—Liaison with the international civil mission and the international security presence;

—Marking/clearing minefields;

—Maintaining a presence at Serb patrimonial sites;

—Maintaining a presence at key border crossings.

Annex 2 of UN Security Council Resolution 1244 (1999) (www.un.org/docs/scres/1999/99sc1244.htm [accessed April 2000]).

7. Safe and free return of all refugees and displaced persons under the supervision of the Office of the United Nations High Commissioner for Refugees and unimpeded access to Kosovo by humanitarian aid organizations.

8. A political process towards the establishment of an interim political framework agreement providing for substantial self-government for Kosovo, taking full account of the Rambouillet accords and the principles of sovereignty and territorial integrity of the Federal Republic of Yugoslavia and the other countries of the region, and the demilitarization of UCK. Negotiations between the parties for a settlement should not delay or disrupt the establishment of democratic self-governing institutions.

9. A comprehensive approach to the economic development and stabilization of the crisis region. This will include the implementation of a stability pact for South-Eastern Europe with broad international participation in order to further promotion of democracy, economic prosperity, stability and regional cooperation.

10. Suspension of military activity will require acceptance of the principles set forth above in addition to agreement to other, previously identified, required elements, which are specified in the footnote below. A military-technical agreement will then be rapidly concluded that would, among other things, specify additional modalities, including the roles and functions of Yugoslav/Serb personnel in Kosovo:

Withdrawal
—Procedures for withdrawals, including the phased, detailed schedule and delineation of a buffer area in Serbia beyond which forces will be withdrawn;
Returning personnel
—Equipment associated with returning personnel;
—Terms of reference for their functional responsibilities;
—Timetable for their return;
—Delineation of their geographical areas of operation;
—Rules governing their relationship to the international security presence and the international civil mission.

FOOTNOTE. Other required elements: a rapid and precise timetable for withdrawals, meaning, e.g., seven days to complete withdrawal and air defence weapons withdrawn outside a 25 kilometre mutual safety zone within 48 hours; return of personnel for the four functions specified above will be under the supervision of the international security presence and will be limited to a small agreed number (hundreds, not thousands).

Suspension of military activity will occur after the beginning of verifiable withdrawals. The discussion and achievement of a military-technical agreement shall not extend the previously determined time for completion of withdrawals.

Military Agreement Ending the War in Kosovo

Military Technical Agreement, 9 June 1999

Between the International Security Force ("KFOR") and the governments of the Federal Republic of Yugoslavia and the Republic of Serbia.

Article I: General Obligations

1. The Parties to this Agreement reaffirm the document presented by President Ahtisaari to President Milosevic and approved by the Serb Parliament and the Federal Government on June 3, 1999, to include deployment in Kosovo under UN auspices of effective international civil and security presences. The Parties further note that the UN Security Council is prepared to adopt a resolution, which has been introduced, regarding these presences.

2. The State Governmental authorities of the Federal Republic of Yugoslavia and the Republic of Serbia understand and agree that the international security force ("KFOR") will deploy following the adoption of the UNSCR referred to in paragraph 1 and operate without hindrance within Kosovo and with the authority to take all necessary action to establish and maintain a secure environment for all citizens of Kosovo and otherwise carry out its mission. They further agree to comply with all of the obligations of this Agreement and to facilitate the deployment and operation of this force.

3. For purposes of the agreement, the following expressions shall have the meanings as described below:

(a) "The Parties" are those signatories to the Agreement.

(b) "Authorities" means the appropriate responsible individual, agency, or organisation of the Parties.

(c) "FRY Forces" includes all of the FRY and Republic of Serbia personnel and organisations with a military capability. This includes regular army and naval forces, armed civilian groups, associated paramilitary groups, air forces, national guards, border police, army reserves, military police, intelligence services, federal and Serbian Ministry of Internal Affairs local, special, riot and anti-terrorist police, and any other groups or individuals so designated by the international security force ("KFOR") commander.

See www.kforonline.com/resources/documents/mta.htm (accessed April 2000).

(d) The Air Safety Zone (ASZ) is defined as a 25-kilometre zone that extends beyond the Kosovo province border into the rest of FRY territory. It includes the airspace above that 25-kilometre zone.

(e) The Ground Safety Zone (GSZ) is defined as a 5-kilometre zone that extends beyond the Kosovo province border into the rest of FRY territory. It includes the terrain within that 5-kilometre zone.

(f) Entry into Force Day (EIF Day) is defined as the day this Agreement is signed.

4. The purposes of these obligations are as follows:

(a) To establish a durable cessation of hostilities, under no circumstances shall any Forces of the FRY and the Republic of Serbia enter into, reenter, or remain within the territory of Kosovo or the Ground Safety Zone (GSZ) and the Air Safety Zone (ASZ) described in paragraph 3. Article I without the prior express consent of the international security force ("KFOR") commander. Local police will be allowed to remain in the GSZ.

The above paragraph is without prejudice to the agreed return of FRY and Serbian personnel which will be the subject of a subsequent separate agreement as provided for in paragraph 6 of the document mentioned in paragraph 1 of this Article.

(b) To provide for the support and authorization of the international security force ("KFOR") and in particular to authorize the international security force ("KFOR") to take such actions as are required, including the use of necessary force, to ensure compliance with this Agreement and protection of the international security force ("KFOR"), and to contribute to a secure environment for the international civil implementation presence, and other international organisations, agencies, and non-governmental organisations (details in Appendix B).

Article II: Cessation of Hostilities

1. The FRY Forces shall immediately, upon entry into force (EIF) of this Agreement, refrain from committing any hostile or provocative acts of any type against any person in Kosovo and will order armed forces to cease all such activities. They shall not encourage, organise or support hostile or provocative demonstrations.

2. Phased Withdrawal of FRY Forces (ground): The FRY agrees to a phased withdrawal of all FRY Forces from Kosovo to locations in Serbia outside Kosovo. FRY Forces will mark and clear minefields, booby traps and obstacles. As they withdraw, FRY Forces will clear all lines of communication

by removing all mines, demolitions, booby traps, obstacles and charges. They will also mark all sides of all minefields. International security forces' ("KFOR") entry and deployment into Kosovo will be synchronized. The phased withdrawal of FRY Forces from Kosovo will be in accordance with the sequence outlined below:

(a) By EIF + 1 day, FRY Forces located in Zone 3 will have vacated, via designated routes, that Zone to demonstrate compliance (depicted on the map at Appendix A to the Agreement). Once it is verified that FRY forces have complied with this subparagraph and with paragraph 1 of this Article, NATO air strikes will be suspended. The suspension will continue provided that the obligations of this agreement are fully complied with, and provided that the UNSC adopts a resolution concerning the deployment of the international security force ("KFOR") so rapidly that a security gap can be avoided.

(b) By EIF + 6 days, all FRY Forces in Kosovo will have vacated Zone 1 (depicted on the map at Appendix A to the Agreement). Establish liaison teams with the KFOR commander in Pristina.

(c) By EIF + 9 days, all FRY Forces in Kosovo will have vacated Zone 2 (depicted on the map at Appendix A to the Agreement).

(d) By EIF + 11 days, all FRY Forces in Kosovo will have vacated Zone 3 (depicted on the map at Appendix A to the Agreement).

(e) By EIF +11 days, all FRY Forces in Kosovo will have completed their withdrawal from Kosovo (depicted on map at Appendix A to the Agreement) to locations in Serbia outside Kosovo, and not within the 5 km GSZ. At the end of the sequence (EIF + 11), the senior FRY Forces commanders responsible for the withdrawing forces shall confirm in writing to the international security force ("KFOR") commander that the FRY Forces have complied and completed the phased withdrawal. The international security force ("KFOR") commander may approve specific requests for exceptions to the phased withdrawal. The bombing campaign will terminate on complete withdrawal of FRY Forces as provided under Article II. The international security force ("KFOR") shall retain, as necessary, authority to enforce compliance with this Agreement.

(f) The authorities of the FRY and the Republic of Serbia will co-operate fully with international security force ("KFOR") in its verification of the withdrawal of forces from Kosovo and beyond the ASZ/GSZ.

(g) FRY armed forces withdrawing in accordance with Appendix A, i.e. in designated assembly areas or withdrawing on designated routes, will not be subject to air attack.

(h) The international security force ("KFOR") will provide appropriate control of the borders of FRY in Kosovo with Albania and FYROM until the arrival of the civilian mission of the UN.

3. Phased Withdrawal of Yugoslavia Air and Air Defence Forces (YAADF):

(a) At EIF + 1 day, no FRY aircraft, fixed wing and rotary, will fly in Kosovo airspace or over the ASZ without prior approval by the international security force ("KFOR") commander. All air defence systems, radar, surface-to-air missile and aircraft of the Parties will refrain from acquisition, target tracking or otherwise illuminating international security ("KFOR") air platforms operating in the Kosovo airspace or over the ASZ.

(b) By EIF + 3 days, all aircraft, radars, surface-to-air missiles (including man-portable air defence systems (MANPADS)) and anti-aircraft artillery in Kosovo will withdraw to other locations in Serbia outside the 25 kilometre ASZ.

(c) The international security force ("KFOR") commander will control and coordinate use of airspace over Kosovo and the ASZ commencing at EIF. Violation of any of the provisions above, including the international security force ("KFOR") commander's rules and procedures governing the airspace over Kosovo, as well as unauthorised flight or activation of FRY Integrated Air Defence (IADS) within the ASZ, are subject to military action by the international security force ("KFOR"), including the use of necessary force. The international security force ("KFOR") commander may delegate control of normal civilian air activities to appropriate FRY institutions to monitor operations, deconflict international security force ("KFOR") air traffic movements, and ensure smooth and safe operations of the air traffic system. It is envisioned that control of civil air traffic will be returned to civilian authorities as soon as practicable.

Article III: Notifications

1. This agreement and written orders requiring compliance will be immediately communicated to all FRY forces.

2. By EIF +2 days, the State governmental authorities of the FRY and the Republic of Serbia shall furnish the following specific information regarding the status of all FRY Forces:

(a) Detailed records, positions and descriptions of all mines, unexploded ordnance, explosive devices, demolitions, obstacles, booby traps, wire entanglement, physical or military hazards to the safe movement of any personnel in Kosovo laid by FRY Forces.

(b) Any further information of a military or security nature about FRY Forces in the territory of Kosovo and the GSZ and ASZ requested by the international security force ("KFOR") commander.

Article IV: Establishment of a Joint Implementation Commission (JIC)

A JIC shall be established with the deployment of the international security force ("KFOR") to Kosovo as directed by the international security force ("KFOR") commander.

Article V: Final Authority to Interpret

The international security force ("KFOR") commander is the final authority regarding interpretation of this Agreement and the security aspects of the peace settlement it supports. His determinations are binding on all Parties and persons.

Article VI: Entry into Force

This agreement shall enter into force upon signature.

Appendices

A. Phased Withdrawal of FRY Forces from Kosovo

For the map showing the order of withdrawal, see www.kforonline.com/resources/documents/bmta-map.jpg.

B. International Security Force ("KFOR") Operations

1. Consistent with the general obligations of the Military Technical Agreement, the State Governmental authorities of the FRY and the Republic of Serbia understand and agree that the international security force ("KFOR") will deploy and operate without hindrance within Kosovo and with the authority to take all necessary action to establish and maintain a secure environment for all citizens of Kosovo.

2. The international security force ("KFOR") commander shall have the authority, without interference or permission, to do all that he judges necessary and proper, including the use of military force, to protect the international security force ("KFOR"), the international civil implementation

presence, and to carry out the responsibilities inherent in this Military Technical Agreement and the Peace Settlement which it supports.

3. The international security force ("KFOR") nor any of its personnel or staff shall be liable for any damages to public or private property that they may cause in the course of duties related to the implementation of this Agreement. The parties will agree a Status of Forces Agreement (SOFA) as soon as possible.

4. The international security force ("KFOR") shall have the right:

(a) To monitor and ensure compliance with this Agreement and to respond promptly to any violations and restore compliance, using military force if required.

This includes necessary actions to:

1. Enforce withdrawals of FRY forces.

2. Enforce compliance following the return of selected FRY personnel to Kosovo.

3. Provide assistance to other international entities involved in the implementation or otherwise authorised by the UNSC.

(b) To establish liaison arrangements with local Kosovo authorities, and with FRY/Serbian civil and military authorities.

(c) To observe, monitor and inspect any and all facilities or activities in Kosovo that the international security force ("KFOR") commander believes has or may have military or police capability, or may be associated with the employment of military or police capabilities, or are otherwise relevant to compliance with this Agreement.

5. Notwithstanding any other provision of this Agreement, the Parties understand and agree that the international security force ("KFOR") commander has the right and is authorised to compel the removal, withdrawal, or relocation of specific Forces and weapons, and to order the cessation of any activities whenever the international security force ("KFOR") commander determines a potential threat to either the international security force ("KFOR") or its mission, or to another Party. Forces failing to redeploy, withdraw, relocate, or to cease threatening or potentially threatening activities following such a demand by the international security force ("KFOR") shall be subject to military action by the international security force ("KFOR"), including the use of necessary force, to ensure compliance.

UN Resolution Ending Koso War

United Nations Resolution 1244 (1999), S/RES/1244, 10 June 1999

Adopted by the Security Council at its 4011th meeting, on 10 June 1999

The Security Council,

Bearing in mind the purposes and principles of the Charter of the United Nations, and the primary responsibility of the Security Council for the maintenance of international peace and security,

Recalling its resolutions 1160 (1998) of 31 March 1998, 1199 (1998) of 23 September 1998, 1203 (1998) of 24 October 1998 and 1239 (1999) of 14 May 1999,

Regretting that there has not been full compliance with the requirements of these resolutions,

Determined to resolve the grave humanitarian situation in Kosovo, Federal Republic of Yugoslavia, and to provide for the safe and free return of all refugees and displaced persons to their homes,

Condemning all acts of violence against the Kosovo population as well as all terrorist acts by any party,

Recalling the statement made by the Secretary-General on 9 April 1999, expressing concern at the humanitarian tragedy taking place in Kosovo,

Reaffirming the right of all refugees and displaced persons to return to their homes in safety,

Recalling the jurisdiction and the mandate of the International Tribunal for the Former Yugoslavia,

Welcoming the general principles on a political solution to the Kosovo crisis adopted on 6 May 1999 (S/1999/516, annex 1 to this resolution) and welcoming also the acceptance by the Federal Republic of Yugoslavia of the principles set forth in points 1 to 9 of the paper presented in Belgrade on 2 June 1999 (S/1999/649, annex 2 to this resolution), and the Federal Republic of Yugoslavia's agreement to that paper,

Reaffirming the commitment of all Member States to the sovereignty and territorial integrity of the Federal Republic of Yugoslavia and the other States of the region, as set out in the Helsinki Final Act and annex 2,

Reaffirming the call in previous resolutions for substantial autonomy and meaningful self-administration for Kosovo,

See www.un.org/docs/scres/1999/99sc1244.htm (accessed April 2000).

Determining that the situation in the region continues to constitute a threat to international peace and security,

Determined to ensure the safety and security of international personnel and the implementation by all concerned of their responsibilities under the present resolution, and *acting* for these purposes under Chapter VII of the Charter of the United Nations,

1. *Decides* that a political solution to the Kosovo crisis shall be based on the general principles in annex 1 and as further elaborated in the principles and other required elements in annex 2;

2. *Welcomes* the acceptance by the Federal Republic of Yugoslavia of the principles and other required elements referred to in paragraph 1 above, and *demands* the full cooperation of the Federal Republic of Yugoslavia in their rapid implementation;

3. *Demands* in particular that the Federal Republic of Yugoslavia put an immediate and verifiable end to violence and repression in Kosovo, and begin and complete verifiable phased withdrawal from Kosovo of all military, police and paramilitary forces according to a rapid timetable, with which the deployment of the international security presence in Kosovo will be synchronized;

4. *Confirms* that after the withdrawal an agreed number of Yugoslav and Serb military and police personnel will be permitted to return to Kosovo to perform the functions in accordance with annex 2;

5. *Decides* on the deployment in Kosovo, under United Nations auspices, of international civil and security presences, with appropriate equipment and personnel as required, and welcomes the agreement of the Federal Republic of Yugoslavia to such presences;

6. *Requests* the Secretary-General to appoint, in consultation with the Security Council, a Special Representative to control the implementation of the international civil presence, and *further requests* the Secretary-General to instruct his Special Representative to coordinate closely with the international security presence to ensure that both presences operate towards the same goals and in a mutually supportive manner;

7. *Authorizes* Member States and relevant international organizations to establish the international security presence in Kosovo as set out in point 4 of annex 2 with all necessary means to fulfil its responsibilities under paragraph 9 below;

8. *Affirms* the need for the rapid early deployment of effective international civil and security presences to Kosovo, and *demands* that the parties cooperate fully in their deployment;

9. *Decides* that the responsibilities of the international security presence to be deployed and acting in Kosovo will include:

(a) Deterring renewed hostilities, maintaining and where necessary enforcing a ceasefire, and ensuring the withdrawal and preventing the return into Kosovo of Federal and Republic military, police and paramilitary forces, except as provided in point 6 of annex 2;

(b) Demilitarizing the Kosovo Liberation Army (KLA) and other armed Kosovo Albanian groups as required in paragraph 15 below;

(c) Establishing a secure environment in which refugees and displaced persons can return home in safety, the international civil presence can operate, a transitional administration can be established, and humanitarian aid can be delivered;

(d) Ensuring public safety and order until the international civil presence can take responsibility for this task;

(e) Supervising demining until the international civil presence can, as appropriate, take over responsibility for this task;

(f) Supporting, as appropriate, and coordinating closely with the work of the international civil presence;

(g) Conducting border monitoring duties as required;

(h) Ensuring the protection and freedom of movement of itself, the international civil presence, and other international organizations;

10. *Authorizes* the Secretary-General, with the assistance of relevant international organizations, to establish an international civil presence in Kosovo in order to provide an interim administration for Kosovo under which the people of Kosovo can enjoy substantial autonomy within the Federal Republic of Yugoslavia, and which will provide transitional administration while establishing and overseeing the development of provisional democratic self-governing institutions to ensure conditions for a peaceful and normal life for all inhabitants of Kosovo;

11. *Decides* that the main responsibilities of the international civil presence will include:

(a) Promoting the establishment, pending a final settlement, of substantial autonomy and self-government in Kosovo, taking full account of annex 2 and of the Rambouillet accords (S/1999/648);

(b) Performing basic civilian administrative functions where and as long as required;

(c) Organizing and overseeing the development of provisional institutions for democratic and autonomous self-government pending a political settlement, including the holding of elections;

(d) Transferring, as these institutions are established, its administrative responsibilities while overseeing and supporting the consolidation of Kosovo's local provisional institutions and other peace-building activities;

(e) Facilitating a political process designed to determine Kosovo's future status, taking into account the Rambouillet accords (S/1999/648);

(f) In a final stage, overseeing the transfer of authority from Kosovo's provisional institutions to institutions established under a political settlement;

(g) Supporting the reconstruction of key infrastructure and other economic reconstruction;

(h) Supporting, in coordination with international humanitarian organizations, humanitarian and disaster relief aid;

(i) Maintaining civil law and order, including establishing local police forces and meanwhile through the deployment of international police personnel to serve in Kosovo;

(j) Protecting and promoting human rights;

(k) Assuring the safe and unimpeded return of all refugees and displaced persons to their homes in Kosovo;

12. *Emphasizes* the need for coordinated humanitarian relief operations, and for the Federal Republic of Yugoslavia to allow unimpeded access to Kosovo by humanitarian aid organizations and to cooperate with such organizations so as to ensure the fast and effective delivery of international aid;

13. *Encourages* all Member States and international organizations to contribute to economic and social reconstruction as well as to the safe return of refugees and displaced persons, and *emphasizes* in this context the importance of convening an international donors' conference, particularly for the purposes set out in paragraph 11 (g) above, at the earliest possible date;

14. *Demands* full cooperation by all concerned, including the international security presence, with the International Tribunal for the Former Yugoslavia;

15. *Demands* that the KLA and other armed Kosovo Albanian groups end immediately all offensive actions and comply with the requirements for demilitarization as laid down by the head of the international security presence in consultation with the Special Representative of the Secretary-General;

16. *Decides* that the prohibitions imposed by paragraph 8 of resolution 1160 (1998) shall not apply to arms and related *matériel* for the use of the international civil and security presences;

17. *Welcomes* the work in hand in the European Union and other international organizations to develop a comprehensive approach to the economic development and stabilization of the region affected by the Kosovo crisis, including the implementation of a Stability Pact for South Eastern Europe

with broad international participation in order to further the promotion of democracy, economic prosperity, stability and regional cooperation;

18. *Demands* that all States in the region cooperate fully in the implementation of all aspects of this resolution;

19. *Decides* that the international civil and security presences are established for an initial period of 12 months, to continue thereafter unless the Security Council decides otherwise;

20. *Requests* the Secretary-General to report to the Council at regular intervals on the implementation of this resolution, including reports from the leaderships of the international civil and security presences, the first reports to be submitted within 30 days of the adoption of this resolution;

21. *Decides* to remain actively seized of the matter.

Annex 1. Statement by the Chairman on the Conclusion of the Meeting of the G-8 Foreign Ministers held at the Petersberg Centre, 6 May 1999

The G-8 Foreign Ministers adopted the following general principles on the political solution to the Kosovo crisis:

—Immediate and verifiable end of violence and repression in Kosovo;

—Withdrawal from Kosovo of military, police and paramilitary forces;

—Deployment in Kosovo of effective international civil and security presences, endorsed and adopted by the United Nations, capable of guaranteeing the achievement of the common objectives;

—Establishment of an interim administration for Kosovo to be decided by the Security Council of the United Nations to ensure conditions for a peaceful and normal life for all inhabitants in Kosovo;

—The safe and free return of all refugees and displaced persons and unimpeded access to Kosovo by humanitarian aid organizations;

—A political process towards the establishment of an interim political framework agreement providing for a substantial self-government for Kosovo, taking full account of the Rambouillet accords and the principles of sovereignty and territorial integrity of the Federal Republic of Yugoslavia and the other countries of the region, and the demilitarization of the KLA;

—Comprehensive approach to the economic development and stabilization of the crisis region.

Notes

Chapter One

1. See Wesley K. Clark, "The United States and NATO: The Way Ahead," *Parameters*, vol. 29 (Winter 1999-2000), p. 10; and *Report to Congress: Kosovo/Operation Allied Force After-Action Report* (U.S. Department of Defense, January 2000), p. 78.

2. Quoted in John T. Correll, "Lessons Drawn and Quartered," *Air Force Magazine* (December 1999), p. 2; and *Report to Congress: Kosovo/Operation Allied Force After-Action Report*, p. 6.

3. "Americans on Kosovo: A Study of U.S. Public Attitudes" (Program on International Policy Attitudes, May 19, 1999) (www.pipa.org/onlinereports/kosovo/kosovo.htm [accessed March 2000]).

4. E. J. Dionne Jr., "A Farewell to Syndromes," *Washington Post*, April 6, 1999, p. A23. See also Miles A. Pomper and Chuck McCutcheon, "As Kosovo Crisis Escalates, Calls Increase to Reconsider Use of Ground Troops," *CQ Weekly*, April 3, 1999, pp. 809–11; and Dan Balz, "U.S. Consensus Grows to Send Ground Troops," *Washington Post*, April 6, 1999, p. A1.

5. David Fromkin, *Kosovo Crossing: American Ideals Meet Reality on the Balkan Battlefields* (Free Press, 1999), pp. 89–95.

6. Noel Malcolm, *Kosovo: A Short History*, rev. ed. (Harper/Perennial, 1999), p. 217.

7. Ibid., pp. 264–66.

8. For more on this history and on what follows below, see ibid., pp. xvii–xxxvi, 111–14, 136–40, 193-201, 228–30, 258, 280–82, 286, 331–32, 337; and *Kosovo: History of a Balkan Hotspot* (U.S. Central Intelligence Agency, Interagency Balkan Task Force, June 1998).

9. For a similar view, see Warren Zimmermann, *Origins of a Catastrophe: Yugoslavia and Its Destroyers* (Time Books, 1996), p. 130. Zimmermann, looking at Kosovo from the perspective of all parties and the vantage point of the early 1990s, suggested that it might ultimately need to be partitioned.

10. For one vivid, yet in the end oversimplified and fatalistic, depiction of these hatreds, see Robert D. Kaplan, *Balkan Ghosts: A Journey through History* (Vintage, 1996), pp. 29–48.

11. Julie A. Mertus, *Kosovo: How Myths and Truths Started a War* (University of California Press, 1999), pp. 17–46.

12. Malcolm, *Kosovo*, pp. 342–48.

13. Mertus, *Kosovo*, p. 319.

14. Quoted in David Binder, "Bush Warns Serbs Not to Widen War," *New York Times*, December 28, 1992, p. A6.

15. Warren Christopher, "New Steps toward Conflict Resolution in the Former Yugoslavia" (U.S. Department of State, February 10, 1993).

16. Richard Caplan, "International Diplomacy and the Crisis in Kosovo," *International Affairs*, vol. 74 (October 1998), pp. 745–61.

17. See Richard Holbrooke, *To End a War* (Random House, 1998), pp. 234, 357; and Pauline Neville-Jones, "Dayton, IFOR, and Alliance Relations in Bosnia," *Survival*, vol. 38 (Winter 1996–97), pp. 58–9.

18. The "outer wall" of sanctions are those that were imposed on Yugoslavia during the Bosnia war and not lifted after the signing of the Dayton Accords. These include barring the country from joining an international institution (such as the United Nations and the Organization for Security and Cooperation in Europe), denying it airline access to U.S. airports, revoking its most-favored-nation trade status, and denying it access to loans from international financial institutions and to U.S. government credits or loans for investment. Under U.S. policy, the sanctions are to remain in place until Belgrade improves the human rights situation in Kosovo (supporting self-government for the territory, among other things), cooperates with the International Criminal Tribunal for the Former Yugoslavia, and resolves outstanding state succession issues relating to the disintegration of Yugoslavia.

19. Richard Holbrooke, interview with the authors, April 7, 2000.

20. See Veton Surroi, "The Albanian National Question: The Post-Dayton Payoff," *War Report*, no. 41 (May 1996), p. 25.

21. Malcolm, *Kosovo*, preface.

22. Malcolm, *Kosovo*, pp. 354–55.

23. See especially Ted Galen Carpenter, ed., *NATO's Empty Victory: A Postmortem on the Balkan War* (Washington, D.C.: CATO Institute, 2000); Michael Mandelbaum, "A Perfect Failure," *Foreign Affairs*, vol. 78 (September-October 1999), pp. 2–8; Michael MccGwire, "Why Did We Bomb Belgrade?" *International Affairs*, vol. 76 (January 2000), pp. 1–23; and Christopher Layne and Benjamin Schwarz, "For the Record: Kosovo II," *National Interest*, no. 57 (Fall 1999), pp. 9–15.

24. The other major 1998 crises involving refugees or internally displaced people were in Angola (300,000–500,000 uprooted that year), Congo-Brazzaville (250,000), Sierra Leone (550,000), and Colombia (300,000). *World Refugee Survey, 1999* (Washington, D.C.: U.S. Committee for Refugees, 1999), p. 1.

25. Recall that in Bosnia the equip and train program began with a huge advan-

tage: the Muslim-led government army was larger, if less well armed, than that of the Bosnian Serbs and was aided by Bosnian Croat and Croatian forces. See for example International Institute for Strategic Studies, *The Military Balance, 1994/1995* (London: Brassey's, 1994), pp. 83–84.

26. George Robertson, "What's Going Right in Kosovo," *Washington Post*, December 7, 1999, p. A31; Statement of Wesley K. Clark, Hearing, *Defense Authorization Request for Fiscal Year 2001*, Senate Armed Services Committee, 106 Cong. 2 sess. (February 29, 2000); and Lord Robertson of Port Ellen, "Kosovo One Year On: Achievement and Challenge" (www.nato.int/kosovo/repo2000/report_cn.pdf [accessed March 2000]).

27. See for example William Cohen, interview, *PBS Frontline, War in Europe* (www.pbs.org/wgbh/pages/frontline/shows/kosovo/interviews/cohen.html [accessed March 2000]). Note: *PBS Frontline, War in Europe* is generally available (www.pbs.org/wgbh/pages/frontline/shows/kosovo/).

28. Other U.S Air Force thinking differs on this subject. Espoused prominently after Operation Allied Force by Lieutenant General Michael Short, who ran the air war against Serbia, it holds that aerial attacks should *not* follow this traditional phased approach but hit a wide range of targets from the opening hours of a conflict. According to this view, doing so maximizes shock and minimizes an enemy's ability to hide key assets or to develop contingency plans for functioning while under attack. However, that was not the body of U.S. Air Force doctrine that influenced war planning most heavily in Operation Allied Force.

29. "Address to the Nation by the President" (White House, Office of the Press Secretary, June 10, 1999). See also William S. Cohen and Henry H. Shelton, "Joint Statement on the Kosovo After-Action Review" (U.S. Department of Defense, October 14, 1999); and James Steinberg, "A Perfect Polemic: Blind to Reality in Kosovo," *Foreign Affairs*, vol. 78 (November-December 1998), pp. 128–33.

Chapter Two

1. "Statement on Kosovo" (London: Contact Group, March 9, 1998). Russia dissociated itself from all punitive measures except the arms embargo.

2. Madeleine K. Albright, "Press Briefing at the Ministry of Foreign Affairs" (Rome: U.S. Department of State, March 7, 1998).

3. "Remarks by the President and UN Secretary-General Kofi Annan in Photo Opportunity" (White House, Office of the Press Secretary, March 11, 1998).

4. Quoted in Walter Isaacson, "Madeleine's War," *Time*, May 17, 1999, p. 29.

5. See Ivo H. Daalder, *Getting to Dayton: The Making of America's Bosnia Policy* (Brookings, 2000), pp. 5–36.

6. Gary Dempsey, "Washington's Kosovo Policy: Consequences and Contradictions," *Policy Analysis*, October 8, 1998, p. 17.

7. Charter flights to the United States by the Yugoslav national airlines were approved, the Yugoslav consulate in the United States was reopened, and member-

ship in the U.S.-sponsored Southern European Cooperation Initiative was offered. R. Jeffrey Smith, "U.S. Assails Government Crackdown in Kosovo," *Washington Post,* March 5, 1998, p. A23.

8. Albright, "Press Briefing at the Ministry of Foreign Affairs" (March 7, 1998).

9. This was clear even at the time. See Ivo H. Daalder, "Kosovo: Bosnia Déjà Vu," *Washington Post,* April 17, 1998, p. A23; Chris Hedges, "Another Victory for Death in Serbia," *New York Times,* March 8, 1998, p. 5; and Warren Zimmermann, "The Demons of Kosovo," *National Interest,* no. 52 (Summer 1998), pp. 3–11.

10. Smith, "U.S. Assails Government Crackdown in Kosovo," p. A23.

11. Senior State Department official, interview by authors, September 24, 1999. See also Jane Perlez, "U.S. Warned Serb Leader Not to Crack Down on Kosovo Albanians," *New York Times,* March 15, 1998, p. 6.

12. See Tom Walker, "Albanians Defy Serb Order for Quick Funerals," *Times* (London), March 10, 1998, p. 12; Chris Hedges, "On a Garage Floor in Kosovo, a Gruesome Serbian Harvest," *New York Times,* March 10, 1998, p. A1; R. Jeffrey Smith, "11 Children among Kosovo Dead," *Washington Post,* March 10, 1998, p. A1; and Bronwen Maddox, "The 80 Days War," *Times* (London), July 15, 1999, p. 43.

13. Quoted in Chris Hedges, "Serbs Claim Victory over a Separatist Militia," *New York Times,* March 8, 1998, p. 6. An unfortunate reference to the KLA as a "terrorist group" was made by Bob Gelbard in press conferences in Pristina and Belgrade weeks before. See Robert S. Gelbard, "Press Conference" (Pristina: U.S. Department of State, February 22, 1998); and Robert S. Gelbard, "Press Conference" (Belgrade: U.S. Department of State, February 23, 1998). Some have since accused Gelbard of essentially giving the Serbs a green light to attack in Kosovo. See, for example, Noel Malcolm, preface to *Kosovo: A Short History,* rev. ed. (Harper/Perennial, 1999); and Patrick Moore, "Why the Kosovo Crisis Now?" *RFE/RL Newsline,* March 2, 1998, pt. 2. But this is a misreading of what Gelbard said both publicly and privately, when he strongly warned against any escalation and openly pointed his finger at the Serb police as the group responsible for "the great majority of [the] violence." See Gelbard, "Press Conference" (February 23, 1998).

14. Barton Gellman, "The Path to Crisis: How the United States and Its Allies Went to War," *Washington Post,* April 18, 1999, p. A30.

15. When during the first Contact Group meeting on March 9 in London Albright's close aide James Rubin suggested that she ought to accept the weaker language for threatening the Serbs proposed by the Italians and French, she snarled, "Where do you think we are, Munich?" Quoted in Isaacson, "Madeleine's War," p. 29. See also Michael Hirsh, "At War with Ourselves," *Harper's Magazine,* vol. 299 (July 1999), pp. 60–69.

16. Madeleine K. Albright, "Statement at the Contact Group Ministerial on Kosovo" (London: U.S. Department of State, March 9, 1998).

17. "Statement on Kosovo" (London: Contact Group, March 9, 1998).

18. "Statement on Kosovo" (Bonn: Contact Group, March 25, 1998).

19. UN Security Council, Resolution 1160 (1998), March 31, 1998. See also John M. Goshko, "Arms Embargo on Yugoslavia; U.N. Security Council Seeks to Prevent More Violence in Kosovo," *Washington Post*, April 1, 1998, p. A24.

20. Days before the third Contact Group meeting since the outbreak of violence in Kosovo, a senior Clinton administration official warned in a background briefing that Washington would "not settle for an agreement just for the sake of an agreement. We will not settle for a lowest common denominator solution. In other words, consensus is not the goal here. A strong substantive package is the goal. . . . [If] there is not an agreement with the Contact Group on this type of substantive package that we are advocating . . . then we would expect, while continuing to work with the Contact Group in the future, to show much more leadership on our own." "Senior State Department Official Holds Background Briefing on U.S. Policy in Kosovo and Bosnia," (U.S. Department of State, April 27, 1998). For agreement on sanctions, see "Statement" (Rome: Contact Group, April 29, 1998); for the May announcement, see "Statement Issued by the UK as Co-ordinator of the Birmingham Contact Group Meeting" (Birmingham, U.K.: Contact Group, May 18, 1998).

21. Asked whether the Christmas warning still stood, State Department deputy spokesman James Foley answered: "We've not commented on press reports on that subject, and I'm not going to be able to today. As I said, we have a broad range of options. I'm not going to specify either in terms of ruling in or ruling out particular options. And I certainly can't comment on that particular subject." "Daily Press Briefing" (U.S. Department of State, March 5, 1998). A week later, Robert Gelbard told Congress, in a fully vetted statement, "We believe that no option should be ruled in or out for now. What we prefer to do . . . is use every possible economic sanction or other kind of tool we have diplomatically, but we're not ruling anything out." Robert S. Gelbard, testimony, Hearing, *The Prospects for Implementation of Dayton Agreements and the New NATO Mission in Bosnia*, Committee on International Relations, 105 Cong. 2 sess. (March 12, 1998), p. 24; and senior State Department official, interview by authors, September 24, 1999. Adding to the confusion was the statement by an administration official that same day that "the United States view remains the same as it was in December 1992—that we're not going to sit back and accept a major Serb military operation in Kosovo." Philip Shenon, "U.S. Says It Might Consider Attacking Serbs," *New York Times*, March 13, 1998, p. A10.

22. This sentiment was particularly strong in the Pentagon, where defense planners concluded almost immediately that force was not the answer: "The first question we had to ask was whether the Christmas warning was still on the table. And the fact is that the Christmas warning was not on the table. We were not prepared for unilateral action." Quoted in Gellman, "The Path to Crisis," p. A30.

23. After Berger's outburst, no one else—not Albright nor her deputy, Strobe Talbott—came to Gelbard's support. U.S. official, interview by authors, May 20, 1998. See also Elaine Sciolino and Ethan Bronner, "How a President, Distracted by Scandal, Entered Balkan War," *New York Times*, April 18, 1999, p. 12.

24. Samuel R. Berger, interview by authors, February 9, 2000.

25. Quoted in Gellman, "The Path to Crisis." See also Sciolino and Bronner, "How a President, Distracted by Scandal, Entered Balkan War."

26. Daalder, "Kosovo: Bosnia Déjà Vu"; and Zimmermann, "The Demons of Kosovo." See also Steven Erlanger, "First Bosnia, Now Kosovo," *New York Times,* June 6, 1998, p. A14.

27. Bob Davis, "Pledging a 'Clinton Doctrine' for Foreign Policy Creates Concerns for Adversaries and Allies Alike," *Wall Street Journal,* August 6, 1998, p. A12.

28. *PBS Frontline, War in Europe* (www.pbs.org/wgbh/pages/frontline/shows/kosovo/ [accessed March 2000]).

29. "Statement on Kosovo," NATO Press Release M-NAC-1(98)61, May 28, 1998.

30. Ibid.

31. Javier Solana, "Remarks to the Press," NATO Press Release, May 28, 1998.

32. "Statement on Kosovo," NATO Press Release M-NAC-D-1(98)77, June 11, 1998.

33. Mike O'Connor, "NATO Jets Patrol Skies Near Serbia in Show of Force," *New York Times,* June 16, 1998, p. A1.

34. "Statement by NATO Secretary-General, Dr. Javier Solana, on Exercise 'Determined Falcon,'" NATO Press Release (98)80, June 13, 1998.

35. Klaus Naumann, interview, *PBS Frontline, War in Europe.*

36. It was no coincidence that the air exercises were undertaken just one day before President Milosevic's visit to Moscow. In his meeting with President Boris Yeltsin on June 16, Milosevic agreed to a number of steps designed to ease the crisis, including providing access to Kosovo for relief groups and international monitors, supporting arrangements for the return of more than 65,000 people to their homes, and resuming talks with the Albanian community on a political solution to the conflict. While Milosevic refused to accede to the Contact Group's key demand that Serb security forces be withdrawn, U.S. intelligence officials later reported "a definite leveling off and possibly even drop in offensive type of operations on the part of the Serbs" following the Moscow visit. "Background Briefing" (U.S. Department of Defense, Office of the Assistant Secretary of Defense, Public Affairs, July 15, 1998). See also O'Connor, "NATO Jets Patrol Skies Near Serbia in Show of Force"; and Michael R. Gordon, "Milosevic Pledges Steps to Hold off Attack from NATO," *New York Times,* June 17, 1998, p. A1.

37. Statement by Klaus Naumann, Hearings, *Lessons Learned from the Military Operations Conducted as Part of Operation Allied Force,* Senate Committee on Armed Services, 106 Cong. 1 sess. (November 3, 1999), p. 3.

38. Craig R. Whitney, "NATO to Conduct Large Maneuvers to Warn off Serbs," *New York Times,* June 12, 1998, p. A1.

39. Klaus Naumann, interview by authors, December 22, 1999; and Wesley Clark, interview, *PBS Frontline, War in Europe.*

40. U.S. official, interview by authors, September 24, 1999; and NATO official, interview by authors, November 9, 1999. See also Steven R. Bowman, *Bosnia and Kosovo: U.S. Military Operations,* no. 93056 (Congressional Research Service, 1998),

p. 10; Dana Priest, "Military Doubtful on Kosovo Strikes; Officials Say Success Requires All-Out Bombardment," *Washington Post*, June 17, 1998, p. A23; R. Jeffrey Smith, "NATO Albania Deployment Less Likely," *Washington Post*, May 28, 1998, p. A30; Thomas E. Ricks and Carla Anne Robbins, "U.S., NATO Allies Plan to Conduct Air-Raid Drill to Halt Serb Attacks," *Wall Street Journal*, June 11, 1998, p. B8; and Michael Evans and Charles Bremner, "NATO to Draw up Kosovo Military Options," *Times* (London), June 25, 1998, p. 17.

41. Naumann, interview by authors, December 22, 1999; and U.S. official, interview by authors, September 24, 1999.

42. *PBS Frontline, War in Europe.*

43. "Background Briefing" (July 15, 1998).

44. R. Jeffrey Smith, "Officials Seek Kosovo Intervention," *Washington Post*, June 6, 1998, p. A17. On June 7 British Foreign Secretary Robin Cook stated that "President Milosevic over the past week has crossed the threshold. The use of tanks, of artillery, of the might of the military army against civilian centers is wholly unacceptable within the modern Europe." Steven Erlanger, "Milosevic Agrees to Let Diplomatic Observers into Kosovo," *New York Times*, June 8, 1998, p. A23.

45. British government officials, interviews by authors, September 7, 1999, November 8, 9, and 12, 1999. See also Smith, "Officials Seek Kosovo Intervention," p. A1; and Ricks and Robbins, "U.S. NATO Allies Plan to Conduct Air-Raid Drill to Halt Serb Attacks," p. B8.

46. Mike O'Connor, "Thousands of Refugees Flee Serb Mountain Attack," *New York Times*, August 5, 1998, p. A3; and Priest, "Military Doubtful on Kosovo Strikes," p. A23.

47. Whitney, "NATO to Conduct Large Maneuvers to Warn off Serbs," p. A1.

48. "Statement on Kosovo" (Washington, D.C.: Contact Group, January 8, 1998).

49. See Michael Igantieff, "The Diplomatic Life: The Dream of Albanians," *New Yorker*, January 11, 1999, pp. 34–39.

50. "Milosevic Agrees to Meet with an Ethnic Albanian over Kosovo," *New York Times*, May 14, 1998, p. A9.

51. Richard C. Holbrooke, interview with authors, April 7, 2000.

52. Guy Dinmore, "U.S. Envoy Arranges Kosovo Peace Talks," *Washington Post*, May 14, 1998, p. A25; and Erlanger, "Milosevic Agrees to Let Diplomatic Observers into Kosovo," p. A3.

53. See "Kosovo Diplomatic Observer Mission" (U.S. Department of State, Bureau of European and Canadian Affairs, July 8, 1998).

54. Barton Gellman, "U.S. Reaching out to Kosovo Rebels," *Washington Post*, July 1, 1998, pp. A25, A32.

55. "Statement" (Bonn: Contact Group, July 8, 1998), paras. 8–9.

56. "Autonomy for Kosovo Is Goal of Envoy's Talks," *Richmond Times-Dispatch*, July 10, 1998, p. 4.

57. R. Jeffrey Smith, "Kosovo Albanians Said to Agree on Negotiating Team," *Washington Post*, July 28, 1998, p. A11.

58. R. Jeffrey Smith, "Discussions of Kosovo's Legal Status Postponed," *Washington Post*, September 3, 1998, p. A48.

59. Quoted in R. Jeffrey Smith, "An Empty Country," *Washington Post*, July 31, 1998, p. A22.

60. John Goshko, "U.S., Allies Inch Closer to Kosovo Intervention," *Washington Post*, September 23, 1998, pp. A21.

61. UN Security Council, Resolution 1199 (1998), September 23, 1998, paras. 3, 4.

62. "Statement by the Secretary-General of NATO," NATO Press Release (98)93, August 12, 1998; and Steven Erlanger, "NATO Approval Renews Threat of Force in Kosovo," *New York Times*, August 4, 1998, p. A3.

63. NATO official, interview by authors, November 9, 1999.

64. "Statement by the Secretary-General of NATO," NATO Press Statement, August 12, 1998; and British government official, interview by authors, September 7, 1999.

65. Quoted in Gellman, "The Path to Crisis," p. A30.

66. Steven Lee Myers, "U.S. Urging NATO to Step up Plans to Act against Yugoslavia," *New York Times*, September 24, 1998, p. A8. See also Craig Whitney, "Allies Inch toward Action against Serbs," *New York Times*, September 25, 1998, p. A8.

67. "Statement by the Secretary-General," NATO Press Statement, Vilamoura, Portugal, September 24, 1998.

68. "Background Briefing: Under Secretary of Defense for Policy Walter B. Slocombe and Ambassador Vershbow" (Vilamoura, Portugal: U.S. Department of Defense, September 24, 1998).

69. Jane Perlez, "Massacres by Serbian Forces in 3 Kosovo Villages," *New York Times*, September 30, 1998, p. A1; and Guy Dinmore, "New Kosovo Massacre May Spur NATO to Act," *Washington Post*, September 30, 1998, p. A1. For complete details, see *Federal Republic of Yugoslavia: A Week of Terror in Drenica—Humanitarian Law Violations in Kosovo* (New York: Human Rights Watch, 1999).

70. Quoted by Madeleine K. Albright, "Remarks on Board Aircraft en Route to Jerusalem" (U.S. Department of State, October 5, 1998). According to Jamie Shea, NATO's spokesman, the allies pegged this threshold at thirty-four dead, the number of people killed by a Serb artillery shell in Sarajevo in August 1995 that turned out to be the trigger for Operation Deliberate Force. Jamie Shea, interview by authors, November 10, 1999.

71. For an overview of these issues, consult especially Catherine Guicherd, "International Law and the War in Kosovo," *Survival*, vol. 41 (Summer 1999), pp. 25–29; and Adam Roberts, "NATO's 'Humanitarian War' over Kosovo," *Survival*, vol. 41 (Autumn 1999), pp. 104–07.

72. Celestine Bohlen, "Russia Vows to Block the U.N. from Backing Attack on Serbs," *New York Times*, October 7, 1998, p. A8.

73. See "FRY/Kosovo: The Way Ahead; UK View on the Legal Base for Use of Force" (London: Foreign and Commonwealth Office, October 7, 1998); Alexander Nicoll, "Cracks Still Appear in NATO's Collective Will for Air Strikes," *Financial Times*,

October 9, 1998, p. 2; Claus Gennrich, "Im Angesicht der Not im Kosovo baut Kinkel neue juristische Brücken," *Frankfurter Allgemeine Zeitung*, October 14, 1998, p. 2; and Roger Cohen, "NATO Shatters Old Limits in the Name of Preventing Evil," *New York Times*, October 18, 1998, p. 3.

74. Quoted in Guicherd, "International Law and the War in Kosovo," p. 28. See also statements by French Defense Minister Alain Richard and German Foreign Minister Joschka Fischer in Horst Teltschik, ed., *Global Security on the Threshold to the Next Millennium* (Berlin: Berlin Verlag, 1999), pp. 43, 53–54.

75. Roger Cohen, "NATO Nears Final Order to Approve Kosovo Strike," *New York Times*, October 11, 1998, p. A8.

76. "Report of the Secretary-General Prepared Pursuant to Resolutions 1160 (1998) and 1199 (1998) of the Security Council," S/1998/912 (UN Security Council, October 3, 1998); and Jane Perlez, "Serb Pullback May Forestall NATO Attack," *New York Times*, October 5, 1998, p. A1.

77. Senior U.S. official, interview by authors, August 24, 1999. See also James Rubin, "Ambassador Holbrooke Travel to Brussels and Belgrade" (U.S. Department of State, October 4, 1998).

78. "Contact Group Discussions on Kosovo: Press Conference by British Foreign Foreign Secretary, Robin Cook" (London: Contact Group, October 8, 1998).

79. Senior U.S. and allied officials indicated that they had had no prior knowledge of what Holbrooke would do in Belgrade aside from demanding Milosevic's compliance. Allied officials also complained that they had had no input into Holbrooke's talks. Interviews by authors: senior U.S. official, August 24, 1999; senior Pentagon official, February 16, 2000; senior German official, October 22, 1999; and senior British official, November 8, 1999.

80. Senior U.S. official, interview by authors, August 24, 1999.

81. Quoted in Roger Cohen, "Americans Rebuke Yugoslav Leader," *New York Times*, October 9, 1998, p. A6.

82. A first draft interim agreement (Hill I) had been circulated to the parties on October 1. A second draft (Hill II) incorporated comments from both sides and was presented to and adopted by the Contact Group on October 8 as an agreed basis for negotiations. For the Contact Group's endorsement of Hill II, see "Contact Group Discussions on Kosovo" (October 8, 1998). Differing versions of the Hill proposal are also reproduced in Marc Weller, *The Crisis in Kosovo, 1989–1999* (Cambridge, England: Documents and Analysis Publishing, Ltd., 1999), pp. 356–82.

83. Jane Perlez, "A U.S. Message to Milosevic Turns into Full-Dress Talks," *New York Times*, October 10, 1998, p. A6; R. Jeffrey Smith, "U.S. Envoys, Milosevic Seek Accord to Avert Airstrikes," *Washington Post*, October 10, 1998, p. A18; R. Jeffrey Smith, "Talks Continue as Serbs Prepare for NATO Airstrikes," *Washington Post*, October 11, 1998, pp. A39, A46; R. Jeffrey Smith and George Lardner Jr., "Accord on Kosovo Remains Elusive," *Washington Post*, October 12, 1998, pp. A14, A22; David Buchan and Guy Dinmore, "Envoy Looks to Close Kosovo Deal," *Financial Times*,

October 13, 1998, p. 1; and Martin Walker and Richard Norton-Taylor, "Kosovo Crisis: How a Fragile Peace Was Won," *Guardian*, October 14, 1998, p. 15.

84. Quoted in Walker and Norton-Taylor, "How a Fragile Peace Was Won," p. 15. Even saber rattling seemed to have no impact on Milosevic. On October 10, U.S. B-52 bombers flew to Britain in preparation for possible air strikes and an aircraft carrier from the Sixth Fleet went on station in the Adriatic. See Jane Perlez, "NATO Raises Its Pressure on the Serbs," *New York Times*, October 12, 1998, p. A8; and Guy Dinmore and Alex Nicoll, "NATO Expected to Issue Yugoslav 'Activation Order,'" *Financial Times*, October 12, 1998, p. 24. When Holbrooke introduced Milosevic to Lieutenant General Mike Short as the man who would run the air campaign, Milosevic's first remark was, "So, General, you're the man who's going to bomb us." General Short responded: "Mr. President, I've got B-52s in one hand, I've got U-2s in the other—I'm going to be ordered to use one of the two of them. I hope you make the right choice." Although the general's statement appeared to have an impact, it would take many more days to convince Milosevic to make that right choice. The anecdote was recounted by Holbrooke in an interview on the *Newshour with Jim Lehrer*, October 14, 1998.

85. Steven Erlanger, "Schröder Tells Clinton He Backs Action by NATO in Kosovo," *New York Times*, October 10, 1998, p. A6.

86. Naumann, interview by authors, December 22, 1999; R. Jeffrey Smith, "Dramatic Kosovo Negotiations Had a Predetermined Last Act," *Washington Post*, October 15, 1998, p. A32; Walker and Norton-Taylor, "How a Fragile Peace Was Won"; and Richard Holbrooke and William Walker, "Briefing on Kosovo" (U.S. Department of State, October 28, 1998).

87. "Statement to the Press by the Secretary-General," NATO Press Statement, October 13, 1998.

88. "Press Conference by Ambassador Richard Holbrooke, and Ambassador Christopher Hill" (Belgrade: U.S. Department of State, October 13, 1998).

89. "Kosovo Verification Mission Agreement between the North Atlantic Treaty Organization and the Federal Republic of Yugoslavia," S/1998/991, annex (UN Security Council, October 23, 1998).

90. "Letter Dated 16 October from the Minister for Foreign Affairs of Poland Addressed to the Secretary-General," S/1998/978, annex (UN Security Council, October 20, 1998).

91. UN Security Council, Resolution 1203 (1998), October 24, 1998. Both Russia and China threatened to veto the original text of the draft resolution, which included the Security Council's right to take all "appropriate steps" in case Yugoslavia failed to meet its obligations. In the end, both abstained, emphasizing that the resolution did not entail "any authorization of using force or threatening to use force against the Federal Republic of Yugoslavia." Quoted in Youssef Ibrahim, "U.N. Measure Skirts Outright Threat of Force against Milosevic," *New York Times*, October 25, 1998, p. 6.

92. Quoted in Steven Erlanger, "Clinton Presses Yugoslavs as NATO's Role Is Hailed," *New York Times*, October 14, 1998, p. A11.

93. "Balkans: Statement by Mrs. Sadako Ogada, UN High Commisioner for Refugees" (Geneva: UNHCR, November 20, 1998). According to the UNHCR, by November 26, 1998, 75,000 of the 250,000 people displaced inside Kosovo had returned to their homes; the remaining 175,000 found shelter elsewhere. "UN Inter-Agency Update on Kosovo Situation Report 72" (UNHCR, November 26, 1998). See also "Report of the Secretary-General Prepared Pursuant to Resolutions 1160 (1998), 1199 (1998) and 1203 (1998) of the Security Council," S/1198/1068 (UN Security Council, November 12, 1998).

94. ABC News, *This Week*, "The NATO Deal on Kosovo," October 18, 1998, transcript. See also Holbrooke and Walker, "Briefing on Kosovo" (October 28, 1998); "Press Briefing by National Security Adviser Samuel Berger" (White House, Office of the Press Secretary, October 13, 1998); and Samuel Berger, "A Chance for Peace," *Washington Post*, October 21, 1998, p. A19.

95. Holbrooke and Walker, "Briefing on Kosovo" (October 28, 1998).

96. See Ivo H. Daalder, "Peace at Any Price," *San Diego Union-Tribune*, October 18, 1998, p. G1; Ivo H. Daalder, "Slouching toward a Breakaway Kosovo," *Washington Times*, November 4, 1998, p. A27; Fred Hiatt, "Phony Deal in Kosovo," *Washington Post*, October 18, 1998, p. C7; Jim Hoagland, "Holbrooke's Deal at the Brink," *Washington Post*, October 14, 1998, p. A15; and Helle Bering, "Why We Are Not Helping Kosovo," *Washington Times*, October 20, 1998, p. A15.

97. See for example James A. Schear, "Arms Control Treaty Compliance: Buildup to a Breakdown?" *International Security*, vol. 10 (Fall 1985), pp. 141–82; Jeanette Voas, "The Arms-Control Compliance Debate," *Survival*, vol. 20 (January-February 1985), pp. 8–31; and Richard N. Haass, "Verification and Compliance," in Albert Carnesale and Richard N. Haass, eds., *Superpower Arms Control: Setting the Record Straight* (Ballinger, 1985), pp. 303–28.

98. As General Clark recalled, when he traveled to Belgrade to finalize the NATO aerial verification agrement, "We weren't sure that there was anything in writing that said that Milosevic was actually going to comply with the UN Security Council resolution [calling for him] to withdraw the excess forces and to stop the excessive violence there. And that wasn't part of the signed agreement." See Wesley Clark, interview, *PBS Frontline, War in Europe*.

99. "Press Briefing by National Security Adviser Samuel Berger" (October 13, 1998).

100. Senior State Department official, interview by authors, September 23, 1999.

101. Steven Lee Myers, "Serb Forces Leaving Kosovo, but at a Slow Pace, U.S. Says," *New York Times*, October 19, 1998, p. A9.

102. "Statement by the NATO Spokesman," NATO Speech, October 16, 1998; and Steven Lee Myers, "Reprieve by NATO Allows Milosevic Another 10 Days," *New York Times*, October 17, 1998, p. A1.

103. Craig R. Whitney, "2 NATO Generals to Warn Milosevic of Air Raids," *New York Times*, October 24, 1998, p. A4.

104. The text of the final agreement did not specify this number, in part because the Pentagon apparently had briefed the Senate on the MUP troop presence in Kosovo,

arguing that the pre-crisis MUP presence was 6,000, rather than 11,000, troops. This discrepancy was discovered only when a draft of the agreement worked out by Clark and Naumann was sent to the United States for final approval, at which time it was decided to omit any specific numbers in the agreement rather than to seek a renegotiation, which was likely to fail. Naumann, interview by authors, December 22, 1999.

105. The text of the agreement, as released by Yugoslav authorities, is reprinted in appendix C. See also "Press Conference by Jamie Shea and General Wesley Clark," NATO Press Conference, April 13, 1999; Michael Evans, "Belgrade to Pull out 5,000 Police," *Times* (London), October 27, 1998, p. 14; Steven Lee Myers, "NATO Is Likely to Extend Deadline for Kosovo Strikes," *New York Times*, October 27, 1998, p. A10; and "Background Briefing" (U.S. Department of Defense, October 29, 1998).

106. Naumann, interview by authors, December 22, 1999. See also James Gow, "Kosovo after the Holbrooke-Milosevic Agreement: What Now?" *International Spectator*, vol. 33 (October-December 1998), p. 21.

107. "Statement to the Press by NATO Secretary-General Dr. Javier Solana," NATO Speech, October 27, 1998; and Evans, "Belgrade to Pull Out 5,000 Police," p. 14.

108. "Press Conference by Jamie Shea and General Wesley Clark," April 13, 1999, slides 1-5.

109. XFOR consisted of a 1,500-person, French-led NATO force that excluded U.S. combat personnel. Its mission was to "extract OSCE verifiers or other designated persons from Kosovo in an emergency." "Press Statement," NATO Press Release (98)139, December 5, 1998. Three levels of response were developed for the force. A tier-1 extraction would be in a local area, occur in a benign environment, and involve only a few monitors; a predeployed XFOR would be able to respond to a tier-1 response on its own. A tier-2 extraction would involve special forces forward deployed as part of XFOR to extract a small number of monitors in a local area but entry and exit would likely be contested. A tier-3 extraction would involve the entire OSCE presence and require large-scale reinforcements with other NATO forces (including a U.S. marine expeditionary unit stationed offshore in the Adriatic Sea). British government official, interview by authors, September 7, 1999.

110. Naumann, interview by authors, December 22, 1999.

111. Quoted in John F. Harris, "Advice Didn't Sway Clinton on Airstrikes," *Washington Post*, April 1, 1999, p. A1.

112. Richard Holbrooke, interview with authors, April 7, 2000. For Vershbow's views, see pp. 54-55.

113. Berger, interview by authors, February 9, 2000; and Hearing, *Nomination of Richard Holbrooke as U.S. Ambassador to the United Nations, Senate Foreign Relations Committee*, 106 Cong. 1 sess. (June 24, 1999), p. 8.

114. Richard Holbrooke, interview with the authors, April 7, 2000.

115. Madeleine Albright, interview, PBS Frontline, *War in Europe*.

116. Cohen statement, *U.S. Policy Regarding Kosovo, and a Revised Strategic Concept for NATO*, Senate Committee on Armed Services, 106 Cong. 1 sess. (April 15, 1999).

117. British government officials, interviews by authors, November 9, 1999.

118. NATO diplomat, interview by authors, November 10, 1999. Similarly, Javier Solana recalled that in October he "kept insisting on the importance of getting NATO involved . . . not only in the air but also on the ground." ABC News, *Nightline*, "The Insiders' Story," August 30, 1999.

119. Michael Hirsh and John Barry, "How We Stumbled into War," *Newsweek*, April 12, 1999, p. 40.

120. Senior U.S. official, interview by authors, August 24, 1999. Quotations from the cable are in Sciolino and Bronner, "How a President, Distracted by Scandal, Entered Balkan War," p. 12.

121. Quoted in Barry Schweid, "NATO Preparing for Bombing Serbs," *Associated Press Headlines*, October 8, 1998 (dailynews.yahoo.com [accessed October 1999]); and Perlez, "NATO Raises Its Pressure on the Serbs," p. A8.

122. NATO and European officials, interviews by authors, November 9–12, 1999.

123. On doubts about the agreement, see also Lord Robertson of Port Ellen, "Kosovo: An Account of the Crisis" (www.mod.uk/news/kosovo/account/[accessed February 2000]).

124. "Press Conference by Ambassador Richard Holbrooke, and Ambassador Christopher Hill" (October 13, 1998). According to Holbrooke, Polish Foreign Minister Bronislaw Geremek was "somewhat taken aback by the size and potential expense of the role devised for the [O.S.C.E.] in Kosovo." Jane Perlez, "Milosevic Accepts Kosovo Monitors," *New York Times*, October 14, 1998, p. A1.

125. ABC News, *This Week*, October 18, 1998.

126. "Statement by the President" (New York: White House, Office of the Press Secretary, October 12, 1998). After the agreement was reached, Clinton was asked, "Given your expressed distrust of Milosevic, how optimistic are you?" The president answered, "I'm neither optimistic, nor pessimistic because I have something better now. We have now a verification system, so we're not dependent upon our hopes. . . . There will be facts—facts on the ground which will tell us whether or not the compliance is there." See "Remarks by the President upon Departure for Forest Knolls Elementary School" (White House, Office of the Press Secretary, October 13, 1998).

127. Among the critics was none other than NATO's top military commander, General Klaus Naumann. See Naumann, interview, *PBS Frontline, War in Europe*.

128. Nathan Gardels, "Putting the Pressure on Milosevic: An Interview with Richard Holbrooke," *Los Angeles Times*, October 22, 1998, p. B9.

129. To be sure, in the five months of operations, Kosovo Verification Mission monitors faced only minor problems, and when all 1,380 were withdrawn on March 20, 1999, their exodus to Macedonia was unimpeded.

130. The one notable exception was an article by Fred C. Iklé, "After Detection—What?" *Foreign Affairs*, vol. 39 (January 1961), pp. 208–20.

131. Richard Holbrooke, interview with authors, April 7, 2000.

132. See Daalder, "Slouching toward a Breakaway Kosovo," p. A27.

133. On October 31, 1998, the Kosovar Diplomatic Observer Mission reported

that the "KLA (UCK) presence is growing in those areas where Serb troops and police have departed, having established its own checkpoints on secondary roads in the Drenica, Podujevo, and Malisevo areas." See "KDOM Daily Report," October 31, 1998 (www.state.gov/www/regions/eur/rpt 981031 kdom.html [accessed March 2000]).

134. Quoted in Mike O'Connor, "Kosovo Rebels Gain Ground under NATO Threat," *New York Times*, December 4, 1998, p. A3.

135. Naumann, interview by authors, December 22, 1999. See Naumann, interview, *PBS Frontline, War in Europe*.

136. Wesley K. Clark, "The United States and NATO: The Way Ahead," *Parameters*, vol. 34 (Winter 1999-2000), p. 8.

137. Klaus Naumann testified before the U.S. Senate that he had "reason to believe that . . . in November 1998 [Milosevic] most probably [took] a decision to not only annihilate the KLA but also to expel the bulk of the Kosovars in order to restore an ethnic superiority for the Serbs." Naumann statement, Hearings, *Lessons Learned from the Military Operations Conducted as Part of Operation Allied Force*, p. 2.

138. Stanisic and Perisic were both critics of the Serb actions in Kosovo, and Perisic told Clark and Naumann of his concerns about using his army in Kosovo for fear that doing so might lead NATO to destroy what he termed the only democratic institution left in Yugoslavia. Naumann, interview by authors, December 22, 1999. See also R. Jeffrey Smith, "Kosovo, Montenegro Alarmed by Firings," *Washington Post*, November 29, 1998, p. A28; and Craig Whitney and Eric Schmitt, "NATO Had Signs Its Strategy Would Fail Kosovars," *New York Times*, April 1, 1999, p. A1.

139. The details of Operation Horseshoe were first made public in R. Jeffrey Smith and William Drozdiak, "Serbs' Offensive Was Meticulously Planned," *Washington Post*, April 11, 1999, pp. A1, A26–27. NATO authorities got wind of the plan only in late February 1999, when German intelligence officials provided them with a copy of the plan apparently obtained from Austrian and possibly Slovenian sources. It was impossible to verify this information before it proved accurate—when Serb forces accelerated the plan's implementation in late March. Senior NATO official, interview by authors, December 21, 1999. See also Coen van Zwol, "Lente in Kosovo," *NRC Handelsblad*, December 18, 1999 (www.nrc.nl/W2/Lab/Kosovo/991218-m.html [accessed December 1999]).

140. Senior State Department official, interview by authors, September 23, 1999. See also *Nomination of Richard Holbrooke as U.S. Ambassador to the United Nations*, p. 15.

141. On these points, see especially Richard K. Betts, "The Delusion of Impartial Intervention," *Foreign Affairs*, vol. 73 (November-December 1994), pp. 20–33; and Stephen J. Stedman, "Alchemy for a New World Order: Overselling 'Preventive Diplomacy,'" *Foreign Affairs*, vol. 74 (May-June 1995), pp. 14–20.

142. Holbrooke, interview with authors, April 7, 2000.

143. Quoted in Tim Weiner, "NATO Warns Time Is Short for Talks on Kosovo," *New York Times*, November 20, 1998, p. A9.

144. "Serbian Government Endorses Accord Reached by President Milosevic,

Belgrade, 13 October 1998," reprinted in Weller, *The Crisis in Kosovo, 1989–1999*, p. 279.

145. Quoted in R. Jeffrey Smith, "Both Sides Resist U.S. Proposals in Kosovo," *Washington Post*, December 30, 1998, p. A16. See also Guy Dinmore, "Kosovo's Plan Removes Serbia's Authority," *Financial Times*, November 19, 1998, p. 2; and "Serbs Reject U.S. Kosovo Plan Despite a Plea for Compromise," *New York Times*, December 9, 1998, p. A5.

146. R. Jeffrey Smith, "A Turnaround in Kosovo," *Washington Post*, November 18, 1999, p. A1; and O'Connor, "Kosovo Rebels Gain Ground under NATO Threat," p. A3.

147. Naumann, interview by authors, December 22, 1999; and "Statement to the Press by NATO Secretary-General Dr. Javier Solana," October 27, 1998.

148. Quoted in Mike O'Connor, "Attack by Serbs Shatters a Cease-Fire in Kosovo," *New York Times*, December 25, 1998, p. A1. See also Misha Savic, "Yugoslav Forces Attack Kosovo Rebel Bastion," *Washington Post*, December 25, 1998, p. A41.

Chapter Three

1. R. Jeffrey Smith, "This Time, Walker Wasn't Speechless; Memory of El Salvador Spurred Criticism of Serbs," *Washington Post*, January 23, 1999, p. A15.

2. Guy Dinmore, "Yugoslavs Eject U.S. Diplomat, Massacre Investigators Thwarted," *Washington Post*, January 19, 1999, p. A1. In late January, the *Washington Post* reported that communication intercepts demonstrated that Serb government officials ordered the security forces to "go in heavy" in Racak. R. Jeffrey Smith, "Serbs Tried to Cover up Massacre; Kosovo Reprisal Plot Bared by Phone Taps," *Washington Post*, January 28, 1999, p. A1.

3. Quoted in Barton Gellman, "The Path to Crisis: How the United States and Its Allies Went to War," *Washington Post*, April 18, 1999, p. A31.

4. For an argument in favor of partition, see John J. Mearsheimer, "The Case for Partitioning Kosovo," in Ted Galen Carpenter, ed., *NATO's Empty Victory* (Washington, D.C.: CATO Institute, 2000), pp. 133–38.

5. See Susan Woodward, *Balkan Tragedy: Chaos and Dissolution after the Cold War* (Brookings, 1995), pp. 330, 341; Warren Zimmermann, *Origins of a Catastrophe: Yugoslavia and Its Destroyers* (Time Books, 1996), p. 130; and International Crisis Group, *Kosovo Spring: The International Crisis Group Guide to Kosovo* (Brussels: 1998), p. 110.

6. Barry Posen, "The War for Kosovo," *International Security*, vol. 24 (Spring 2000), pp. 45–46.

7. See Joseph S. Nye Jr., "Redefining the National Interest," *Foreign Affairs*, vol. 78 (July-August 1999), p. 34.

8. "Daily Press Briefing" (U.S. Department of State, December 1, 1998). When asked what he thought of Rubin's statement, Holbrooke "rolled his eyes. He knew that the Administration, and particularly Albright, had to avoid seeming to be cozy

with Milosevic. Yet there was no realistic prospect of overthrowing his regime. That left only one alternative: talking to the dictator." Michael Ignatieff, "The Dream of Albanians," *New Yorker*, January 11, 1999, p. 36.

9. Quoted in Gellman, "The Path to Crisis," p. A31.

10. Jane Perlez, "Defiant Yugoslav Orders Expulsion of U.S. Diplomat," *New York Times*, January 19, 1999, p. A8.

11. Senior official, interview by authors, November 10, 1999.

12. Perlez, "Defiant Yugoslav Orders Expulsion of U.S. Diplomat," p. A8; and senior State Department official, interview by authors, September 21, 1999.

13. Quoted in Gellman, "The Path to Crisis," p. A1. See also Elaine Sciolino and Ethan Bronner, "How a President, Distracted by a Scandal, Entered Balkan War," *New York Times*, April 18, 1999, p. 13.

14. Both quotations in Gellman, "The Path to Crisis," p. A31.

15. Senior Pentagon official, interview by authors, February 16, 2000.

16. Senior State Department official, interview by authors, September 21, 1999; and senior U.S. official, interview by authors, August 24, 1999. See also Gellman, "The Path to Crisis," p. A31; and Sciolino and Bronner, "How a President, Distracted by a Scandal, Entered Balkan War," p. A13.

17. Gellman, "The Path to Crisis," p. A31.

18. In an interview with Michael Dobbs, Albright recounted why it took so long to succeed: "You need to understand how the process works. I am a very active Secretary of State and a great believer in the American role and power." But to succeed in harnessing that power to her diplomatic efforts, Albright argued, required policymakers to overcome both the "Vietnam syndrome," which cautions against getting involved, and the "Gulf War syndrome," which argues for getting involved only with "half a million Marines" to guarantee victory. "If you are going counter to where the chairman of the Joint Chiefs of Staff is, it takes a while to get your argument across," she said. "You never get decisions just like that. . . . This is a process which is consensual, incremental, [and] takes a while." Quoted in Michael Dobbs, "Annals of Diplomacy: Double Identity," *New Yorker*, March 29, 1999, p. 55.

19. On January 17, the North Atlantic Council strongly condemned the killings in Racak and called on Milosevic to comply with his commitments. However, while the NAC "reaffirmed that the ACTORDS for air operations remain in effect," it underscored allied unease about using force by sending Generals Clark and Naumann to Belgrade for discussions with Milosevic. "Statement by the Secretary-General of NATO, Dr. Javier Solana on Behalf of the North Atlantic Council Following Its Meeting on Sunday 17th January 1999," NATO Press Release 99(003), January 17, 1999.

20. Senior U.S. official, interview by authors, August 24, 1999. See also Dana Priest, "Allies Balk at Bombing Yugoslavia," *Washington Post*, January 23, 1999, p. A18.

21. Quoted in Priest, "Allies Balk at Bombing Yugoslavia," p. A1.

22. Quoted in Gellman, "The Path to Crisis," p. A31. See also Helene Cooper, Thomas E. Ricks, and Carla Anne Robbins, "Military Action in Kosovo Moves Closer as U.S., Allies Plan to Force Settlement," *Wall Street Journal*, January 28, 1999, p. A20.

23. Senior U.S. official, interview by authors, August 24, 1999. Until the Rambouillet conference, the official U.S. position, as agreed by the NSC Deputies Committee, was to tie air strikes to Serb rejection of the accords. However, during the conference, the principals met and agreed that, in addition, the Kosovars would have to accept the accords before the employment of NATO airpower. Senior State Department official, interview by authors, September 23, 1999. That latter position was stated publicly by Secretary Albright on February 21: "If this [Rambouillet] fails because both sides say 'No,' there will not be bombing of Serbia." Quoted in Jane Perlez, "Albright Foresees No Raids on Serbs If 2 Sides Bar Pact," *New York Times*, February 22, 1999, p. A1.

24. Thomas W. Lippman, "U.S. Could Join Force to Manage Postwar Kosovo," *Washington Post*, January 27, 1999, p. A15.

25. Elizabeth Becker, "U.S. Refining Plans for Troops in Kosovo," *New York Times*, February 4, 1999, p. A10; "Remarks by the President at Baldrige Quality Awards Ceremony" (White House, Office of the Press Secretary, February 4, 1999); and "Radio Address by the President to the Nation" (White House, Office of the Press Secretary, February 13, 1999).

26. Gellman, "The Path to Crisis," p. A31.

27. Madeleine K. Albright and Igor Ivanov, "Joint Press Conference on Kosovo" (Moscow: U.S. Department of State, January 26, 1999).

28. Quoted in Roger Cohen, "Germany's Pragmatic Ex-Radical Thinks Globally," *New York Times*, January 28, 1999, p. A3.

29. "Press Release Issued by No. 10 Downing Street Following Dinner between the French President, M. Jacques Chirac, and the British Prime Minister, Mr. Tony Blair, London, 28 January 1999" (January 28, 1999).

30. James Rubin, "Contact Group Ministerial Meeting on Crisis in Kosovo" (U.S. Department of State, January 27, 1999).

31. Norman Kempster, "U.S. Pushes 2-Track Plan for Kosovo Peace," *Los Angeles Times*, January 28, 1999, p. A4.

32. "Secretary-General Calls for Unconditional Respect for Human Rights of Kosovo Citizens, in Statement to North Atlantic Treaty Organization," UN Press Release SG/SM/6878, January 28, 1999.

33. "Statement to the Press by NATO Secretary-General Dr. Javier Solana," NATO Press Release (99)11, January 28, 1999.

34. "Transcript: NATO Secretary-General's Press Conference Jan. 28" (U.S. Information Agency, January 29, 1999).

35. "Contact Group Conclusions" (London: Contact Group, January 29, 1999).

36. Madeline K. Albright, "Press Conference" (London: U.S. Department of State, January 28, 1999).

37. "Statement by the North Atlantic Council on Kosovo," NATO Press Release (99)12, January 30, 1999.

38. Madeleine K. Albright, "Remarks at the U.S. Institute of Peace" (U.S. Department of State, February 4, 1999).

39. R. Jeffrey Smith and William Drozdiak, "NATO Approves Strikes in Yugoslavia," *Washington Post*, January 31, 1999, p. A27; and Marc Weller, "The Rambouillet Conference on Kosovo," *International Affairs*, vol. 75 (April 1999), p. 226.

40. The principles are reprinted in Marc Weller, *The Crisis in Kosovo, 1989–1999* (Cambridge, England: Documents and Analysis Publishing, Ltd., 1999), p. 417.

41. Weller, "The Rambouillet Conference on Kosovo," p. 228.

42. Coen van Zwol, "Lente in Kosovo," *NRC Handelsblad*, December 18, 1999, p. 4 (www.nrc.nl/W2/Lab/Kosovo/991218-m.html [accessed December 1999]).

43. Ibid., p. 3.

44. See Jane Perlez, "As Kosovo Talks Continue, NATO Troop Plan Lags Badly," *New York Times*, February 9, 1999, p. A6; and Jane Perlez, "Trickiest Divides Are among Big Powers at Kosovo Talks," *New York Times*, February 11, 1999, p. A8.

45. Senior White House official, meeting with authors, February 9, 1999.

46. Jane Perlez, "Albright Brings Foes Face to Face at Kosovo Talks," *New York Times*, February 15, 1999, p. A1.

47. Charles Trueheart, "Serbian Leader Rejects Kosovo Peace Force, Autonomy Plan," *Washington Post*, February 16, 1999, p. A11.

48. Jane Perlez, "U.S. Negotiator at the Kosovo Talks Visits Milosevic," *New York Times*, February 17, 1999, p. A3.

49. The Hill mission occurred without any consultations with his co-negotiators. Petritsch even tried vainly to stop Hill from going to the airport, while Mayorski packed his bags and left for the Russian embassy. Tom Walker, "U.S. Stance on Kosovo Talks and 'Secret Flight' Infuriate Diplomats," *Times* (London), February 18, 1999, p. 17; and Gunter Hofmann, "Wie Deutschland in den Krieg geriet," *Die Zeit*, May 12, 1999, p. 12.

50. Van Zwol, "Lente in Kosovo," p. 5.

51. Weller, "The Rambouillet Conference on Kosovo," p. 229.

52. Jane Perlez, "Serbs Yield No Ground; Envoys Seem Resigned," *New York Times*, February 20, 1999, p. A6.

53. "Joint Press Conference by President Clinton and President Jacques Chirac of France" (White House, Office of the Press Secretary, February 19, 1999).

54. Since the French had barred NATO from participating at Rambouillet, the briefing was held at a military airfield near the chateau. Jane Perlez, "Talks on Kosovo Near Breakdown; Deadline Is Today," *New York Times*, February 23, 1999, p. A8.

55. Weller, "The Rambouillet Conference on Kosovo," p. 232.

56. "Interim Agreement for Peace and Self-Government in Kosovo, 23 February 1999," Chapter 8, Article I (3), reprinted in Weller, *The Crisis in Kosovo, 1989–1999*, p. 469.

57. Letter reprinted in Weller, *The Crisis in Kosovo, 1989–1999*, p. 452.

58. R. Jeffrey Smith, "Rebels' Intransigence Stymied Accord," *Washington Post*, February 24, 1999, p. A17.

59. Statement reprinted in Weller, *The Crisis in Kosovo, 1989–1999*, p. 471.

60. Perlez, "Albright Foresees No Raids on Serbs If 2 Sides Bar Pact," p. A1.

61. "Statement Rambouillet Accords: Co-Chairmen's Conclusions" (Rambouillet, France: Contact Group, February 23, 1999), pp. 1–2.

62. Jane Perlez, "Kosovo Albanians, in Reversal, Say They Will Sign Peace Pact," *New York Times*, February 24, 1999, p. A1; and Philip Shenon, "U.S. Says Kosovo Rebels Are Ready to Sign Peace Pact," *New York Times*, March 9, 1999, p. A3.

63. Carlotta Gall, "U.S. Official Sees 'Collision Course' in Kosovo Dispute," *New York Times*, March 10, 1999, p. A1.

64. William Claiborne, "U.S. Kosovo Plan Faces 2-Front Fight," *Washington Post*, March 11, 1999, p. A27.

65. Craig R. Whitney, "Ethnic Albanians Move to Accept Kosovo Pact," *New York Times*, March 16, 1999, p. A8; and Craig R. Whitney, "Serbs Reinforce Kosovo Forces, Clouding Talks," *New York Times*, March 17, 1999, p. A1. For specific changes in the text suggested by the Serb delegation, see the proposed draft agreement, reprinted in Weller, *The Crisis in Kosovo, 1989–1999*, pp. 480–90.

66. Statement reprinted in Weller, *The Crisis in Kosovo 1989–1999*, p. 493.

67. A whispering campaign of this sort has been attributed by Albright's aides to Holbrooke himself. See Warren Bass, "Cold War," *New Republic*, December 13, 1999, pp. 16–18.

68. See for example Christopher Layne and Benjamin Schwarz, "Kosovo: For the Record," *National Interest*, no. 57 (Fall 1999), pp. 10–11.

69. "Statement by the North Atlantic Council on Kosovo" (January 30, 1999).

70. Michael Mandelbaum, "A Perfect Failure: NATO's War against Yugoslavia," *Foreign Affairs*, vol. 78 (September-October 1999), p. 4. See also Alan Kuperman, "Botched Diplomacy Led to War," *Wall Street Journal*, June 17, 1999, p. A27.

71. "Interim Agreement for Peace and Self-Government in Kosovo, 23 February 1999," reprinted in Weller, *The Crisis in Kosovo, 1989–1999.*

72. General Wesley Clark, interview with authors, April 20, 2000.

73 "Rubin, Hill on Kosovo at U.S. Institute of Peace March 23" (U.S. Department of State, International Information Programs' Washington File, March 24, 2000).

74. Senior British official, interview by authors, November 8, 1999.

75. See, for example, Fred Hiatt, "A U.S. Retreat . . ." *Washington Post*, February 14, 1999, p. C7; Jim Hoagland, "Kosovo Disaster," *Washington Post*, February 28, 1999, p. B7; Robert E. Hunter, "NATO Gave Milosevic Advantage," *Los Angeles Times*, February 26, 1999, p. B7; and Mark Danner, "Endgame in Kosovo," *New York Review of Books*, May 6, 1999, pp. 8–11.

76. Hoagland, "Kosovo Disaster," p. B7.

77. See "Kosovo Rebels Clash with Serbs," *New York Times*, February 13, 1999, p. A4; Peter Finn, "Thousands Flee Ethnic Fighting," *Washington Post*, February 23, 1999, p. A16; Dana Priest and Thomas W. Lippman, "U.S. Speaks More Softly after Failed Kosovo Talks," *Washington Post*, February 25, 1999, p. A17; and Eric Schmitt, "Serb Army Masses 4,500 Armored Troops," *New York Times*, February 26, 1999, p. A11.

78. See, for example, Jane Perlez, "Diplomat vs. Rebels," *New York Times*, February 25, 1999, p. A10.

79. Samuel R. Berger, interview by authors, February 9, 2000.

80. Quoted in Joseph Fitchett, "Main Winner: U.S. Support for EU," *International Herald Tribune*, June 11, 1999, p. 1. See also Michael Hirsh, "At War with Ourselves," *Harper's Magazine*, vol. 299 (July 1999), pp. 60–69, esp. p. 66; and Walter Isaacson, "Madeleine's War," *Time*, May 17, 1999, p. 34.

81. "Remarks by the President on the Situation in Kosovo" (White House, Office of the Press Secretary, March 22, 1999).

82. "Political and Military Objectives of NATO Action with Regard to the Crisis in Kosovo," NATO Press Release 1999(043), March 23, 1999.

83. "Statement by the President to the Nation" (White House, Office of the Press Secretary, March 24, 1999).

84. Quoted in R. Jeffrey Smith, "Belgrade Rebuffs Final U.S. Warning," *Washington Post*, March 23, 1999, p. A1.

85. See "Press Conference by President Clinton" (White House, Office of the Press Secretary, June 25, 1999); Berger, interview by authors, February 9, 2000. Indeed, others in the U.S. government, including Secretary Albright's inner circle, considered the odds of Milosevic hunkering down and riding out a long air campaign at less than 25 percent. See Thomas W. Lippman, "Albright Misjudged Milosevic on Kosovo," *Washington Post*, April 7, 1999, p. A1.

86. Madeleine K. Albright, interview, PBS, *Newshour with Jim Lehrer*, March 24, 1999 (www.pbs.org/newshour/bb/europe/jan-june99/albright_3-24.html [accessed January 2000]).

87. When General Naumann informed Defence Minister George Robertson that a strike restricted to cruise missiles would enable the Serbs to redeploy their air defense systems and thus render the neutralization of that system more difficult, Robertson turned to the British chief of staff, General Sir Charles Guthrie, and asked, "Why haven't you ever told me that?" Klaus Naumann, interview by authors, December 22, 1999.

88. The one clear exception to this consensus that we encountered was from Richard Holbrooke. Although Holbrooke publicly declared that the bombing would be "swift, severe, and sustained," he privately warned that the initial NATO bombing plans were not sufficiently robust and would leave NATO worse off than before if Milosevic stood up to them, which he would have little difficulty doing. Believing that Milosevic had no incentive to give in after a few days, Holbrooke told the White House on March 20 that if a short campaign was all that NATO could muster, it might be better not to bomb at all. Richard Holbrooke, interview with the authors, April 7, 2000.

89. Albright, "Remarks at the U.S. Institute of Peace."

90. "Press Conference by the President" (White House, Office of the Press Secretary, April 24, 1999). A widely read National Intelligence Estimate issued in November 1998 similarly concluded that "the October agreement indicates that Milosevic is susceptible to outside pressure." Quoted in Sciolino and Bronner, "How a President, Distracted by a Scandal, Entered Balkan War," p. A13.

91. See also Adam Roberts, "NATO's 'Humanitarian War' over Kosovo," *Survival,* vol. 41 (Autumn 1999), p. 111. In assuming that the similarities between Bosnia and Kosovo would override their differences, the Clinton administration appears to have made a classic mistake in reasoning by historical analogy. On this point more generally, see Ernest May, "*Lessons of the Past: The Use and Misuse of History in American Foreign Policy* (Oxford University Press, 1973).

92. Zimmermann, *Origins of a Catastrophe,* p. 13.

93. Madeleine K. Albright, interview, *PBS Frontline, War in Europe* (www.pbs.org/wgbh/pages/frontline/shows/kosovo/ [accessed March 2000]).

94. For further details, see Ivo H. Daalder, *Getting to Dayton: The Making of America's Bosnia Policy* (Brookings, 2000), pp. 127–29.

95. Senior State Department official, interview by authors, September 23, 1999. Generals Clark and Naumann also confirmed that, compared to their last contact with Milosevic in late October 1998, he was a changed person on January 19, when they met with him at the North Atlantic Council's request after the Racak massacre. A similar sense was reported by Richard Holbrooke about his final meetings with Milosevic on March 22–23, 1999, which Holbrooke characterized as "the most bleak and the least engaged that we've ever had" in three-and-a-half years of exchanges. Naumann, interview by authors, December 22, 1999; and Wesley Clark, interview, *PBS Frontline, War in Europe;* and Richard Holbrooke, interview, ABC News, *Nightline,* March 24, 1999 (abcnews.go.com/onair/nightline/NightlineIndex.html [accessed March 1999]).

96. See Jane Perlez, "Kosovo Situation Worsens as Serbs Press Offensive," *New York Times,* March 21, 1999, p. A1.

97. "Press Conference by General Wesley Clark and NATO Secretary-General Javier Solana," NATO Press Conference, April 13, 1999, slide 5.

98. Van Zwol, "Lente in Kosovo," p. 7; Priest and Lippman, "U.S. Speaks More Softly after Failed Kosovo Talks"; and Schmitt, "Serb Army Masses 4,500 Armored Troops."

99. Senior German official, interview by authors, October 27, 1999.

100. Madeleine K. Albright and Lamberto Dini, "Press Conference" (Rome: U.S. Department of State, March 7, 1998).

101. Quoted in Blaine Harden, "A Long Struggle That Led Serb Leader to Back Down," *New York Times,* June 8, 1999, p. A13.

102. Naumann, interview by authors, December 22, 1999; Berger, interview by authors, February 9, 2000; and senior Pentagon official, interview by authors, February 16, 2000.

103. See John F. Harris, "Advice Didn't Sway Clinton on Airstrike," *Washington Post,* April 1, 1999, p. A1.

104. Senior U.S. official, interview by authors, September 24, 1999. Also senior Pentagon official, interview by authors, February 16, 2000; Bradley Graham, "Cohen Wrestles with a Mission Far Harder than Predicted," *Washington Post,* April 11, 1999, p. A24; and Bradley Graham, "Joint Chiefs Doubted Air Strategy," *Washington Post,* April 5, 1999, p. A1.

105. Quoted in Sciolino and Bronner, "How a President, Distracted by Scandal, Entered Balkan War," p. 13. The main reason for ruling out the use of ground forces at this time was London's fear (shared by other allies) that Washington might support the option by urging the small military presence in Macedonia, deployed there to extract the civilian monitors from Kosovo in an emergency, to form the nucleus of an invasion force. Already unhappy to have deployed a NATO force on the ground without any U.S. participation, Britain was loath to extend that precedent to a possible ground force option. If there was going to be a war on the ground in Kosovo, American soldiers would have to fight alongside European troops. Senior British official, interview by authors, November 8, 1999.

106. "Address by the President to the Nation" (White House, Office of the Press Secretary, March 24, 1999).

107. Admiral James Ellis, who commanded U.S. naval forces in Europe and was the overall NATO commander of allied forces in south Europe during the war, went further than that: "The lack of a credible threat of ground invasion probably prolonged the air campaign." The lesson: "Never say never . . . or deny yourself credible options." James O. Ellis, "A View from the Top," briefing, summer 1999. See also "Statement of General Klaus Naumann," Hearing, *Lessons Learned from the Military Operations Conducted as Part of Operation Allied Force*, Senate Armed Services Committee, 106 Cong. 1 sess. (November 3, 1999), p. 3.

108. Berger, interview by authors, February 9, 2000.

109. Quoted in Eric Schmitt, "The Powell Doctrine Is Looking Pretty Good Again," *New York Times*, April 4, 1999, p. 5.

110. Quoted in Graham, "Cohen Wrestles with a Mission Far Harder than Predicted," p. A24.

111. Senior U.S. official, interview by authors, September 24, 1999; and Berger, interview by authors, February 9, 2000.

112. Senate staff member, interview by authors, September 8, 1999.

113. See Lord Robertson of Port Ellen, "Kosovo: An Account of the Crisis" (www.mod.uk/news/kosovo/account/ [accessed February 2000]); and Roger Cohen, "Elite Forces Standing by If Air Power Won't Work," *New York Times*, April 3, 1999, p. A7.

114. "Statement by the President" (White House, Office of the Press Secretary, April 5, 1999).

115. Quoted in John Broder, "In Grim Week, Pep Talk from the President," *New York Times*, April 1, 1999, p. A1.

Chapter Four

1. "Statement by the President to the Nation" (White House, Office of the Press Secretary, March 24, 1999).

2. "The Situation in and around Kosovo," NATO Press Release M-NAC-1(99)51, April 12, 1999.

3. Text of the peace agreement appears as Annex 2 to UN Security Resolution 1244, June 10, 1999 (www.un.org/docs/scres/1999/99sc1244.htm [accessed March 2000]).

4. Adam Roberts, "NATO's 'Humanitarian War' over Kosovo," *Survival,* vol. 41 (Autumn 1999), pp. 105–09; and Ivo H. Daalder, "NATO, the UN, and the Use of Force," *International Peacekeeping,* vol. 5 (January-April 1999), pp. 27–35.

5. "Press Conference by Jamie Shea and General Wesley Clark," NATO Press Conference, April 13, 1999; Roberts, "NATO's 'Humanitarian War' over Kosovo," pp. 111–13.

6. See International Institute for Strategic Studies, *The Military Balance, 1998/99* (Oxford University Press, 1998), pp. 99–100, 295.

7. *Report to Congress: Kosovo/Operation Allied Force After-Action Report* (U.S. Department of Defense, 2000), pp. 31–32.

8. About 3,000 coalition planes, including combat helicopters but not other types of helicopters, participated in Operation Desert Storm; if one counts all fixed-wing and rotary aircraft, the United States alone deployed 3,800 aircraft to the conflict. See Thomas A. Keaney and Eliot A. Cohen, *Gulf War Air Power Survey Summary Report* (Government Printing Office, 1993), pp. 4, 181–205. The clearest indication of what the United States would now use in a major theater war, at least for combat aircraft, is given in Les Aspin, *Report on the Bottom-Up Review* (U.S. Department of Defense, 1993), p. 19.

9. Roughly 350 Western aircraft were in place during Operation Desert Fox. Steve Vogel, "U.S. Trimming Size of Iraq Attack Force," *Washington Post,* December 23, 1998, p. A18.

10. Eric Schmitt, "NATO Dismisses a Milosevic Bid and Steps up Raids," *New York Times,* April 7, 1999, p. A1.

11. See John Pike, "Where Are the Carriers?" (Federation of American Scientists, December 27, 1999) (www.fas.org/man/dod-101/sys/ships/where.htm [accessed November 1999]).

12. Statement of Daniel Murphy, Hearings, Senate Armed Services Committee, Subcommittee on Sea Power, October 13, 1999, excerpted in "The Navy in the Balkans," *Air Force Magazine,* vol. 82 (December 1999), pp. 48–49.

13. Barton Gellman, "In the End, Allies See No Credible Alternative," *Washington Post,* March 23, 1999, p. A12. See also Steven Lee Myers, "NATO Plan Calls for Widening Strikes on Air Defenses and Heavy Weapons," *New York Times,* March 20, 1999, p. A4.

14. James O. Ellis, "A View from the Top," briefing slides, summer 1999, emphasis in original.

15. Klaus Naumann, "Statement on Kosovo After-Action Review," Hearings, *Lessons Learned from the Military Operations Conducted as Part of Operation Allied Force,* Senate Armed Services Committee, 106 Cong. 1 sess. (November 3, 1999), p. 5.

16. See Bradley Graham, "Joint Chiefs Doubted Air Strategy," *Washington Post,* April 5, 1999, p. A1.

17. Craig R. Whitney, "For NATO, Doubts Nag," *New York Times*, March 31, 1999, p. A1; and Patrick Wintour and Peter Beaumont, "Revealed: The Secret Plan to Invade Kosovo," *Observer*, July 18, 1999, p. 17.

18. John F. Harris, "Clinton, Aides Vague on Plans for Troops," *Washington Post*, April 6, 1999, p. A20.

19. Blaine Harden, "The Long Struggle That Led the Serb Leader to Back Down," *New York Times*, June 6, 1999, p. 1.

20. In chapter 6 we take issue with certain other parts of the Powell doctrine. For General Powell's own words on his doctrine, see Colin L. Powell, "U.S. Forces: Challenges Ahead," *Foreign Affairs*, vol. 71 (Winter 1992–93), pp. 36–41; and Colin L. Powell with Joseph E. Persico, *My American Journey* (Random House, 1995), pp. 564, 605. See also Richard N. Haass, *Intervention: The Use of American Military Force in the Post–Cold War World*, rev. ed. (Brookings, 1999), p. 15.

21. William Cohen, interview, *PBS Frontline, War in Europe* (www.pbs.org/wgbh/pages/frontline/shows/kosovo/ [accessed March 2000]). See also Bradley Graham, "Cohen Wrestles with Mission Far Harder than Predicted," *Washington Post*, April 11, 1999, p. A24; Bradley Graham, "General Says War Stretches U.S. Forces," *Washington Post*, April 30, 1999, p. A1; Steven Lee Myers and Eric Schmitt, "Pentagon Works to Keep Allies United and Congress on Board," *International Herald Tribune*, May 31, 1999, p. 2; John A. Tirpak, "The NATO Way of War," *Air Force Magazine*, vol. 82 (December 1999), pp. 24–27; "Statement of Senator John Warner," Hearings, *Lessons Learned from the Military Operations Conducted as Part of Operation Allied Force*, Senate Committee on Armed Services, 106 Cong. 1 sess. (October 21, 1999).

22. Dana Priest, "The Commanders' War: Bombing by Committee," *Washington Post*, September 20, 1999, p. A1; Dana Priest, "Soldiering on in a War of Constraints," *Washington Post*, May 30, 1999, p. A1; and Dana Priest, "Target Selection Was Long Process," *Washington Post*, September 20, 1999, p. A11.

23. Senior British official, interview by authors, November 8, 1999.

24. See Barry Posen, "The War for Kosovo," *International Security*, vol. 24 (Spring 2000), pp. 39–84.

25. Johanna McGeary, "The Road to Hell," *Time*, April 12, 1999, pp. 42–43; Klaus Naumann, interview by authors, December 22, 1999; and Samuel R. Berger, interview by authors, February 9, 2000. Berger stated that the Clinton administration had not anticipated that more than 350,000 Kosovar Albanians would be forced from their homes in 1999—that is, a number not much larger than had been forced out in 1998.

26. Quoted in R. Jeffrey Smith and William Drozdiak, "Serbs' Offensive Was Meticulously Planned," *Washington Post*, April 11, 1999, p. A1.

27. See ABC News, *Nightline*, August 30, 1999 (abcnews.go.com/onair/nightline/NightlineIndex.html [accessed August 1999]).

28. Quoted in Elaine Sciolino and Ethan Bronner, "How a President, Distracted by Scandal, Entered Balkan War," *New York Times*, April 18, 1999, p. 1.

29. Prepared statements, George J. Tenet and Patrick M. Hughes, Hearings, *Current and Projected National Security Threats of the U.S.*, Senate Armed Services Com-

mittee, 106 Cong. 1 sess. (February 2, 1999); and Sciolino and Bronner, "How a President, Distracted by Scandal, Entered Balkan War," p. 1.

30. *Report to Congress: Kosovo/Operation Allied Force After-Action Report*, p. 6.

31. As Berger explained, "We had an advantage of 100 to 1 to 1,000 to 1 from the air.... If we were forced to go in on the ground in deep summer, it would have been maybe 3 to 1 or 2 to 1. Milosevic would have been able to be on much more equal grounds with NATO as we came over these mountains, through the caves that Tito had built in Yugoslavia." See Samuel 'Sandy' Berger, interview, *PBS Frontline, War in Europe.*

32. "Ethnic Cleansing in Kosovo" (April 22, 1999) (www.state.gov/www/regions/eur/kosovomore.html [accessed March 2000]).

33. Jamie Shea, interview by authors, November 10, 1999.

34. Steven Erlanger with Christopher S. Wren, "Early Count Hints at Fewer Kosovo Deaths," *New York Times*, November 11, 1999, p. A6; and "Ethnic Cleansing in Kosovo" (December 1999).

35. James M. Dorsey, "From Serb Paramilitaries, Tales of Killing and Cash," *Wall Street Journal*, September 1, 1999, p. A18; and "Ethnic Cleansing in Kosovo" (March 31, 1999).

36. "Ethnic Cleansing in Kosovo" (March 31 and April 5, 1999); and Eric Schmitt with Steven Lee Myers, "Pentagon Says Yugoslav Army Is Now Cut Off," *New York Times*, April 9, 1999, p. A1.

37. John Diamond, "US: Yugoslavia Has Chemical Agents," *Associated Press Headlines*, April 15, 1999 (dailynews.yahoo.com [accessed April 1999]).

38. "Press Conference by NATO Secretary-General Javier Solana and General Wesley K. Clark, SACEUR," NATO Press Conference, April 1, 1999; Mark Dennis and others, "A Tragic Exodus ... and No Exit!: The Nightmare," *Newsweek*, April 12, 1999, pp. 27-28; "Press Conference of NATO Spokesman, Jamie Shea, and Air Commodore, David Wilby, SHAPE," NATO Press Conference, March 28, 1999; and "Press Conference by Jamie Shea and Brigadier General Giuseppe Marani," NATO Press Conference, April 20, 1999.

39. See John Kifner, "How Serb Forces Purged One Million Albanians," *New York Times*, May 29, 1999, p. A1; John Daniszewski, "The Death of Belanica," *Los Angeles Times*, April 25, 1999, p. S3; and Smith and Drozdiak, "Serbs' Offensive Was Meticulously Planned," p. A1.

40. Thomas W. Lippman and Dana Priest, "NATO Hits Yugoslav Ground Forces," *Washington Post*, April 9, 1999, p. A1.

41. Massimo Calabresi, "My Tea with Arkan the Henchman," *Time*, April 12, 1999, p. 49.

42. Peter Finn, R. Jeffrey Smith, and Daniel Williams, "Voices Blend in a Chorus of Suffering: Refugees Describe Campaign of Terror," *Washington Post*, March 30, 1999, p. A1; and Kifner, "How Serb Forces Purged One Million Albanians," p. A1.

43. David E. Rosenbaum, "U.S. Official Calls Tallies of Kosovo Slain Too Low," *New York Times*, April 19, 1999, p. A10.

44. "Press Conference by NATO Secretary-General Javier Solana and General Wesley K. Clark, SACEUR," April 1, 1999; "Ethnic Cleansing in Kosovo" (March 31, 1999); and Norman Kempster and John-Thor Dahlburg, "Crisis in Yugoslavia: NATO Targets Yugoslavia's Tanks, Troops," Los Angeles Times, March 29, 1999, p. A1.

45. "Ethnic Cleansing in Kosovo" (April 22, 1999). See also "Ethnic Cleansing in Kosovo" (March 31, 1999).

46. "Press Conference by NATO Secretary-General Javier Solana and General Wesley K. Clark, SACEUR," April 1, 1999.

47. "Press Conference of NATO Spokesman Jamie Shea and Air Commodore David Wilby, SHAPE," March 28, 1999; and Francis X. Clines, "NATO Hunting for Serb Forces; U.S. Reports Signs of 'Genocide,'" New York Times, March 30, 1999, p. A1.

48. Thomas W. Lippman and Dana Priest, "NATO Builds Forces for 24-Hour Airstrikes," Washington Post, March 30, 1999, p. A1.

49. For a view on this issue with which we disagree, see Christopher Layne and Benjamin Schwarz, "For the Record: Kosovo II," National Interest, no. 57 (Fall 1999), pp. 9–15; for a response, see Ivo H. Daalder, "Argument: NATO and Kosovo," National Interest, no. 58 (Winter 1999–2000), pp. 113–16; and Ivo H. Daalder and Michael E. O'Hanlon, "Kosovo—The True Test: Lives Were Saved," Washington Post, March 26, 2000, p. B1.

50. International Institute for Strategic Studies, The Military Balance, 1998/99, pp. 99–100.

51. See for example Dusko Doder and Louise Branson, Milosevic: Portrait of a Tyrant (Free Press, 1999), pp. 145–74.

52. Smith and Drozdiak, "Serbs' Offensive Was Meticulously Planned," p. A1.

53. See for example Andrew F. Krepinevich, The Army and Vietnam (Johns Hopkins University Press, 1986), pp. 158–70.

54. John Pike, "Kosovo Background" (Federation of American Scientists, May 23, 1999) (www.fas.org/man/dod-101/ops/kosovo_back.htm [accessed May 1999]).

55. Smith and Drozdiak, "Serbs' Offensive Was Meticulously Planned," p. A1; "Press Conference by Jamie Shea and Brigadier General Giuseppe Marani," NATO Press Conference, April 19, 1999.

56. Paul Richter, "Crisis in Yugoslavia: Ground War an Unknown Equation," Los Angeles Times, March 30, 1999, p. A18; and Smith and Drozdiak, "Serbs' Offensive Was Meticulously Planned," p. A1.

57. Smith and Drozdiak, "Serbs' Offensive Was Meticulously Planned"; and Steven Erlanger, "Monitors' Reports Provide Chronicle of Kosovo Terror," New York Times, December 5, 1999, p. A1.

58. Peter Finn and R. Jeffrey Smith, "Rebels with a Crippled Cause," Washington Post, April 23, 1999, p. A1; and Stacy Sullivan, "A Look at . . . Prospects for Peace: Convince the KLA the War Is Over," Washington Post, June 6, 1999, p. B3.

59. See Warren Zimmermann, "Milosevic's Final Solution," New York Review of Books, vol. 46 (June 10, 1999), pp. 41–43.

60. William Drozdiak, "NATO Ministers Press on Diplomatic Front," Washington Post, April 13, 1999, p. A1.

61. Bob Drogin and Joel Havemann, "Crisis in Yugoslavia: U.S. May Call up Reservists in Escalation of Allied Air War," *Los Angeles Times*, April 14, 1999, p. A1.

62. Eric Schmitt, "Legislators Told Air Plan Needs Time," *New York Times*, April 16, 1999, p. A10.

63. "Statement by the President to the Nation" (March 24, 1999), p. 3.

64. Quoted in Mark Matthews and Tom Bowman, "Next Step Unclear If Airstrikes Don't Work," *Baltimore Sun*, March 24, 1999, p. A21

65. Quoted in John A. Tirpak, "Short's View of the Air Campaign," *Air Force Magazine*, vol. 82 (September 1999), pp. 43–47.

66. Quoted in Roberts, "NATO's 'Humanitarian War' over Kosovo," p. 111.

67. Michael O'Hanlon, "Should Serbia Be Scared?" *New York Times*, March 23, 1999, p. A31.

68. See Michael R. Gordon, "Allied Air Chief Stresses Hitting Belgrade Sites," *New York Times*, May 13, 1999, p. A1; William Drozdiak and Dana Priest, "NATO's Cautious Air Strategy Comes under Fire," *Washington Post*, May 16, 1999, p. A26; and Michael C. Short, interview, *PBS Frontline, War in Europe.*

69. "Press Conference by NATO Secretary-General Javier Solana and Gen. Wesley Clark, SACEUR," NATO Press Conference, March 25, 1999.

70. Wesley Clark, interview with authors, April 20, 2000.

71. See for example Layne and Benjamin, "For the Record: Kosovo II."

72. Jim Garanome, "Cohen Rejects Revisionists' Views of Kosovo Operation," *American Forces Information Service News Articles*, February 7, 2000 (www.defenselink.mil/news/Feb2000 [accessed February 2000]).

73. NATO's operational plan (OPLAN) for Operation Allied Force consisted of five phases overall: "Phase 0 was the deployment of air assets into the European theater. Phase 1 would establish air superiority over Kosovo . . . and degrade command and control . . . over the whole of the Federal Republic of Yugoslavia [FRY]. Phase 2 would attack military targets in Kosovo and those Yugoslav forces south of 44 degrees latitude, which were providing reinforcement for Serbian forces into Kosovo. . . . Phase 3 would expand air operations against a wide range of high-value military and security targets throughout the [FRY]. Phase 4 would redeploy forces as required. A Limited Air Response relying predominantly on cruise missiles to strike selected targets throughout the [FRY] was developed as a stand-alone option. . . . [and] was integrated into Phase 1." William S. Cohen and Henry H. Shelton, "Joint Statement on the Kosovo After-Action Review," Hearing, *Lessons Learned from the Military Operations Conducted as Part of Operation Allied Force*, Senate Armed Services Committee, 106 Cong. 1 sess. (October 14, 1999), pp. 7–8

74. These attacks, together with numerous strikes earlier in the decade against Iraq and Osama bin Laden's terrorist network, depleted the air force supply of cruise missiles (it reportedly had only 100 left by April 1999). More than 2,000 navy Tomahawk cruise missiles of similar capability remained. See Lawrence J. Korb, "Not Enough Cruise Missiles to Go Around?" *New York Times*, April 6, 1999, p. A27; and Lord Robertson of Port Ellen, "Kosovo: An Account of the Crisis" (www.mod.uk/news/kosovo/account/ [accessed February 2000]).

75. *Report to Congress: Kosovo/Operation Allied Force After-Action Report*, pp. 31–32. According to Pentagon data, the 50,000 U.S. personnel deployed included 21,000 air force, 14,000 navy, 10,000 army, and almost 5,000 marines.

76. House Armed Services Committee, "Kosovo Backgrounder," June 30, 1999 (www/house.gov/hasc/Publications/106thCongress/Kosovobackgrounder.pdf [accessed July 1999]); "Press Conference by NATO Secretary-General Javier Solana and Gen. Wesley Clark, SACEUR," March 25, 1999; "Press Conference by NATO Spokesman Jamie Shea and Air Commodore David Wilby, SHAPE," NATO Press Conference, March 26, 1999; and "Press Conference of NATO Spokesman Jamie Shea and Air Commodore David Wilby, SHAPE," NATO Press Conference, March 27, 1999.

77. Michael C. Short, interview, *PBS Frontline, War in Europe*.

78. Dana Priest, "Air War Honed NATO Strike Forces and Commanders," *Washington Post*, June 5, 1999, p. A16; and Steven Lee Myers, Chinese Embassy Bombings: A Wide Net of Blame," *New York Times*, April 17, 2000, pp. A1, A10.

79. See statements by Daniel J. Murphy Jr., commander of the U.S. Navy's Sixth Fleet and NATO's Striking and Support Forces, southern Europe, during Operation Allied Force, in "The Navy in the Balkans," *Air Force Magazine*, vol. 82 (December 1999), pp. 48–49. Moreover, in recent years air force strategists have increasingly argued in favor of "parallel warfare," in which many target sets would be attacked from the outset of a campaign. Our thanks to David Ochmanek of the RAND Corporation for this point. Similar logic undergirded one idea for attacking Iraq during the Gulf War, the air force plan known as Instant Thunder. See Michael R. Gordon and Bernard E. Trainor, *The Generals' War: The Inside Story of the Conflict in the Gulf* (Little, Brown, 1995), pp. 77–97.

80. "Press Conference by NATO Spokesman Jamie Shea and Air Commodore David Wilby, SHAPE," NATO Press Conference, March 29, 1999.

81. "U.S. Confirms Yugoslavs Downed Stealth Fighter," *Washington Post*, November 25, 1999, p. A18.

82. Thomas E. Ricks, "Milosevic Pursues Strategy of Conserving Missiles and Mounting Ground Offensive," *Wall Street Journal*, March 29, 1999, p. A4; and Vago Muradian, "Stealth Compromised by Not Destroying F-117 Wreckage," *Defense Daily*, April 2, 1999, p. 3.

83. Roberto Suro and Thomas E. Ricks, "Pentagon: NATO Kosovo Air War Data Leaked," *Washington Post*, March 10, 2000, p. A2.

84. Dana Priest, "U.S. Forces Raced Enemy to Reach Pilot," *Washington Post*, March 29, 1999, p. A1.

85. Robert Burns, "Belgrade May Have Sold Downed Stealth Fighter," *Philadelphia Inquirer*, September 18, 1999, p. A4.

86. House Armed Services Committee, "Kosovo Backgrounder"; "Press Conference by NATO Secretary-General Javier Solana and Gen. Wesley Clark, SACEUR," March 25, 1999; "Press Conference of NATO Spokesman Jamie Shea and Air Commodore David Wilby, SHAPE," March 28, 1999; "Press Conference by NATO Spokesman, Jamie Shea and Air Commodore David Wilby, SHAPE," March 29, 1999; and

"Press Conference by NATO Spokesman Jamie Shea and Air Commodore David Wilby, SHAPE," NATO Press Conference, March 30, 1999.

87. See BBC News, *Newsnight*, "NATO's Inner Kosovo Conflict," August 20, 1999 (news.bbc.co.uk/hi/english/world/europe [accessed August 1999]).

88. NATO dropped more than 23,000 bombs and missiles (about 35 percent being precision guided). NATO's air armada roughly tripled, from 366 to 912 planes, over the course of the conflict. The allies also fired 329 cruise missiles. Total sorties numbered 37,465 (the total was 112,235 in Operation Desert Storm). Strike sorties numbered 10,808 (there were 47,630 in the Gulf War, averaging almost ten times as many per day as the Allied Force norm). See Wesley K. Clark, "The United States and NATO: The Way Ahead," *Parameters*, vol. 29 (Winter 1999–2000), p. 10; Air Force Association, "Learning the Right Lessons from Operation Allied Force," Issue Brief, July 15, 1999; and Ken Bacon, Thomas Wilson, and Chuck Wald, "DoD News Briefing" (U.S. Department of Defense, April 12, 1999). Sometimes slightly different aircraft numbers and sortie totals are presented. For example, apparently counting unmanned aircraft and manned aircraft, the Pentagon has stated that total aerial vehicles increased from 344 to about 1,050 over the course of the war. *Report to Congress: Kosovo/Operation Allied Force After-Action Report*, pp. 31, 32, 78.

89. By the end of the first month of the war, air defense and command, control, and communications (c-cubed) assets represented about half of all targets that had been struck at least once. Together, about 250 such targets were hit. Serb forces in the field constituted the next largest target set, with just under 200 targets. The remaining 200 or so targets were a combination of supply lines and petroleum-oil-lubricant facilities. See "Echoes from Allied Force," *Air Force Magazine*, vol. 82 (August 1999), p. 60.

90. "Press Conference by NATO Spokesman, Jamie Shea and Colonel Konrad Freytag, SHAPE," NATO Speech, April 23, 1999 (Washington, D.C.); "Press Conference by NATO Spokesman Jamie Shea and Colonel Konrad Freytag, GEAF, SHAPE," NATO Press Conference, April 24, 1999 (Washington, D.C.); Steven Lee Myers, "Pentagon Details New Damage and Says It Is Succeeding in Demoralizing the Serb Forces," *New York Times*, April 23, 1999, p. A11; and Tirpak, "Short's View of the Air Campaign," p. 45.

91. Michael Ignatieff, "The Virtual Commander," *New Yorker*, August 2, 1999, p. 35.

92. House Armed Services Committee, "Kosovo Backgrounder," June 30, 1999; "Press Conference by Secretary-General, Dr. Javier Solana and SACEUR, Gen. Wesley Clark," March 25, 1999; "Press Conference of NATO Spokesman Jamie Shea and Air Commodore, David Wilby, SHAPE," March 28, 1999; and Keaney and Cohen, *Gulf War Air Power Survey Summary Report*, p. 173.

93. "Press Conference of the NATO Spokesman, Jamie Shea and Air Commodore David Wilby," NATO Press Conference, March 31, 1999.

94. "Press Conference by NATO Spokesman, Jamie Shea and Air Commodore, David Wilby, SHAPE," NATO Press Conference, April 6, 1999; "Press Conference by NATO Spokesman, Jamie Shea and Air Commodore David Wilby," NATO Press Con-

ference, April 9, 1999; "Press Conference by NATO Spokesman, Jamie Shea and Colonel Konrad Freytag," NATO Press Conference, April 10, 1999; "Press Conference by Jamie Shea and General Wesley Clark," April 13, 1999; Steven Lee Myers, "Leaders of NATO Reject Plan to Fire on Ships that Defy Oil Embargo," *New York Times*, May 5, 1999, p. A11. See also Mike Doubleday and Charles Wald, "DoD News Briefing" (U.S. Department of Defense, April 12, 1999).

95. Tim Youngs and others, "Kosovo: Operation 'Allied Force,'" Research Paper 99/48 (London: House of Commons Library, April 29, 1999), p. 25; "Prepared Statement of the United States European Command before the Senate Armed Services Committee," Hearings, *Lessons Learned from the Military Operations Conducted as Part of Operation Allied Force*, Senate Committee on Armed Services, 106 Cong. 1 sess. (October 21, 1999); Dana Priest, "Yugoslav Air Defenses Mostly Intact," *Washington Post*, April 13, 1999, p. A1; Bill Gertz, "Remote Radar Allows Serbs to Keep Firing at NATO Jets," *Washington Times*, April 13, 1999, p. A1; and Thomas W. Lippman, "NATO Expands Fleet of Aircraft," *Washington Post*, April 11, 1999, p. A1.

96. Craig R. Whitney, "Clash of the Spokesmen, Confusion of the Media," *New York Times*, April 17, 1999, p. A10.

97. "Press Conference by Jamie Shea and General Wesley Clark," April 13, 1999; Steven Lee Myers, "Pentagon Plans to Add 300 Planes to Battle Yugoslavia," *New York Times*, April 13, 1999, p. A1; and Rowan Scarborough, "Clark Reports Yugoslavia Pours Troops into Kosovo," *Washington Times*, April 28, 1999, p. A1.

98. Keaney and Cohen, *Gulf War Air Power Survey Summary Report*, pp. 61–62.

99. Jim Garamone, "Cohen Rejects Revisionists' Views of Kosovo Operation," *American Forces Information Service News Articles*, February 7, 2000 (www.defenselink.mil/news/Feb2000 [accessed February 2000]).

100. See Elizabeth Becker, "Rights Group Says NATO Killed 500 Civilians in Kosovo War," *New York Times*, February 7, 2000, p. A10; and Human Rights Watch, "Civilian Deaths in the NATO Air Campaign," *Human Rights Watch Report*, vol. 12 (February 2000).

101. "U.S. Jets Used Controversial Ammunition in Kosovo War," *Los Angeles Times*, March 22, 2000, p. 4.

102. Tirpak, "Short's View of the Air Campaign," p. 47.

103. William M. Arkin, "Challenge to the '15,000-Foot Myth' Consumes Air Force Planners," *Defense Daily*, March 2, 2000.

104. Senior British official, interview by authors, November 8, 1999.

105. Senior NATO official, interview by authors, November 10, 1999.

106. Craig R. Whitney, "U.S. Military Acted outside NATO Framework during Kosovo Conflict, France Says," *New York Times*, November 11, 1999, p. A6.

107. Senior French officials, interviews by authors, October 7 and November 11, 1999.

108. See Elizabeth Becker, "With Aid Effort Overwhelmed, NATO Will Take over Coordination," *New York Times*, April 7, 1999, p. A11; "Press Conference by NATO Spokesman, Jamie Shea and Air Commodore, David Wilby, SHAPE," NATO Press

Conference, April 7, 1999; "Press Conference by Jamie Shea and Brigadier General Giuseppe Marani," April 19, 1999; "NATO's Role in Relation to the Conflict in Kosovo," NATO Basic Fact Sheet, April 1999, updated January 26, 2000 (www.nato.int/docu/facts/2000/kosovo.htm); and Humanitarianism and War Project and Humanitarian Law Consultancy, "The Interaction of NATO-Related Military Forces with Humanitarian Actors in the Kosovo Crisis," paper prepared for a workshop convened by the Foreign Ministry of the Netherlands, The Hague, November 15–16, 1999, p. 40.

109. "Press Conference by NATO Spokesman, Jamie Shea and Air Commodore, David Wilby, SHAPE," April 6, 1999; "Press Conference by NATO Spokesman Jamie Shea and Air Commodore David Wilby," April 9, 1999; "Press Conference by NATO Spokesman Jamie Shea and Colonel Konrad Freytag," April 10, 1999; "Press Conference by Jamie Shea and General Wesley Clark," April 13, 1999; Rowan Scarborough, "Bombs Ruin Serb Oil Output, but Reserves Called 'Substantial,'" *Washington Times*, April 13, 1999, p. A15.

110. Roberta Cohen and David A. Korn, "Failing the Internally Displaced," *Forced Migration Review*, August 1999, p. 12.

111. Michael R. Gordon and Eric Schmitt, "Crisis in the Balkans: Military Strategy—Pentagon Withholds Copters from Battlefields in Kosovo," *New York Times*, May 16, 1999, p. 1.

112. Dana Priest, "Risks and Restraints: Why the Apaches Never Flew in Kosovo," *Washington Post*, December 29, 1999, p. A1; and John Kifner, "With Fanfare, First Attack Copters Arrive but Active Role Is Days Away," *New York Times*, April 22, 1999, p. A14.

113. Cohen and Shelton, "Joint Statement on the Kosovo After-Action Review," p. 13.

114. Priest, "Risks and Restraints," p. 1. Before Operation Desert Storm, most independent analysts estimated that the U.S.-led coalition would lose several thousand American troops; press quotes of Pentagon estimates ranged from 10,000 to 30,000; actual losses were 400 killed, including those lost in accidents before and during the war. See Congressional Budget Office, "Costs of Operation Desert Shield," January 1991, p. 15.

115. Senior U.S. official, interview by authors, November 12, 1999; and Priest, "Risks and Restraints," p. 1.

116. See Gordon with Schmitt, "Pentagon Withholds Copters from Battlefields in Kosovo," p. 1; and Molly Moore, "Earthbound Apaches," *Washington Post*, May 21, 1999, p. A25.

117. Bradley Graham and William Drozdiak, "Temp Quickens Air Campaign; 2 U.S. Pilots Killed in Helicopter Crash," *Washington Post*, May 5, 1999, p. A1; and Paul Richter and Lisa Getter, "Mechanical Failure, Pilot Error Seen as Causes of Apache Crashes," *Los Angeles Times*, May 13, 1999, p. A14.

118. Barton Gellman, "U.S., Allies Launch Air Attack on Yugoslav Military Targets," *Washington Post*, March 25, 1999, p. A1.

119. Michael Wines, "Hostility to U.S. Is Now Popular with Russians," *New York Times*, April 12, 1999, p. A1.

120. Youngs and others, "Kosovo: Operation 'Allied Force,'" p. 11.

121. "UN Sec-Gen Kofi Annan on NATO Air Strikes," March 24, 1999 (www.usia.gov/products/washfile.htm [accessed March 2000]); and Gellman, "U.S., Allies Launch Air Attack on Yugoslav Military Targets," p. A1.

122. "Press Conference of the NATO Spokesman, Jamie Shea, and Air Commodore David Wilby," March 31, 1999.

123. Judith Matloff, "Russia's Tough Talk Unsettles West," *Christian Science Monitor*, April 12, 1999, p. 1.

124. "Press Conference by NATO Secretary-General Javier Solana and General Wesley K. Clark, SACEUR," April 1, 1999.

125. Steven Erlanger, "Support for Homeland up as Sirens Wail and News Is Censored," *New York Times*, March 29, 1999, p. A1; and Michael Dobbs, "Serbian Nationalism Lifts Milosevic," *Washington Post*, March 30, 1999, p. A1.

126. Stacy Sullivan, "Milosevic Is One Problem: National Denial Is the Other," *New York Times*, August 21, 1999, p. A23.

127. "Press Conference by the President" (White House, Office of the Press Secretary, June 25, 1999).

128. James Rupert, "Montenegro Media Warned to Toe Milosevic Party Line," *Washington Post*, April 12, 1999, p. A18.

129. Youngs and others, "Kosovo: Operation 'Allied Force,'" p. 23.

130. "Press Conference by NATO Spokesman, Jamie Shea, and Air Commodore David Wilby," NATO Press Conference, April 3, 1999.

131. "Statement on Kosovo Issued by the Heads of State and Government Participating in the Meeting of the North Atlantic Council in Washington, D.C. on 23rd and 24th April 1999," NATO Press Release S-1(99)62, April 23, 1999.

132. "Press Conference Given by NATO Spokesman, Jamie Shea, and Colonel Konrad Freytag, SHAPE," NATO Press Conference, April 25, 1999 (Washington, D.C.); Youngs and others, "Kosovo: Operation 'Allied Force,'" p. 9.

133. Youngs and others, "Kosovo: Operation 'Allied Force,'" p. 14.

134. William Drozdiak, "NATO's Newcomers Are Shaken by Air Strikes," *Washington Post*, April 12, 1999, p. A17.

135. "Statement by the President to the Nation" (March 24, 1999), p. 4.

136. Bradley Graham and Guy Gugliotta, "Administration Seeks to Reassure Congress on Air War," *Washington Post*, April 16, 1999, p. A25; and Myers and Schmitt, "Pentagon Works to Keep Allies United and Congress on Board," p. 2.

137. Harris, "Clinton, Aides Vague on Plans for Troops," *Washington Post*, p. A20; Lippman and Priest, "NATO Hits Yugoslav Ground Forces," p. A1; and Joyce Howard Price, "NATO Has Ground Plan for Kosovo Troop Option," *Washington Times*, April 12, 1999, p. A1.

138. Al Gore, interview, "Second in Command," *Newsweek*, April 19, 1999, p. 39.

139. Berger, interview by authors, February 9, 2000.

140. For example, Richard N. Haass and the authors held a press conference at the Brookings Institution on March 29, 1999, which raised these issues (www.brookings.edu/comm/transcripts/19990329.htm [accessed April 2000]).

141. For a good discussion, albeit one that appeared in the war's second month, see J. Bryan Hehir, "A Look at . . . What Makes a Just War?: NATO's Laudable Goals and Questionable Means," and Jean Bethke Elshtain, "A Look at . . . What Makes a Just War?: Whose Lives Are We Sparing?" both, *Washington Post*, May 16, 1999, p. B3. See also Paul W. Kahn, "War and Sacrifice in Kosovo," *Philosophy and Public Policy*, vol. 19 (Spring-Summer 1999), pp. 1–6.

142. See Bill Frelick, "Genocide by Mass Starvation," *Los Angeles Times*, April 25, 1999, p. M5; and "Press Conference by Mr. Peter Daniel and Colonel Konrad Freytag," NATO Press Conference, May 1, 1999.

143. Rowan Scarborough, "Military Experts See a Need for Ground Troops," *Washington Times*, March 30, 1999, p. A1; and George C. Wilson, "Exit Strategy a Must for Army Invasion Endorsement," *Army Times*, May 10, 1999, p. 16.

144. "Assessing the Situation," *Newshour with Jim Lehrer*, April 2, 1999 (www.pbs.org/newshour/bb/europe/jan-june99/assessment_4-2.html [accessed April 1999]); and "Military Options," *Newshour with Jim Lehrer*, March 23, 1999 (www.pbs.org/newshour/bb/europe/jan-june99/kosovo_3-23.html [accessed March 1999]).

145. Chuck Hagel, "Victory: The Only Exit Strategy," *Washington Post*, March 31, 1999, p. A29; Bill Sammon and Joyce Howard Price, "Pentagon Considers Ground Operations," *Washington Times*, March 29, 1999, p. A1; and Graham and Gugliotta, "Administration Seeks to Reassure Congress on Air War," p. 25.

146. Senior State Department official, interview by authors, September 21, 1999.

147. Elizabeth Becker, "A Leader Who Climbed the Ranks, as His Father Did, to Become the Chief of Staff," *New York Times*, March 29, 1999, p. A9.

148. British Embassy, communication with authors, February 9, 2000.

149. Some recent U.S. studies may go too far in making this point, suggesting that the American public would accept hundreds of casualties in humanitarian military operations. Such polling data must be approached with caution. It is one thing to determine views on such an emotional subject in the abstract and quite another to determine them for real-life circumstances. But the broader point is valid nonetheless: Americans will accept combat casualties if they believe them necessary to achieve a valid objective in ways that minimize risks and maximize success. See Peter D. Feaver and Christopher Gelpi, "A Look at . . . Casualty Aversion: How Many Deaths Are Acceptable? A Surprising Answer," *Washington Post*, November 7, 1999, p. B3; and Steven Kull and I. M. Destler, *Misreading the Public: The Myth of a New Isolationism* (Brookings, 1999), pp. 106–09.

150. American Forces Information Service, *Defense Almanac 97* (U.S. Department of Defense, 1997), p. 44.

151. For a good discussion, see Fareed Zakaria, "Wage a Full War—Or Cut a Deal," *Newsweek*, April 12, 1999, p. 44; and Richard N. Haass, "Modest Objectives, Ambitious Means," *Washington Post*, April 19, 1999, p. A19. See also Michael O'Hanlon, "Invade Serbia, but Let Serbs Keep a Slice," *Wall Street Journal*, April 6, 1999, p. A26.

152. Bradley Graham, "Bombing Spreads; Kosovo Exodus Grows," *Washington Post*, March 29, 1999, p. A1; and Bradley Graham, "As Ground Forces Build, Questions Linger," *Washington Post*, April 14, 1999, p. A1.

153. See Joshua M. Epstein, "Dynamic Analysis and the Conventional Balance in Europe," *International Security*, vol. 12 (Spring 1988), p. 156; James T. Quinlivan, "Force Requirements in Stability Operations," *Parameters*, vol. 25 (Winter 1995–96), pp. 59–69; and Michael O'Hanlon, *Saving Lives with Force: Military Criteria for Humanitarian Intervention* (Brookings, 1997), pp. 38–42.

154. Sammon and Price, "Pentagon Considers Ground Operations."

155. Thomas W. Lippman, "NATO Expands Fleet of Aircraft," *Washington Post*, April 11, 1999, p. A1.

156. Graham and Gugliotta, "Administration Seeks to Reassure Congress on Air War," p. A25.

157. "Americans on Kosovo: A Study of US Public Attitudes" (Program on International Policy Attitudes, May 19, 1999) (www.pipa.org/onlinereports/kosovo/kosovo.htm [accessed March 2000]); and Bruce W. Jentleson, "Normative Dilemmas and Political Myths: The Contemporary Political Context of the Use of Military Force," paper presented at the international conference, Employing Air and Space Power at the Turn of the Millennium: Lessons and Implications, Fisher Institute for Air and Space Strategic Studies, Tel Aviv, December 1999.

158. See International Institute for Strategic Studies, "NATO's Campaign in Yugoslavia," *Strategic Comments*, vol. 5 (April 1999); John Barry, "Why Troops Take Time," *Newsweek*, April 26, 1999, p. 30; and Steven Komarow, "Viable Ground Option Would Take Months," *USA Today*, April 19, 1999, p. A3.

159. John Keegan, "Milosevic Keeps Allies Guessing as He Prepares to Play Waiting Game," *London Daily Telegraph*, April 21, 1999, p. 5. For a similar argument, though perhaps too optimistic about how fast the United States could have moved forces to the region and how many casualties NATO would likely suffer in subsequent fighting, see Robert Killebrew, "Objective Kosovo: How Would a Ground War Work?" *Washington Post*, April 25, 1999, p. B1.

160. Thomas E. Ricks and Carla Anne Robbins, "NATO Develops a Plan to Dispatch Troops into Kosovo after Bombing," *Wall Street Journal*, May 5, 1999, p. A3.

161. The 101st Air Assault Division has 380 helicopters, of which roughly 100 are attack helicopters and the rest transport and utility aircraft. The latter can, depending on the type, carry eleven to thirty-three people and five to thirteen tons of cargo, allowing roughly 10–20 percent of the division's strength to be transported at a time. Additional helicopters can also be devoted to support the 101st; for example, the army also has four corps-level formations, each with roughly as many helicopters as the 101st. See Frances Lussier, *An Analysis of U.S. Army Helicopter Programs* (U.S. Congressional Budget Office, 1995), pp. 14–15, 66–67. In Desert Storm, the 101st moved roughly 150 kilometers in one day's time, setting up a supply base about 100 kilometers short of the main objective. See Robert H. Scales Jr., *Certain Victory: The U.S. Army in the Gulf War* (Washington, D.C.: Brassey's, 1994), pp. 217–21.

162. International Institute for Strategic Studies, "NATO's Campaign in Yugoslavia."

163. Harris, "Clinton, Aides Vague on Plans for Troops," p. A20.

164. Adam Clymer, "Allies Shifting Focus to Halting Atrocities Reported in Kosovo," *New York Times*, March 29, 1999, p. A1; Drozdiak, "NATO Ministers Press on Diplomatic Front," p. A1; and Michael W. Doyle and Stephen Holmes, "Arm the K.L.A.," *New York Times*, May 25, 1999, p. A27.

Chapter Five

1. Samuel R. Berger, interview by authors, February 9, 2000.

2. "NATO Press Briefing by Peter Daniel and Colonel Konrad Freytag," NATO Press Release, May 1, 1999.

3. Berger, interview by authors, February 9, 2000.

4. See the comments of Joseph Ralston, vice chairman of the Joint Chiefs of Staff, in John T. Correll, "The Use of Force," *Air Force Magazine*, vol. 82 (December 1999), p. 39.

5. William Jefferson Clinton, "A Just and Necessary War," *New York Times*, May 23, 1999, p. 17.

6. Senior U.S. official, interview by authors, September 24, 1999. See also William S. Cohen and Henry H. Shelton, "Joint Statement on the Kosovo After-Action Review," Hearing, *Lessons Learned from the Military Operations Conducted as Part of Operation Allied Force*, Senate Armed Services Committee, 106 Cong. 1 sess. (October 14, 1999), p. 9.

7. For an overview of Russia's Kosovo policy, see Oleg Levitin, "Inside Moscow's Kosovo Muddle," *Survival*, vol. 42 (Spring 2000), pp. 130–40.

8. House Armed Services Committee, "Kosovo Backgrounder," June 30, 1999, p. 4 (www.house.gov/hasc/Publications/106thCongress/kosovobackgrounder.pdf [accessed January 2000]).

9. To support the expanded aerial effort, President Clinton authorized the activation of up to 33,000 U.S. reservists in late April. Until then, the 1,000 or so air force reservists involved in the war had responded on a voluntary basis only. By mid-May, 5,000 reserve personnel had been activated. Kosovo Task Force, "Kosovo Situation Reports: April 1999" (Congressional Research Service, updated May 3, 1999), p. 33; and Kosovo Task Force, "Kosovo Situation Reports: May 1999" (Congressional Research Service, updated May 3, 1999), p. 25.

10. *Report to Congress: Kosovo/Operation Allied Force After-Action Report* (U.S. Department of Defense, 2000), p. 60.

11. In Operation Desert Storm, only 10 percent of coalition aircraft were capable of dropping precision munitions like laser-guided bombs; in Operation Allied Force, the fraction was 90 percent. Ibid., pp. 79, 88.

12. Eric Schmitt and Steven Lee Myers, "NATO Planes Flying Lower, Increasing Risk of Being Hit," *New York Times*, May 4, 1999, p. A19; Kosovo Task Force, "Kosovo Situation Reports: May 1999," p. 31; and "Press Conference by Jamie Shea and General Giuseppe Marani," NATO Press Conference, April 28, 1999.

13. Lord Robertson of Port Ellen, "Kosovo: An Account of the Crisis" (www.mod.uk/news/kosovo/account/nato/html [accessed March 2000]); "Lucky Day," *Inside the Pentagon*, September 16, 1999, p. 1; and "NATO Press Conference by Jamie Shea and Major General Walter Jertz, SHAPE," NATO Press Conference, June 1, 1999.

14. "Press Conference Given by NATO Spokesman Jamie Shea and SHAPE Spokesman Major General Walter Jertz; Video Press Conference with NATO Secretary General, Dr. Javier Solana from Skopje," NATO Press Conference, May 12, 1999 (Skopje).

15. "Press Conference given by NATO Spokesman Jamie Shea and SHAPE Spokesman Major General Walter Jertz," NATO Press Conference, May 23, 1999; and "Press Conference by Mr. Jamie Shea, NATO Spokesman, and Major General Walter Jertz, SHAPE," June 1, 1999.

16. "Press Conference Given by Mr. Jamie Shea, NATO Spokesman, and SHAPE Spokesman Major General Walter Jertz, SHAPE," NATO Press Conference, May 25, 1999.

17. William M. Arkin, "Ask Not for Whom the Phone Rings," washingtonpost. com, October 11, 1999 (www.washingtonpost.com/wp-srv/national/dotmil/ arkin101199.htm [accessed March 2000]).

18. See Dana Priest, "The Commanders' War: Bombing by Committee; France Balked at NATO Targets," *Washington Post*, September 20, 1999, p. A1; NATO, "Operation Allied Force Update," various days (www.nato.int/kosovo/press [accessed September 1999]); House Armed Services Committee, "Kosovo Backgrounder," June 30, 1999, pp. 2, 7; Kosovo Task Force, "Kosovo Situation Reports: May 1999," pp. 1, 33; "Press Conference by Jamie Shea and General Wesley Clark," NATO Press Conference, April 27, 1999; and "Press Conference by Mr. Peter Daniel and Major General Walter Jertz, Mr. Isa Zymberi in Brussels, and Mr. Fatmir Gashi in Kukes," NATO Press Conference, May 24, 1999 (Kukes, Albania).

19. *Report to Congress: Kosovo/Operation Allied Force After-Action Report*, p. 87.

20. "Remarks as Prepared for Delivery Secretary of Defense William S. Cohen to the International Institute for Strategic Studies, Hotel del Coronado, San Diego, California" (U.S. Department of Defense, September 9, 1999), p. 3; Paul Richter, "B-2 Drops Its Bad PR in Air War," *Los Angeles Times*, July 8, 1999, p. A1; and *Report to Congress: Kosovo/Operation Allied Force After-Action Report*, p. 97.

21. "Echoes from Allied Force," *Air Force Magazine*, vol. 82 (August 1999), p. 61; and "Press Conference by Mr. Jamie Shea, NATO Spokesman, and Major General Walter Jertz, SHAPE," NATO Press Release, May 27, 1999.

22. Daniel Williams, "Serbs Release POWs to Jackson; U.S. Confirms Downing of F-16; Pilot Rescued," *Washington Post*, May 2, 1999, p. A1; and Kosovo Task Force, "Kosovo Situation Reports: May 1999," pp. 1, 3, 5.

23. In Operations Desert Shield and Desert Storm, the United States suffered a total of 383 deaths: 84 in Desert Shield from "nonhostile" causes such as accidents and 299 during the conflict and its aftermath, distributed about equally between hostile and nonhostile causes (148 from "hostile" or direct enemy action, 151 from

accidents and such). See American Forces Information Service, *Defense Almanac 97* (U.S. Department of Defense, 1997), p. 44.

24. Kosovo Task Force, "Kosovo Situation Reports: May 1999," pp. 1, 21.

25. Steven Lee Myers, "Leaders of NATO Reject Proposal by General Clark to Fire on Ships That Defy Oil Embargo," *New York Times*, May 5, 1999, p. A11; Kosovo Task Force, "Kosovo Situation Reports: May 1999," p. 2; and "Press Conference by Mr. Jamie Shea and Colonel Konrad Freytag," NATO Press Conference, May 2, 1999.

26. "Press Conference by Mr. Jamie Shea, NATO Spokesman and Major General Walter Jertz, SHAPE," NATO Press Release, May 26, 1999.

27. William M. Arkin, "The Cyber Bomb in Yugoslavia," washingtonpost.com, October 25, 1999 (www.washingtonpost.com/wp-srv/national/dotmil/arkin102599.htm [accessed October 1999]); and Bradley Graham, "Military Grappling with Guidelines for Cyber Warfare; Questions Prevented Use on Yugoslavia," *Washington Post*, November 8, 1999, p. A1.

28. Ted Galen Carpenter, "Damage to Relations with Russia and China," in Ted Galen Carpenter, ed., *NATO's Empty Victory: A Postmortem on the Balkan War* (Washington, D.C.: CATO Institute, 2000), pp. 82–86.

29. John Sweeney, Jens Holsoe, and Ed Vulliamy, "NATO Bombed Chinese Deliberately," *Observer*, October 17, 1999; and Michael Laris, "U.S. Details Embassy Bombing for Chinese," *Washington Post*, June 17, 1999, p. A30.

30. See the in-depth analysis of the bombing in Steve Lee Myers, "Chinese Embassy Bombing: A Wide Net of Blame," *New York Times*, April 17, 2000, pp. A1, A10.

31. "Operations Allied Force/Allied Harbour/Joint Forge-Order of Battle/Basing 1 June 1999,"compiled by Tim Ripley, *Jane's Defence Weekly*, June 1999 (www.janes.com/defence/features/kosovo/airassets.html [accessed June 1999]).

32. *Report to Congress: Kosovo/Operation Allied Force After-Action Report*, p. 78.

33. "Prepared Statement of the Honorable William S. Cohen to the Senate Armed Services Committee," Hearing, *U.S. Policy and Military Operations Regarding Kosovo*, Senate Committee on Armed Services, 106 Cong. 1 sess. (July 20, 1999), pp. 5–6; Damian Kemp, "Kosovo War Makes UAVs Part of All 'Future Combat,'" *Jane's Defence Weekly*, June 30, 1999, p. 10; and Nick Cook, "NATO Battles against the Elements," *Jane's Defence Weekly*, April 21, 1999, p. 4. The allies used some 23,000 bombs and missiles during the war, of which 35 percent, or about 8,000, were precision munitions (early in the war, about 90 percent of all munitions were precision guided); see William S. Cohen, "DoD News Briefing" (U.S. Department of Defense, June 10, 1999).

34. International Institute for Strategic Studies, *The Military Balance, 1998/99* (Oxford University Press, 1998), pp. 12–72.

35. "Remarks as Prepared for Delivery, Secretary of Defense William S. Cohen to the International Institute for Strategic Studies, Hotel del Coronado, San Diego, California," September 9, 1999, p. 3.

36. Joseph Fitchett, "Allies Emphasize Need to Prepare for Kosovo-Style Air Wars," *International Herald Tribune*, November 12, 1999, p. 8.

37. Klaus Naumann, "Testimony on Kosovo After-Action Review," Hearings, *Lessons Learned from the Military Operations Conducted as Part of Operation Allied Force*, Senate Armed Services Committee, 106 Cong. 1 sess. (November 3, 1999), p. 6.

38. "Press Conference given by NATO Spokesman, Jamie Shea and SHAPE Spokesman, Colonel Konrad Freytag," NATO Press Conference, May 22, 1999; and "Press Conference by Jamie Shea, NATO Spokesman, and Major General Walter Jertz, SHAPE," NATO Press Conference, June 8, 1999.

39. "Family Says Slain Albanian Leader Had Been Seized by Serbs," *New York Times*, May 9, 1999, p. 11.

40. "Press Conference Given by NATO Spokesman, Jamie Shea and SHAPE Spokesman, Major General Walter Jertz," May 23, 1999.

41. "Press Conference by Jamie Shea, NATO Spokesman, and Major General Walter Jertz, SHAPE," NATO Press Conference, June 6, 1999.

42. Kosovo Task Force, "Kosovo Situation Reports: May 1999," pp. 19, 22, 25, and Elizabeth Becker, "U.S. Plans Airdrops to Refugees inside Kosovo," *New York Times*, May 11, 1999, p. 12.

43. Steven Erlanger with Christopher S. Wren, "Early Count Hints at Fewer Kosovo Deaths," *New York Times*, November 11, 1999, p. A6; and U.S. State Department, "Ethnic Cleansing in Kosovo: An Accounting," December 1999 (www.state.gov/www/global/human_rights/kosovoii/homepage.html [accessed March 2000]).

44. Mark Heinrich, "UN Official in Kosovo: 11,000 in Mass Graves," *Washington Times*, August 3, 1999, p. A12; and Carlotta Gall, "Rebel General Planning a New Army for Kosovo," *New York Times*, June 22, 1999, p. A12.

45. "The Kosovo Refugee Crisis: An Independent Evaluation of UNHCR's Emergency Preparedness and Response," UN High Commissioner for Refugees, February 2000 (www.unhcr.ch/evaluate/kosovo/ch1.htm [accessed March 2000]); also UN High Commissioner for Refugees, cited in Elizabeth Becker and David Rohde, "Refugees Are Skeptical of Pledges," *New York Times*, June 4, 1999, p. A21.

46. "Ex-Croat Army Man Leads KLA," *Financial Times*, May 4, 1999, p. 2.

47. Kosovo Task Force, "Kosovo Situation Reports: May 1999," pp. 1, 3, 31.

48. *CIA Report to Congress Pursuant to Sec. 312 of the Intelligence Authorization Act for Fiscal Year 2000.*

49. William Claiborne, "KLA Improving Its Status, Pentagon Says," *Washington Post*, May 28, 1999, p. A31.

50. Dana Priest and Peter Finn, "NATO Gives Air Support to Kosovo Guerrillas, but Yugoslavs Repel Attack from Albania," *Washington Post*, June 2, 1999, p. A1. There were also unconfirmed reports of NATO Special Forces working inside of Kosovo with the KLA; see Philip Sherwell, "War in the Balkans: SAS Teams Move in to Help KLA 'Rise from the Ashes,'" *London Daily Telegraph*, web version, April 18, 1999.

51. William Drozdiak, "B-52 Strike Devastates Field Force in Kosovo," *Washington Post*, June 9, 1999, p. A19; Dana Priest, "The Commander's War: A Decisive Battle That Never Was," *Washington Post*, September 19, 1999, p. A1; and Richard J. Newman, "The Bombs That Failed in Kosovo," *U.S. News and World Report*, September 20, 1999, pp. 28–30.

52. Cohen, "DoD News Briefing" (June 10, 1999).

53. House Armed Services Committee, "Kosovo Backgrounder," June 30, 1999, p. 3; and "Press Conference on the Kosovo Strike Assessment by General Wesley K. Clark, Supreme Allied Commander, Europe and Brigadier General John Corley, Chief, Kosovo Mission Effectiveness Assessment Team," NATO Press Conference, September 16, 1999.

54. Clinton, "A Just and Necessary War," p. 17; and Cohen, "DoD News Briefing" (June 10, 1999).

55. Cohen, "Prepared Statement," Senate Armed Services Committee, July 20, 1999.

56. "Press Conference on the Kosovo Strike Assessment," NATO Press Conference, September 16, 1999.

57. "Maps and Aerial Views of Post- and Pre-Strikes Used during the Press Conference by General Wesley K. Clark, 'Kosovo Strike Assessment,'" NATO Press Conference, September 16, 1999.

58. Thomas A. Keaney and Eliot A. Cohen, *Gulf War Air Power Survey Summary Report* (U.S. Government Printing Office, 1993), pp. 126–28.

59. *Report to Congress: Kosovo/Operation Allied Force After-Action Report*, pp. 84–86.

60. Rowan Scarborough, "NATO Exaggerated Weapons Hit in Kosovo but Clark Says Mission Accomplished," *Washington Times*, September 17, 1999, p. A3.

61. Michael Dobbs, "A War-Torn Reporter Reflects," *Washington Post*, July 11, 1999, p. B1.

62. General Wesley Clark, interview with authors, April 20, 2000.

63. "Press Conference Given by NATO Spokesman, Jamie Shea and General Konrad Freytag, SHAPE," NATO Press Conference, April 25, 1999; Kosovo Task Force, "Kosovo Situation Reports: May 1999," pp. 23, 25, 27, 29; "Press Conference by Dr. Jamie Shea and Colonel Konrad Freytag," NATO Press Conference, May 2, 1999; and "Press Conference Given by NATO Spokesman, Jamie Shea and SHAPE Spokesman, Major General Walter Jertz," NATO Press Conference, May 19, 1999. About 80 percent of Yugoslav troops are conscripts.

64. See, for example, Steven Erlanger, "Belgrade's People Still Defiant, but Deeply Weary," *New York Times*, May 24, 1999, p. A1.

65. See also Wesley Clark, interview, *PBS Frontline, War in Europe* (www.pbs.org/wgbh/pages/frontline/shows/kosovo/ [accessed March 2000]).

66. Thomas Lippman and Bradley Graham, "NATO Takes a New Look at Options for Invasion," *Washington Post*, April 22, 1999, p. A1.

67. Klaus Naumann, interview by authors, December 22, 1999.

68. Senior U.S. official, interview by authors, August 24, 1999.

69. It is conceivable that ninety days were not enough to load and unload ships (and hire them, in the case of most European militaries, since they generally lack their own sealift), prepare roads and other facilities as required, and move forces into position. It could have taken longer, depending on the availability of commercial sealift, the availability of ports and other infrastructure in Greece, and the speed with which engineering equipment could be moved to Kosovo. For some of the

Pentagon's concerns in this regard, see *Report to Congress: Kosovo/Operation Allied Force After-Action Report,* pp. 102–03.

70. Steven Erlanger, "NATO Was Closer to Ground War in Kosovo Than Is Widely Realized," *New York Times,* November 7, 1999, p. 6; Michael Hirsh and others, "NATO's Game of Chicken," *Newsweek,* July 26, 1999, pp. 58–61; Priest, "The Commander's War: A Decisive Battle That Never Was," p. A1; and Patrick Wintour and Peter Beaumont, "Revealed: The Secret Plan to Invade Kosovo," *Observer,* July 18, 1999, p. 17.

71. "Remarks by the President and His Majesty Abdullah II, King of the Hashemite Kingdom of Jordan in Photo Opportunity" (White House, Office of the Press Secretary, May 18, 1999).

72. Senior U.S. official, interview by authors, September 24, 1999.

73. See John F. Harris, "Clinton Says He Might Send Ground Troops," *Washington Post,* May 19, 1999, p. A1.

74. Clinton, "A Just and Necessary War," p. D17; and Kosovo Task Force, "Kosovo Situation Reports: May 1999," pp. 31–32, 35.

75. Berger, interview by authors, February 9, 2000; Clark, interview, and Samuel Berger, interview, *PBS Frontline, War in Europe.*

76. Originally planned for deployment in Macedonia, Task Force Hawk had to deploy to Albania when the Macedonian government objected. In Albania, the Tirana airport had room for only one or two transport aircraft at a time (the task force required 550 C-17 flights for deployment); furthermore, it was frequently used for relief supplies and initially was unusable at night. Another complicating factor in Albania was the mud, which required that hardened helipads be built. See "Operation *Allied Force:* Lessons Learned" (Congressional Research Service, September 3, 1999), p. 15; and Dana Priest, "Risks and Restraints: Why the Apaches Never Flew," *Washington Post,* December 29, 1999, p. A1.

77. Kosovo Task Force, "Kosovo Situation Reports: April 1999," pp. 15, 31; Kosovo Task Force, "Kosovo Situation Reports: May 1999," p. 15; and Kosovo Task Force, "Kosovo Situation Reports: June 1999" (Congressional Research Service, 1999), pp. 7, 21, 25.

78. Michael Evans, "Peace Force Is Still Not Ready for Settlement," *Times* (London), May 12, 1999, p. 10.

79. General Wesley Clark, interview with authors, April 20, 2000; "Morning Briefing by Jamie Shea," NATO Morning Briefing, May 26, 1999; Priest, "The Commanders' War: Bombing by Committee," p. A1; and Jane Perlez, "Clinton Is Pushing for 50,000 Troops at Kosovo Border," *New York Times,* May 22, 1999, p. A1.

80. Senior British official, interview by authors, November 8, 1999. See also Erlanger, "NATO Was Closer to Ground War in Kosovo Than Is Widely Realized," p. 6.

81. See Steven Lee Myers, "Cohen and Other Ministers Size up Possible Ground Force," *New York Times,* May 29, 1999, p. A6; and Hirsh and others, "NATO's Game of Chicken."

82. Coen van Zwol, "Lente in Kosovo," *NRC Handelsblad,* December 18, 1999 (www.nrc.nl/W2/Lab/Kosovo/991218-m.html [accessed December 1999]), p. 23.

83. *Report to Congress: Kosovo/Operation Allied Force After-Action Report*, pp. 101–02.

84. General Wesley Clark, interview with authors, April 20, 2000.

85. Those present at the meeting included former U.S. ambassador to the United Nations Jeanne Kirkpatrick, former congressman Lee Hamilton, former U.S. ambassadors to NATO William Taft and Robert Hunter, former NATO commander General George Joulwan, former White House and State Department official Helmut Sonnenfeldt, and former National Security Council officials Stephen Larrabee, Jeremy Rosner, and Ivo Daalder. Quotations in the text are taken from notes taken at the meeting by Daalder. See also Erlanger, "NATO Was Closer to Ground War in Kosovo Than Is Widely Realized," p. A6.

86. Hirsh and others, "NATO's Game of Chicken"; and John Harris and Bradley Graham, "Clinton Is Reassessing Sufficiency of Air War," *Washington Post*, June 3, 1999, p. A1.

87. Berger, interview by authors, February 9, 2000.

88. Ibid. See also *Newshour with Jim Lehrer*, June 11, 1999 (www.pbs.org/newshour/bb/europe/jan-june99/clinton_6-11.htm [accessed June 1999]).

89. Erlanger, "NATO Was Closer to Ground War in Kosovo Than Is Widely Realized," p. 6.

90. Ibid.

91. Hirsh and others, "NATO's Game of Chicken."

92. See Kosovo Task Force, "Kosovo Situation Reports: April 1999," pp. 4, 6, 8, 28, 36; Kosovo Task Force, "Kosovo Situation Reports: May 1999," pp. 14, 34, 38; and Kosovo Task Force, "Kosovo Situation Reports: June 1999," p. 10.

93. See Pat Towell, "Congress Set to Provide Money, but No Guidance, for Kosovo Mission," *CQ Weekly*, May 1, 1999, pp. 1036–40; and E. J. Dionne Jr., "War as an Opening for Partisan Payback," *Washington Post*, May 3, 1999, p. A25.

94. James M. Lindsay, "Congress and the Use of Force in the Post–Cold War Era," in Aspen Strategy Group, *The United States and the Use of Force in the Post–Cold War Era* (Washington, D.C.: Aspen Institute, 1995), p. 75. See also Robert B. Zoellick, "Congress and the Making of U.S. Foreign Policy," *Survival*, vol. 41 (Winter 1999–2000), pp. 31–34.

95. Kosovo Task Force, "Kosovo Situation Reports: April 1999," pp. 34, 36; quote taken from Kosovo Task Force, "Kosovo Situation Reports: June 1999," p. 14.

96. Kosovo Task Force, "Kosovo Situation Reports: April 1999," p. 36.

97. Senior French officials, interviews by authors, October 7 and November 11, 1999.

98. Senior French official, interview by authors, November 11, 1999.

99. Senior U.S. official, interview by authors, November 11, 1999. Also senior Italian officials, interviews by authors, October 23, 1999.

100. "Dini Sparks Row over Kosovo Policy," *International Herald Tribune: Italy Daily*, May 29–30, 1999, p. 1; and Kosovo Task Force, "Kosovo Situation Reports: May 1999," pp. 14, 20, 22, 24, 26, 30, 32, 40.

101. "Press Conference by NATO Secretary-General, Mr Javier Solana, and German Chancellor Gerhard Schroeder," NATO Speech, May 19, 1999.

102. Senior German official, interview by authors, November 10, 1999.

103. Senior British official, interview by authors, November 8, 1999.

104. "Press Conference by the President" (White House, Office of the Press Secretary, June 25, 1999).

105. Senior British official, interview by authors, November 12, 1999.

106. "The Situation in and around Kosovo," NATO Press Release M-NAC-1(99)51, April 12, 1999.

107. German official, interview by authors, October 22, 1999. See also Blaine Harden, "A Long Struggle That Led Serb Leader to Back Down," New York Times, June 6, 1999, p. 12.

108. German Ministry of Foreign Affairs, "Deutsche Initiative für den Kosovo," April 16, 1999 (www.auswaertiges-amt.de/6_archiv/inf-kos/hintergr/initia.htm [accessed March 2000]).

109. Daniel Williams, "German Proposal Rejected by U.S.; Plan Offered Pause in Bombing," Washington Post, April 15, 1999, p. A27.

110. John F. Harris and Charles Babington, "Despite Peace Push, Bombing Continues; Clinton Demands Yugoslav Retreat," Washington Post, May 4, 1999, p. A1.

111. "Press Conference of the President and Prime Minister Obuchi" (White House, Office of the Press Secretary, May 3, 1999).

112. Quoted in Jane Perlez, "Clinton's Quandary: No Approach to End War Is Fast or Certain of Success," New York Times, April 29, 1999, p. A16.

113. The plan also called for an immediate and verifiable end of violence and repression in Kosovo, safe return of all refugees and displaced persons, free access in Kosovo for aid organizations, a political process leading to autonomy, and an economic development plan. See "Statement by the Chairman on the Conclusion of the Meeting of the G8 Foreign Ministers on the Petersberg" (Bonn: May 6, 1999) (www.seerecon.org/keyspeeches/keyspeeches-002.htm [accessed March 2000]).

114. See Barton Gellman and Steven Mufson, "Ambiguity Wins in Agreement in Kosovo," Washington Post, May 7, 1999, p. A35.

115. Daniel Williams, "Belgrade Announces Kosovo Troop Cut," Washington Post, May 11, 1999, p. A1.

116. Harden, "A Long Struggle That Led Serb Leader to Back Down," p. 12; and Brownen Maddox, "The 80 Days War," Times (London), July 15, 1999, p. 47. In addition to these two excellent accounts of the Ahtisaari-Chernomyrdin-Talbott talks, see also William Drozdiak, "The Kosovo Peace Deal: How It Happened," Washington Post, June 6, 1999, pp. A1, A22; Tyler Marshall and Richard Boudreaux, "Crisis in Yugoslavia: How an Uneasy Alliance Prevailed," Los Angeles Times, June 6, 1999, p. A1; and Martin Walker, "Revealed: How Deal Was Done in Stalin's Hideaway," Guardian, June 5, 1999. Talbott gave his own account in an interview on PBS Frontline, War in Europe. Unless otherwise noted, what follows is drawn from these sources.

117. Steven Mufson and John F. Harris, "Turmoil May Hamper Kosovo Mediation, U.S. Officials Say," Washington Post, May 13, 1999, p. A22.

118. Van Zwol, "Lente in Kosovo," p. 26.

119. Daniel Williams, "Milosevic Hears Terms for Peace," *Washington Post*, June 3, 1999, p. A1; and Richard Norton-Taylor and Martin Walker, "Prospect of Split Kosovo," *Guardian*, May 26, 1999.

120. "Statement on Kosovo Issued by the Heads of State and Government Participating in the Meeting of the North Atlantic Council in Washington, D.C. on 23rd and 24th April 1999," NATO Press Release S-1(99)62, April 23, 1999.

121. See Walker, "How Deal Was Done in Stalin's Hideaway"; and Guy Dinmore and John Lloyd, "Milosevic Agrees to Allow NATO Troops into Kosovo," *Financial Times*, May 31, 1999, p. 1.

122. Talbott interview, *PBS Frontline, War in Europe*.

123. Ibid.

124. Walker, "How Deal Was Done in Stalin's Hideaway."

125. Hirsch and others, "NATO's Game of Chicken."

126. Dinmore and Lloyd, "Milosevic Agrees to Allow NATO Troops in Kosovo," p. 1; and Williams, "Milosevic Hears Terms for Peace," p. A1.

127. Drozdiak, "The Kosovo Peace Deal," p. A22. See also Talbott interview, *PBS Frontline, War in Europe*.

128. See text of the agreement on principles for a solution to the Kosovo crisis, Annex 2 to UN Security Council Resolution 1244 (1999), reprinted in appendix C.

129. Talbott interview, *PBS Frontline, War in Europe*.

130. Van Zwol, "Lente in Kosovo," p. 28.

131. Paraphrased text of the agreement on principles for a solution to the Kosovo crisis, Annex 2 to UN Security Council Resolution 1244 (1999).

132. Harden, "A Long Struggle That Led Serb Leader to Back Down," p. 12; and Walker, "How Deal Was Done in Stalin's Hideaway."

133. Quoted in Marshall and Boudreaux, "How an Uneasy Alliance Prevailed," p. A1.

134. Daniel Williams, "Yugoslavs Yield to NATO Terms," *Washington Post*, June 4, 1999, p. A1.

135. Harden, "A Long Struggle That Led Serb Leader to Back Down," p. 12.

136. R. Jeffrey Smith and Molly Moore, "Kosovo Pullout Set to Start Today; NATO-Led Contingent to Enter Province," *Washington Post*, June 10, 1999, p. A1.

137. Paul Watson, "Just Outside Kosovo, Ethnic Albanians Still Live in Fear," *Los Angeles Times*, November 30, 1999, p. A1; and Steven Erlanger, "Kosovo's Rebels Regrouping Nearby in Serbia," *New York Times*, March 2, 2000, pp. A1, A10.

138. Kosovo Task Force, "Kosovo Situation Reports: June 1999," pp. 5–18, esp. pp. 13, 15; and "Press Conference by Mr. Jamie Shea, NATO Spokesman," NATO Press Conference, June 11, 1999.

139. Zbigniew Brzezinski, Hearings, *The Lessons of Kosovo*, Senate Foreign Relations Committee, 106 Cong. 2 sess. (October 6, 1999).

140. Steven Erlanger, "Russia Enters Kosovo Early but Moscow Calls It a Mistake," *New York Times*, June 12, 1999, p. 1.

141. Robert G. Kaiser and David Hoffman, "Russia Had Bigger Plan in Kosovo,"

Washington Post, June 25, 1999, p. A1; and Zbigniew Brzezinski, "The Lessons of Kosovo," testimony, Senate Foreign Relations Committee, 106 Cong 1 sess (October 6, 1999).

142. Celestine Bohlen, "Accord Is Reached on Integrating Russian Troops in Kosovo Force," *New York Times,* June 19, 1999, p. 1.

143. Toni Marshall and Bill Gertz, "Briton Refused Clark's Order to Intercept Russians in Kosovo," *Washington Times,* August 3, 1999, p. A1; and Elizabeth Becker, "U.S. General Was Overruled in Kosovo," *New York Times,* September 10, 1999, p. A6.

144. Berger interview, *PBS Frontline, War in Europe.*

145. Steven Lee Myers with Michael Wines, "Accord with NATO Lets Moscow Add Troops in Kosovo," *New York Times,* July 6, 1999, p. A1.

146. David R. Sands, "Lasting Peace Seems Far Away in Kosovo," *Washington Times,* September 10, 1999, p. A15; Wesley K. Clark, "Prepared Statement," Hearings, *Situation in Bosnia and Kosovo,* Senate Armed Services Committee, February 2, 2000, 106 Cong. 1 sess. p. 7; Richard Norton-Taylor, "Kosovo: After the War—Killings Show up Police Shortage," *Guardian,* July 27, 1999; and Michael O'Hanlon and Kori Schake, "Winning the Peace in Kosovo," *Christian Science Monitor,* November 8, 1999, p. 11.

147. *Law Enforcement Management and Administrative Statistics, 1993: Data for Individual State and Local Agencies with 100 or More Officers* (U.S. Department of Justice, 1993), pp. 1–12.

148. "Statement by the President" (White House, Office of the Press Secretary, February 24, 2000); and "Fact Sheet on PDD 71: Strengthening Criminal Justice Systems (In Support of Peace Operations & Other Complex Contingencies)" (www.usia.gov/products/pdq/wfarchive.htm [accessed March 2000]).

149. International Crisis Group, *Violence in Kosovo: Who's Killing Whom?* Balkans Report 78, amended version (Washington, D.C.: November 2, 1999).

150. R. Jeffrey Smith, "Kosovo's Youth Blamed for Brutal Ethnic Crimes," *Washington Post,* December 6, 1999, p. A1; and Steven Erlanger, "Monitors' Reports Provide Chronicle of Kosovo Terror," *New York Times,* December 5, 1999, p. 1.

151. Organization for Security and Cooperation in Europe, "Assessment of the Situation of Ethnic Minorities in Kosovo" (February 14, 2000) (www.osce.org/kosovo/publications/ethnic_minorities/minorities4.htm [accessed March 2000]); and Edward Cody, "Out of Work and Hope, Serbs Evacuate Kosovo," *Washington Post,* February 17, 2000, p. A21.

152. David Holley, "Serbs Make Last Stand in Divided Kosovo City," *Los Angeles Times,* August 17, 1999, p. A1.

153. "Milosevic Opponent Assails NATO Effort," *Washington Post,* August 5, 1999, p. A20.

154. For examples of Western news stories that accurately identified many individual problems in Kosovo in the fall of 1999 but failed to acknowledge the accomplishments of the international community and the former KLA, see Steven Erlanger, "Chaos and Intolerance Prevailing in Kosovo Despite UN's Efforts," *New York Times,* November 22, 1999, p. A1; and R. Jeffrey Smith, "Kosovo Rebels Make Own Laws,"

Washington Post, November 24, 1999, p. A1. For a useful and fair rendition of the accomplishments to date, see "Press Briefing by National Security Advisor, Samuel 'Sandy' Berger, and UNMIK Principal Deputy Special Representative of the Secretary-General, Jock Covey" (Camp Bondsteel, Kosovo: White House, Office of the Press Secretary, November 23, 1999).

155. "KFOR Press Update by Major Ole Irgens, KFOR Spokesman," November 10, 1999 (Pristina); Alex Todorovic, "Unhappy with KFOR, Serbs Bolster Milosevic," *Christian Science Monitor*, September 15, 1999, p. 7; Dan Eggen, "NATO 'Duds' Keep Killing in Kosovo," *Washington Post*, July 19, 1999, p. A1; Lord Robertson of Port Ellen, "NATO and Kosovo: Kosovo One Year On" (Brussels: March 21, 2000) (www.nato.int/kosovo/repo2000/index.htm [accessed March 2000]); U.S. Department of Commerce, *Statistical Abstract of the United States, 1999*, 119th ed. (U.S. Government Printing Office, 1999), p. 99; Federal Bureau of Investigation, "Uniform Crime Reports," November 21, 1999 (www.fbi.gov/ucr.htm [accessed November 1999]); and Clark, "Prepared Statement," February 2, 2000, p. 6.

156. David S. Cloud, "Albright's Spokesman Helped Shape Kosovo Pact—James Rubin Wooed the Rebels," *Wall Street Journal*, June 29, 1999, p. A11. For a good overview of the KLA, see International Crisis Group, *What Happened to the KLA?* (Washington, D.C.: March 3, 2000).

157. Wade Boese, "Belgrade, KLA Move Forward on Arms Control, Disarmament," *Arms Control Today*, vol. 29 (September-October 1999), p. 37.

158. Chris Hedges, "As U.N. Organizes, Rebels Are Taking Charge of Kosovo," *New York Times*, July 29, 1999, p. A1.

159. Zoran Kusovac, "Interview with General Agim Ceku, Commander of Kosovo Protection Corps (KPC)," *Jane's Defence Weekly*, October 20, 1999, p. 32.

160. Carlotta Gall, "Kosovo Rebel Leader Basking in Warmth of Deal's Reception," *New York Times*, September 22, 1999, p. A8; Carlotta Gall, "Russia Assails Accord for New Kosovo Force," *International Herald Tribune*, September 23, 1999; and Andrew Gray, "NATO's Boss Sees No Free Kosovo," *Washington Times*, September 28, 1999, p. A16.

161. On the crime problem in Albania and Kosovo, see Frank Cilluffo and George Salmoiraghi, "And the Winner Is . . . the Albanian Mafia," *Washington Quarterly*, vol. 22 (Autumn 1999), pp. 21–25. See also Steven Erlanger, "U.N. Chief in Kosovo Says Lack of Money Imperils Mission," *New York Times*, March 4, 2000, p. 7.

162. International Crisis Group, *What Happened to the KLA?*

163. Karl Vick, "Africa Has Refugees, Kosovo Gets Money," *Washington Post*, October 8, 1999, p. A24.

164. Matthew Kaminski, "Kosovo Assessment Highlights Damage to Housing Stock," *Wall Street Journal*, July 26, 1999, p. A20.

165. Timothy Garton Ash, "Anarchy & Madness," *New York Review of Books*, February 10, 2000, pp. 48–53.

166. Noel Malcolm, *Kosovo: A Short History* (Harper/Perennial, 1999), p. 337.

167. Michael B. G. Froman, "Building a Sustainable Economy in Kosovo," in Rob-

ert Zoellick and Philip Zelikow, eds., *America and the Balkans: Memos to a President* (W. W. Norton, 2000); and Matthias Rueb, "Reconstructing Kosovo: On the Right Track—But Where Does It Lead?" *NATO Review* (Autumn 1999), p. 22.

168. R. Jeffrey Smith, "Specter of Independent Kosovo Divides U.S., European Allies," *Washington Post*, September 28, 1999, p. A19; and David R. Sands, "Ethnic Albanians Seek Independent Kosovo," *Washington Times*, August 12, 1999, p. A1.

169. Jane Perlez, "NATO Expects Separate Kosovo, without Yugoslav Police or Taxes," *New York Times*, June 11, 1999, p. A1.

170. For a concurring view, see International Institute for Strategic Studies, "The Future of Kosovo: An Indefinite NATO Presence," *Strategic Comments*, vol. 6 (January 2000).

171. Barbara Crossette, "UN Council Urged to Debate Political Future of Kosovo," *New York Times*, March 7, 2000, p. A6.

172. For a similar concept, see Jeffrey Gedmin, "Kosovo without Serbia: The Time for Independenc Is Now," *Washington Times*, March 28, 2000, p. A21.

Chapter Six

1. Although it may have been theoretically possible to have addressed the issue at Dayton, the task of forging a Bosnian peace was more than sufficient to occupy even the most dogged and inexhaustible negotiators.

2. However, following the first instances of violence in late summer 1997, the Contact Group did issue a statement expressing deep concern about rising tensions and warned "against any resort to violence to press political demands." "Statement on Kosovo of Contact Group Foreign Ministers" (New York: Contact Group, September 24, 1997).

3. "Statement on Kosovo" (Washington, D.C.: Contact Group, January 8, 1998); and "Statement on Kosovo" (Moscow: Contact Group, February 25, 1998).

4. Quoted in David Binder, "Bush Warns Serbs Not to Widen War," *New York Times*, December 28, 1992, p. A6.

5. See Ivo H. Daalder, "Kosovo: Bosnia Déjà Vu," *Washington Post*, April 17, 1998, p. A23. At the time, Michael O'Hanlon was not prepared to consider using force, a possibility he seriously entertained only in July, when Serb attacks on Kosovars escalated significantly. See Michael E. O'Hanlon, "Dying for Kosovo," *Washington Times*, July 1, 1998, p. A17.

6. See, for example, statements made by Senator Bob Dole (R-Kans.), Senator Don Nickles (R-Okla.), and Senator Chuck Hagel (R-Nebr.), in Craig R. Whitney, "Balkan Powder Keg Watches the Fuse," *New York Times*, May 25, 1993, p. A6; in Steven Erlanger, "First Bosnia, Now Kosovo," *New York Times*, June 10, 1998, p. A14; and in Bob Dole, "We Must Stop the Kosovo Terror," *Washington Post*, September 14, 1998, p. A19.

7. In the end, the war in Kosovo did not undermine the peace process in Bosnia.

If anything, the opposite may be closer to true if it convinced the Bosnian Serb leadership that its fate lay in Sarajevo rather than Belgrade.

8. Michael O'Hanlon had, and continues to have, reservations about the use of air strikes at this point in 1998. In retrospect, however, it seems to be an option that was worth considering.

9. Samuel R. Berger, interview by authors, February 9, 2000. See also R. W. Apple Jr., "A Domestic Sort with Global Worries," *New York Times*, August 25, 1999, p. A1.

10. See Madeleine K. Albright, "Remarks and Q & A Session at the U.S. Institute of Peace" (U.S. Department of State, February 4, 1999).

11. See Bruce W. Jentleson, "Normative Dilemmas and Political Myths: The Contemporary Political Context of the Use of Military Force," paper prepared for the international conference, "Employing Air and Space Power at the Turn of the Millennium: Lessons and Implications," Fisher Institute for Air and Space Strategic Studies, Tel Aviv, December 1999, pp. 9–12; and Program on International Public Attitudes, *Americans on Kosovo: A Study of U.S. Public Attitudes* (Washington, D.C.: 1999).

12. In the end, the administration was prepared to consider the use of ground forces even in the absence of a NATO decision or consensus. As Sandy Berger told a group of former government officials (including Ivo Daalder) who met with him on June 2, 1999, "A consensus within NATO is valuable, but it is not an absolute requirement."

13. Michael Hirsh and others, "NATO's Game of Chicken," *Newsweek*, July 26, 1999, pp. 58–61.

14. See Michael Mandelbaum, "A Perfect Failure: NATO's War against Yugoslavia," *Foreign Affairs*, vol. 78 (September-October 1999), pp. 2–8. See also Ted Galen Carpenter, ed., *NATO's Empty Victory: A Postmortem on the Balkan War* (Washington, D.C.: Cato Institute, 2000).

15. Yahya Sadowski, *The Myth of Global Chaos* (Brookings, 1998), p. 86.

16. Christopher Layne and Benjamin Schwarz, "For the Record: Kosovo II," *National Interest*, no. 57 (Fall 1999), pp. 9–15.

17. Christopher Layne and Benjamin Schwartz, "We Were Suckers for the KLA," *Washington Post*, March 25, 2000, p. B15; Peter Finn, "War Left Kosovo Serbs in Limbo," *Washington Post*, March 24, 2000, p. A1; Richard Meerten, "In Kosovo, a Hard Year All Around," *Christian Science Monitor*, March 22, 2000, p. 1; and Tariq Ali, "Crimes, Lies, and Misdemeanors," *Financial Times*, April 2, 2000, p. 5.

18. "Address to the Nation by the President" (White House, Office of the Press Secretary, June 10, 1999); and James Steinberg, "A Perfect Polemic," *Foreign Affairs*, vol. 78 (November-December 1999), pp. 128–33.

19. Mark Kramer, "What Is Driving Russia's New Strategic Concept," Memo 103 (Harvard University, Program on New Approaches to Russian Security, January 2000).

20. Ted Galen Carpenter, "Damage to Relations with Russia and China," in Carpenter, ed., *NATO's Empty Victory*, pp. 77–91. See also Mandelbaum, "A Perfect Failure," pp. 2–8.

21. Michael Gordon, "Imitating NATO: A Script Is Adapted for Chechnya," *New York Times*, September 28, 1999, p. A3.

22. See also Celeste A. Wallander, "Russian National Security Policy in 2000," Memo 102 (Harvard University, Program on New Approaches to Russian Security, January 2000). While Wallander is critical of NATO's war against Serbia for its effects on Russia, she agrees that in the end the Kosovo precedent was not the main cause of the war over Chechnya.

23. Michael McFaul, "Getting Russia Right," *Foreign Policy*, no. 117 (Winter 1999-2000), pp. 58–73; and Dmitry Shlapentokh, "The Illusions and Realities of Russian Nationalism," *Washington Quarterly*, vol. 23 (Winter 2000), pp. 173–86.

24. Sharon LaFraniere, "Russia Mends Broken Ties with NATO," *Washington Post*, February 17, 2000, p. A1.

25. Dana Priest, "The Commanders' War: The Battle Inside Headquarters; Tension Grew with Divide over Strategy," *Washington Post*, September 21, 1999, p. A1; Wesley Clark and Michael C. Short, interviews, *PBS Frontline, War in Europe* (www.pbs.org/wgbh/pages/frontline/shows/kosovo/ [accessed March 2000]); Don D. Chipman, "The Balkan Wars: Diplomacy, Politics, and Coalition Warfare," *Strategic Review*, vol. 28 (Winter 2000), pp. 28–31; and Alan D. Zimm, "Desert Storm, Kosovo, and 'Doctrinal Schizophrenia,'" *Strategic Review*, vol. 28 (Winter 2000), pp. 37–39.

26. Alan Kuperman, "Botched Diplomacy Led to War," *Wall Street Journal*, June 17, 1999, p. A27; Layne and Schwartz, "For the Record: Kosovo II," p. 11; Mandelbaum, "A Perfect Failure," p. 4; and Barry Posen, "The War for Kosovo," *International Security*, vol. 24 (Spring 2000), pp. 80–81.

27. Appendix B, "Military-Technical Agreement between International Security Force ('KFOR') and the Government of the Federal Republic of Yugoslavia and the Republic of Serbia," June 9, 1999: "Notwithstanding any other provision of this Agreement, the Parties understand and agree that the international security force ('KFOR') commander has the right and is authorised to compel the removal, withdrawal, or relocation of specific Forces and weapons, and to order the cessation of any activities whenever the international security force ('KFOR') commander determines a potential threat to either the international security force ('KFOR') or its mission, or to another Party. Forces failing to redeploy, withdraw, relocate, or to cease threatening or potentially threatening activities following such a demand by the international security force ('KFOR') shall be subject to military action by the international security force ('KFOR'), including the use of necessary force, to ensure compliance" (www.nato.int/kosovo/docu/a990609a.htm [accessed March 2000], reprinted in appendix C).

28. Kosovo Task Force, "Kosovo Situation Reports: April 1999" (Congressional Research Service, 1999), p. 36; Paul Richter, "Crisis in Yugoslavia: Milosevic War Machine Has a Lot of Fight Left," *Los Angeles Times*, April 29, 1999, p. A1; Steven Erlanger, "Bombing Unites Serb Army as It Debilitates Economy—Production Cut in Half, Experts Say," *New York Times*, April 30, 1999, p. A1; and "Press Conference

Given by Mr. Jamie Shea and Major General Walter Jertz," NATO Press Conference, May 5, 1999.

29. Wesley K. Clark, "When Force Is Necessary: NATO's Military Response to the Kosovo Crisis," *NATO Review,* vol. 47 (Summer 1999), p. 17.

30. Barry R. Posen, "Measuring the European Conventional Balance," *International Security,* vol. 9 (Summer 1985), pp. 47–88, reprinted in Steven E. Miller, *Conventional Forces and American Defense Policy* (Princeton University Press, 1986), p. 92.

31. For similar analyses, see Anthony Cordesman, *The Lessons and Non-Lessons of the Air and Missile Campaign in Kosovo* (Washington, D.C.: Center for Strategic and International Studies, 1999); and *Operation Allied Force: Lessons Learned* (Congressional Research Service, Foreign Affairs, Defense, and Trade Division, 1999), p. 7.

32. "Statement by the President" (White House, Office of the Press Secretary, April 28, 1999).

33. See Thomas Friedman in Thomas Friedman and Ignacio Ramonet, "Dueling Globalizations," *Foreign Policy,* no. 116 (Fall 1999), p. 124; Charles Krauthammer, "The Short, Unhappy Life of Humanitarian War," *National Interest,* no. 57 (Fall 1999), p. 5; and Short, interview, *PBS Frontline, War in Europe.*

34. See statements of Strobe Talbott, "The Insiders' Story," *Nightline,* "The War in Kosovo," August 30, 1999.

35. Senior Italian official, interview by authors, October 23, 1999; and senior U.S. official, interview by authors, November 11, 1999.

36. *Operation Allied Force: Lessons Learned,* p. 6.

37. See Dana Priest, "The Commanders' War: A Decisive Battle That Never Was," *Washington Post,* September 19, 1999, p. A1. Moreover, the road upgrades were needed just to supply refugee camps; see "Press Conference Given by NATO Spokesman, Jamie Shea and SHAPE Spokesman, Major General Walter Jertz; Video Press Conference with the NATO Secretary General Dr. Javier Solana from Skopje," NATO Press Conference, May 12, 1999 (Skopje); "Press Conference Given by NATO Spokesman, Jamie Shea and SHAPE Spokesman, Major General Walter Jertz and Commander Fabrizio Maltinti," NATO Press Conference, May 13, 1999; and Steven Erlanger, "NATO Was Closer to Ground War in Kosovo Than Is Widely Realized," *New York Times,* November 7, 1999, p. 6, and authors' conversation with Kori Schake.

38. Patrick Wintour and Peter Beaumont, "Revealed: The Secret Plan to Invade Kosovo," *Observer,* July 18, 1999, p. 1.

39. Michael R. Gordon, "NATO Moves Ahead on a Kosovo Force of 50,000 Troops," *New York Times,* May 26, 1999, p. A1.

40. Michael Dobbs, "For Milosevic, a Choice Whose Time Had Come," *Washington Post,* June 4, 1999, p. A1.

41. Flora Lewis, "A Clash with Russia in Kosovo Came Too Close for Comfort," *International Herald Tribune,* October 1, 1999; and Zbigniew Brzezinski, Testimony, Hearings, *The Lessons of Kosovo,* Senate Foreign Relations Committee, 106 Cong. 1 sess. (October 6, 1999).

42. Steven Erlanger, "Word of Indictment Stuns Serbs and Blights Hopes," *New York Times*, May 27, 1999, p. A12; Jane Perlez, "Some Fears over Talks; Aides Worry," *New York Times*, May 28, 1999, p. A10; and David Hoffman, "Russia Says Talks Sideswiped; Milosevic Indictment Deepens Pessimism over Peace Efforts," *Washington Post*, May 28, 1999, p. A28.

43. These lessons draw and expand on Ivo H. Daalder and Michael E. O'Hanlon, "Unlearning the Lessons of Kosovo," *Foreign Policy*, no. 116 (Fall 1999), pp. 128–40.

44. See Christopher Layne and Benjamin Schwarz, "Argument: NATO and Kosovo; Reply," *National Interest*, no. 58 (Winter 1999-2000), p. 116.

45. The classic statement on compellance is Thomas C. Schelling, *Arms and Influence* (Yale University Press, 1966), p. 69 ff. Also see Richard N. Haass, *Intervention: The Use of American Military Force in the Post–Cold War World*, rev. ed. (Brookings, 1999), pp. 53–55.

46. Bradley Graham and Dana Priest, "U.S. Details Strategy, Damage," *Washington Post*, December 18, 1998, p. A1; and "The 70-Hour War," *Washington Post*, December 21, 1998, p. A28.

47. "Remarks by the President on the Situation in Kosovo" (White House, Office of the Press Secretary, March 22, 1999).

48. Quoted in R. Jeffrey Smith, "Belgrade Rebuffs Final U.S. Warning," *Washington Post*, March 23, 1999, p. A1.

49. Bradley Graham, "Joint Chiefs Doubted Air Strategy," *Washington Post*, April 5, 1999, p. A1; and General Charles Krulak, interview, *PBS Frontline, War in Europe*.

50. See Lawrence Freedman, *The Revolution in Strategic Affairs*, Adelphi Paper 318 (Oxford University Press for the International Institute for Strategic Studies, 1998); and Michael O'Hanlon, *Technological Change and the Future of Warfare* (Brookings, 2000).

51. Colin Powell is a former chairman of the Joint Chiefs of Staff and a former national security adviser. The White House officials are quoted in Barton Gellman, "The Kosovo Peace Deal: What It Means," *Washington Post*, June 6, 1999, p. A1; see also in Blaine Harden and John Broder, "Clinton's Aims: Win the War, Keep the U.S. Voters Content," *New York Times*, May 22, 1999, p. A1.

52. One might have therefore expected Weinberger to be among those opposed to Operation Allied Force, given its largely humanitarian orientation. Ironically, Weinberger supported the war against Serbia on the grounds that NATO had a vital interest in the stability of southeastern Europe. We would describe the interests as important but not vital in the proper national security sense. Caspar W. Weinberger, "Losing Track of the Main Objective of War," *New York Times*, April 12, 1999, p. A25.

53. Colin L. Powell, "U.S. Forces: Challenges Ahead," *Foreign Affairs*, vol. 71 (Winter 1992-93), pp. 32–45.

54. Ibid., p. 40.

55. Quoted in Michael Dobbs, "Annals of Diplomacy: Double Identity," *New Yorker*, March 29, 1999, p. 55. See also Les Aspin, "The Use and Usefulness of Military Force in the Post–Cold War, Post-Soviet World," address, September 21, 1992, excerpted in

Haass, *Intervention*, pp. 207–14; and Jim Hoagland, "August Guns: How Sarajevo Will Reshape U.S. Strategy," *Washington Post*, August 9, 1992, pp. C1–C2. One of us has not been immune from making this charge. See Ivo H. Daalder, "The United States and Military Intervention in Internal Conflict," in Michael E. Brown, ed., *The International Dimensions of Internal Conflict* (MIT Press, 1996), pp. 469–72.

56. See Steven Kull and I. M. Destler, *Misreading the Public: The Myth of a New Isolationism* (Brookings, 1999), pp. 106–10.

57. This notion effectively became official U.S. policy in 1994, when the Clinton administration announced its policy on peace operations. A declassified version of this presidential directive is *Clinton Administration's Policy on Reforming Multilateral Peace Operations* (U.S. Department of State, 1994). See also Ivo H. Daalder, "Knowing When to Say No: The Development of U.S. Policy for Peacekeeping," in William J. Durch, ed., *UN Peacekeeping and the Uncivil Wars of the 1990s* (St. Martin's Press, 1996), esp. pp. 52–53.

58. For the change in U.S. policy toward Bosnia, see Ivo H. Daalder, *Getting to Dayton: The Making of America's Bosnia Policy* (Brookings, 2000), pp. 177–78. For good critiques of the exit schedule notion, see Haass, *Intervention*, pp. 76–77; and Gideon Rose, "The Exit Strategy Delusion," *Foreign Affairs*, vol. 77 (January-February 1998), pp. 56–67.

59. International Institute for Strategic Studies, *The Military Balance, 1999/2000* (Oxford University Press, 1999), pp. 48–78; and American Forces Information Service, *Defense Almanac, 1999* (www.defenselink.mil/pubs/almanac/almanac/at_a_glance.html [accessed February 2000]).

60. On this issue, see Stephen John Stedman, "Spoiler Problems in Peace Processes," *International Security*, vol. 22 (Fall 1997), pp. 5–53.

61. Michael O'Hanlon, "Transforming NATO: The Role of European Forces," *Survival*, vol. 39 (Autumn 1997), pp. 5–15; David Gompert and Richard Kugler, "Free-Rider Redux: NATO Needs to Project Power (and Europe Can Help)," *Foreign Affairs*, vol. 74 (January-February 1995), pp. 7–12; John E. Peters and Howard Deshong, *Out of Area or Out of Reach? European Military Support for Operations in Southwest Asia* (Santa Monica, Calif.: RAND, 1995), pp. 97–117; and International Institute for Strategic Studies, *The Military Balance, 1999/2000*, p. 78.

62. Helsinki European Council, "Presidency Conclusions," December 10–11, 1999.

63. See Chester A. Crocker, "Afterword: Strengthening African Peacemaking and Peacekeeping," in David R. Smock, ed., *Making War and Waging Peace* (Washington, D.C.: U.S. Institute of Peace, 1993), pp. 263–69.

64. See Janet E. Heininger, *Peacekeeping in Transition: The United Nations in Cambodia* (New York: Twentieth Century Fund Press, 1994), pp. 129–30.

65. See Barbara F. Walter, "Designing Transitions from Civil War: Demobilization, Democratization, and Commitments to Peace," *International Security*, vol. 24 (Summer 1999), pp. 127–55.

66. See Adekeye Adebajo and Michael O'Hanlon, "Africa: Toward a Rapid-Reaction Force," *SAIS Review*, vol. 17 (Summer-Fall 1997), pp. 153–64; "African Crisis Response Initiative (ACRI)" (Department of State, Bureau of African Affairs, March

27, 1998); Jim Fisher-Thompson, "Rice Briefs Congress on Support for Nigerian-Led ECOMOG Force," U.S. Information Service, March 26, 1999 (www.eucom.mil/africa/usis/99mar26.htm [accessed January 2000]); and "Proposed U.S. Budget Cut Would Undercut African Peacekeeping" (U.S. Information Service, October 29, 1999) (www.eucom.mil/programs/acri/usis/99oct29.htm [accessed January 2000]).

67. Kofi A. Annan, "Two Concepts of Sovereignty," *Economist*, September 18, 1999, pp. 49–50.

68. See Mandelbaum, "A Perfect Failure," p. 7; and Carpenter, "Damage to Relations with Russia and China," pp. 77–91.

69. See Dana Priest, "The Commander's War: Bombing by Committee: France Balked at NATO Target Series," *Washington Post*, September 20, 1999, p. A1.

70. William Drozdiak, "Allies Need Upgrade, General Says," *Washington Post*, June 20, 1999, p. A20.

71. General Klaus Naumann, "Prepared Statement on Kosovo After-Action Review," Hearing, *Lessons Learned from the Military Operations Conducted as Part of Operation Allied Force*, Senate Armed Services Committee, 106 Cong. 1 sess. (November 3, 1999), p. 5.

72. William S. Cohen and Henry H. Shelton, "Joint Statement on the Kosovo After-Action Review," Hearing, *Lessons Learned from the Military Operations Conducted as Part of Operation Allied Force*, Senate Armed Services Committee, 106 Cong. 1 sess. (October 14, 1999), p. 9; and Priest, "The Commanders' War: Bombing by Committee," p. A1.

73. On April 24, the House voted on four different measures in a wholly contradictory manner. By 249 to 180 it voted to require the president to seek authorization for the use of ground forces in the war. It rejected declaring war on Yugoslavia (2 to 427) and set the war powers clock in motion by requiring U.S. troops to cease operations and return home (139 to 290). The House also failed to support the air campaign (213 to 213). However, it appropriated $13 billion for the costs of the war!

74. For a good documentation and explanation of this argument, see William C. Wohlforth, "The Stability of a Unipolar World," *International Security*, vol. 24 (Summer 1999), pp. 5–41.

Appendix B

1. Nick Cook, "Serb Air War Changes Gear," *Jane's Defence Weekly*, April 7, 1999, p. 25.

2. William S. Cohen and Henry H. Shelton, "Joint Statement on the Kosovo After-Action Review," Hearing, *Lessons Learned from the Military Operations Conducted as Part of Operation Allied Force*, Senate Armed Services Committee, 106 Cong. 1 sess. (October 14, 1999), p. 14.

3. *Report to Congress: Kosovo/Operation Allied Force After-Action Report* (U.S. Department of Defense, January 31, 2000), pp. 26, 38–39, 55.

4. Ibid., pp. 26, 46–50.

5. See John Pike, "Where Are the Carriers?" (Federation of American Scientists, December 27, 1999) (www.fas.org/man/dod-101/sys/ship/where.htm [accessed March 2000]).

6. See statement by Daniel J. Murphy Jr., "The Navy in the Balkans," *Air Force Magazine,* vol. 82 (December 1999), pp. 48–49.

7. Bradley Graham, "General Says War Stretches U.S. Forces," *Washington Post,* April 30, 1999, p. A1.

8. See Michael O'Hanlon, *How to Be a Cheap Hawk* (Brookings, 1998), pp. 48–74.

9. See Michael E. O'Hanlon, "Military Dimensions of a Ground War in Kosovo" (unpublished paper, April 26, 1999) (www.brookings.edu/views/articles/ohanlon/ 1999unp.htm [accessed April 2000]).

10. *Report to Congress: Kosovo/Operation Allied Force After-Action Report,* p. 121.

11. Bryan Bender, "U.S. Weapons Shortages Risked Success in Kosovo," *Jane's Defence Weekly,* October 6, 1999, p. 3.

12. U.S. Department of Defense, "FY 2001 Defense Budget," briefing slides, February 2000 (www.defenselink.mil/news/Feb2000 [accessed February 2000]); Henry H. Shelton, "Posture Statement," Hearings, *Defense Authorizations Request for Fiscal Year 2001,* Senate Armed Services Committee, 106 Cong. 2 sess. (February 8, 2000), p. 9; and William S. Cohen, Hearings, *Defense Authorizations Request for Fiscal Year 2001,* Senate Armed Services Committee, 106 Cong. 2 sess. (February 8, 2000).

13. Dan Crippen, director, Congressional Budget Office, letter to Congress, April 15, 1999; Steven Kosiak, "Total Cost of Allied Force Air Campaign: A Preliminary Estimate" (Washington, D.C.: Center for Strategic and Budgetary Assessments, June 10, 1999).

14. House Armed Services Committee, "Kosovo Backgrounder," June 30, 1999, p. 15 (www.house.gov/hasc [accessed July 1999]).

15. Thomas W. Lippman and Dana Priest, "NATO Hits Yugoslav Ground Forces," *Washington Post,* April 9, 1999, p. A1.

16. William S. Cohen, "News Briefing," U.S. Department of Defense, June 10, 1999.

17. Kosovo Task Force, "Kosovo Situation Reports: April 1999" (Congressional Research Service, 1999), p. 33.

18. See R. Jeffrey Smith and William Drozdiak, "Serbs' Offensive Was Meticulously Planned," *Washington Post,* April 11, 1999, p. A1; O'Hanlon, "Military Dimensions of a Ground War in Kosovo"; and "Press Conference by Jamie Shea and Brigadier General Giuseppe Marani," NATO Press Conference, April 20, 1999.

19. William Drozdiak and Thomas W. Lippman, "Clinton Joins Allies on Ground Troops," *Washington Post,* April 23, 1999, p. A1.

20. Johanna McGeary, "The Road to Hell," *Time,* April 12, 1999, p. 46.

21. Thomas A. Keaney and Eliot A. Cohen, *Gulf War Air Power Survey Summary Report* (U.S. Government Printing Office, 1993), p. 70.

22. Federation of American Scientists, Washington, D.C. (www.fas.org); Human Rights Watch, "Civilian Deaths in the NATO Air Campaign," February 2000; and NATO "Kosovo One Year On: Achievement and Challenge," March 21, 2000 (www.nato.int/kosovo/repo2000/index.htm [accessed April 2000]).

Index